WILD guide

Morocco

Adventures through Mountain, Coast and Desert

Lola Culsán, John Weller & Danny Weller

For Jenny: Mum & Nana

The Monkey Fingers Loop (p269)

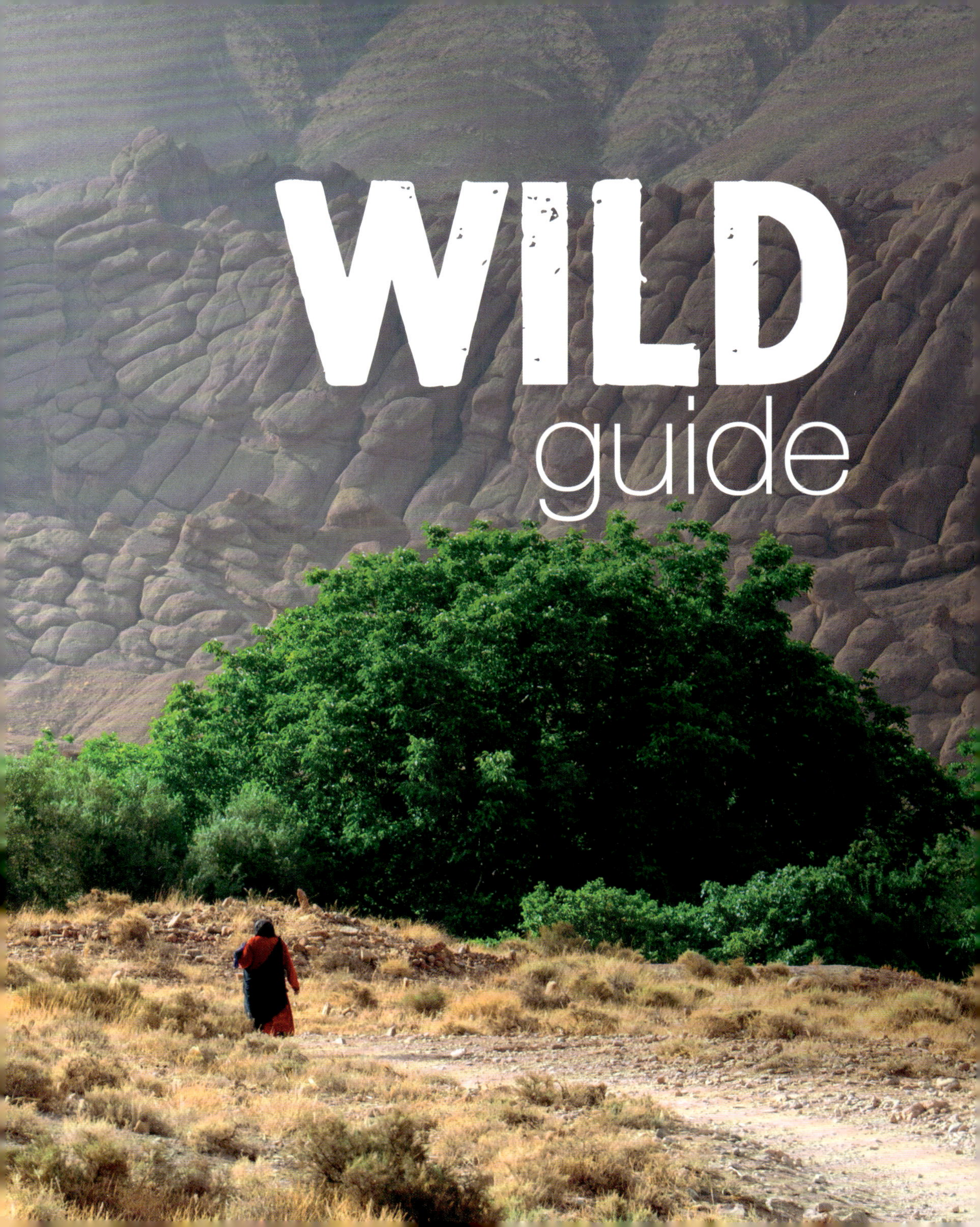
WILD
guide

Plage Ettrakna (p77)

Contents

Regions

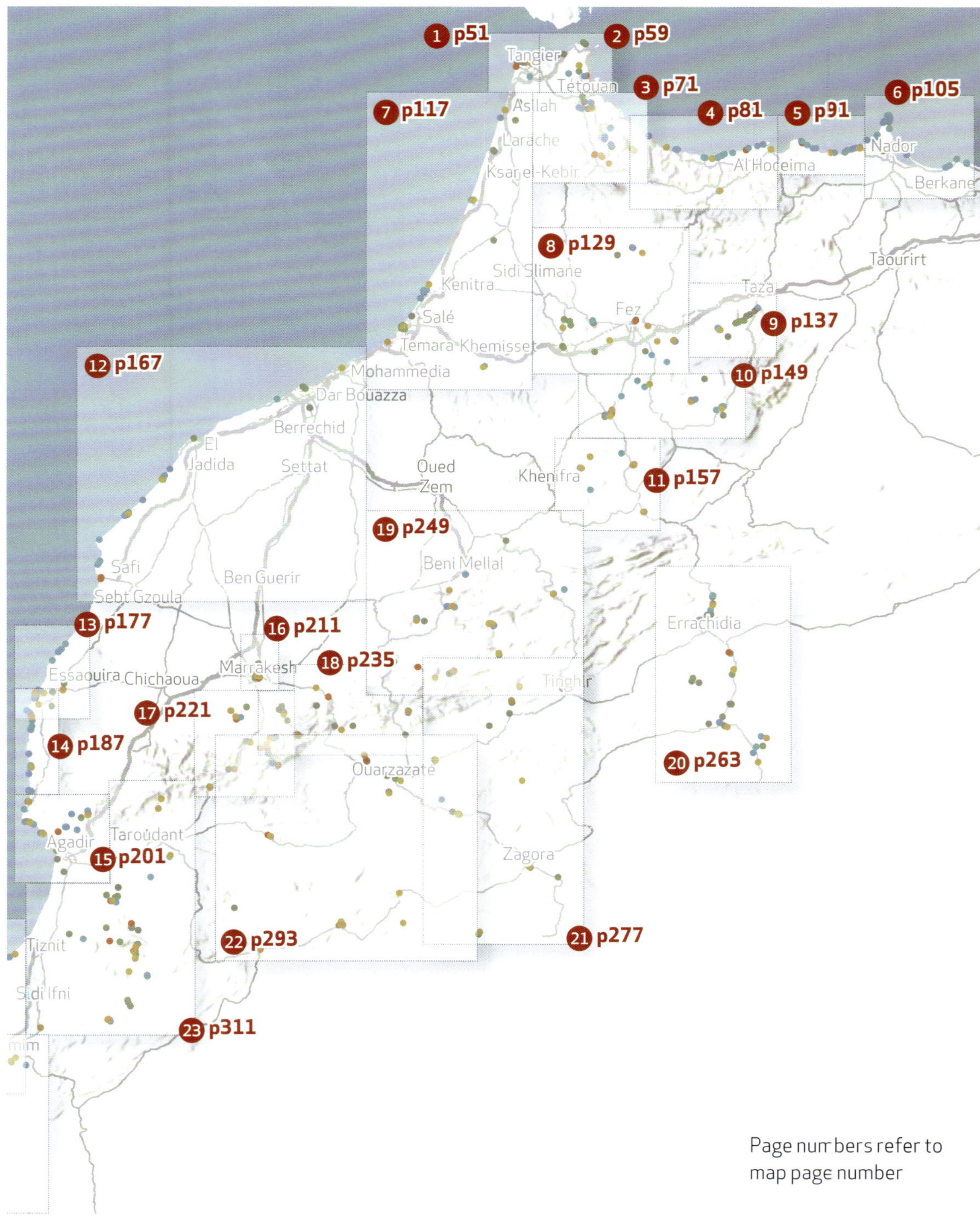

Page numbers refer to map page number

Agadir Aguellouy (p306)

Introduction

Morocco's diverse landscapes unfold like a storybook, every chapter rich with beauty, mystery and vibrant illustrations. Towering forests and glacial lakes nestle high within the snow-dusted Atlas Mountains, where rugged peaks pierce the sky. Encounter deep red-rock gorges carved into the landscape and hidden valleys cradling villages seemingly unconcerned by the outside world and the passage of time. Donkeys and camels are more common than cars in rural Morocco, demonstrating lifestyles worlds apart from the oft-travelled landscapes of Europe.

Along the Atlantic coast, rocky cliffs stand resolutely against the ocean's fierce embrace. In the north, the Mediterranean caresses secluded sandy coves and tranquil bays, frequented only by an occasional fisherman. In contrast, the Sahara stretches out endlessly, punctuated by the miracle of oases where olive groves and date palms flourish .

Morocco's wildlife reflects its diverse landscapes. In the desert, catch a glimpse of the elusive fennec fox, its oversized ears alert, or the delicate tracks of a dorcas gazelle etched into golden sand. while camels, the ships of the desert, roam gracefully, Barbary macaques frolic among the branches in cedar forests, while eagles soar majestically above Along the coasts, playful bottlenose dolphins leap through the waves, and, in winter, wetlands come alive with flocks of flamingos, spoonbills and other migrating birds.

This book invites the adventurous spirit to explore lesser-known destinations. Danny travelled along the Atlantic coast from Sidi Ifni to Tangier, using shared taxis, buses and hitchhiking, as well as trekking along deserted beaches and cliffs. Riding the waves at every opportunity, he followed the 'surfer's trail' from Agadir to Essaouira, where he discovered secret coves and hidden beaches that few visit.

Qued El Kannar (p67)

Meanwhile, John and Lola navigated their campervan through the Rif Mountains, the High and Anti-Atlas Mountains, the Draa valley and along the Mediterranean coast. They swam in secret waterholes and bathed by hidden beaches, trekked through rocky mountains and ancient forests Travelling down unmarked roads and paths not found on maps, they visited remote villages where inhabitants were surprised to see foreign visitors.

In rural communities, we were met with extraordinary generosity and warm hospitality. After getting a puncture in a remote village, the entire male population emerged with makeshift tools to help us get back on the road. When we offered payment for their help, they declined: 'We didn't do it for money. We did it from the heart.' This spirit of kindness is woven into the very fabric of Moroccan culture.

In our quest for sustainable tourism, we sought accommodations that are ecologically sound and benefit local people. You don't usually need to book hotels, *gites* and campsites far in advance, but if you do, tell them what you want and they'll go out of their way to provide. Food, treks, transfers, guides, donkeys, visits to villages/co-operatives/markets, workshops in bread-making/cooking/weaving, bikes, entertainment, information – if it's in their power, they'll secure the best they can. More than anything, Moroccans want to help you.

As you make your way through this magnificent land, especially its wilder regions, approach with an open heart. A wave, smile or hand to the chest often brings a warm *salaam* (peace) and an invitation to share tea or a meal from a family. We encourage you to accept these heartfelt invitations: drink their strong, sweet mint tea, share a tagine or a biscuit, enjoy the slower and more convivial way of life. Embrace spontaneity, take chances on the unknown and you will create memories to cherish for a lifetime.

We share these experiences, insights and suggestions with the hope of opening the way for you to craft your own journey through Morocco. We hope you enjoy our book.

Lola, John & Danny

Finding Your Way & Transport

Each place in this book can be located using the overview map provided at the end of each chapter, along with the detailed directions and latitude and longitude provided. These are given in decimal degrees (WGS84) correct to 10m and can be entered straight into any web-based mapping program, such as Google Maps or Streetmap. The latter will also provide Ordnance Survey mapping if you select that option. Print out the map before you go, or save a 'screen grab' and email it to yourself, so you're not reliant on phone signal. Some routes include roads or tracks that are not recognised by Google Maps and, in these cases, we have provided detailed turn-by-turn instructions. Approximate walk-in times are given, for one way only (we allow approximately 20 mins per kilometre, depending on terrain) and abbreviations in the directions refer to left and right (L, R) and north, east, south and west (N, E, S, W).

Moroccan Stop Sign

Moroccan Arabic and Tashlhit words and place names are typically translated into Roman alphabet with much inconsistency, creating multiple spellings, so you may find places spelt in many ways on maps and signs. We've prioritised usefulness over consistency and used the spellings most likely to help you find your way. We hope you agree with our approach.

Driving in Morocco: What to Expect

Driving in Morocco is a unique experience, distinct from most European driving norms. While drivers in Europe often adhere strictly to road rules, in Morocco, it's best to 'expect the unexpected'. Vehicles may pull out in front of you on motorways, drivers might not yield to oncoming traffic on narrow roads and pedestrians often step into the road in towns without warning. In rural areas, expect to encounter sheep, goats, donkeys and camels at every turn. Despite these quirks, Moroccan drivers are usually good-natured and tolerant. Once you venture outside urban areas and off the main routes, traffic thins out considerably – just be cautious of heavily laden donkeys and slow-moving carts on rural roads. If you see a stop sign (see photo on left), be sure to come to a complete stop as police will give you an on-the-spot fine for an infringement.

Cycling

Cycling is a great way to see the sights in Moroccan towns and many offer hiring options. For those wanting a serious challenge, the High Atlas, Anti-Atlas and Rif Mountains offer scenic adventures and you will be met with warm hospitality in rural villages.

Msoura (p113)

Speed Limits and Police Checks

Speed limits change frequently, especially near towns, and it's crucial to stay alert to these signs. Although there are few speed cameras, police frequently monitor speed with radars and impose on-the-spot fines for violations. Police checkpoints are common, particularly when entering or leaving towns. Often, you'll see signs indicating speed reductions from 60 to 40 to 20km/h; it's essential to slow as directed and acknowledge the police officer with eye contact. Usually, a nod from the officer lets you pass, but failure to follow these cues may result in a fine. Occasionally, drivers will flash their lights to warn you of an upcoming police presence.

Road Conditions

Road quality in Morocco varies from world-class to downright dangerous. Toll roads and major highways are generally well-maintained, while other roads may have frequent potholes or uneven surfaces. In mountainous or rural areas, paved roads often give way to stony or gravel tracks, requiring slower, more cautious driving. For 4x4 routes or narrow, winding roads, be sure to check local advice if travelling in a large or heavy vehicle. In our experience, driving a six-metre camper van, most main routes were manageable, though we've specified areas where 4x4s or smaller vehicles are recommended. It's also worth being mindful that, in winter, mountain routes may be covered in snow or ice and some are completely impassable, so always check weather conditions.

Vehicle Entry and Exit Requirements

A vehicle can remain in Morocco for up to six months without a special visa. However, unless you have a residence visa, you must exit and re-enter the country every three months.

Cara Blanca (p100)

Car Insurance

Most UK insurers don't provide comprehensive coverage for Morocco. For third-party coverage, they often charge higher premiums. You're legally required to have at least third-party insurance to drive in Morocco and authorities may request your insurance documents. You might find it easier and more affordable to buy temporary third-party coverage at entry points such as Tangier Port. This coverage is often renewable in larger towns providing an accessible option for extended stays.

Public Transport

Collective taxis are a primary form of travel and are cheap. There is no app, there is no schedule, they will appear when they appear. They largely follow a specific route like buses and will drop off and pick up people along the way. Don't be surprised when a seven-seater fills up with 11 people. Taxis won't leave the terminus until the taxi is full. Taxis at the terminus sometimes take hours to leave, so it can be better to wait somewhere en route. To flag shared taxis down, put up the number of fingers of seats required. White or yellow is the most common colour.

Smaller four-seaters **local taxis** operate in bigger towns and cities. They operate only within the city boundaries. These are either private or collective and if you are the first one in the car, the driver will likely ask if you mind if they pick someone else up. You can refuse but it isn't common to do so. However, the driver must drop you off before the people he picked up, unless they're stopping on the way to your destination.

In some tourist towns, taxis are available at the terminus for **private hire**, taking you on a tour of and waiting with you while you explore. Be sure to negotiate a price before heading out. In cities, ride-hailing apps are becoming popular, especially InDrive.

Trains: the big cities are all connected by rail. Trains in Morocco are an enjoyable experience. Getting on and off trains can be a bit of a scrum so if you're set on getting a seat, be prepared for a bit of push and shove. At the time of writing there no train lines south of Marrakech. High speed lines are planned along the Atlantic Coast.

CTM coaches are the most reliable choice, offering comfortable seating, air conditioning and scheduled departure times. CTM are useful for reaching a your destination with minimal hassle, a convenient choice for both Moroccans and tourists. Book tickets online via CTM's website (ctm.ma) or at coach stations.

Local buses and the ubiquitous **Mercedes vans** provide budget-friendly alternatives. Buses operate in many smaller towns and regions but don't follow strict schedules, often departing only when full, which can make them crowded and unpredictable

Hitchhiking

Hitchhiking is a widely accepted way to get around, especially in rural areas. Danny hitchhiked extensively and found Moroccan drivers to be welcoming and generous. (See Solo Women Travellers - p18.)
Hitchhiking signals: If you're hitching a long distance, extend your thumb. For shorter trips to a nearby town, use an arc motion with your index finger, and if staying within the same area, point downward.

Solo Women Travellers

A rewarding experience if approached with awareness and preparation. First, research and plan your itinerary. Dress modestly to respect local customs. Engage with locals, but remain cautious about trusting strangers too quickly. Family groups are best. Consider joining guided tours for excursions to explore the countryside or desert safely. Learning a few basic Moroccan Arabic or French phrases can enhance your interaction and show respect for the culture. Stay in reputable accommodations. Always keep emergency contact information handy and share your travel plans with someone you trust. Most importantly, trust your instincts – if something feels off, it's okay to walk away or seek help.

The following is an account from Layla Besellam, a Moroccan-American woman who Danny met in Tangier, on her experiences while hitchhiking solo through Morocco:

'Hitchhiking in Morocco is a common means of transportation and many Moroccans all over the country use it to travel between cities, and even shorter distances in rural and mountain areas where cars are rare. I always say that Morocco is sort of stuck in the 70s, in the best way possible. The old cars, slower adaptation to modern technology, personable people and little idiosyncrasies, such as hitchhiking, transport me to this beautiful way of life that I actually much prefer. As a 21-year-old woman, the idea of getting into a car with a stranger can be quite terrifying.
It requires a heightened sense of awareness and a strong intuition to gauge the energy and trustworthiness of the person offering a ride. I have learned to carefully assess each situation, ensuring that I feel secure before accepting a ride. Despite these initial apprehensions, my experiences with solo and group hitchhiking have been overwhelmingly positive. Each encounter I've had has reinforced my confidence and showed that, with caution, hitchhiking can be a great and safe way to travel around. My hitchhiking interactions, so deeply personal and unfiltered, were far beyond what any tourism group could offer. Each ride felt like a new chapter, with its own characters and narratives. The openness and generosity of every person I've met along the way have reinforced the notion that human connections transcend borders

La Cathedrále Imsfrane (p239)

Customs & Culture

Amazigh or Berber? The terms 'Amazigh' and 'Berber' both refer to the indigenous people of north Africa, but 'Amazigh' is the preferred term used by the people themselves. 'Amazigh' means 'free people' or 'noble me' in the Tamazight language and reflects their self-identity and cultural pride. 'Berber,' derived from the Greek word 'barbaros', has historically been used by outsiders and is considered less accurate and sometimes pejorative. Therefore, we will be using the terms Amazigh and Tamazight throughout the guide, although there are three main Amazigh languages used in Morocco: Tashelhit, Tamazight, and Tarifit. All use the Tifinagh alphabet, completely different from Arabic, and you will see this on signs, schools and government buildings in mountain areas.

Erg Chigaga (p273)

Dress for men: Shorts are uncommon outside tourist areas, especially in more traditional or rural settings, and can draw curious looks or comments. Danny found that in remote areas, wearing long, lightweight trousers was the best choice for blending in and avoiding unwanted attention.

Dress for women: While tourists aren't expected to follow Islamic dress codes strictly, dressing modestly is appreciated and shows respect for local customs. In areas outside of European-style hotels and tourist spots, it's advisable to wear long, loose trousers and tops that cover the shoulders – practical not only for cultural respect but also for sun protection. When swimming in rivers or lakes near local people, Lola typically wore a long-sleeve surfing costume and surf shorts,

Beaches: When visiting wilder beaches, remember they're often the place of work and sometimes the home of the fishing community. Enjoy yourself respectfully, particularly in more remote areas where they aren't exposed to as many tourists. Be mindful of local customs and cultures, particularly when it comes to dress. Women don't have to go into the sea in their clothes, but this isn't the kind of place to try out your new skimpy bikini.

Women: As an Islamic country, Morocco has traditional expectations for women's dress, especially in rural and conservative areas. In these regions, women typically cover their hair and wear modest clothing that covers their arms and legs, though they don't commonly cover their faces. It's also common to see women working hard in the fields or carrying large loads of harvested crops.

In rural cafés or restaurants, Lola found she was often the only woman present, though men were generally friendly and respectful. We were frequently invited to join family picnics, which included both women and men, allowing us a welcoming view of family life.

Aït Bouguemez (p240)

In larger cities such as Tangier and Casablanca, women's lifestyles are evolving, with increasing visibility in public and greater independence. For example, we met a group of women aged 40 to 70 from Casablanca who had travelled to a mountain village specifically to go trekking, a reflection of the growing interest among Moroccan women in outdoor activities and solo travel.

Mosques: These aren't museums and aren't like churches in Europe. The vast majority of mosques in Morocco are closed to non-Muslims and tourists cannot enter. Some mosques are open to the public, such as the Hussein II Mosque in Casablanca, but this is the exception rather than the rule.

Ramadan: During this holy month, Muslims don't eat or drink from sunrise to sunset. As a result, most restaurants and food shops are closed during the day, only opening again at sunset. Plan your trips to the shops accordingly and stock up on food and water. Restaurants in tourist areas will remain open. If you're eating and drinking openly while walking around in public, some people may ask you to stop out of respect for those who are fasting. A couple of times, we were invited to join a family 'iftar', the meal families have when they break their fast at sunset. This was a real treat, consisting of hrira (tomato-based soup with chickpeas and lentils), dates, sweet and savoury pastries and fruit.

Alcohol: Only available in tourist areas or bigger towns and cities and has a larger price tag than in Europe. You can buy alcohol in some European-style restaurants. Big supermarkets sometimes stock alcohol, but you have to ask for it as they have a separate room, usually round the back. During Ramadan or Eid, it's virtually impossible to buy alcohol.

Guardians: At all major historical sites, a guardian will let you into the site and offer to show you around for a fee. A fee is also expected for letting you into the precincts. Give what you think is appropriate and remember this is an important income for the guardian, his family and the wider community. The ever-present cousin to the site guardian is the parking guardian. Ever-present outside points of interest, beaches and high streets, parking guardians will help you park and watch your car in exchange for a small fee – 5dh is appropriate for short stays.

Toilets: In Morocco, you'll find that many modern hotels and tourist accommodations, as well as some homestays, offer European-style (or 'western-style') toilets. In major cities, especially in places frequented by tourists, cafés and restaurants often provide these conveniences, although it's best to check beforehand if this is important for you. However, once you venture into rural or less tourist-centric areas, stand-up or squat toilets are much more common. In these locations, it's typical for toilet paper not to be provided, so bringing your own can be helpful. Instead, there may be a small water bucket or hose provided for personal hygiene, in line with traditional practices. It's also a good idea to carry hand sanitiser and tissues, as soap may not always be available in more basic facilities.

Wild and Responsible

Wild camping is legal away from big cities and tourist areas. We parked our campervan beside lakes, in woods, on country roads and in small villages without any difficulty. Often someone will come and say hello (you're never alone in Morocco) and we just asked if we were OK to park there and were never refused. This usually means that they'll keep an eye out for you. One kind gentleman brought us soup and dates from his own house because the restaurants were closed while people broke their fast during Ramadan. In some mountain areas, guides are recommended for your own safety. We met a young Frenchman who had been travelling all over Morocco and sleeping in a hammock for two months. (Make sure you buy one with a built-in mosquito net – he had suffered from bites during the night in some places.) Obviously be careful with fires, which should be thoroughly doused with water, and leave no trace.

Litter: It's unfortunate, but you are likely to notice a lot of litter around Morocco due to limited waste collection systems. In cities, bins and pick-up services are few, leading to more rubbish along roadsides and in public areas. In rural and mountain regions, it's even tougher – families often have no choice but to burn or bury plastic waste, as formal disposal options simply don't exist. The good news is environmental awareness is growing, with locals and visitors starting small clean-up efforts to help tackle the problem. You can help by disposing of your own rubbish responsibly.

Lac Lalla Takerkoust (p215)

Phrases & Glossary

The most common word we heard in Morocco was marhaba (welcome) or marhaba bik (welcome to you).

Tapping of the heart with the right hand when saying hello or goodbye is a symbol of peace and respect – prevalent all over Morocco.

Greetings, Goodbyes & Polite Expressions
Salaam alaykum – Peace be upon you (and the response, Alaykum salaam – And also upon you)
Sbah al-khayr – Good morning
Masaa al-khayr – Good evening
Maa salaama – Goodbye
Yaum sayeed – Have a good day
Layla sayeeda – Have a good night
Kidayr? – How are you?
Mizyaan – Great
Bikhayr – Happy
La bas – All good (can be used as a statement or a question)
Alhamdulillah – Good by the grace of God
Aefak – Please
Shukran bizaaf – Thank you very much
La, shukran – No, thank you
Naam, aefak – Yes please
Afwan – You're welcome
Asif – Sorry
Mumkin nsawrek? – Can I take a photo of you?

Getting Around
Fayn toilet? – Where is the bathroom?
Fayn…? – Where is…?
Kayn taxi? – Is there a taxi?
Mechi – Let's go (useful when giving directions)
Liyasar – Left
Liyemin – Right
Asif/ Smahli – Excuse me or pardon

Shopping & Bargaining
Bsh'hal? – How much?
Mumkin + price? – Is … possible?
Bsh'hal hada? – How much is this?
Ghali/rahh ghali – Expensive/It's too expensive
Bshwiya bshwiya – Little by little (when haggling)
Khelliha b… – Give it to me for…
Maakayn mushkil – No problem
Bsh'hal tkhali hali? – How much can you do it for?

Eating & Dining
Bismillah – In the name of God (said before meals)
Shwiya bshwiya – A little bit (when serving food)
Hnaya – Here you go (when offering something).
Lma – Water
Atay – Tea (a staple of Moroccan hospitality)
Khobz – Bread
Bla suker – without sugar

Making Friends
Shno smiytak? – What's your name?
Ismi… – My name is…
Ana min… – I'm from…
Sbar Alaya – Wait for me.

Emergency Phrases
Musa'ada! – Help!
Mchali baztam – I lost my wallet
Ana bghit doctor – I need a doctor
Baraka – *Enough!* (Useful if someone won't take no for an answer)

Money & Bargaining

The majority of shops, restaurants and businesses don't accept cards, so carrying a ready supply of dirhams is essential (although Morocco's central bank is encouraging adoption of digital payments in shops so this may change in the next few years). In some rural areas, there won't be a cash machine for miles around, so be sure to plan accordingly and stock up before heading off the beaten track. You can change cash in banks and access ATMs in most small towns.

Bargaining is a key part of everyday life in Morocco. It's part of the social fabric of every community and is how residents get to know and build relationships with the business owners in the neighbourhood. In the markets and souks, it's the responsibility of the stallholders to get the best price for themselves and they will charge you more as a tourist, as you have the money to travel to Morocco. Equally, it's your responsibility to get the best price for yourself and the stallholder will respect you more for haggling. The best strategy is to offer half of whatever their initial price was and meet in the middle. However, there is no need to bargain in restaurants, supermarkets, cafés or sweet shops.

In markets and towns, people may approach persistently, eager to sell their wares; it's worth remembering that there is no welfare safety net here – selling may be a matter of sustenance. Be warm yet resolute. If needed, a clear *baraka* (enough) and stop signal with the hand will convey your answer.

Souk El Had du Drâa (p175)

Food

Moroccan food is always fresh and delicious. Tagines are an integral part of the cuisine, featuring a variety of styles such as chicken, vegetable, beef with prunes, lamb, and more. If you're by the sea, expect freshly grilled fish and prawns. In the mountainous areas, particularly in the south where the soil isn't fertile enough for cattle, chicken or lamb tagines are the staples, all prepared using fresh, locally sourced ingredients and traditional home-cooking methods. Bread is a key component of the Moroccan diet, used in place of utensils to scoop food from the shared tagine pot. However, in rural and mountain areas restaurants and cafés are harder to find.

Breakfast in Morocco is hearty, typically including fresh orange juice, bread, honey, jams, olives, olive oil and mint tea or coffee. Sugar is usually added to tea and orange juice. If you don't want it or would prefer to add your own say: bla suker (without sugar).

If you find a café with large stewing pots outside, don't hesitate to eat there. These local eateries serve a variety of rich and flavourful bean and lentil stews, providing a delicious alternative to tagines. In some towns, fried fish is offered by weight in cafés and in our experience, a cheap, tasty and filling option.

Vegetarians will find vegetable tagines and stews. For those who are lactose intolerant, dairy is not a significant part of the Moroccan diet, as most dishes are prepared using high-quality olive oil.

Honey holds a special place in Moroccan cuisine, particularly in its many regional varieties such as wild thyme, orange blossom, and eucalyptus, each offering a unique flavour profile. Honey enhances traditional dishes such as *rfissa*, a spiced chicken stew with lentils and fenugreek, and *seffa*, which layers steamed vermicelli or couscous with sweet notes of honey, cinnamon, and almonds. Valued for its health benefits, honey is often used to alleviate colds and aid digestion. While quality honey can be pricey, some of the best pure, organic, and occasionally certified honey can be found in rural areas.

Photography & Phones

Morocco is a photographer's paradise. However, photographing people can require some care, as many Moroccans prefer not to be treated as photo subjects without their consent. In markets and medinas, always ask before capturing someone's face, as religious or personal reasons often affect their response. Some people may be open to photos in exchange for a small tip, typically around 10 dirhams, while others may decline altogether. Women, in particular, often prefer not to be photographed. If permission is granted, a friendly smile and showing appreciation go a long way in creating a positive exchange. It's also recommended to avoid photographing police, soldiers and other official facilities to prevent potential issues, as these are often restricted for security reasons.

Drones aren't permitted for personal use in Morocco, a restriction established in 2015. If you bring a drone into the country, customs will confiscate it, but you might be able to retrieve it when you leave, assuming you declared it upon entry. Companies can use drones in Morocco, but they must secure aviation permits beforehand.

SIM cards: Maroc Telecom, Orange, and Inwi are the main mobile service providers. Maroc Telecom tends to have the widest network coverage, especially in rural and mountainous areas, making it a popular choice for travellers visiting remote locations. We also used Inwi and had excellent coverage on our travels. Using a combination of suppliers will maximise coverage.

SIM cards are easily available at most Moroccan airports and at international ferry terminals, convenient for getting connected upon arrival. Purchase SIMs and top-ups at supermarkets and smaller convenience shops throughout Morocco.

Barrage Sidi Chahed (p121)

These smaller shops are useually helpful in setting up data top-ups via scratch cards or direct credits.

Ambulance - 15
Police - 19 (city) or 177 (Outside of city: Royal Gendarmerie)
Fire - 15
Mountain Rescue Team Tafraout - +212 673-701247

Best for
Secret Beaches & Surfing

Morocco's coastline is an untapped treasure trove for intrepid beach explorers. The Atlantic coast stretches for miles, featuring vast, unspoiled beaches ideal for walking and picnics. Secluded spots such as Cap Sim boast big waves and dramatic scenery, while the secluded Plage Blanche, a 40km stretch where the Sahara meets the sea, is perfect for camping by the dunes. Along the Mediterranean, east of Tangier, rocky coves and sea caves await divers and adventurers.

For surfers, Morocco is legendary. The informal surf route from Agadir to Essaouira includes Taghazout and Imsouane, Morocco's twin surf hubs. In between, a bevy of iconic beaches catering to all skill levels will have surfers and body boarders salivating for the salty sting of the waves. Beginners can start at Taghazout Bay, while experienced surfers flock to Madraba, The Cathedral and Panorama Beach. With no bars or restaurants at many spots, visitors should bring ample food, water and shade.

Madraba Beach (p192)

Be safe

1 Don't swim alone.

2 Be aware that rip currents can form when there is heavy swell or surf. These circulate water out to the back of the breaking waves.

3 Rips occur along the edge of coves or stacks, or between surf breaks on longer beaches.

4 To exit a rip current swim parallel to the shore.

Best for

Wild Swimming, Waterfalls & Cliff Jumping

Morocco is rich in natural water spots that beckon wild swimmers, adventurers, and nature enthusiasts. Below the grand Cascades d'Ouzoud, smaller waterfalls and secluded pools provide refreshing escapes from the busier areas, perfect for a tranquil dip. For those willing to climb, the rocky pools of the Amtoudi River flow in gentle steps through a striking gorge, punctuated by pink oleanders that bloom along the water's edge. Closer to the desert, the clear, green waters of Cascades Attiq offer a refreshing retreat from the surrounding heat and dry landscape, while the serene River of Aït Mansour winds through a landscape of dense palm groves, providing shaded peace.

In the Atlas Mountains, remote natural lakes such as Ifni and the fabled Isli and Tislit are hidden treasures, rewarding visitors with raw beauty and solitude far from well-trodden paths.

La Rivière Amtoudi (p300)

Be safe

1 Never swim alone, and keep a constant watch on weak swimmers.

2 Cold water can dramatically decrease swimming ability, create cold shock and cause drowning through panic. Know your limits, enter slowly and stay close to the shoreline.

3 Never jump into water unless you have thoroughly checked for depth and obstructions.

4 Avoid strong currents, such as those directly under large waterfalls or weirs, or those found in river rapids during floods: they can drag you under.

5 Always make sure you know how you will get out before you get in.

6 Wear footwear if you can.

7 Avoid direct contact with blue-green algae, and be wary of water quality in lowland areas during droughts and heavy rain. Cover cuts with plasters if worried, and if you develop flu-like symptoms tell your doctor you have been in a river.

Best for
Ancient & Sacred Wonders

From neolithic cave paintings and rock carvings to ancient cities such as Lixus, first built by the Phoenicians in the seventh century BC and spanning Carthaginian, Roman and Amazigh (Berber) civilisations, monuments reflect the storied past of Morocco. Some are well known, ticketed and staffed, while others are hidden away in tiny villages, protected only by a semi-official 'guardian' who will appear, like Mr Benn, with a key, unlock a door or gate and show you around. The memory of others, such as Setti Fatma Mausoleum, dedicated to a local 'saint', is kept alive and passed down orally by descendants.

Kasbahs and ksars, the fortified homes of important and wealthy individuals and fortified villages where for many years Jews and Muslims shared resources and safety, are a fascinating feature, described orally by a helpful 'guardian'. Meanwhile, hilltop agadirs like those in Amtoudi, built to store and defend the crops, valuables and important documents of local tribes, reveal Amazigh engineering and communal organisation.

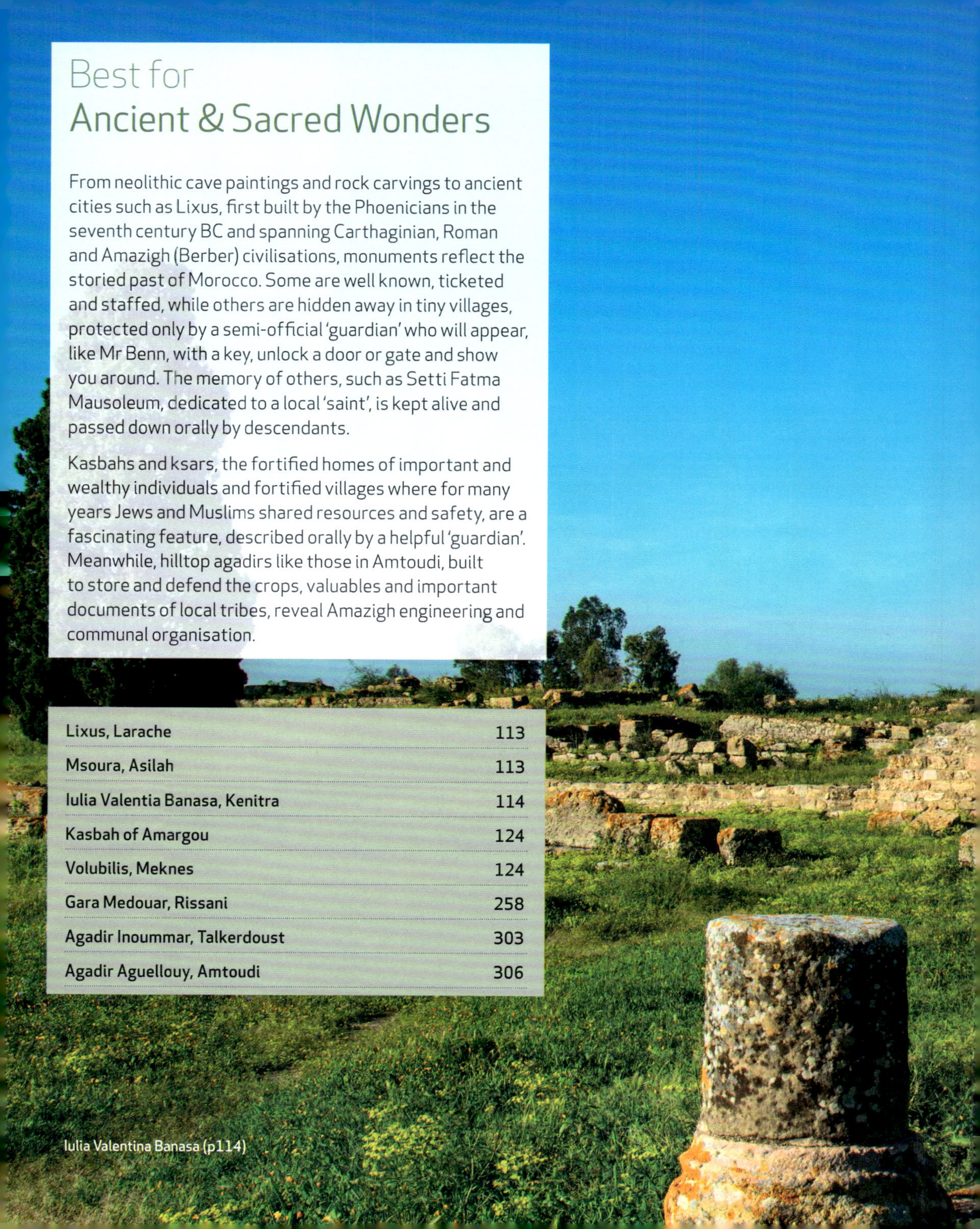

Iulia Valentina Banasa (p114)

Best for
Sunset Views & Highpoints

There's a reason why Morocco is known as 'The Land of the Setting Sun'. From the highest peaks in the mountains to isolated stretches of sand along the Atlantic coast, the sunsets in Morocco are nothing short of breathtaking, filling the horizon with a warm golden glow. At Nid d'Aigle (Eagle's Nest) gaze out over the vast expanse of the Atlantic Ocean as the sun transforms the water into shimmering gold. Alternatively, experience the striking silhouette of the Kasbah des Oudayas from Rabat Marina as the sun dips below the horizon, casting a magical light over the scene. The Atlas Mountains offer countless vantage points to admire this beauty.

At Oukaïmeden, a popular ski resort, and at Jbel Tagtout, let the wind carry away your cries of joy as you lose yourself in the expansive sky, punctuated by the rugged peaks surrounding you.

Oukaïmeden Lookout Point (p231)

Best for
Walks & Treks

Put your best foot forward and step out on to the path of adventure. Morocco has an array of walks and treks on offer, with something to suit the needs of the leisure stroller to the hardened mountain climber. The Tinghir Palmeraie offers a relaxing stroll through palm groves, bisected by little rivers and dotted with the memories of ruined ksars, while Mount Toubkal and The Monkey Fingers Loop are tough scrambles up steep cliffs, with views worth the beads of sweat on your brow and the blisters on your feet.

Many walks and treks can be completed with a map or satnav, but some of the more mountainous routes can prove challenging and, unless you are experienced in navigating and mountaineering, we recommend hiring the services of a local guide. On the other hand, Moroccan hospitality is the stuff of legend, so if you're out on a walk and someone offers you a glass of tea or a portion of their food, why not take them up on it. Who knows what new experiences could lie in store?

Shrine of Sidi Moussa (p245)

Be safe

1 On high ground be prepared for the weather to deteriorate and make descent or retreat difficult.

2 Carry waterproofs, warm clothes, whistle, compass, GPS device, map, torch, snacks and water.

3 Don't hesitate to turn back if you don't feel confident on a trek.

4 Protect your skin, head and eyes from the sun.

Best for
Desert Adventures & Oases

Morocco offers much more than just vast deserts; its sandy Sahara and rocky Agafay regions should definitely be on any visitor's itinerary. Tinfou Dunes near Zagora provide a perfect introduction to Morocco's desert magic. Arrive early for the quietest moments, with only the wind's soft whistle as company. Further south, Erg Chigaga demands a challenging trek, but sunrise at its summit is otherworldly, as the sun lights up golden waves of sand stretching endlessly. Its counterpart, Erg Chebbi, is equally as breathtaking, with sandy slopes reaching 150m. These vast dunes, which even camels avoid due to their steep and shifting sands, feel surreal, like a painter's bold strokes. In the valleys, sparse bushes and the tracks of small birds hint at life clinging to the sands. By contrast, Agafay is rocky and arid, with rugged hills and barren stretches offering a unique desert escape. Here, camel or horseback rides bring solitude and a peaceful connection with nature, while camps range from simple tents to luxury setups, complete with Moroccan cuisine, stargazing, and cultural performances – a peaceful retreat into Morocco's untamed beauty. No desert is complete without oases to escape to: palm groves, traditional mud brick buildings and, at Fint, a cooling pool to swim in.

Erg Chigaga (p273)

Be safe

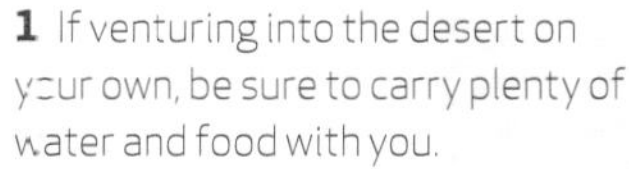

1 If venturing into the desert on your own, be sure to carry plenty of water and food with you.

2 Research your route and resting places before you set out.

3 Pack warm clothes as well as light-weight clothing - deserts get cold at night..

4 If driving into the desert, fill up with fuel and carry reserves.

5 Watch our for scorpions and other animals.

6 Pack a survival kit & a compass.

7 Protect your head, skin and eyes from the sun

Best for

Travellers With Disabilities

Travelling in Morocco with a disability can present challenges. Although Morocco ratified the UN Convention on the Rights of Persons with Disabilities in 2009, accessible infrastructure is limited, particularly outside urban centres. In rural areas, wheelchair ramps, Braille signage, and accessible transport options are rare, and public buildings are rarely adapted for mobility needs. However, locals are generally friendly, understanding and willing to assist wherever possible. We've included accessibility information wherever feasible to help travellers navigate these challenges.

Le Jardin Secret (p205)

Best for

Slow Food, Gardens & Markets

Markets across Morocco bustle with activity, the lifeblood of the Moroccan social entity. Shouted greetings, heated but good-natured haggling and mandatory glasses of mint tea are common sights. Take in the sounds and smells of Souk el Had du Drâa, a bustling market visited even by Moroccans from big cities for a taste of tradition, which starts its busy day with the trading and butchering of camels, cows and sheep. Amid the carnage, vibrant produce and a myriad of merchandise, vendors shout their prices, creating an overwhelming sensory experience. Green gems stud the brown hem of Morocco's high neckline: gardens filled with towering cacti and sweet-smelling flowers, put together in an intricate pattern. Spanning several hectares, Donabo Gardens near Tangier, blends nature and sustainability with features such as the hibiscus garden, mint maze, and garden of chili peppers. Visitors can enjoy eco-friendly tours, workshops, and organic meals made from fresh, garden-grown produce.

Tizi n'Tichka Pass (p232)

Erg Chigaga (p273)

AROUND TANGIER

Our perfect adventure

- **Explore** the streets of the old medina on foot, or jump on a bicycle and pedal along the seafront promenade
- **Drink** mint tea in the legendary Cafe Hafa and watch the twinkling lights of Spain
- **Taste** your own mortality and take a step back in time at the Phoenician Tombs, complete with a panoramic Mediterranean vista
- **Stroll** through the sweetly smelling paths of the Donabo Gardens and tuck into a delicious organic salad and slice of cheesecake
- **Breathe** in salty air and imagine yourself a hero at the mythological Caves of Hercules
- **Strike** a pose by the sign identifying the meeting of the Atlantic Ocean and the Mediterranean Sea
- **Dive** into the cooling embrace of the waves at the beach in the réserve du Cap Spartel
- **Admire** Moroccan artworks and decor at Villa Harris, before picnicking in the park
- **Watch** the sunset over the Atlantic from the lighthouse of Cap Spartel

2

2

21

'Tangier is the spot where the dream of the Arabian Nights comes true, and one wonders if the wild, impossible tales in the books of travel are not true also.'

Mark Twain, The Innocents Abroad

Originally inhabited by Amazigh tribes, Tangier became a vital trading post for the Phoenicians and Carthaginians in about the fifth century BCE. Under Roman rule, it flourished as 'Tingis' and developed into a commercial centre connecting the Mediterranean and Atlantic trade routes. Following the Arab conquest in the seventh century, Tangier evolved into a centre of Islamic culture and commerce. The city later passed through Portuguese and British hands before returning to Moroccan rule in 1684. The nineteenth century saw European artists and writers seduced by Tangier's captivating beauty. Eugène Delacroix's visit in 1832 and his vivid depictions of Moroccan life ignited attention among the Romantic painters. Henri Matisse, fascinated by the golden hues, created some of his best works here.

In the twentieth century, Tangier became a haven for bohemians and a home to literary figures such as Paul and Jane Bowles and William Burroughs. In the 1960s, the city drew actors and musicians seeking artistic freedom and an escape from sexual hypocrisy, embracing the city's eclectic spirit. Cafe Hafa was a favourite spot for many of these artists. Opened in 1921, this laid-back café, with terraced seating, is famous for its sea views. We sipped a cup of mint tea, imagining Joe Orton or the Beat poets who also frequented the café, while gazing over the Straits of Gibraltar, and looking back at the twinkling lights of Spain.

Like previous visitors, we were captivated by Tangier's exotic charm. We cycled along the seafront Corniche Gardens to the Villa Harris gallery, where we learned how foreign visitors in the 20th century supported local artists, all while our bikes were safely guarded. Our cycle ride continued west along the coast to Cap Spartel, where, legend has it, Hercules once lived in a cave. We stopped off at the Danobo Gardens, a peaceful retreat where paths are lined with fragrant flowers and bees hum; storks clacked in nearby trees as we savoured a salad sourced from the garden itself, alongside an unforgettable homemade lemon cheesecake.

FOREST, PARKS & GARDENS

1 RÉSERVE DU CAP SPARTEL

This nature reserve, dotted with pine and eucalyptus trees and wildflowers, is a tranquil escape. At the northern coastal end, a small beach awaited, sheltered by rugged rocks that rose boldly from the sea, reminiscent of mythical sea creatures such as Dandan, the 'biggest of all fishes and the fiercest of our foes' according to *The Thousand and One Nights*. The area is also rich in history, including the 1936 Battle of Cap Spartel, an early naval clash of the Spanish Civil War where Republican and Nationalist forces engaged off the coast where the Atlantic and Mediterranean converge. From the lookout platform above, we watched a group of boys leaping from the rocks into the sea. A great spot to watch the sunset. From Tangier, take the Rte des Grottes d'Hercule for 1km; at the roundabout take 1st exit for 1.5km; turn R on to the coast road; after 2.3km turn L at sign for Cap Spartel and park (35.7850, -5.9294)

2 mins, 35.7862, -5.9291

2 DONABO GARDENS

Spanning several hectares, the gardens are a delightful blend of nature and sustainability, featuring the Hibiscus Garden, Mint Maze and Garden of Chili Peppers, among others. What struck us most was its eco-friendly approach, using sustainable methods to grow herbs and vegetables. After exploring the gardens, we enjoyed organic sandwiches and salads at the café, all made from fresh produce grown right there in the gardens; De-lish-ous. The homemade cakes were a particular highlight, each one crafted with care and packed with flavour. Donabo Gardens offers guided tours, gardening workshops and bread-making plus special events. Highly recommended. From Tangier Port, head W for 8km; the gardens are signposted on your R. Donabo Gardens, Cap Spartel Road Km10, Tangier. donabogardens.com +212 539-939393

2 mins, 35.7878, -5.8834

3 PERDICARIS PARK

Also known as Rmilat Forest, this is a public space covering 70 hectares. The park is home to hundreds of different botanical species and features wide paths for strolls and panoramic sea views. No facilities inside, so stock up on food and water before you head in. From Tangier Port, head W for 7.5km; park is on your R

2 mins, 35.7876, -5.8656

3

3

6

5

7

4 MENDOUBIA GARDEN

Dating back to the late nineteenth century, Mendoubia Garden was originally established as part of a palace complex for Sultan Moulay Hassan I. The gardens were named after 'Mendoub', a title given to the sultan's ambassador to European courts. At the summit of the hill stands a monument, flanked by cannons, featuring the speech made by Mohammed V calling for independence. The garden is home to an ancient banyan tree, believed to be over 800 years old. Free entry. The garden is a two-minute walk N of Grand Socco. Place du 9 Avril 1947, Tanger 90000.

2 mins, 35.7851, -5.8141

VIEWPOINTS

5 ATLANTIC & MEDITERRANEAN SIGN

Yes, it's an imaginary line in the water, but there was still something quite special about the point where two seas meet. A wooden plaque marks the spot above Cap Spartel; we took a photo and left happy. Directions as for Cap Spartel; park where you can

1 min, 35.78774, -5.92718

6 CAP SPARTEL LIGHTHOUSE

Historical landmark offering panoramic views of the union of the Atlantic Ocean and the Mediterranean Sea. Built in 1864, the lighthouse has helped countless ships navigate the strategic, rock-strewn waters. Often bustling with tourists and vendors. Arrive early to avoid the crowds. From Cap Spartel (549); head N for 500m to parking spot (35.7895, -5.9239). Route de Cap Spartel, Tangier 90000

2 mins, 35.79118, -5.92358

7 PLACE FARO

Often referred to as 'La Terrasse des Paresseux' (Idler's Terrace), Place Faro is where locals gather to enjoy mint tea in the cafés, while visitors are transfixed by the views over the Strait of Gibraltar. Historical brass cannons, remnants from colonial days, stand watch over the promenade. Telescopes aimed at the northern horizon gave us a good view of Spain just across the water. Opposite 6-17 Bd Pasteur, Tangier.

1 min, 35.7810, -5.8117

8 POINT D'OBSERVATION CAP MALABATA

Europe and Africa, all in one vista and with a lighthouse standing majestically beside you. What more could you need? Take the time to relax with a cup of mint tea at the café on the clifftop and look out at the international cargo ships crisscrossing the Strait of Gibraltar. Turn off the N16 on to Sidi Mnari at the roundabout

(35.8108, -5.7390) and follow for five minutes until reaching the lighthouse car park.

1 min, 35.8167, -5.7482

9 LIGHTHOUSE CAP MALABATA

With the Moroccan star emblazoned on its walls, The Malabata Lighthouse is an iconic beacon that has guided countless ships along the coastline and is a proud symbol of the district's maritime legacy. Visitors can delve into its history through guided tours and discover its significance to Tangier's maritime commerce. Turn off the N16 on to Sidi Mnari at the roundabout (35.8108, -5.7390) and follow for five minutes until reaching the lighthouse car park.

1 min, 35.8167, -5.7491

CULTURAL HOTSPOTS

10 AMERICAN LEGATION MUSEUM

Housed in a magnificent building dating back to 1821, this museum is the only US National Historic Landmark outside the United States. Originally a diplomatic mission, complete with a peaceful courtyard, fountain and gardens, it was established after Morocco became the first nation to recognise US independence in 1777. The museum showcases a collection of Moroccan and American history, featuring art,

historical documents and cultural artefacts. Artwork from local and international artists is also on display. The museum serves as a centre for cultural exchange, hosting events that promote literacy and understanding of Moroccan-American relations. Entry for foreign visitors is 50dh. 8 Rue d'Amerique, Tanger. legation.org +212 539-935317
2 mins, 35.7841, -5.8106

11 LIBRAIRIE DES COLONNES

Since 1949, the Librairie des Colonnes bookshop has been a Tangier institution steeped in history. A haven for writers and artists such as Samuel Beckett, Jack Kerouac and Paul Bowles who found inspiration among the shelves. Today, the shop remains an essential destination for book lovers, offering a unique blend of old-world charm and contemporary titles. 54 Boulevard Pasteur, Tangier 90020. +212 539-936955
2 mins, 35.7798, -5.8093

12 RIF CINEMA

The Rif Cinema was established in the 1930s and is famous for its art deco architecture. The cinema hosts film festivals, art events and community screenings as well as showing classic and contemporary films. An adjoining café is home to Cinémathèque de Tangier, a non-profit organisation dedicated to Moroccan film development. Grand Socco, Place du 9 Avril 1947, Tangier, 90000. cinemathequedetanger.com +212 539-934683
2 mins, 35.7838, -5.8131

13 MOHAMED DRISSI GALLERY

Located in a historical building that used to be the residence of the former consul general of the United Kingdom, the gallery showcases both local and international artists. Place de la Kasbah, Tanger 90030. +212 539-936073
2 mins, 35.7820, -5.8159

14 KASBAH MUSEUM

Established in 1997, the museum is housed in a former Sultan's palace. Exhibits include archaeological artefacts, traditional Moroccan ceramics, textiles and artworks that highlight the influences of Amazigh, Arab and European cultures. The museum has several rooms dedicated to the history of Tangier and its role as a major port city. Head to the western edge of the medina; at the highest point, go through the Bab Kasbah gate until you reach the museum. Pl. de la Kasbah, Tanger 90030. +212 539-912092
3 mins, 35.7882, -5.812

14

15

15 VILLA HARRIS MUSEUM

An impressive collection of north African art housed in the exquisite, recently restored villa of Walter Burton Harris (1866-1933) and surrounded by extensive, shady public gardens. A British journalist, author and travel writer, Harris was celebrated for his vivid portrayals of life in north Africa and his engagement with the cultural and political landscapes of Morocco. Highly recommended. Rent a bike from MJ Bike Morocco or walk E along the corniche for 5km; park and Villa are opposite Hôtel Tarik. Avenue Mohammed VI, Tangier, Morocco. +212 763-074502

2 mins, 35.7827, -5.7642

LAKES & RIVERS

16 BARRAGE SIDI HSSEIN

A dirt track leads to the quiet lake, bordered on one side by a wood of Aleppo pine, eucalyptus, wild olive trees and broom. A family group sat in the shade below the trees, while others strolled around the lake: an obvious escape from the city, with a great view of Tangier. Dotted around the lake were locals fishing. On this spring day the grass was scattered with wildflowers, including purple valerian and bright yellow of common sunflowers. Sheep calmly grazed in the fields below the ridge, which separated the lake from the fields. From Tangier, head S on P4602; at roundabout, take the 1st exit onto P4600 for 400m; entrance and parking (35.6930, -5.8274) is on your R; walk along path to lake

2 mins, 35.6936, -5.8278

ANCIENT

17 CAVE OF HERCULES

Mythology claims that the Greek hero Hercules found refuge in this cave before embarking on his 11th task: retrieving the golden apples of the Hesperides in nearby Lixus (513). Legend also has it that the cave marks one end of a subterranean tunnel stretching 24km to St Michael's Cave in Gibraltar, a passageway supposedly used by Barbary macaque monkeys to migrate. Meanwhile, back in the real world, the cave boasted two entrances: one to the sea, famously called 'The Map of Africa', and another to the land. Intricate stalactites and rock formations have created a breathtaking spectacle. Popularity has led to crowds, so arrive early to fully appreciate the power and the magic. From Tangier head S on N1 for 14km to Spartel where you will see signs for the cave; take City Tour bus from Tangier; Grottes D'Hercule Tour (tanger.city-tour.com); hire a bike from MJ Bike Morocco. Rte des Grottes d'Hercule, Tanger +212 606-703374

4 mins, 35.7599, -5.9392

15

12

21

25

26

18 PHOENICIAN TOMBS

Established by the Phoenicians between1000 and 800 BC, Tangier has few physical remnants of its founders. Most Punic relics were looted, destroyed or eroded, but thankfully these tombs survived. The Hafa Necropolis, originally home to an estimated 98 graves carved into the rock, dates back 3,000 years. Excavations from 1910 to 1960 revealed the tombs; 20 are still visible today. The necropolis offers an incredible view across the Strait of Gibraltar towards the Spanish town of Tarifa. From the outskirts of the old medina, take the Avenue Ibn Al Abbar, which becomes the Avenue A Imam Malik; after 800m, turn R at the stadium and the parking will be on your L (35.7893, -5.8216); walk N towards Avenue Hadj Mohamed Tazi, turn R and then the first L at the sign for the *Tombeaux Phéniciens*.

5 mins, 35.7907, -5.8201

19 CHÂTEAU DE MNAR

Perched atop the headland that gave the castle its name, this building stands out like a particularly well-fortified thumb next to the anodyne-looking petrol station. The building is a Portuguese fort from the 1600s. Turn off the N16 about 12km out of Tangier (35.8115, -5.7385), opposite the Shell petrol station; follow the track down to the castle to the parking spot.

1 min, 35.8144, -5.7393 £

ADVENTURE

20 MJ BIKE MOROCCO

A fun and eco-friendly way to explore Tangier. Enthusiastic and helpful staff can arrange city and coastal tours to Cap Spartel. We hired a couple of bikes for an afternoon and had an unforgettable ride along the promenade to Villa Harris gallery and gardens. Standard and E-bikes for hire. Rue du Port, Tangier 90000. +212 639-394957

1 min, 35.7856, -5.8087 £

CAFÉS & EATERIES

21 CAFE HAFA

Perched on a cliff top just outside Tangier's old medina, Cafe Hafa offers unparalleled views of the Bay of Tangier. Opened in 1921, it has retained its original decor, with levels of terraced seating facing the Strait of Gibraltar, with Spain visible in the distance. Once a favoured haunt of the Beat Generation, Café Hafa has hosted notable figures such as Paul Bowles, William S. Burroughs and The Rolling Stones. Renowned for its mint tea, Café Hafa serves a special Tangier brew that attracts locals and tourists alike. Rue Hafa, Tangier.

35.7913, -5.8218 £

22 SUNSET CAFE

Do as Hercules did; enjoy a mint tea on the balcony beneath colourful parasols overlooking both the Mediterranean and Atlantic. Next door to the Cave of Hercules. Rte des Grottes d'Hercule, Tanger

35.7599, -5.9389 £

23 ABOU TAYSSIR

A cosy little corner where you can enjoy a slice of Syria, with falafels, shawarma and a wide variety of other tasty Middle Eastern dishes. The owner is warm and welcoming, taking time to chat with customers. 11 rue Italie Bab el Fahs, Tangier 90000. +212 644-660292

35.7864, -5.8133 £

17

19

24 CAFÉ MNAR

Nothing to see here apart from the views. Good mint tea. Directions as for Lighthouse Cap Malabata. +212 620-687696

35.8167, -5.7486 £

PLACES TO STAY

25 CAMPING MIRAMONTE

With the sea on one side and the city of Tangier on the other, this hilltop family-run campsite offers a welcome retreat. Well-maintained, tree-filled gardens provide shade for relaxing. Hotel rooms are also available. The swimming pool, overlooked by sun terraces, is seriously impressive. We spent a memorable morning jumping and diving from the diving board. The pool is open to day visitors for a fee. The on-site restaurant serves decent food made from locally sourced ingredients. If you're driving, there's a very steep road with a hairpin bend leading to the campsite entrance. Camping Miramonte, Route de la Plage Merkala, Tangier 90000. +212 695-075127

35.7903, -5.8313

26 HOTEL CONTINENTAL

Grandly overlooking the Port of Tangier, the Hotel Continental transports you back in time. Built in 1870, the hotel's rich history is palpable from the moment you step inside. With views of the Mediterranean Sea and the Strait of Gibraltar, it offers a unique connection to Tangier's past, where literary figures such as Paul Bowles and William Burroughs found inspiration. Walking through its corridors, it's easy to imagine Tennessee Williams and Henri Matisse soaking up the atmosphere that permeates this charming old hotel. We particularly loved having breakfast on the terrace, overlooking the ocean – a scene straight out of a 1950s film. Despite its age, Hotel Continental makes an effort to be eco-friendly, with solar panels and energy-efficient lighting discreetly blending into its historic architecture. The hotel uses locally sourced ingredients in its restaurant. Park near the port (35.7845, -5.8083) and get tokens from the hotel. Rue Dar Baroud N° 36, Ancienne Medina, Tanger (90000). hcontinental-tanger.com +212 539-931024

35.7873, -5.8095 £££

20

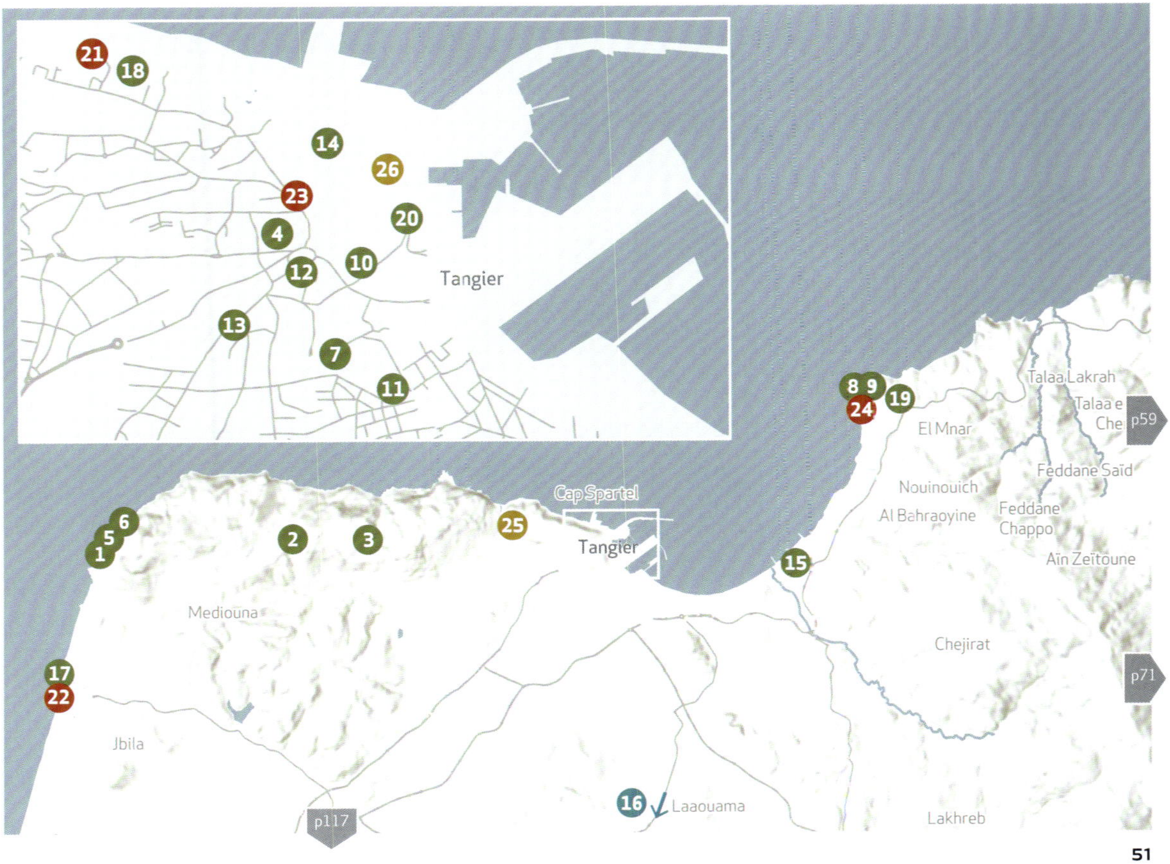

Tangier

Cap Spartel

Tangier

Mediouna

Jbila

El Mnar

Nouinouich

Al Bahraoyine

Talaa Lakrah

Talaa e Che

Feddane Saïd

Feddane Chappo

Aïn Zeïtoune

Chejirat

Laaouama

Lakhreb

p59

p71

p117

AROUND BOUJMIL MOUNTAINS

Our perfect adventure

- **Refresh** yourself in the waters of the Mediterranean at Zrarae beaches
- **Wander** through antiquity at the coastal fortress of Ksar-es-Sghir
- **Witness** three countries, two continents in one view from Belyounech Panorama and Mirador del Estrecho
- **Climb** the curves of Belyounech's 'Sleeping Woman'
- **Hike** through misty mountains and meet monkeys and wild horses on Boujmil Mountain Peak
- **Sample** legendary Moroccan hospitality and take in the mountain and sea views from Boujmil Guest House
- **Glide** through the mountain-fringed waters of Barrage Asmir
- **Dine** on tasty tagines and watch the horses prance in the paddock at Café Fadaa Dadash

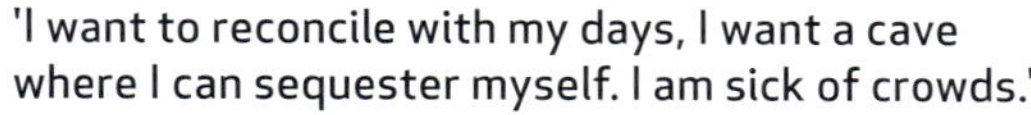

'I want to reconcile with my days, I want a cave where I can sequester myself. I am sick of crowds.'

El Habib Louai, Poetic Justice

The Boujmil Mountain range is full of hiking trails, hidden valleys and silvery peaks; their beauty eerily reminiscent of scenes from Lord of the Rings. Around every corner, we expected to see Frodo, Aragorn or Legolas striding majestically towards us. We took a hike up to the Boujmil Mountain peak early one morning, the sun peeking its head over the tops of the mountains. The paths snaked through grassy valleys, fringed by silver-white rocks. Just before cresting a verge, we looked back at the valleys below us, stretching all the way to the sea. We gasped, taking in its majesty and the feeling of romantic solitude. At that very moment, a man in corduroy trousers, a Paris Saint-Germain jacket and flip-flops strode over the crest of a verge, giving us a wave and a salaam. As we have learned in Morocco, whether you're on an isolated beach or high on a mountain, as if by magic, someone will appear.

Cresting that same verge, laughing at ourselves, we saw what we had been looking for: wild horses – a mare and two foals, grazing in the valley below us. To our left came the single cry of a monkey, warning his troop that there were humans around, before streaking off into the rocks. The horses paid us little mind though, and with a haughty aloofness and a toss of her mane, the mare continued grazing to her heart's content. We took in the panorama of mountain peaks, leading down to the sea to our left and encompassing the wide waters of the Barrage Asmir and, beyond it, the cold heights of the White Mountain.

The coastline surrounding Boujmil is rich with treasures, both natural and man-made. Family-friendly beaches such as Zrarae and Fardioua fringe the coastline, with the nearby fortified medieval bastion of Ksar-es-Seghir standing squat and resolute in the defence of its lands. From the seaside village of Belyounech, take a hike into the nearby mountains, reaching a peak known locally as 'The Sleeping Woman,' named for its silhouette resembling a reclining figure against the sky. Belyounech also offers breathtaking vistas of two continents and three countries.

BEACHES

1 ZRARAE BEACH #1

The first of the two Zrarae beaches is nestled beneath cliffs that roll down to its sands, covered in gorse, wildflowers and the occasional roaming donkey. Zrarae Beach is popular with local families, with children throwing themselves into the water as a vast array of ships pass through the Strait of Gibraltar. The water was clear and still and the entry was gentle. From Tangier, head E on N16 for 40km, taking the L exit and park near Station Afriquia petrol station (35.8303, -5.6747); walk 100m down path towards the beach; at bottom of cliff follow LH fork to beach

10 mins, 35.8327, -5.6746

2 ZRARAE BEACH #2

Smaller and cosier than its more accessible counterpart, this beach is ideal if you prefer silence and solitude for your day on the coast. Golden sands and clear blue Mediterranean water. Directions as for Zrarae #1; at the fork at the bottom of the cliff, follow path along the clifftop; after 100m you will pass an auxiliary station on L; continue to beach.

15 mins, 35.8323, -5.6719

3 FARDIOUA BEACH

A lovely place to spend an afternoon on the sand or even just to enjoy a quick glass of mint tea and some sweet biscuits from the café. Entry into the water is gradual and gentle, making this an ideal spot for families with young children to cool off from the heat of the day with a refreshing dip. Take the N16 40km E from Tangier; take L down unmarked road (35.8272, -5.6111); follow to electricity relay and parking spot (35.8301, -5.6132); walk L to borders of the electricity relay; turn R for 30m towards the beach

10 mins, 35.8324, -5.6153

LAKES & RIVERS

4 BARRAGE ASMIR

A vast, sprawling reservoir surrounded by mountains, popular with locals of all ages to cool off in the midday sun. Boys and girls throw themselves headlong into the water, carefree and with shouts of delight, while elderly couples sit beneath parasols with their toes in the water, sipping tea or coffee. The bottom of the lake is slightly muddy but it still makes for a delicious swim. No roads in this area have names, so follow GPS co-ordinates.

2 mins, 35.6974, -5.3931

1

1

5

4

6

5 BARRAGE HASSAN BEN EL MAHDI

Calm, reflective waters stretch out towards the horizon, framed by arid, rocky landscapes interspersed with patches of greenery.
At the far end of the reservoir, opposite the dam, a flat stretch of land offers a perfect vantage point to gaze over the turquoise waters towards hills dotted with colourful buildings.
In the distance, the white limestone cliffs of the Rif Mountains rise dramatically above the rippling waters. The sound of seagulls fills the air as they fly off in a cloud of wings as a man rides past with two donkeys, while sheep graze peacefully on the slopes. Wind turbines spin lazily, adding a modern touch to the tranquil scene. Walking around most of the reservoir is possible but the terrain is exposed, with little shade or facilities, so it's essential to bring your own food and drink if you plan to spend the day here. Don't forget your sunscreen. Though not officially designated as a campsite, visitors have been known to camp here. Head E out of Tétouan, follow the N2 for 4km until reaching the roundabout; turn right on to the P4701, follow it for 21km until you see the reservoir on your L. Turn down a dirt track on to flat ground where you can park (35.7138, -5.5192).

1 min, 35.7142, -5.5192

VIEWPOINTS

6 BELYOUNECH PANORAMA

The most northerly point of Morocco, with expansive views across the water towards Europe and Gibraltar. From the pharmacy in the centre of Belyounech, take the road N for 1.8km past the mosque and the epicerie, until reaching the very end of the road on the headland. Park where you can.

3 mins, 35.9204, -5.4034

7 MIRADOR DEL ESTRECHO

Three countries, two continents, one view: what more could you ask for? Located near the Spanish exclave of Ceuta, the fishing town of Belyounech is a hidden gem for all those who are suckers for a scintillating view, taking in Morocco, Spain and the rock of Gibraltar. Also popular with hikers as it is located at the base of Jbel Musa, an 842m mountain also known as the 'The Sleeping Woman', its profile resembling a woman at rest. Take the N16 east from Tangier, towards Fnideq. 20km before the town there is a junction with a police checkpoint and signs for Belyounech. Turn L and follow road for 6km before entering the town. Upon entering town, take first L and follow coast road for 300m to parking (35.9096, -5.3870).

1 min, 35.9096, -5.3870

8

8

8

8 BOUJMIL MOUNTAIN PEAK

The view from the peak has to be seen to be believed. The landscape encompasses rolling hills, sprawling lakes and the vast expanse of the Mediterranean; majestic mountains, hidden valleys and silvery peaks. Hiking trails snake through grassy valleys, past grazing cows and horses and foraging monkeys amid the silver-white rocks. The hike is a brisk two-hour round trip – ask at Boujmil Guest House for directions. Follow GPS co-ordinates as no roads in this area have names. Parking available in the village.

120 mins, 35.7671, -5.4373

9 OUED ZARJOUNE

Peaceful mountain village, complete with its own water source and a café run by a local woman who refused to let us pay for our coffee and lemonade: 'Pay me when you come back next time.' This village is surrounded by silvery-white mountains and is popular with hikers. No roads in this area have names, so follow GPS co-ordinates. Parking in village.

2 mins, 35.7286, -5.4373

ANCIENT

10 KSAR ES SEGHIR

Ksar es Seghir, a small, squat fortress at the mouth of a river, is known for its unusual circular design with thick walls, bastions and monumental gates built by the Marinid Sultan in 1287. Originally established as a Phoenician colony and later controlled by Romans, Byzantines and various Islamic dynasties and caliphates, the ksar served as a major embarkation port for troops heading to Spain. In 1458, the Portuguese captured the town from the pirates operating from behind its walls, fortifying it for nearly a century before abandoning it in 1549. In subsequent centuries, it declined into a small fishing village. The town of Ksar es Seghir has seen renewed significance this century with the construction of a Moroccan naval base and the nearby Tanger Med port. Turn L off the N16 near the river at the roundabout (35.8408, -5.5575) and the parking will be on your L (35.8425, -5.5569) just after the campsite; follow the signs for the castle from there, just behind the Plage Publique. Alternatively, walk 1.7km SW from Ksar es Seghir train station.

1 min, 35.8430, -5.5590

PLACES TO STAY

11 BOUJMIL GUEST HOUSE

Perched on the side of the Boujmil mountain, the terrace offered views down through the foothills and out to the sea. Cosy cabins with en suite bathrooms and showers are available, as well as a delicious lamb tagine. Follow GPS as no roads in this area have names. Douar Boujmil Commune Alalyiyene M'diq, Fnideq 93055. +212 661-590707

35.7683, -5.4376 ££

PLACES TO EAT

12 FADAA DADACH CAFÉ

A lovely place to get some refreshments after a morning spent hiking or swimming. We had a healthy-sized lemon, olive and chicken tagine and some fresh orange juice in the open air, with ducks and horses grazing in the fields around us. Follow GPS as no roads in this area have names.

35.6980, -5.3793 £

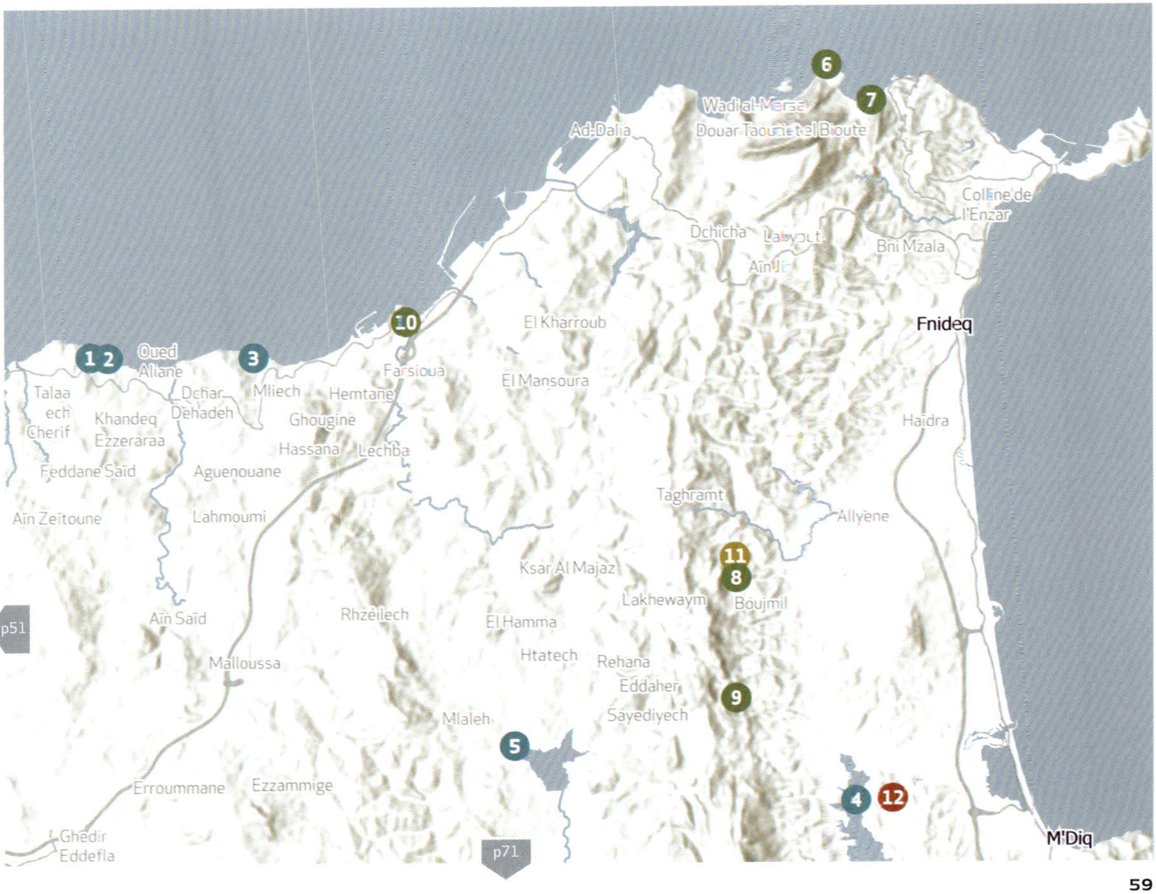

TETOUAN, CHEFCHAOUEN & RIF MOUNTAINS

Our perfect adventure

- → **Gaze** over the city of Tetouan from the cloud-shrouded heights of Jbel Ajnane
- → **Paddle** to your heart's content in the blue waters of Ain Zarka
- → **Picnic** on the reed-lined shores of the Oued Hajera at Sahtariiyn, in the shadow of the Rif Mountains
- → **Splash** through the waterfalls of Akchour and take an adrenaline-fuelled jump off the side of the dam
- → **Soak** in the awe-inspiring views from the heights of The God's Bridge, where Morocco's natural beauty stretches before you
- → **Swim** in perfect solitude and serenity at the river pool of Baofa, in the mountain's embrace
- → **Stroll** through the painted streets of the legendary blue village of Chefchaouen
- → **Relax** after a long day of adventuring and wandering in the cosy beauty of the Riad Bin Souaki, in the heart of Chefchaouen's old medina

'My country is a poem written in the colours of the sun and the shadows of the mountains.'

Mohammed Bennis, The Silence of the Body

Nestled among the green slopes and the untamed rivers of the Rif Mountains lies the village of Chefchaouen. The blue aesthetic has made it a popular tourist stop but it is nonetheless an unmissable visit and a great place to base yourself while you go in search of wilder adventures. The surrounding mountains are teeming with hikes and hidden trails and the nearby river of Oued Laou provides several wild swimming spots, including the isolated green waters of Baofa and the calmer pools of Oued Laou Familial.

The Rif Mountains have adventure in store for all those who want it; from the vast waterscapes of Embalse de la Palmera, where you can enjoy a mid-road trip dip, the hike up to The God's Bridge and the Akchour Waterfalls, complete with tranquil swimming holes perfect for families and jump spots for the more intrepid. Be sure to take a break from your journey at Café Karim, and enjoy a revitalising glass of sweet mint tea, looking out over the expansive panorama provided by Embalse de la Palmera. We took a road trip up into the mountains above the Tétouan and watched in wonderment as clouds cascaded off the peaks surrounding the city as the sun cast its final rays across the scene. The white houses of Tétouan were stacked up against the hillsides like shelves. We passed a herd of wild horses taking refuge from the wind in the concrete shell of a bus stop. What bus would be making it all the way into the depths of these mountains, we could not tell.

Coming down from our mountain stopover, we took a detour to Ain Zarka, a natural pool teeming with families on a hot summer's day. Boys and girls jumped with screams of delight from a cliff above the pool. One nine-year-old boy, braver or more foolish than the rest, climbed higher and higher up the cliff. 'There's no way he's going to jump from up there,' we whispered to each other – hoping he would. From 30 feet, the boy placed his back against the cliff face and, after only a few moments of deliberation, launched himself into the abyss and the applause that we had waiting for him.

LAKES & RIVERS

1 SAHTARIIYN

Pretty picnic spot along the banks of the Oued Hajera. Reeds and oleander line the banks. A small rabbit path takes you downstream before the river gets taken over by reeds. Walk downriver to find a good place to swim. Make sure you have worked out where to get out before you get in. From Bounane Bridge in Tetouan, take the N13 W for 6km; take third exit off roundabout by Paloma's Hotel on to N2; after 9km (ignoring Google maps) turn R at crossroads by Épicerie Ben Karrich; drive down steep hill for 1.4km; 20m after the road turns sharply right you will see a dirt track on the left where you can turn in and park (35.4874, -5.4382); walk along riverbank

2 mins, 35.4879, -5.4368

2 EMBALSE DE LA PALMERA

This vast, sprawling reservoir dominated our vision as we looked out across its sparkling waters, with the white heights of Monte Kelti at our back and the green peaks of the Rif Mountains ringing the shores of the lake before us. After walking over the hill from the parking spot and heading down towards the shore, a large tree offered shade. We saw people swimming and diving in from the shoreline. Take the N2 S from Tetouan, the reservoir lies between the towns of Dar Ben Karrich and Zinat; once you reach the reservoir, follow the N2 along its shore for 750m until you see a café on the LH side of the motorway and a hill leading to a promontory on the right; park at the base of the hill (35.4843, -5.41382) and follow the path over the hill down to the waters; the nearest beach on your R is fenced off and private, follow the path to your L towards the trees, you will find a publicly accessible shoreline.

10 mins, 35.4812, -5.4154

3 AIN ZARKA

A recreation area developed from a natural pool in the mountains, buzzing with energy on a scorching summer day. Boys and girls leapt from a cliff above the water, their joyous screams echoing through the air as their parents watched with eagle eyes. Made up of two pools, joined by the stream, one is deeper and fit for jumping, while the lower is shallower and suitable for younger children. Arrive early to avoid the crowds. There were cafés and stalls surrounding the pools. Park where you can in the village.

1 min, 35.5203, -5.3412

5

4

7

7

4 OUED IFERTEN

An offshoot of the Oued Laou river, winding its way toward the sea. As the river narrows, it becomes a peaceful stream, perfect for paddling rather than swimming. The water flows steadily and the bankside greenery and pink oleanders add that touch of colour. Overhead, a tall mosque minaret stands as a silent guardian, its presence adding reverence to the scene. The river was partially dammed with stones creating small cascades where the water rushed over the rocks. Take the P1405 from A Oued for 15km until you reach the bridge over the Oued Laou near Beni Ifertan; turn off on to the shingle path before the bridge and park next to the river (35.3529, -5.1855); on your R is Oued Iferten and straight ahead of you is Oued Laou Familial.

1 min, 35.3535, -5.1843

5 OUED LAOU FAMILIAL

While some sections of the Oued Laou river can be difficult to access, with steep descents into mountain valleys, Oued Laou Familial is next to the road. Ideal for those travelling with young children, the river becomes a wide lake and the entry into the water is gentle with little current. Wide shingle beach with huts to sit at. Popular wild swim spot with locals and perfect for a mid-trip dip. Directions as for Oued Iferten.

1 min, 35.3518, -5.1862

6 BAOFA RIVER VIEW

Hop out of your car and take in the panorama that the river and mountains have created for you. Small stall selling cold drinks and local wicker products. From Oued Laou SW on N16 for 23km to parking spot on L (35.2948, -5.2290).

1 min, 35.2948, -5.2290

7 BAOFA

Nestled deep in a lush mountain valley, the Oued Laou river winds its course towards the sea. A stone bridge arches over the river, offering a perfect vantage point to take in the scenery. From the bridge, a trail snakes down to a secluded swimming spot, where smooth rocks meet the river's edge. The water was cool and crystal clear. Just downstream, small rapids ripple and splash, adding a gentle soundtrack. As we settled in and got ready to take the plunge, a young boy appeared, leading a small herd of ten goats down to the riverbank. After guiding them into the water to cool off from the sun's heat, he pulled out a simple fishing rod, casting his line with a hopeful glance, eager to see what the river might offer. Directions as for Baofa River View, walk back from the parking at the viewpoint to the turn off to the R by the bus stop to Baofa; follow steep and rocky path 200m down to the river.

20 mins, 35.2935, -5.2309

8 CASCADE OUED LAOU

From a vantage point high on a cliff, the emerald-green waters of the Oued Laou river tumbled over rocks below. Mountains rose all around us, covered in green vegetation stretching down to the water's edge where fans of ferns and clusters of pink flowers lined the banks, their vibrant colours contrasting with the deep green of the water. At a bend in the river, a hydroelectric plant stands as a testament to human ingenuity, harnessing the river's power to provide electricity to the villages, hamlets and homes scattered throughout the mountains. The plant's presence adds a sense of purpose to the otherwise serene setting, but it also means that this particular stretch of the river is inaccessible, its powerful currents and infrastructure making it unfortunately off-limits to swimmers and adventurers alike. Nonetheless, the beauty of the scene is untarnished, the river an essential artery flowing through the heart of the mountains. Turn off the N2 on to the P4105; follow it for 14km, passing through the town of Al Oued; the river and the hydroelectric station will come into view on your L and there is a space next to the road to park (35.2801, -5.23380); there is a rocky path down to the cliff's edge where you can get a better view of the landscape.

1 min, 35.2800, -5.2338

10
10
10
10

9 AKCHOUR WATERFALLS

A breathtaking natural wonder, the area features a series of cascades and pools, with the most famous being the 'Grand Cascade', which plunges energetically from 100m into a clear, turquoise basin. The hike through Talassemtane National Park to the falls took us through a picturesque landscape of narrow trails, rocky paths and quaint wooden bridges crossing over streams, all enveloped by the soothing sounds of flowing water. The crystal-clear waters at the base of the falls are perfect for a refreshing swim. Beauty brings crowds. Early birds get peaceful swims. From the village Al Oued (35.2653, -5.2310), turn R on to the Route d'Akchour and follow it for 6km until reaching the parking spot (35.2393, -5.1822); follow the signposted trail into the mountains; there are a range of waterfalls to choose from along the path.

60 mins, 35.2432, -5.1819 (trailstart)

10 OUED EL KANNAR

The water was crystal clear and there was a deluge of deep blue pools in which to dip, swim and dive. In summer, there were many shacks selling cold drinks, tagines and cookies. Other shacks offered tents to sleep in for 200dh for two people a night. We walked up the river for half an hour and found ourselves ensconced in the wild belly of the river gorge, with towering cliffs on either side. We had been warned, though, that we needed to wade through water up to our necks and hold our bags above our heads to reach the higher pools. The river was a rite of passage – young children splashed about at the lower pool, older kids further upstream. Teenage daredevils practised their jumps and dives from high up on the hillside. In one pool, we watched a young woman in trousers and a long-sleeved top practising her breaststroke while her husband watched proudly. Remembering our childhood life-saving lessons swimming in pyjamas, we mused on how much more difficult it must have been for her to learn. Also known as Wadi El Qanar.

From Steha, head SW on N16 for 5.2km; turn R on to P4111 for 13.5km; after 1.5km take the R fork; follow road for 6.5km to parking spot (35.2155, -5.0145).

5 mins, 35.2153, -5.0156

TREKS

11 THE GOD'S BRIDGE

A rare red rock formation within Talassemtane National Park, which towers 25m above the river Oued Farda; it almost beggars belief that this bridge was carved by nature and not by human hand. Over countless millennia, the river flowed as an underground watercourse, eroding the rock and carving a path deeper and deeper,

11

9

leaving the bridge high and dry. Directions as for Akchour Waterfall; follow the signposted trail to God's Bridge.

60 mins, 35.2283, -5.1754

12 BOUHACHEM NATURE RESERVE

A protected area celebrated for its biodiversity, forests and rugged mountains. The reserve is home to a number of plant species, including the endemic Moroccan cedar as well as yellow oak, cork oak, and various wildflowers. The park supports wildlife such as the endangered Barbary macaque, wild boar, and birds, including the Bonelli's eagle. Established to promote conservation and sustainable tourism, Bouhachem offers hiking trails to explore its breathtaking scenery. Roads are very basic. No facilities so take water and food. Best visited between October and March. From Chefchaouen take the N2 W for 60km then turn L into the park. If you need a guided tour, contact Eco Rando Chefchaouen +212 672-743347

10 mins, 35.1737, -5.3131

ANCIENT

13 ARCHAEOLOGICAL SITE TAMUDA

Tamuda was an ancient Amazigh city in Mauretania Tingitana, located near present-day Tetouan. Looking at the site facing north, the modern city provides an impressive urban backdrop to the double arches that have been excavated. Founded in the 3rd century BC, the city likely had a Phoenician presence for commerce, as indicated by artefacts like a clay jar with Phoenician seahorse iconography. The Romans occupied Tamuda under Emperor Augustus, but after a local insurrection around AD42, Roman forces destroyed the city and established a fortified settlement. Under Roman rule, Tamuda became a significant city, known for fish salting and purple dye production. The city's ruins were near fortifications that later evolved into Tetouan. Follow the Route Torreta out of Tetouan for 2km; the entrance to the site will be on your L. +212 539-969703

3 mins, 35.5591, -5.4109

VIEWPOINTS

14 JBEL AJNANE

Above the clouds. Sublime views across the valley towards Tetouan and beyond. Accessed by steep and winding mountain roads. From Tetouan, follow Route Torreta S for 6km; parking place on your R.

2 mins, 35.5250, -5.3956

15 AL KHANOOS

Another great viewpoint across the valley. A solitary concrete shell of a bus stop stood firm against the buffeting winds, presumably servicing the tiny mountain hamlet that lay below. Although it is doubtful they got any use out of it, as a herd of horses had taken up residence in and around the bus stop shelter, staring with eyes that seemed to dare us to come closer and relieve them of their spot. Directions as for Jbel Ajnane, then continue S for 5.7km; at the fork, take the LH road and continue for 1km; at the fork, the viewpoint will be on your R.

1 min, 35.4784, -5.3660

CAFÉS & EATERIES

16 FROMAGERIE CHEFCHAOUEN

The fromagerie specialises in the production of cheese made from goat's milk. It has a diversified range of freshly made products, including cured hard goat cheese, goat gouda and goat feta. Yoghurt is also for sale. Km 60 route de Tetouan/Ouzzane Amlay. +212 641-991320

35.1759, -5.3115

17 CAFÉ KARIM

Rustic café with traditional decorations overlooking Embalse de la Palmera. The sweetest place for a mint tea and orange juice while soaking up the view of the lake and surrounding mountains. Food is also available. FHMP-RV, Zinat

35.4843, -5.4130

PLACES TO STAY

18 DAR DYAFA ELKHANOS

Rustic homestay after a breathtaking journey over the mountains from Tetouan. An authentic Amazigh experience in a family home, complete with a goat yard. Tasty tagine, olives and msemen. No shower. Cross Bouanane Bridge out of Tetouan; at roundabout take third exit on to Route Torreta; at roundabout after 1.3km take first exit, bear L; after 17km turn right across scrubland to house. +212 639-828333

35.4834, -5.3366

19 GÎTE TALASSEMTANE & ECO RANDO

Family-run ecolodge committed to eco-tourism. Features rustic stone walls, colourful tiles, and cosy, simple rooms. Incredible mountain views from the breakfast terrace. A warm, welcoming atmosphere and home-cooked, locally sourced food. Through the owners' venture, Eco Rando Chefchaouen, day or longer treks can be organised throughout Talassemtane National Park, to Amazigh villages and to the peaks of Jbel Lakraa (2,159m) and Jbel Tissouka (2,122m). Zaouiyat Hapteene, Commune, Bab Taza 91000. gitetalassemtane.com +212 672-743347

35.1162, -5.1982

20 RIAD BIN SOUAKI

Located in the heart of Chefchaouen's blue medina, Riad Bin Souaki is decorated in a simple yet beautiful Moroccan style, with its en suite rooms and common areas tiled with mosaics and beautifully carved arched doors. Our host

15

12

15

21

was engaging and welcoming, telling us how this house had belonged to his grandfather and had been in his family for generations. We ate a hearty Moroccan breakfast on the rooftop terrace overlooking the clustered roofs of Chefchaouen, before exploring the rest of the village. Park on the edge of medina (35.1697, -5.2658) Free Wi-Fi. Mohamed taleb, 15 Derb Rue Bin Souaki, Chefchaouen 91000. +212 661-448904

35.1698, -5.2627 ££

21 HAVEN HILLS SOCIAL CLUB

Set in the hills above Chefchaouen, this riad has fantastic views over the green and white slopes of the Rif Mountains. Designed by Spanish architects and built by local craftsmen, Haven Hills is a tasteful blend of European and Moroccan and has a focus on ecological practices. There was a well-stocked kitchen with vegetables and herbs from their own garden for guests to prepare their meals. It has only been open two years and their visions for the future include an outdoor kitchen to run cooking classes, a social centre and a Greco-Roman gym with stone weights. Free Wi-Fi. Private rooms and dorm rooms are available. Rte de Loubar, Chefchaouen 91000. havenhills8@gmail.com +212 718-330008

35.1614, -5.2516 ££

22 CAMPING LES FRÈRES

Restaurant and budget campsite at the bottom of the gorge beside the river, Oued El Kannar. Tents with basic bedding are provided. Tagines and grilled fish when available. Moroccan breakfast. Friendly and hospitable. From Oued El Kannar parking spot, walk 100m upstream. +212 605-061094

35.2152, -5.0197 £

23 GÎTE D'ÉTAPE OUED KANNAR

Incredible views over the mountains and valleys from the roof terrace where the stars clearly do come out at night. A basic hostel with three rooms of four, five and six beds and hot showers. The owner, Nuredin, was a kind and helpful host who cooked great food including imaginative vegetarian options such as lentil stew with fresh soft cheese. All the food was organic and sourced locally in the Thursday souk. Nuredin can organise a guide and transport to Oued El Kannar and speaks excellent French, Spanish and English. From Bni Bouzra head W on N16 for 3.7km; turn L on to P4111 for 13.5km; take the R fork just after Épicerie Khmiss Louta and after 800m your destination will be on the right signposted Hotel Kanar. +212 660-970567

35.2036, -4.9959 £

22

23

19

23

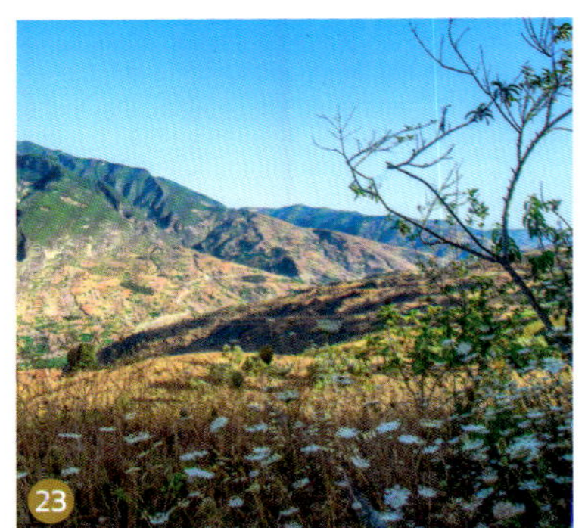

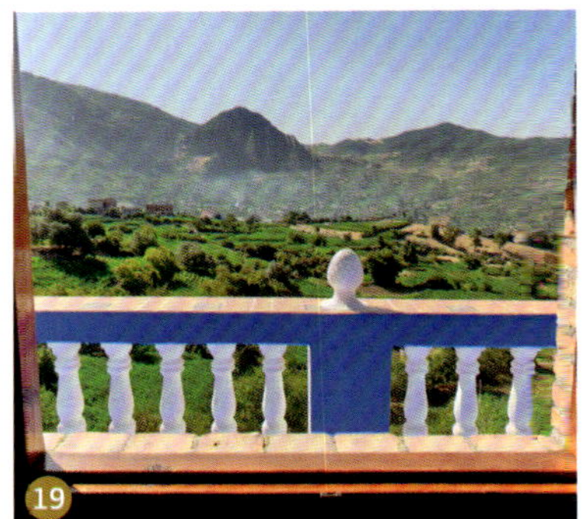

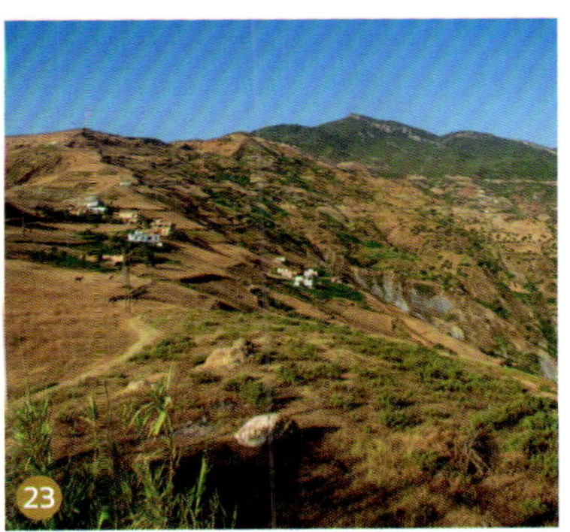

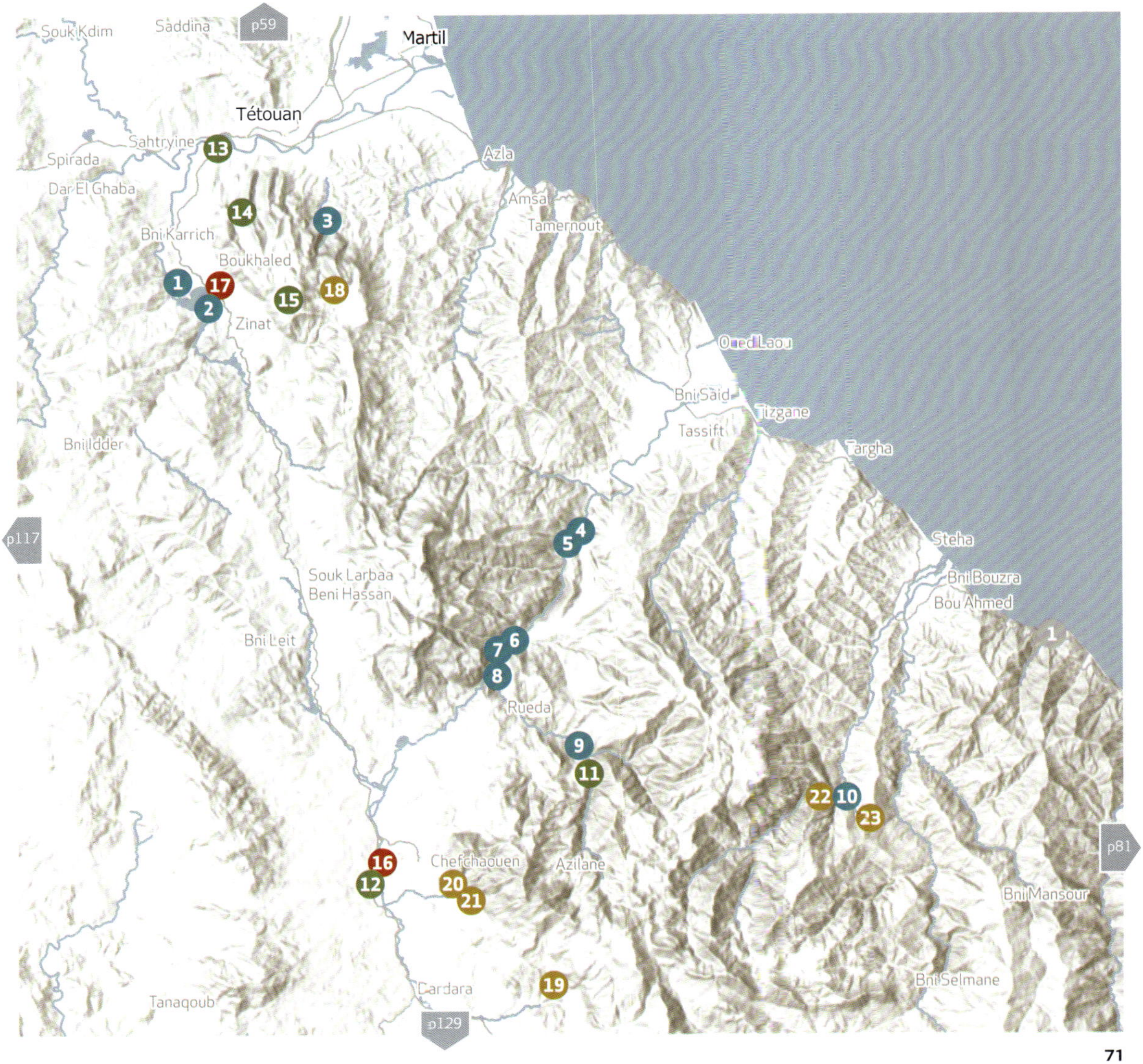
Souk Kdim
Saddina
p59
Martil
Tétouan
Sahtryine
13
Spirada
Dar El Ghaba
14
3
Bni Karrich
Boukhaled
1
17
2
15
18
Zinat
Azla
Amsa
Tamernout
Oued Laou
Bni Said
Tizgane
Tassift
Targha
Bni Idder
p117
4
5
Souk Larbaa
Beni Hassan
Steha
Bni Bouzra
Bou Ahmed
1
Bni Leit
6
7
8
Rueda
9
11
22
10
23
p81
16
Chefchaouen
Azilane
12
20
21
Bni Mansour
Cardara
19
Bni Selmane
Tanaqoub
p129

15

OUED LAOU TO AL HOCEÏMA

Our perfect adventure

- **Wake** to the soothing sounds of the sea at Taghassa Camp
- **Roar** along the coastal highway, the wind in your ears and the sea in your sight
- **Watch** the world go by beneath you from the heights of the ruined El Jebha watchtower
- **Hike** along the shore from Marsdar Beach, taking in the hidden beauties of Playa Monika and Plage Lhwat
- **Discover** the shortest international land border in the world at Plage de Badès
- **Descend** to the challenge of the 700 steep steps down to Plage Taoussarte
- **Plot** up at Camping Amis de Cala Iris, an eco-conscious retreat perched above Almarsa Ighaniman beach
- **Devour** the view and the *sardinne shwa* (grilled sardines) with cumin-infused salsa at Taoussarte Mira Meditiranie

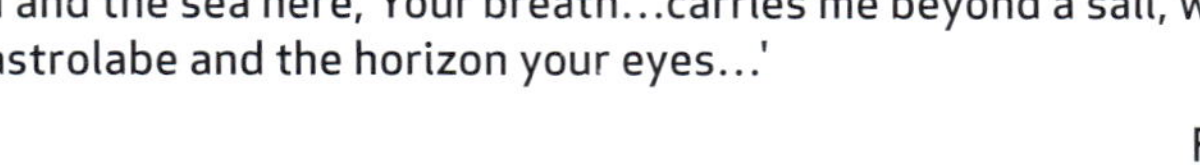

'I and the sea here, Your breath...carries me beyond a sail, without astrolabe and the horizon your eyes...'

Fatiha Morchid

The Rif Mountains tumble into the Mediterranean Sea, eager to catch a glimpse of its shimmering waters. In stark contrast to the flat, sandy beaches of the Atlantic coast, these shingly shores are harder to reach, lying at the base of steep cliffs, offering the promise of solitary swims. The several secretive sea caves that intersperse the northern coastline beckon adventurers to explore their depths. The sinuous N16 coastal road snakes from Tangier to Saïdia near the Algerian border, gifting drivers and passengers panoramic vistas of the sea.

Perched high on the cliffs among the seagulls, an ancient watchtower stands sentinel over the bay at El Jebha. This little port holds a hidden trove of treasures for travellers, deriving its name from its location at the foot of a mountain range. In Arabic, 'El Jebha' means 'forehead,' a reflection of how the surrounding mountains resemble a forehead. Even in ruins, the watchtower retains a majestic presence.

Far below, rocky promontories of Marsdar Beach form a natural bay, complete with a steep path leading down to the stony shore. The beach is easily accessible by boat from nearby El Jebha – an option the vast majority of visitors seem to prefer. However, we are made of sterner stuff and chose to hike the full distance from the watchtower to Plage Lhwat, taking in Playa Monika and the sea caves of El Jebha along the way.

We watched local boys dive and perform somersaults off the headlands while fishermen brought in the day's catch. Upon reaching the pebbly shores of Playa Monika, we paused to catch our breath, listening to the soothing sound of waves filtering back through the pebbles. The sea caves of El Jebha extend deep into the rocks and they are eerily hypnotic to behold as the waves roll in and out, revealing potential passages to unknown secrets.

As we traversed the final headland of our hike, Lhwat Beach stretched into the distance, its grey, sandy expanses framed by low clouds. Headland after headland faded into the mist, resembling an infinity mirror.

BEACHES

1 PLAGE SIDI YAHYA AARAB

This region of Morocco's northern coast seems to break from the established rules for fishing vessels. While almost everywhere else boats are painted a deep blue, perhaps in homage or deference to the sea they sail upon, fishing craft here are painted a distinctly earthy, deep red, with a white line along the rail. Defiance perhaps? As we strolled along the pebbly beach, we made sure to avoid interrupting the sacred sanctity of the football game in full swing. We found ourselves drawn by an irresistible urge: skimming stones. A happy half hour spent reliving our childhoods flinging stones out across the water, laughing in delight at our triumphs and failures in equal measure. Equipped with a café selling mint tea and grilled sardines, this beach is the perfect place to let the world out of your head for a while and simply enjoy the moment. Turn off the N16 on to the access road (35.2978, -4.8849) and turn L into the village; follow the track for 2 mins until you reach the parking spot on your R (35.2995, -4.8825).

3 mins, 35.3002, -4.8793

2 PLAGE TAGHASSA

This wide cove embraces all those who love the sea, with mountains to the north providing a dramatic backdrop to your swim. As we looked out across the small waves of the Mediterranean, clouds tumbled off the mountains like an avalanche in the sky, set on fire by the light of the setting sun. The beach has a short but steep entry into the water and is made of grey shingle. Turn off the N16 (35.2191, -4.7355) follow the track down to the shore, turn L at the sea and drive along the coastal path for 4 mins to the parking spot (35.2243, -4.7366).

1 min, 35.2243, -4.7397

3 MARSDAR BEACH

The rocky mountain promontories form a natural bay with a steep path leading down from the parking to the stony shore below. This beach is also accessible by boat from nearby El Jebha. As we walked down the path to the beach, we watched local boys execute dives and somersaults off the headlands next to fishermen bringing in the day's catch. These contrasting activities of work and joy were set against the backdrop of vast sea caves that puncture the headlands, a testament to the power of the sea. Ruined towers and huts sit on the heights of the dusty yellow cliffs behind the beach, speaking to a time when this bay was significantly more populated. Turn off the N16 in the town of El Jebha (35.2069, -4.6651) and follow the road up on to the cliffs above the town; take a left at the first fork and follow the road until you reach the auxiliary forces station at the tip of the headland and park (35.2116, -4.6623); walk out of the parking area and towards the auxiliary station; follow the path running next to it heading down the cliff; the path is rocky with no steps or handrails; continue for 200m and includes two switchbacks, after which the full expanse of the bay will come into view; the path continues on the northern side of the bay under an overhang, before reaching a steep descent and some rough-hewn steps cut into the cliff itself just before reaching the beach.

20 mins, 35.2100, -4.6594

4 PLAYA MONIKA

A tiny beach hidden between two headlands looking out onto the sea caves of El Jebha. Secluded and serene, the only sound to be heard was the waves filtering back through the pebbles. Hike 500m R across Marsdar Beach and over the headland down into the cove.

45 mins, 35.2118, -4.6535

6

9

8

7

5 SEA CAVES OF EL JEBHA

These caves can be seen from the land, but this involves a precarious scramble across a cliff face with very unsure footholds. The easiest way is to get a boat out from the town of El Jebha. The caverns penetrate deep into the rocks and are eerily hypnotising as the waves roll in and out of them, potential passages to unknown secrets. Unfortunately, you can't swim into them as the entrances have been blocked with nets by local authorities. Scramble along the cliffs at Playa Monika or take a boat from El Jebha.

45mins, 35.2122, -4.6531

6 LHWAT BEACH

Grey mountain sands stretched far into the distance and Al-Hwat beach lay below us. Headland after headland disappeared into the low clouds like an infinity mirror. The number of parasols on the beach suggested that someone had been expecting crowds, yet apart from two young boys kicking a ball around, there was no one else in sight in June. Far in the distance sat a solitary silver 4x4, the only evidence this beach was accessible by the steep and rocky road that doesn't appear on Google Maps. You could also access this beach by boat. We hiked along the coast from Marsdar Beach. To drive to it turn off the N16 in the town of El Jebha (35.2069, -4.6651) and follow the road up onto the cliffs above the town; take a right at the first fork (35.2081, -4.6481) and follow the cliff top path round the cliffs of Marsdar Beach before dropping down steeply into Lhwat beach.

55 mins, 35.2111, -4.6491

7 PLAGE MESTASSA

A quiet, wide bay (500m) flanked on either side by gentle hills. At the centre, there was a small, ruined building resembling a mosque. The beach has large pebbles with smaller ones near the water. The shallow waters quickly drop off into a deep shelf. Turn off N16 at sign for Plage Mestassa; drive 4km along a dirt track to the beach; park where you can on the road at the back of the beach.

2 mins, 35.1546, -4.4295

8 AZROU 'N AQNOUSH

A long, wild, narrow pebble beach where people wild camped at the far end. The beach has a short drop into deep water. Directions as for Plage Mestassa, walk to the far L and climb over the large rocks or follow the path over the hill to the beach.

15 mins, 35.1572, -4.4402

9 ALMARSA IGHANIMAN

Small pebble beach just below Eco Camping Amis de Cala Iris. A great escape from the tourist crowds if the popular Plage Cala-Iris on the other side of the port is busy. No services, so come prepared with food and drinks. From Beni Boufrah follow P5205 signs for Cala Iris for 9km; second turning off roundabout then straight up hill; road turns into dirt track; at fork bear R; park just before beach (35.1480, -4.3746).

5 mins, 35.1484, -4.3746

10 PLAGE SBAE BIBANE

This quiet beach sits beneath high cliffs and the imposing Forteresse Torres de Alcalá. Take first turning R off P5204 after Torres-de-Alcala (35.1518, -4.3296) on to steep, sandy track for 600m; go past the fortress to the L; steep 400m track down to the beach with two tight hairpin bends so not suitable for motorhomes.

3 mins, 35.1566, -4.3310 

11 PLAGE MARSA CHARQI

A rocky beach east of the busy Plage de Torres, predominantly used by fishermen with their bright blue fishing boats, but also good for swimming and snorkelling. From Plage de Torres, walk and clamber over the rocks along the coast to the beach; if you are a strong swimmer, you could also swim round.

30 mins, 35.1618, -4.3204

12 PLAGE DE BADÈS

Surrounded by rugged cliffs that contrast sharply with the deep blue sea. The beach is divided into two areas: a cove between the islet of Peñón de Vélez de la Gomera and another beach to the west with a large rock where local youths jumped and dived. The islet is a tiny Spanish exclave with a small population of military personnel, which sits at the top of a narrow isthmus. At just 85m, this is the shortest international land border in the world. In summer, Plage de Badès comes alive with food and snack stalls selling grilled fish, churros and mint tea. From Rouadi, head W on N16 for 18km until you reach the beach.

2 mins, 35.1705, -4.2952

13 TARAKHSOUNT BEACH

Among the cleanest and isolated beaches on the Mediterranean coast. To get there you have to charter a day boat from Plage de Badès. Negotiate the price of the trip beforehand.

3 mins, 35.1796, -4.2766

14 PLAGE ETTRAKNA

Remote, uninhabited virgin beach surrounded by cliffs. You could be in Bali or Hawaii. To get there you have to charter a day boat from Plage de Badès. Negotiate the price of the trip beforehand.

5 mins, 35.1879, -4.2102

15 PLAGE TAOUSSARTE (700 STEPS)

This secluded beach required a challenging 40-minute hike through untamed countryside, followed by a descent of 700 steep steps. These steps had originally been carved out by local Amazigh communities to access the coast for fishing and trade. Although the journey was demanding, it rewarded us with a gorgeous

14

15

14

coastal retreat set against a dramatic backdrop of headlands and towering mountains. A large rock stood defiantly in the water about 20 metres from the shore, while the beach itself was made up of large grey pebbles with a steep incline leading into the sea. Water shoes are advisable for navigating the stony shoreline. The beach's strong waves made it a popular destination for experienced swimmers and adventurous beachgoers. Camping permitted. Remember the ascent up the 700 steps is harder than the descent. From Al Hoceïma take P5211 W for 7km; at the roundabout turn R on to N16 for 14km; at sign for Taoussarte Beach turn R for 11km; turn R at the sign for parking 700 la plaj (35.2044,-4.0960) for 500m; the car park is on R (35.2077, -4.0936); from car park follow path and steps down to beach.

45 mins, 35.2195, -4.0855

16 BOUMEHDI BEACH

A beautiful bay beneath rocky headlands. Dark sand and large pebbles make it great for snorkelling. There were a handful of shacks selling food and drinks. Walk over the rocks to the right to find the wilder side, or to the left for ten minutes to discover a secluded sandy cove where people camped with tents. Wear sturdy shoes. There was a car park at the top, with a guardian present in summer. From Al Hoceïma, head W on Cor maritime de Sabadia for 9km; parking spot is on your R (35.2322, -4.0135); follow path down to beach.

5 mins, 35.2330, -4.0125

17 PLAGE RMOD

A small, sandy crescent just outside the town of Al Hoceïma where families swam together in the clear waters while young boys threw themselves off low cliffs. Those boys were brave to launch themselves in headfirst, as when I jumped feet-first I touched the sandy floor of the sea. Maybe they knew a trick I didn't. Turn off the Cor Maritime de Sabadia at the roundabout (35.2445, -3.9650) and the parking will be immediately on your R (35.2444, -3.9655).

2 mins, 35.2434, -3.9656

COASTAL FORTS

18 EL JEBHA WATCHTOWER

Perched high on the cliffs among the seagulls, this ancient watchtower stands sentinel over the bay. Even in ruins, it cuts a majestic figure. We entered the small observation post and watched seagulls and tourist boats pass beneath us. Directions as for Marsdar Beach; from the parking spot (35.2116, -4.6623), walk up the cliffs to the L.

5 mins, 35.2117, -4.6632

19 FORTERESSE TORRES DE ALCALÀ

Sitting majestically on a hillside, the fortress offers panoramic views of the Mediterranean, the beaches and the Rif Mountains. Originally constructed by the Almoravids in the twelfth century, the fortress played a crucial role in defending the empire against invaders and uprisings. In the sixteenth century, it was fortified by the Spanish during its north African expansion, becoming a site of resistance against Amazigh tribes and European colonial forces during the Rif War. Take first turning R off P5204 after Torres-de-Alcala (35.1518, -4.3296) on to steep, sandy track for 600m.

5 mins, 35.1558, -4.3300

LAKES & RIVERS

20 BARRAGE AL JOMOAA

This long narrow lake is the lifeblood of the surrounding villages. Beautiful views from the bridge across the dam, particularly at sunset, when the lake and entire valley are lit with an orange glow. From Place Mohamed VI de Targuist, head S along the road through Targuist for 850m until you reach a T-junction overlooking a football pitch; turn R and then L down a dusty path for 50m, which will lead you to the bank of the lake. Park in town.

12 mins, 34.9322, -4.3175

17

19

17

CAFÉS & EATERIES

21 COSTA DEL SOL

Laid-back beachfront café selling locally caught charcoal grilled fish. We watched a football match on TV with a group of enthusiastic Moroccan kids in the backroom. Great atmosphere, mint tea and churros. On the LH side of Plage de Torrès. Dr Torres, Beni Boufrah. +212 771-030483.

35.1572, -4.3274

22 CAFÊ ISMAIL

Enjoy freshly cooked churros and mint tea while overlooking the tiny Spanish exclave of Peñón de Vélez de la Gomera on Plage de Badès. Peñón de Vélez de la Gomera, Plage de Badès.

35.1707, -4.2973

23 TAOUSSARTE MIRA MEDITIRANIE

Sumptuous views over Taya Beach and the tree-covered headlands of the Al Hoceïma National Park. We had sardinne shwa, (grilled sardines) with a bowl of cumin-infused salsa on the side, chips and salad with fresh orange juice. Delicious. Directions as for Plage Taoussarte, but carry on past *parking 700 la plaj* signpost for 850m.

35.2058, -4.1052

PLACES TO STAY

24 TAGHASSA CAMP

Unzip your tent, rub your eyes and meet the Mediterranean. The restaurant's warmly lit tables and chairs adorn the beach, providing a fantastic place to watch the sunset over the mountains. Access road is quite rough and the campsite doesn't have space for motorhomes. However, it can provide tents if given notice. Turn off N16 at (35.2191, -4.7355) and follow track down to sea, turn L and drive along coastal path for 4 mins to parking (35.2243, -4.7397). +212 665-624421

35.2242, -4.7398

25 CAMPING AMIS DE CALA IRIS

An eco-conscious retreat perched above Almarsa Ighaniman beach. The grounds boast native flora and olive trees, coupled with environmentally friendly initiatives such as solar power and temperature-controlled showers. Accommodation options range from rustic tents to eco-cabins, crafted from local, sustainable materials. Directions as for Almarsa Ighaniman, but continue for 180m to campsite on R at the blue gate flanked by white rocks. Boite 81, Beni Boufrah 32102. amisdecalairis.com +212 066-2036718

35.1493, -4.3769

26 CASA PACA

Two terraces complete with sofas provide a cliff-top view of the surrounding area. Our host, Joaquín, was helpful and accommodating. The en suite rooms were cosy and comfy with beautiful views out over the bay. Free Wi-Fi. From Al Hoceïma, head S on P5211 for 8km; turn L on to an unnamed road (35.2041, -3.9160), follow down the switchbacks to the bottom of the hill; turn off road onto the track (35.2071, -3.9055) and follow the road up the hill, bearing R at the fork to the guest house. Plage de Sfiha, Ajdir, Al Hoceïma 32003. casapacamarruecos.com +212 673-867501

35.2106, -3.9057 ££

27 SENHAJA SUITE

Beautifully furnished apartment in the town of Targuist in the heart of the Senhaja Mountains, next to the Barrage Al Jomoaa. Equipped with mosaic-patterned living room, family room, kitchen and open courtyard. Run by Discover Senhaja, this company provides a modern recording studio in town for those who are musically inclined, boasting an array of traditional Moroccan and international instruments. Create something special on your trip through Targuist. discoversenhaja.ma +212 618-801721

34.9342, -4.3112 ££

Steha
Bni Bouzra
Bou Ahmed
Amtar
Bni Mansour
Bni Smih
Izaouiaten
Beni Boufrah
Bni Gmil
Senada
Adouz
Tafansa
Izemmouren
Azghar
Al Hoceïma National Park
Aït Kamra
Aït Hichem
Sidi Bouafif
Tizi Ayache
Idardouchen
Bni Abdellah
Issoufiyen
Bni Hadifa
Iounane
Bab Berred
Bni Rzine
Ouaouzgane
Bni Gmil Maksouline
Moulay Ahmed Cherif
Tizi Itchene
Issaguen
Tamorot
Sidi Boutmim
Zouaiat Sidi Abdelkader
Chakrane
Bni Boukhlef
Aït Erouadi

p71
p91
p129

11

GULF OF HOCEÏMA TO IAAZZANENE

Our perfect adventure

- → **Sample** a slice of paradise at Plage Ihttaryen, take a dip in its clear refreshing waters and lose yourself in its solitude
- → **Dine** on fish delicacies overlooking the golden sands of Ghanso Beach at Restaurant Asmak Rif
- → **Wander** through the abandoned resort at Playa 'n Tijathar and glide through the Mediterranean waves
- → **Snorkel** the rock formations of Playa Marsa 'n Tarist, then relax on the secluded shingle beach
- → **Leap** from rocks into the crystal-clear waters of Ghanso Beach bordered by cacti and orange cliffs
- → **Escape** the crowds at Plage Sidi Driss and take a stroll along the boundless beach
- → **Dive** from a rock at Playa Lâabdounen – watch a local first
- → **Enjoy** traditional Moroccan cuisine, a small pool and playground at Motel Resto la Rocade

1

3

4

'O creature of the earth
go to the pond and the water
to the blue in the eye of the phoenix
and you will find the man bending
under the burden of the earth.'

Malika Al-Assimi, Creation

The coastline between Al Hoceïma and Iaazzanene was described to us as 'Morocco's forgotten coast'. We found only two hotels along the entire 90km stretch. The N16 coastal highway was only constructed ten years ago and this lack of development means one thing for certain: lots of hidden and pristine beaches for us to explore. The coastal road took us up and around tall cliffs overlooking the Mediterranean; every few kilometres we were jumping out of the van and exploring another beach. At Plage Sidi Driss, we met a fellow campervan traveller. Yousef, a Moroccan from Casablanca, was doing much the same as we were: travelling the length and breadth of the country: 'I have lived here all my life, yet I have seen so little of my own country. It is time to change that.' Even in a country as beautiful and diverse as Morocco, it is easy to get stuck in one place and in your routines. Time to get out and see the world.

Of all the beaches we visited – Ajetti, Agharabo Yarzn and Ghanso, to name but a few – there was but one clear winner. Plage Ihttaryen. Hidden from view behind two enormous red cliffs and with a 20-minute walk down steep, rocky paths to reach the prize; the exertion was more than worth it. A young family was playing around their father's fishing boat, their feet crunching on the pebbly shore; waves lapping; and statuesque rock formations standing proudly from beneath the sea's surface. Around a small rocky outcrop, more treasures lay waiting to be discovered: a sliver of sandy beach, complete with a room-sized cave at the back, crying out to be explored. Fallen rocks formed tunnels and passages, their ceilings covered with tiny crabs, which scuttled back and forth above the water. Our own patch of paradise.

This may be the forgotten coastline, but hungry travellers still need food. The enterprising locals have set up a plethora of small shacks and restaurants, serving fresh charcoal-grilled fish to all. At the end of a long day of beach hunting, we sat in a hut on the clifftop Restaurant Asmak Rif, which overlooks Ghanso Beach. We enjoyed one of the most sumptuous and delicious meals of our entire Moroccan adventure; prawns, calamari, grilled dorado, sardines and salad left our fingers messy, but our bellies very happy. A must-visit.

BEACHES

1 PLAGE ICHARDAD

A long, sandy beach with a tall emblematic rock for good measure. Deserted in summer. From Al Hoceïma, head E on N16 to Rte de Yawmzir for 36km; turn L and continue on Rte de Yawmzir for 1.6km till you reach the parking spot (35.2662, -3.6623); scramble down rocks to the beach.

5 mins, 35.2666, -3.6620

2 PLAGE AGHARABO YARZN

Quiet beach occupied by a single family on a windless afternoon. Sand and shingle shoreline and devastatingly clear waters. Provides a quieter alternative to the beaches to the east. Directions as for Plage Ichardad, but head R along the path around the headland and walk down across the rocks where safe.

15 mins, 35.2649, -3.6586

3 PLAGE AJETTI

The western end of the sand and pebble beach is very pretty with a huge rocky headland sticking out into the sea. Café at the entrance to the beach. From Al Hoceïma, head E on N16 for 38km; turn off L by Restaurant Ajetti (35.2387, -3.6147) on to track; take L by restaurant parking onto the track for 100m down on to the beach.

3 mins, 35.2408, -3.6162

4 PLAGE SIDI DRISS

Crystalline waters with a steep entry both at the shoreline and within the water itself. Plage Sidi Driss is the least developed section of a long beach. Accessible by car right up to the shore, we enjoyed a quick walk across the pebbles, surrounded by mountains. From Al Hoceima, head E on N16 for 46km and turn L off the N16 (35.2123, -3.5409), on to a sandy track; after 50m, at the fork, turn R and follow this track for 500m down to the beach.

1 min, 35.2196, -3.5487

5 PLAGE SIDI DRISS #2

A quiet and relaxing spot by the sea. The beach attracts both locals and visitors. From Al Hoceïma, head E on N16 for 43km; turn L (35.2164, -3.5667) near the mosque in the village of Aït Tayar; take first L down to the beach.

2 mins, 35.2195, -3.5685

6 PLAGE IHTTARYEN

Walking down the rocky path, the beach appeared between the vast rock formations. Crystal-blue sea with rocks like statues in the water; a small slice of paradise hiding away from the world. Surrounded by cliffs, this hidden bay is calm and serene, carpeted with sand and small pebbles. A blue fishing boat added to the picturesque scene. A room-size cave on the left provided shelter from the sun. Walk or swim to the western end to find artistic rock formations in layers of white, yellow and grey – at times resembling gold, from other angles, marble. Two tiny, magical bays within a bay. We could be in Thailand. There were no facilities, so bring water, food and shade. From Al Hoceïma head E on N16 for 70km before turning L (35.1862, -3.3936); after the gap in the cliffs, drive along the path for 100m to parking spot (35.1879, -3.3954). From the parking spot, walk down towards the police station for 100m, the path will be on the left.; follow the path for 50m until reaching a fork, take the RH fork round a boulder, then after 30m follow the path round to your left where you will see the sea. Follow this path for 100m passing two forks on your L, bear right all the way to the edge of the cliff until the path bends round to your left and heads down towards the beach for another 50m.

20 mins, 35.1901, -3.3970

6

10

7

7 GHANSO BEACH

Wide, clean and family-friendly beach bordered by cacti and orange cliffs. Reached by a winding, dusty track. We joined locals rock jumping at the eastern end of the beach. Bring food, drink and shade or visit Asmak Rif fish restaurant on the top of the cliff. From Nador, head W on N16 for 45km; turn R (35.1933, -3.3125) and follow track down to beach for 500m.

5 mins, 35.1949, -3.3150

8 PLAYA LÂABDOUNEN

Sandy beach with a layer of shingle by the shoreline. Be careful of the steep shelf into deep water. Popular but not busy in mid-summer. Water shoes were helpful, especially for climbing up the big rock about 50m out where Danny and John joined locals diving and jumping into the sea. Did we mention the incredibly clear blue water? From Nador, head W on N16 for 45km; turn R (35.2002, -3.3043) down unmarked road, which turns into a steep but drivable track for 400m; park overlooking beach.

2 mins, 35.1999, -3.3084

9 PLAYA MARSA 'N TARIST

Steep climb down a narrow track, followed by a scramble over rocks to the first of two pretty shingle beaches. Very secluded so bring your own water and food. From Nador, head W on N16 for 43km; turn R (35.2046, -3.3008) on to unmarked track and park (35.2050, -3.3005); scramble down steep rocks to the beach.

5 mins, 35.2049, -3.2993

10 PLAYA MEZIAN

The neighbour of Playa Marsa 'n Tarist and the more secluded of the two conjoining coves, but no less gorgeous. Directions as for Playa Marsa 'n Tarist. Playa Mezian is the LH of the two coves.

5 mins, 35.2049, -3.2998

11 PLAYA ISADEN

Cute sand and shingle cove edged by high cliffs, which provide welcome shade from the afternoon sun. Deep turquoise water stippled with large rocks. From Nador, head W on N16 for 42km; turn R (35.2055, -3.2929) at unmarked track to parking spot (35.2061, -3.2933); walk east for 1 min to find steep path to beach.

2 mins, 35.2062, -3.2948

8

8

12 IFRI 'N ODHADHEN

Long, narrow, shingle beach. From Nador, head W on N16 for 39km and turn R (35.2109, -3.2615) down unmarked track to parking spot (35.2116, -3.2617) at top of cliff; walk down rough path on LHS of parking spot down to the beach.

5 mins, 35.2121, -3.2616

13 BOUYZEGAREN BEACH

Long, sand and shingle beach surrounded by impressive layered cliffs. Crystal-clear turquoise waters with shallow entry and rocky seabed about 5m out. From Nador, head W on N16 for 38km; turn R (35.2157, -3.2521) down unmarked track to parking spot (35.2157, -3.2523) at top of cliff; path at the L of the parking spot down on to the beach.

5 mins, 35.2155, -3.2532

14 PLAYA IFRI IFOUNASSEN

Sand and shingle 300m-long family beach. We watched a group of teenagers rock jumping and diving on the furthest rocks. Parking attendant sells cold drinks on a hot day. Head W from Nador for 35km; turn R down unmarked track to parking spot (35.2207, -3.2332); walk down obvious path to beach.

5 mins, 35.2215, -3.2316

15 SIDI EL BACHIRI BEACH

About 250m-long sand and shingle beach with parking space at the top. From Nador, head W on N16 for 35km; turn R down unmarked track (35.2217, -3.2237) to parking spot (35.2221, -3.2234); follow obvious path to beach.

4 mins, 35.2220, -3.2250

16 PLAYA 'N TIJATHAR

A tiny sandy beach lies in front of an abandoned holiday resort. The shallow entry into the crystal-clear water was flanked by rocky platforms occupied by a plethora of haughty seabirds. While this was not a picture-postcard location, we stayed for hours, the beach to ourselves – if you didn't count the seabirds who hopped from perch to perch in the rockbools and onto the decaying hull of a fishing boat. From Nador, head W on N16 for 20km; follow P6202 and Rte Plage Bouyafar el - Kallat for 13km to parking spot (35.2728, -3.1417); follow path at RH side of parking spot, which bears R for 400m.

3 mins, 35.2743, -3.1400

14

LAKES & RIVERS

17 L'EMBOUCHURE DE OUED KERT

The mouth of the Oued Kert forms a natural lake. We had a long chat with the fishermen, who complained about plastic driving away all the sardines. From Nador, head W on N16 for 32km; take a R off the N16 at the Motel Delta Kert; follow track to beach for 750m and park (35.2229, -3.2010); turn R and walk 10 mins along shore to mouth of river.

10 mins, 35.2254, -3.1966

CAFÉS & EATERIES

18 RESTAURANT ASMAK RIF

The basic but private shacks offered an intimate dining experience with arguably the best sunset views over the Mediterranean. We chose our own seafood from the cabinet, which was then charcoal-cooked to perfection. The staff were friendly and helpful. Excellent value and highly recommended. Directions as for Ghanso Beach, but carry on west for 300m; the restaurant is on R.

35.1923, -3.3156 ££

19 CAFÉ RESTAURANT VUE SUR MER

Fresh fish ordered by weight. A glass-fronted cold cabinet filled with different types of fish: from squid and prawns to a variety of white fish – just point and they weigh and cook. Reasonable price and good service. Directions as for Plage Ichardad but stay on N16 for 500m; restaurant is on R. Small fee for parking.

35.2529, -3.6564

PLACES TO STAY

20 MOTEL RESTO LA ROCADE

Basic motel, ideally situated for travellers as there is limited accommodation along the N16 coastal road. We were able to park our campervan by prior arrangement. There is also a children's playground, a small swimming pool and green area. From Nador head W on N16 for 60km; motel is on your R. Irangouyane Assihel Tazaghine, 62250. +212 661-574609

35.1890, -3.4330

21 MOTEL DELTA KERT

Sparkling clean hotel with great food and excellent service. The hotel was full but the owner let us park our van outside for the night. Great sea views over L'Embouchure de Oued Kert. From Nador, take the N16 west for 32km; hotel is on your R. +212 661-376378

35.2185, -3.1977

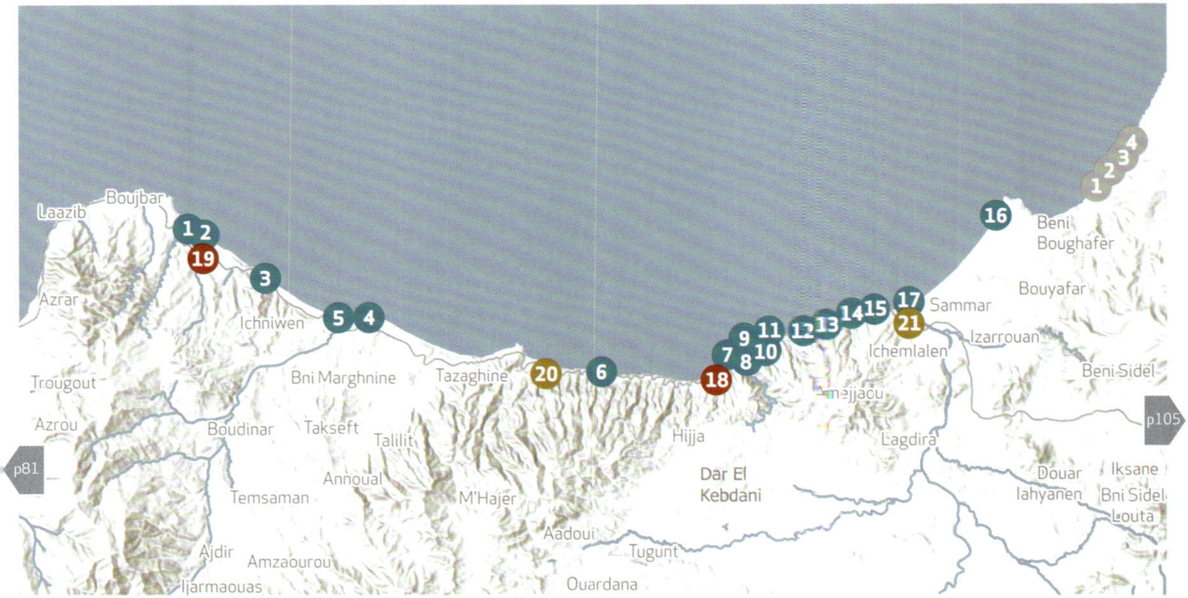

p81
p105

NADOR HEADLAND TO MOULOUYA NATIONAL PARK

Our perfect adventure

- → **Explore** the pristine beaches and coves of the Nador headland
- → **Dive** from the rocks at Cara Blanca into the turquoise Mediterranean waves
- → **Wolf** down a calamari sandwich in contented silence at Café Tibouda after a day on Thisith Beach
- → **Check-out** the cheeky Barbary macaques monkeys on Mount Gourougou (do NOT feed the monkeys)
- → **Imbibe** the panoramic views from the top of Mount Gourougou
- → **Walk** in the footsteps of history in the ruins of Tazouda Tower
- → **Roar** with fear and delight as you watch or join the cliff jumpers at Cap de l'Eau-les-Rochers
- → **Hike** around the headland from Thisith Beach to Mina Rosita Beach

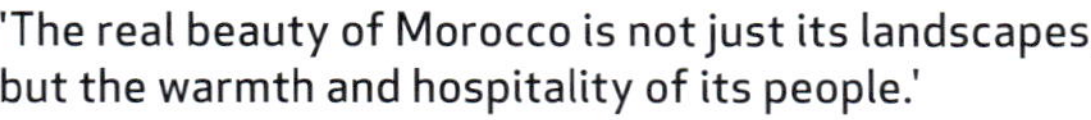
'The real beauty of Morocco is not just its landscapes, but the warmth and hospitality of its people.'

Anthony Bourdain

The headland that juts out into the Mediterranean Sea north of Nador is waiting to be discovered. Out of all the fabulous beaches, cliff jumps and panoramic viewpoints, our favourite was Cara Blanca (White Face). Bright yellow, almost white sandstone cliffs form a breathtaking coastal promenade from where thrill-seekers from far and wide launched themselves into the turquoise sea.

Standing tall above the headland and the city of Nador sits Mount Gourougou, reaching a height of almost 1,000m. The mountain offers breathtaking views of the surrounding area and is dotted with ancient mosques and fortresses dating back to the Middle Ages. The mountaintop is home to a large population of macaque monkeys, known to steal food from cars, so be sure to close your windows and doors, or your car might become infested with monkeys seeking snacks while you take photos of their kin. The mountain's height has provided a strategic advantage to scouts and generals throughout history, playing a significant role during the Rif War between the Amazigh and Spain, with the Battle of Annual in 1921 being partially fought on its slopes.

East of Nador, the Moroccan coastline continues toward the Algerian border. Boufadisse Beach is one of the more popular spots. For a lively atmosphere, Red Beach is perfect, where local families gather on the sandy shore. For a more serene setting, Embouchure Oued Moulouya features a discrete sandy beach at the river's mouth, where fishing boats are moored and children can swim safely in the sheltered estuary. Nature lovers will be captivated by the Moulouya National Park, an ornithological treasure that serves as a peaceful haven for migratory birds travelling from Europe to Africa.

Adventure seekers will love Cap de l'Eau-les-Rochers, where they can watch or participate in rock jumping, diving and flipping off cliffs into the swirling sea below. A young man performed a spectacular somersault into the sea, to the roaring appreciation of the crowds. As he emerged, we asked him if we could take a picture of his next leap. He politely replied, 'No, thank you. I don't do this for the pictures.' A true love of the sport. Respect. The energy and adrenaline from both jumpers and spectators create an exhilarating experience, which visitors can enjoy from the Café Restaurant Les Rochers while tucking into traditional Moroccan fish dishes and watching the divers.

BEACHES

1 PALOMAS BEACH

A small strip of sand nestled among the rocky cliffs, where families gathered to enjoy a day by the sea. The main attraction was the cliffs themselves where groups of young boys competed to throw themselves in ever more extravagant ways into the waves, only to emerge seconds later, grinning and ready to go again. From Nador, head NW on N15, P6209 and P6200 for 30km; turn R off P6200 at the garage (35.2902, -3.0407) and follow the roads through the village and down the cliff until you reach the shoreline; follow the road round to L; go past the larger Playa de las Japonesas and continue for 4 mins and the beach and parking will be on your R.

2 mins, 35.2950, -3.06685

2 PLAYA DE LAS JAPONESAS

Perched atop the headland, a green fisherman's hut overlooked the small, curved beach. The rocks at the northern end provided platforms for daredevils to leap into the air, only to be caught by the inevitable embrace of the waves below. This beach hummed with life and vibrancy, beachgoers weaving past blue fishing craft to the water's edge. It was also a favourite among local families. Although this beach was oddly named the Beach of the Japanese, we failed to spot anyone from that particular nation. Maybe we just weren't looking hard enough. Directions as for Palomas Beach.

1 min, 35.2992, -3.0626

3 PLAYA BOUGHABA

Popular with locals and Moroccan tourists; not many foreigners made it out this far east. Sandy beach with a gradual entry into the water, ideal for families with children. Singers gathered around a drum circle, creating a natural and authentic vibe. Two young men rode their horses down to the beach, a pleasant change to see horses used for transportation rather than pleasure rides. The scene was shattered when one of the horses, irked by being tied to a particularly large rock, proceeded to gallop off with the stone still attached to its reins. This rock clattered dangerously close to beachgoers until the horse was caught, calmed down and ridden into the sea to cool off. The horse was then brought to where the riders were sitting, making them feel like members of the family. A clear case of FOMO. Turn off the P6200 at Café Tardin (35.2958, -3.0407) towards the village of Douar Izemmouren; turn L into the village after the panoramic view (35.2991, -3.04727) and head W towards the sea; after 300m turn L at the fork then after 150m turn right and follow road to beach and park.

3 mins, 35.3027, -3.0602

4 PLAGE MARSA YAWYAN

A delightful sandy cove, surrounded by low cliffs, with shallow entry into the water. Deserted on a sunny afternoon in summer, ideal for a secluded dip. From Nador, drive along N15, P6209 and P6200 for 27km; turn R opposite Café Tardin (35.2958, -3.0407); after 1.9km the parking spot (35.3046, -3.0515) will be in front of you; walk down the track to the beach for 600m.

10 mins, 35.3080, -3.0561

5 PLAYA TCHARRANA

A striking cliff that juts out into the sea, its rugged surface worn smooth by the relentless waves. Locals and visitors joyfully fling themselves off the rocks, performing flips and dives. Their delighted shouts echo off the cliff as they plunge into the foamy waves below. It was wonderful to see Moroccan women, sporting burkinis, diving in headfirst, their smiles radiating with pleasure and exhilaration, as they broke the surface. From Nador, follow N15 and P6209 for 28km; turn L off the P6209 (35.3667, -2.9901); (expect a police checkpoint at this turning so have passports/ID ready); follow the road all the way down to the beach.

1 min, 35.3893, -3.0086

6 PLAGE TAZMENTE

We emerged from a steep valley and on to the tucked-away Tazmente Beach, populated only by locals and those in the know. The beach was studded with ubiquitous blue fishing boats, grounded for the day in the late afternoon, with the day's catch either stowed or sold. Beach dogs and donkeys laid claim to the territory as the last beachgoers took their leave. From Nador, drive along N15 and P6209 for 28km; turn L at police checkpoint; follow the road for 7.5km along a dirt track.

1 min, 35.3935, -3.0052

7 THANAWAT ALAAL BEACH

Clear waters, perfect for swimming, diving and snorkelling. If you're lucky, you might be able to purchase fresh fish from a returning fisherman for a bargain. From Nador, drive along N15 and P6209 for 28km; turn L at the police checkpoint; follow the road for 7.3km – the last 15 minutes of the drive is along a single-lane road/dirt track to parking spot (35.3971, -3.0017).

2 mins, 35.3983, -3.0032

8 PLAGE DES TROIS FOURCHES

A four-minute drive from the lighthouse of the same name, Plage des Trois Fourches is another secluded spot on our Nador headland tour, frequented predominantly by locals and some far-faring Moroccans. The western end is decorated with fishermen's huts, their craft forging a path through the waves.

A path leads up on to the headland, offering an encapsulating view of sea, sand and the mountains behind. From Nador head N on N15 and P6209 for 34km; turn L 1.3km before the lighthouse (35.4336, -2.9658); follow the dirt track to the beach for 1.5km

1 min, 35.4375, -2.9761

9 MARSA 'N THRAGHT

Directly below the Faro Trois Fourches lies a secret sliver of sand. An exclusive maritime excursion is often available here, although off-duty auxiliary officers and children from the local hamlet might make an appearance. Directions as for Plage des Trois Fourches, but park on the bend before the lighthouse; next to the parking spot (35.4336, -2.9659) there is a steep track leading down to the beach; 50m down, the path splits into two; take the RH fork round the back of the beach; follow down to the base of the cliff where there is a slight scramble down the rocks on your L.

5 mins, 35.4358, -2.9655

9

10

11

13

16

10 TIBOUDA BEACH

A small fishing village whose beach has been populated by local families. Fishermen's huts surround the bay, their boats scattered across the beach. The smell of barbecued sardines was tantalising to the tongue – the aroma added another layer to the beach's cosiness. You can catch a boat from Tibouda to Plage Mina Rosita or Thisith Beach. From Nador, drive along N15 and P6209 for 39km; park where you can near Café Restaurant Tibouda; take the first R down the dirt track to the beach. Paid parking is available by the beach or park on either side of the road leading to the beach.

2 mins, 35.4230, -2.9544

11 THISITH BEACH

Lovely, long stretch of golden sand parked in front of the resplendent Mediterranean. Sun-drenched bliss. At the right-hand side of the beach, you will see a narrow path that leads around the headland to Plage Mina Rosita – only the adventurous need apply. From Nador, drive along N15 and P6209 for 36km; guardian parking spot (35.4082, -2.9677) is on your R; follow obvious narrow track down to beach for 500m.

10 mins, 35.4082, -2.9641

12 PLAGE MINA ROSITA

This sheltered cove and gentle waves were ideal for swimming and snorkelling and revealed an abundance of marine life beneath the surface. From Nador, drive along N15 and P6209 for 36km; turn R down the unmarked track (35.3993, -2.9672); continue to the parking spot (35.4042, -2.9610) for 750m; walk down the obvious path down to the beach for 300m.

6 mins, 35.4059, -2.9613

13 CHIMNEY BEACH

Accessible only by hiking over the headland from Plage Mina Rosita, this small section of sand is most definitely a wild beach. It has no name recorded on any map, although it does have a very distinctive feature. About 100m out from the shore, a large, brick, chimney-looking structure juts out above the waves, purpose unknown. A unique beach to say the least. Although difficult to access, it is ideal for those who desire a solitary swim. Directions as for Plage Mina Rosita, but walk over the headland on your R for 200m.

8 mins, 35.4041, -2.9592

14 PLAYA MOUHANDIS

She sells sea shells on the sea shore. Popular with Moroccan families. The poor access road and long walk keeps this beach to itself.

The further you walk around the lagoon, the more secluded it becomes. Park at (35.1202, -2.7368) on Playa Taourirt and walk north along the coast for 5.5km. Roads to this beach are in very poor condition.

90 mins, 35.1779, -2.8214

15 BOUFADISSE BEACH

One the more popular beaches east of Nador. However, due to the shelf, current and access, it may not be the best option for families with young children. From Nador, head E on N16 for 60km; turn L (35.0891, -2.4769) down unmarked track and follow for 3.8km to parking spot (35.0922, -2.5086); walk down steep path to beach for 140m.

5 mins, 35.0924, -2.5118

16 RED BEACH

We joined lots of local families enjoying themselves on a sandy beach. Nice vibe. Waves can get a bit rough and there were some big stones along the shore, so mind your feet if you're swimming. From Nador, head E for 55km; turn L down unmarked track (35.1018, -2.4546); follow for 2.4km to parking spot (35.1045, -2.4792); follow obvious path down to beach for 150m.

5 mins, 35.1047, -2.4808

19

17

19

18

18

17 PLAGE L'EAU-LES-ROCHERS

For those not as thrill-seeking as the cliff jumpers on the other side of the headland, this beach offers a more gradual entry to the water and a more relaxing swim. Directions as for Cap de l'Eau-les-Rochers but walk R at the headland.

2 mins, 35.1479, -2.4234

18 EMBOUCHURE OUED MOULOUYA

Discrete sandy beach at the mouth of the Oued Moulouya river where fishing boats were moored. The sheltered cove was ideal for kids to swim. A parking guardian wearing an FBI cap and a faded Brazilian football shirt politely took our 5dh. From Nador, head E on N16 for 68km and turn L on to a dusty path (35.1186, -2.3720); follow track for 3km until reaching the sea.

2 mins, 35.1230, -2.3452

CLIFF JUMPING

19 CAP DE L'EAU-LES-ROCHERS

A cool place for people to gather and watch thrill-seekers jump, dive and flip from the cliffs into the swirling sea below. However, the most impressive part was watching the brave souls fish themselves out of the sea and back on to land when the waves were high. If you're even slightly tempted to jump, be sure to watch the locals jump first. From Nador, head E on N16 for 60km; at the roundabout, take the third exit; after 1.5km park by Cap de l'Eau-les-Rochers car park (35.1475, -2.4234); walk L for 100m across rocks to cliffs.

2 mins, 35.1479, -2.4242

20 CARA BLANCA

Yellow sandstone formed a breathtaking natural coastal promenade. Large boulders were spaced intermittently along the sandstone shelf, looking like huge art installations, sculpted by Mother Nature herself. The waters here were clear, with submerged rock formations making this a snorkeller's paradise. Plenty of jump spots where boys and girls vied with each other to carry out the greatest feats of daring. It was nice to see many women jumping in, rather than the male-dominated sport it can be. Remember, while cliff jumping safety should always be your top priority. Enjoy the incredible views and the rush of adrenaline. Not the easiest descent, but the effort was well worth it. From Nador, head N on N15 and P6209 for 27km; turn R (35.3538, -2.9951) off the P6209 in Taourirt at the road before the school; drive down a narrow, rough, winding track for 350m to Parking Cara Blanca (35.3464, -2.9641); walk down a steep, zigzag path down a cliff to access the beach for 1km.

15 mins, 35.3491, -2.9600

20

20

20

VIEWPOINTS

21 FARO TROIS FOURCHES

At the northernmost tip of Nador's headland stands the Three Forks Lighthouse, a solid white and grey bastion, built in 1864 to provide safety for ships passing through the sometimes treacherous Alboran Sea. The name Three Forks is a reference to the three prominent rocky points jutting out into the sea near the building. This lighthouse could be viewed from the outside but could not be accessed, as it is used by the military to survey Morocco's northern border. Directions as for Plage des Trois Fourches but continue on P6209 for 1.3km; you can't miss the lighthouse.

1 min, 35.4378, -2.9629

22 ROSITA VIEWPOINT

Park up for great views over the Mediterranean and the headland back towards Nador. From Nador, drive along N15 and P6209 for 39km; park on R

1 min, 35.3939, -2.9660

23 MOUNT GOUROUGOU

Shaded by Aleppo pines, this is a cool spot to pause and enjoy the surroundings. But watch out for the cheeky Barbary macaque monkeys – they're everywhere and will be after your snacks. Many people feed the animals bread, but this is not part of their natural diet and can lead to obesity, aggression and diabetes. While it's tempting to watch and interact with the monkeys, it's important not to feed them as it discourages them from foraging for their own food. From Nador, follow R610 and P6209 W for 13km.

2 mins, 35.2047, -2.9984

24 GOUROUGOU PANORAMA

More gorgeous views over the majestic Gourougou Mountains towards Nador and the Mediterranean. Directions as for Mount Gourougou; park by picnic spot and walk up to the viewpoint on your L.

3 mins, 35.2058, -2.9982

25 GOUROUGOU HIDDEN VIEWPOINT

Passing through the picnic tables and the hordes of hungry monkeys, Cresting the rise, yet another panorama, hidden from the road and available only to the adventurous, will be laid out before you. Directions as for Mount Gourougou, head SW through the clearing and up the pine-strewn slope.

2 mins, 35.2043, -2.9976

26 MIRADOR ACHAOUEN

Flat stone platform with a parking spot and railings at the top of Mount Gourougou. Look out over the blue of the Nador lagoon with its spit of land, tall grey rocky outcrops and the mountain peaks and valleys that hide the Spanish exclave of Melilla. Aleppo pines are scattered over the hillsides. Beyond the town of Nador are flat plains of fields and misty mountains can be seen far in the distance. From Nador, follow R610 and P6209 west for 13k; platform is on your R.

1 min, 35.2072, -2.9942

ANCIENT

27 TAZOUDA TOWER

An eleventh-century fortress on the slopes of Mount Gourougou. The walls of the small, ruined fort are more or less intact, featuring narrow slit lookout points on three levels. Visitors can climb the stairs into the tower and imagine sentries peering out, anxiously over the landscape. Enjoy 360° views over the Mediterranean, the surrounding Rif Mountains and far, far beyond. From Nador, follow R610 and P6209 W for 15km; park by Ecological Centre (35.2009, -3.0085) and walk W down track to the castle.

10 mins, 35.2005, -3.0126

23

27

BIRDWATCHING

28 DEAD MAN'S WHARF

Moulouya National Parc is a peaceful place to watch birds that migrate between Europe and Africa. Binoculars are essential. Our well-travelled feathery guests included marbled teal, marsh harrier and northern shoveler. From Nador, head E on N16 for 63km; after crossing Oued Moulouya, turn L at roundabout on to Route el Halg for 1.4km; park on RH side of road (35.1152, -2.3420); cross road and follow roped off boardwalk for 200m to observation tower.

5 mins, 35.1175, -2.3440

CAFÉS & EATERIES

29 CAFÉ RESTAURANT TIBOUDA

Dishing up the usual seaside Moroccan food with excellent views over the sea and Punta de los Farallones peninsula. Directions as for Tibouda Beach. +212 699-918248

35.4210, -2.9563 £

30 CAFÉ RESTAURANT LES ROCHERS

Moroccan fishy dishes with ringside seats of the cliff divers. Directions as for Cap de l'Eau-les-Rochers. Restaurant Les Rochers Cap de l'Eau, Ras El Ma 62602. +212 630-253671

35.1474, -2.4240 ££

27

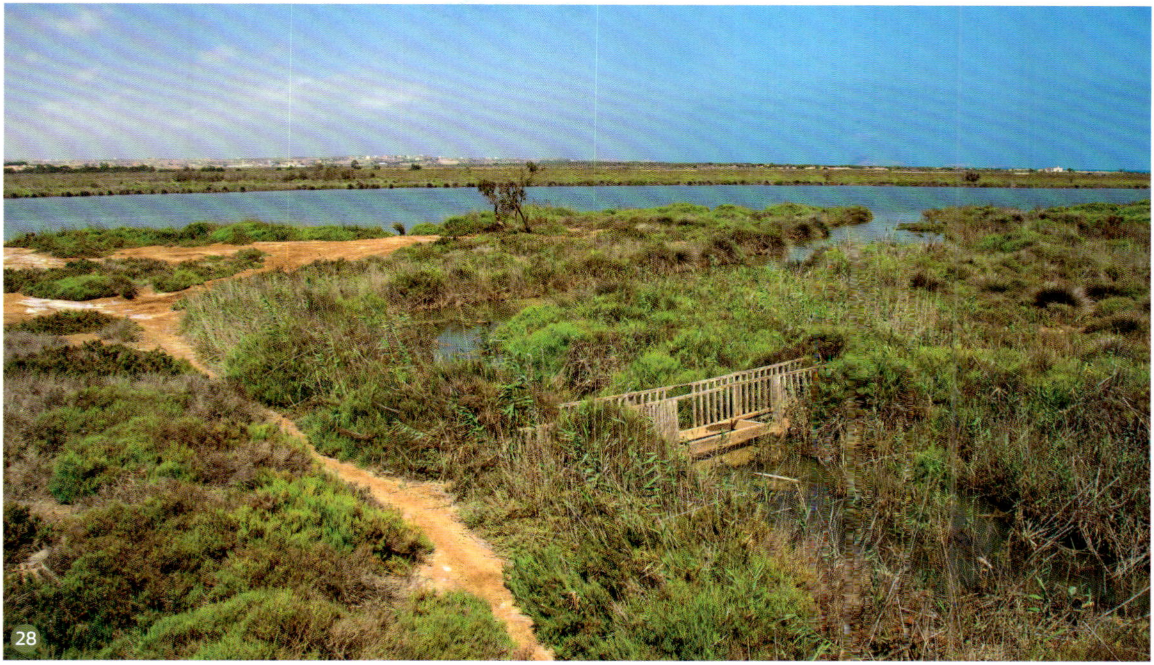
28

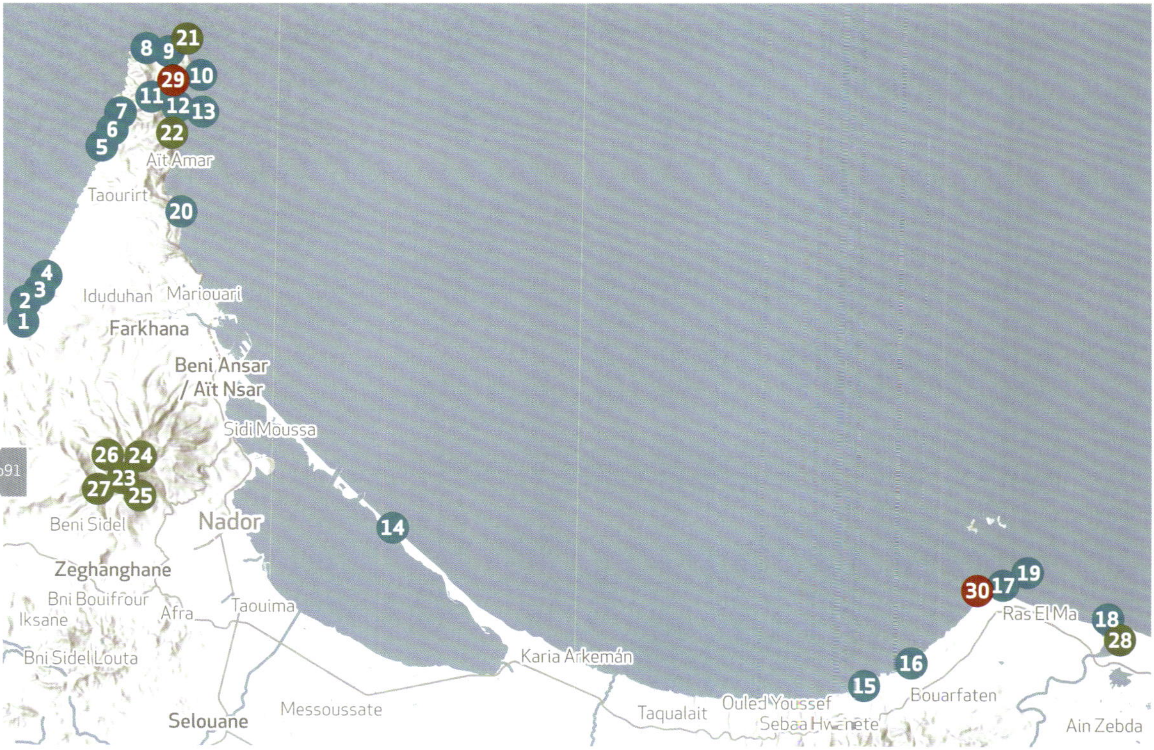
8
9
21
29
10
11
12
13
7
6
5
22
Aït Amar
Taourirt
20
4
3
2
1
Iduduhan
Mariouari
Farkhana
Beni Ansar
/ Aït Nsar
Sidi Moussa
p91
26
24
23
27
25
Beni Sidel
Nador
14
Zeghanghane
Bni Bouifrour
Iksane
Afra
Taouima
Bni Sidel Louta
Selouane
Messoussate
Karia Arkemán
Taqualait
Ouled Youssef
Sebaa Hwenete
15
16
Bouarfaten
30
17
19
Ras El Ma
18
28
Ain Zebda

1

ASILAH TO RABAT

Our perfect adventure

- **Marvel** at the monoliths of Msoura and wander through this remnant of Morocco's ancient past
- **Imagine** yourself a citizen of the Roman Empire as you stroll through the once-majestic city streets of Lixus
- **Gaze** out across the lagoon of Merja Zerga and hear the calls of hundreds of birds flocking over the water
- **Tuck** into a hearty meal on the hilltop at Laila's Farm, overlooking the vast, golden sands of Plage Chlihat
- **Splash** through the waters of Lake Dayet Roumi, cooling off from the scorching heat of the day
- **Breathe** deeply in the Jardins d'Essai Botanique in Rabat, and let the scents of fresh herbs and sweet-smelling flowers fill your nostrils
- **Relax** in the stained-glass luxury of Riad Alhambra, a five-minute walk from the beach
- **Sigh** with pleasure on the banks of Rabat Marina, as the setting sun silhouettes the Kasbah des Oudayas in a gorgeous glow

**'Our steps invent the path as we proceed; behind us they leave no trace.
So we shall always look ahead and trust our feet.
They will take us as far as our minds will go...'**

Tahar Ben Jelloun, The Sand Child

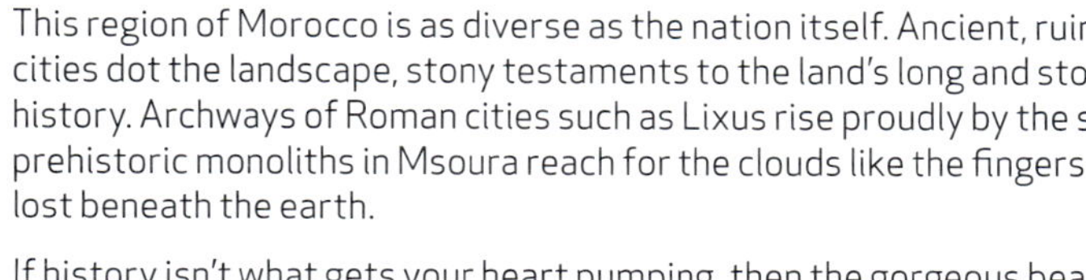

This region of Morocco is as diverse as the nation itself. Ancient, ruined cities dot the landscape, stony testaments to the land's long and storied history. Archways of Roman cities such as Lixus rise proudly by the sea, while prehistoric monoliths in Msoura reach for the clouds like the fingers of those lost beneath the earth.

If history isn't what gets your heart pumping, then the gorgeous beaches are sure to pique your excitement. The Sebou River spills its azure waters into the green depths of the Atlantic. Blue fishing boats continually cross this divide, bringing in the day's catch, passing by beachgoers on Plage Chlihat and Sidi Boughaba on opposite sides of the river mouth. Excited to get down to the beaches, I strolled down the steep hill overlooking the small seaside town of Mehdia, the tranquil waters of Sidi-Boughaba Lake beckoning my attention. Children chased each other while their parents enjoyed a well-earned rest beneath the canopy of trees. Continuing my journey over the sand dunes, I unwittingly disturbed a young couple taking advantage of the privacy offered by the grassy mounds. On the sands below, a group of teenagers controlled massive powerful horses with the merest touch of their knees as they galloped saddleless along the shoreline.

Morocco's capital city lies on this stretch of coast; taking the title from Fes in 1912. Rabat has a rich history dating back to the third century BC when it was first settled by the Phoenicians, later becoming an important Roman port. In the twelfth century, the Almohad dynasty fortified the city and constructed significant landmarks, including the Kasbah des Oudayas, well worth a visit, its terrace providing panoramic views of Rabat beach and the Lighthouse. Rabat boasts an array of exotic gardens, mostly free to visit and a lovely place to take a picnic – the cool shade of the plants a welcome relief from the hot sun. Take a stroll along the marina by the river and watch the sun set behind the fortified old city, as water taxis carry their passengers across the river, with the cries of 'Salé! Salé! Salé!' leaving you in no doubt as to their destination.

4

BEACHES

1 PARADISE BEACH

Long and isolated beach in a glorious location beneath hillsides covered in wildflowers. The road to the beach is quite difficult and you may have to park halfway and walk the rest. Well worth the effort. From Asilah, head S on N1 for 1.4km; take R fork on to R415 for 2.2km; turn R at sign for R'milat Beach along Piste Rmilat Kahf Hmam for 1.6km to parking spot (35.4303, -6.0483); walk along path to beach for 1.8km.

25 mins, 35.4208, -6.0630

2 PLAGE CHLIHAT

A vast expanse of sand next to a long, man-made pier on either side of the river mouth, which protects the harbour of the Sebou River and its boats emerging on to the sea. A family sat together on a colourful blanket as sand billowed around them, the only people on this beach for miles, except for a solitary wandering cow, who made its ponderous way along the shore. The beach slopes gently down to the sea, allowing for gradual entry into the waves. Take the P4201 out of Kenitra, crossing the bridge over the Sebou River in the industrial sector; after crossing the bridge, follow the road for 3km before turning L on to the P4262 by a small grocery shop; follow this road for 10km until reaching the village of Chlihat; at the fork after Café Louna take the LH fork and follow the road until you reach a T-junction; turn R and follow the road all the way down; parking available on L just after the school at the end of the village (34.2829, -6.6447); walk SE along the same road until you hit the river, the track will bend around the river; keep it to your L and follow the path for 15 minutes until you come out on to the beach.

30 mins, 34.2688, -6.6724

3 SIDI BOUGHABA BEACH

This expanse of sand extends from the nearby seaside town of Mehdia. The beach accommodated everyone, from those who sought a solitary swim to those performing doughnuts and wheelies on quad bikes. If, like myself, you belong to the former group, you will want to head further south to access the beach, as the town can become very busy, especially on Eid, as it was when I arrived. The Atlantic water was cool and refreshing, with a gradual entry. From Mehdia, head SE on P4266 for 4km; turn off the P4266 (34.2164, -6.6906) and follow the track for 450m to the beach. Park by the beach.

3 mins, 34.2146, -6.6960

4 RABAT BEACH

A popular destination for both locals and tourists: a lovely stretch of sandy shore, perfect for relaxation and beach activities. As I sat and watched the waves come in, a couple sprinted down the sands, hand in hand before crashing into the water together. They emerged spluttering and laughing, with big smiles. The impressive Hassan Tower and the historical Kasbah des Oudayas provided a scenic backdrop. To the left of the beach is The Lighthouse of Rabat, standing tall above the waves, warning off all wayward ships from the rocks that jut far out into the sea. Walk E along the coast from the parking spot for 3 mins (34.0319, -6.8396); turn L on to the beach before going into the cemetery beneath the kasbah.

3 mins, 34.0332, -6.8386

LAKES & RIVERS

5 MERJA ZERGA

We arrived at Port de Moulay Bouselham at sunset during Ramadan, the streets deserted as people went in for iftar (breaking of the fast). Across the mud flats before the orange sunset, hundreds and thousands of birds flocked up into the sky, circling and sweeping over the horizon. These flats are a rest stop on the northern migration of an array of avian species,

including flamingos, herons, marsh harriers and peregrine falcons. The saltwater lake of Lagune de Moulay-Bousselham is vast and dotted with blue fishing boats. The lake is tidal and, when the tide is out, reveals huge marsh flats. Watch the march of the crabs as hundreds crowd out of the water and then scramble back again. You can take a boat trip around the lake or relax on nearby Moulay Bousselham beach. Park here for the night for 100dh and watch the sunset. Thursday is a fish market day. From the R406 in Moulay Bousselham, head S to Port de Moulay Bouselham.

1 min, 34.8699, -6.2799

6 SEBOU RIVER PORT

At the mouth of the Sebou River lies a busy fishing port, where modern trawlers rubbed boards with the more traditional Moroccan craft. Local boys threw themselves into the blue waters between the hulls, as an old lady and her husband were helped on to the bank from one of the water taxis plying their trade across the river. With the nearest road bridge a half-an-hour's drive away, this is the easiest method to get across the water. For the southern side, turn off the Route de Mehdia from Kenitra at the signs for the port, or for the northern side, take the P4262 to the village of Chlihat and walk across the sands. Park in the port (34.2663, -6.6568) and walk back along the Route de Mehdia from the parking spot for 1km.

15 mins, 34.2717, -6.6463

7 SEBOU RIVER PANORAMA

Set above the glistening blue curves of the Sebou River, with its busy port and shoals of passing fishing craft, stands the ruined Kasbah Moulay Ismail. It clearly once cut an imposing figure, with its commanding position over both sea and river. Time and lack of protection have welcomed decay; although some of its stone walls and towers still stand proud, a testament to the power this hilltop fortress once held. Take the Avenue Antara out of Kenitra to the parking spot by the cemetery (34.2630, -6.6562); walk across the road towards the river, and the panorama and the kasbah will be in front of you.

2 mins, 34.2652, -6.6553

8 LAGUNE DE MOULAY-BOUSSELHAM

Standing on top of the dunes, the view was nothing short of idyllic: a picture-postcard scene. Shockingly blue waters of the lagoon curled out into a channel towards the sea while small fishing craft made their way in and out of the channel, bringing the catch into the bustling port and fish market. We enjoyed a picnic on the bank of the lagoon and took a walk in the woods of the national park. When the tide went out, hundreds of seagulls gathered on the emerging sand flats. Something spooked the birds and they all took to the air, sweeping and twirling like fighter pilots. From Ouled Mesbah head N on P4211 for 9km to parking spot (34.8680, -6.2929).

2 mins, 34.8720, -6.2924

9 DAYET ROUMI

The only low-altitude natural lake in Morocco. Surrounded by green hills and a mixture of Aleppo pine, eucalyptus and acacia trees, the lake has provided water for crops and livestock for centuries, while its shores have been a gathering place for generations of families and friends. The lake has obviously been fuller but was deep enough to swim and its water enveloped me reassuringly. There is something special about swimming in a lake: the silence, the frog's-eye view and total immersion. It was Ramadan, so Lola wore trousers and a shirt in the water to be respectful, but saw a young local woman with the young men, stripping down to sports shorts and throwing herself in. The lake is stream-fed, with cold currents alternating with warm, like a shower in a mid-priced campsite. From Ait Ouribel, head SW on R404 towards P4325 for 6.5km; turn L on to P4314; after 450m the lake will be on the R; park and walk down the beach to the lake.

2 mins, 33.7527, -6.1856

10 SIDI BOUGHABA LAKE

The path to the lake was alive with crickets and flanked by tall ferns. I stepped aside in respect as a group of teenage horse riders trotted down the path towards me, effortlessly controlling their enormous stallions between their knees as they rode bareback away from the lake. Families laughed and played along the shores, the trees and reeds providing relief from the heat of the midday sun. The waters, green with reflected light from the surrounding trees, beckoned me to cool off. However, I learned to my disappointment that the lake was not swimmable; the only reason given is simply, danger. In my experience, when a Moroccan describes something as dangerous or even difficult, it is a good idea to heed their warnings. Nevertheless, this is still a beautiful place for a picnic. From Mehdia turn off the P4266 (34.2593, -6.6638) and follow until you reach the parking spot (34.2510, -6.6658) by the lake.

2 mins, 34.2509, -6.6676

FORESTS, PARKS & GARDENS

11 JARDINS EXOTIQUES DE BOUKNADEL

An exciting botanical garden founded by French horticultural engineer Marcel François in the 1950s and peppered with informative signs educating visitors on diverse plant species.

There is a wild feel to the nature gardens, subdivided into different regions of the world. The small maze was fun. The cultural gardens – Japan, China, Andalusía – are landscaped and orderly, while the didactic area includes an aviary, vivarium (reptiles and spiders) and plant nursery. Accessible to most visitors and the modest entrance fee contributes to the maintenance of the gardens. From Rabat take Avenue Hassan 11/N1 for 1km to the roundabout by Top Dar Fleur on L; take third exit back on N1. Km13 Rte de Rabat, Salé 11000. jardinsexotiques.com

2 mins, 34.0935, -6.7650

12 JARDINS D'ESSAI BOTANIQUES

Established and designed by Jean-Claude Nicolas Forestier in 1914, the gardens are home to an estimated 600 plant species and more than 1,000 varieties. Fountains tinkle along the main thoroughfare, lined with golden flowers. We sought refuge from the heat of the afternoon sun under the generous plant canopies. Follow the smell of lavender through the herb gardens and across into the palmeraie. Free entry. Av. Annasr, Rabat. From the parking spot, walk W on Rue Ibn Hajar towards Avenue Ibn al Ouazzani; turn R and then R again onto Avenue de la Victoire; gardens will be on your R.

2 mins, 34.0092, -6.8484

13 ANDALUSIAN GARDEN

The large pond at the garden's heart, with conveniently placed benches, makes a perfect spot for a picnic or reading a book. Across the water is the Pavillon Neo-Mauresque, a stunning piece of architecture that creates an eye-catching backdrop for this tranquil setting. Not to be confused with the Andalusian Gardens of the same name in the Kasbah des Oudayas precincts. Free entry. Botanical Garden, Av. Annasr, Rabat. Directions: as for Jardins d'Essai Botaniques but when you are on the Avenue de la Victoire; the gardens will be on your L.

2 mins, 34.0106, -6.8496

ANCIENT

14 IULIA CONSTANTIA ZILIL

Excavated in 1958, the Roman/Amazigh city was built by Emperor Augustus between 33 and 25 BC. Its purpose was to house veterans of the Battle of Actium, where Augustus defeated Mark Antony and became ruler of the Roman Empire. The area had been occupied for much longer though, with excavations showing evidence of habitation as far back as 300 BC. The guardian took us around the 25-hectare site and pointed out where the temple, amphitheatre, thermae, a surrounding wall and housing had been excavated. Apart from

the ruins themselves, there was an incredible 360-degree view over the valley. The grass-covered hills looked like waves rolling across a green sea. I had a lovely chat with the guardian, Abdell Salim, who spoke Spanish, French, English and Darija. He gave me a map; I gave him 50dh for his time and expertise. Park at the E end of Had Al Gharbia (35.5232, -5.9191); walk E taking the R fork for 100m; cut across a field for 150m to the ruins; a guide will magically appear and offer to show you the way.
5 mins, 35.5222, -5.9159

15 MSOURA

Some experts identify the large stone circle of Msoura as Neolithic, while others believe that the central tumulus was a burial ground for one of the first Mauritanian kings during the fourth or third century BC. Some researchers think the stones have an astronomical orientation, but others point out that the axis is directed at the Jbel si Habib mountain in the distance. Local legends have the circle as either evil or medicinal. Other myths suggest the giant Antaeus was buried here after his defeat by Hercules. Whatever the truth, the site is impressive and well worth a visit. Yellow lupins stand tall, alongside viper's bugloss and many other wildflowers. Walking around the stone circle as the sun set, we wondered at how an ancient culture managed to move so many obelisks. Msoura is surrounded by a fence and you'll need to get the guardian to open it. Don't worry if no one seems to be around, someone will appear, as if by magic, like the shopkeeper in Mr. Benn. Don't expect a visitors' centre or a gift shop. In the village of Msoura, park at the parking spot on the green on Rte de Msoura (35.4043, -5.9450); the gate is in front of you.
3 mins, 35.4041, -5.9439

16 LES SALINES DE LARACHE

Located along Morocco's coastline, Les Salines de Larache, is known for salt production and diverse wildlife. The unique ecosystem is an essential habitat and breeding ground for migrating and resident birds, including flamingos, herons and waders. Salt was vital to preserve food in the past and as an antiseptic for Roman soldiers. The salt flats are best viewed from the Archaeological Site of Lixus.
1 min, 35.2054, -6.1207

17 LIXUS

We took a step back in time and explored the ancient secrets of Lixus. Dating back to the twelfth century BC, this city was originally established by the Phoenicians, making it one of the oldest urban centres in north Africa. After centuries of grandeur and cultural exchange, Lixus fell under the sway of the mighty Roman

13

16

Empire in the first century BC. As Roman influence waned, the Amazigh people made their home within its ancient walls. Lixus was eventually abandoned. Thanks to extensive restoration efforts, this archaeological jewel now welcomes visitors. Spanning an impressive 62 hectares, Lixus stands as one of the largest sites of Roman remains in north Africa and boasts the only fully round amphitheatre in Morocco. Intricate mosaics adorn the floors of the amphitheatre and baths and, amazingly, much of the original colour on the tiles was still visible. A museum with two exhibition halls showcases archaeological artefacts from the Phoenician, Mauritanian, Roman and Islamic periods. Lixus is also believed to be the location of the Secret Gardens of Hesperides, a legendary site where Hercules is said to have completed one of his famous labours. Knowledgeable guides are available for free – we gifted a tip for the insights he provided. From Larache, head E on N1 for 4.8km; turn L at the roundabout and follow the road for 1.8km; at the fork by the riverbank, take a sharp L and follow the road for 1.4km, park on your L.

2 mins, 35.1981, -6.1128

18 IULIA VALENTIA BANASA

One of three Roman-Amazigh cities founded by Emperor Augustus between 33 and 25 BC for veterans of the Battle of Actium.

The site is renowned for its well-preserved ruins, which included thermal baths and an aqueduct. Children often pass through on their way home from school and a young girl rode her bike through the ruins while turkeys and a donkey grazed in the tall grass. Butterflies flitted among the yellow wildflowers, and palms and shrubs flourished around the site. It was clear that very few tourists travelled this far into the countryside and the trip was far sweeter for that knowledge. If the front gate is closed, try the back gate. From Ouled Slimane head W on P4234 for 1.2km; turn R for 1.5km; slight L for 300m; entrance is on the R. Parking front gate (34.5990, -6.1158), parking back gate (34.6034, -6.1158).

2 mins, 34.6023, -6.1149

19 KASBAH DES OUDAYAS

In its commanding position high above the city, the Kasbah des Oudayas is a UNESCO World Heritage Site and a fantastic viewpoint. Built in the thirteenth century as a small military fort to protect the ancient necropolis of Chellah and the Bou Regreg River mouth, it has since evolved into a major fortress and citadel. Abandoned and reoccupied over time, it was restored during the French protectorate. Visitors enter through the Bab Oudaya gate, stepping into a serene world of white and blue. Highlights include the Andalusian Gardens,

inspired by mediaeval Arab culture and the former palace of Sultan Moulay Ismail, now the Oudayas Museum. Narrow alleys lead to an old mosque with a prominent minaret and art galleries. The Place des Oudayas offers sublime views of Salé and Rabat's beaches, the lighthouse and the river mouth.
From Rabat, head E along Av Al Marsa to parking spot (34.0314, -6.8372); walk back along the Av Al Marsa for 50m and then take the first left down the slope and through the Bab Oudayas, the gate into the Kasbah.

3 mins, 34.0319, -6.8361

20 CHELLAH NECROPOLIS

Chellah is a mediaeval fortified Muslim necropolis on the outskirts of Rabat, which has long captivated visitors with its blend of Mauritanian, Roman and Islamic heritage. Originally a Roman colony known as Sala Colonia, it later became used as a dynastic necropolis for the Marinids. Upon entering, I was greeted by an imposing gateway leading to a tranquil garden filled with flowers. The site features Roman ruins, including remnants of temples, a forum and a triumphal arch. Among the highlights were the well-preserved minaret, and the remains of a mosque and royal tombs from the Marinid dynasty. The clacking call of storks reverberated across the ancient grounds from their roosts in nearby towers and trees. From the southeast tower, I enjoyed excellent views over the river valleys.
Make sure you make the acquaintance of Kanfood, a hedgehog lovingly cared for by the local gardener. In Rabat, turn off the R401 at onto the Chellah access road.
challah-billetterie.ma

2 mins, 34.0068, -6.8231

Higher sections of thenecropolis are accessible by wheelchair ramps, lower sections by stairs

VIEWPOINTS

21 TRAVERSÉE DU BOU REGREG

The Rabat Marina is an ideal place for a sunset stroll. With the Kasbah des Oudayas (679) at my back, I took my time making my way up the riverbank, absorbing the sights and sounds; the keowing of seagulls, the children playing on the corniche, the water taxis ferrying passengers to the nearby city of Salé and the water lapping at the stones on the river banks. The pontoon of the Traversée du Bou Regreg, the departure point for many water-bound craft, is the spot to take in the sunset scenario, with the old medina and kasbah silhouetted in orange, their shadows extending across the river. Picturesque didn't even come close to describing the scene. From Rabat, take the

20

19

22

23

26

R322 Avenue Marsa along the river and park next to the marina (34.0289, -6.8333); walk back up the river to the Traversée du Bou Regreg.

5 mins, 34.0275, -6.8278

22 PLACE OUDAYA

A large courtyard at the front of the kasbah, facing out towards the sea. A perfect place to watch the sunset behind Rabat Lighthouse and over the golden sands of Rabat Beach. Directions as for Kasbah des Oudayas; walk along the front of the kasbah for 3 mins to get to the viewpoint.

3 mins, 34.0330, -6.8356

CULTURAL HOTSPOTS

23 MUSEUM OF PHOTOTOGRAPHY, RABAT

Housed within the remains of the Burj Kebir Fortress, the national photography museum overlooks the Atlantic. The museum, opened in 2020, showcases the history of photography in Morocco and also exhibits international photographers. Educational programs and workshops are offered. 61 Avenue Mokhtar Gazoulit, Ocean District, Rabat. +212 641-172794

3 mins, 34.0248, -6.8508 £

PLACES TO STAY

24 CAMPING ECHRIGUI

No frills, budget campsite on the edge of Asilah. Very handy stopover after we'd arrived in Morocco on the Tangier ferry (50km) and were heading south. The helpful owners cooked us up a mean tagine at late notice. Av. Khalid Ibn Oualid, Asilah 90050 +212 661-397589

35.4722, -6.0278 £

25 LE NID DU HIBOU

Cosy family campsite offering tree-shaded pitches and apartments. Food available on demand. Arriving during Ramadan we were invited into the family home to break the fast (iftar) with hrira (soup), dates, tagine and sweets. Boat trips on Lagune de Moulay-Bousselham can be organised. Le Nid du Hibou Campsite, Moulay Bousselham, 14302. lagunedeshibou@gmail.com +212 663-095358

34.8728, -6.2776 £

26 LAILA'S CHLIHAT FARM

Set on top of a hill overlooking Plage Chlihat, this woman-owned farm has cabins, space for campervans and tents. Little thatched huts stand in a row facing the sea, where you can enjoy a glass of mint tea and your dinner while you watch the sunset. I had delicious lamb skewers and chops, left over from Eid al-Adha (The Feast of Sacrifice), where each family sacrifices and eats a sheep to honour the willingness of Abraham to sacrifice his son as an act of obedience to God's command. Take the P4201 out of Kenitra, crossing the bridge over the River Sebou in the industrial sector; after crossing the bridge, follow the road for 3km before turning L on to the P4262 by a small grocery shop; follow this road for 5km and the gates to the farm will be on your left. +212 698-984336

34.3062, -6.6299 ££

21

27 SAM HOSTEL

This hostel and guesthouse, situated in the heart of Rabat Medina, was a perfect base to explore the city. Although the main hostel was full, Oussama set me up in the overflow guesthouse, which was decorated with traditional Moroccan mosaics and a fountain in the central courtyard. As it was Eid al-Adha (The Feast of Sacrifice) and there were no restaurants open, the family who lived upstairs generously provided me with breakfast, as it is customary to invite neighbours to eat during this religious festival. 23 Rue Moulay Brahim, Rabat 10000. +212 654-031536

34.0265, -6.8338 £

28 RIAD ALHAMBRA

Located in the town of Harhoura, just outside Rabat and only a five-minute walk from the beach, this is the perfect retreat. Complete with swimming pool, mosaics and stained-glass windows and ceilings that transform the Moroccan sunshine into a shining array of shades and colours. The hrira and chicken and vegetable couscous were delicious. Friendly, welcoming personnel. 35 Rue Bouregreg Lot Beethoven, El Harhoura 12024 riadalhambra.com +212 613-897719

33.9188, -6.9600 £££

29 HOTEL DAR EDDAYA

Luxurious hotel overlooking Dayet Roumi Lake. The hotel's staff provide excellent service to their guests.
dareddayahotel.ma +212 661-487834

33.7442, -6.1982 £££

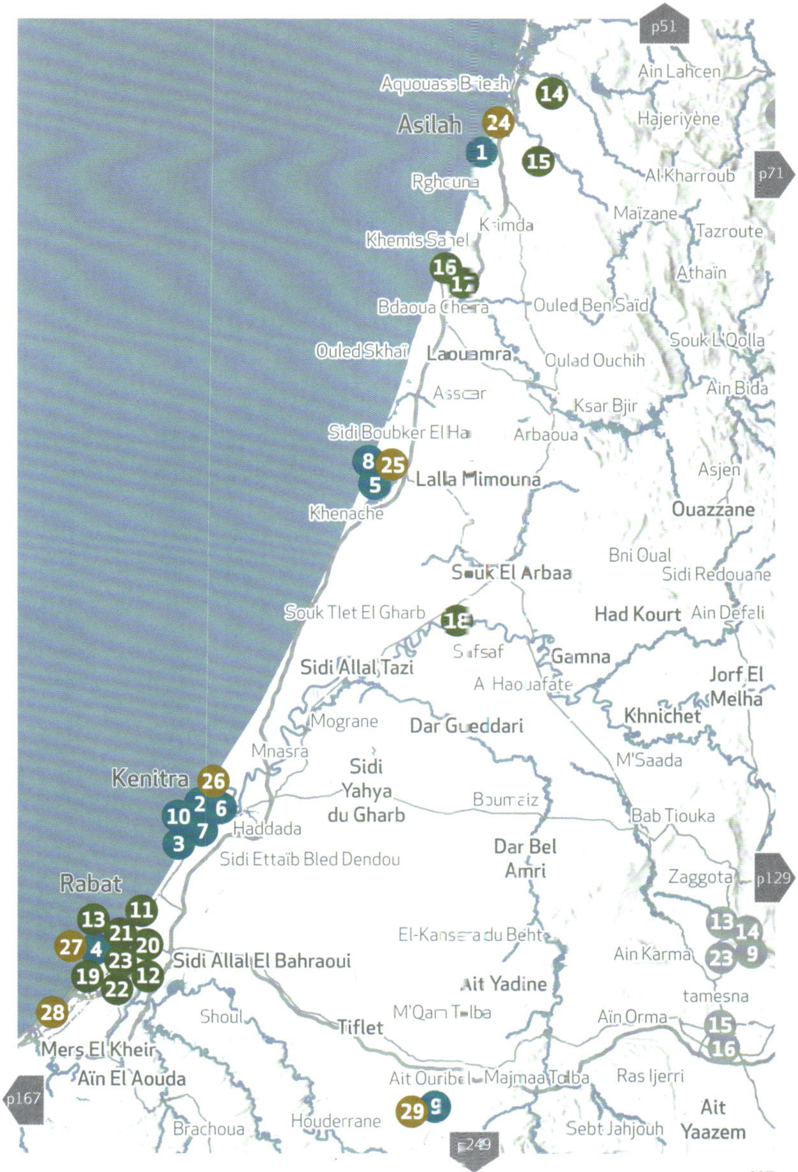

p51
Asilah
Ain Lahcen
Hajeriyène
Al Kharroub
p71
Maïzane
Tazroute
Khemis Sahel
Athaïn
Ouled Ben Saïd
Souk L'Qolla
Ouled Skhaï
Laouamra
Oulad Ouchih
Ain Bida
Ksar Bjir
Sidi Boubker El Ha
Arbaoua
Lalla Mimouna
Asjen
Khenache
Ouazzane
Bni Oual
Sidi Redouane
Souk El Arbaa
Souk Tlet El Gharb
Had Kourt
Ain Defali
Sidi Allal Tazi
Gamna
Jorf El Melha
Khnichet
Mograne
Dar Gueddari
Mnasra
M'Saada
Kenitra
Sidi Yahya du Gharb
Bab Tiouka
Haddada
Sidi Ettaïb Bled Dendou
Dar Bel Amri
Zaggota
p129
Rabat
Ain Karma
Sidi Allal El Bahraoui
Ait Yadine
tamesna
Shoul
Tiflet
Aïn Orma
Mers El Kheir
Aïn El Aouda
Ras Ijerri
p167
Majmaa Tolba
Ait Yaazem
Brachoua
Houderrane
Sebt Jahjouh
p249

AROUND MEKNES & FES

Our perfect adventure

- → **Explore** the well-preserved Roman ruins of the once-mighty Volubilis and imagine yourself a gladiator
- → **Stroll** through the shady forests of Bab Rmila Natural Park, smell the pine and eucalyptus and listen to birdsong
- → **Eat** fish freshly caught and cooked by the side of the sparkling Sidi Chahed reservoir after a refreshing dip
- → **Gaze** out over the old city of Fes at sunset from the monumental Marinid Tombs
- → **Swim** in thermal pools housed in the startling brutalist structure of Sidi Harazem
- → **Stay** at Terre de Traces Ecolodge and paddleboard in their huge irrigation pool
- → **Dive** from a boat into the vast turquoise Barrage Allal el Fassi amid lush, green hills
- → **Sip** mint tea and eat fresh doughnuts beside Cascades de Sefrou among olive and fig trees
- → **Bake** bread and experience traditional mountain village life in Dar Lala Zhour

2

2

2

'If Aphrodite chills at home in Cyprus for most of the year, then Fes must be the goddess's playground.'

Raquel Cepeda

The Middle Atlas region differs from the rest of Morocco, combining a temperate climate and lush vegetation with rugged mountains, forests, deep valleys and lakes. Regular rainfall and the fertility of the land support varied agriculture, including vast olive groves, vineyards and fruit orchards. In June, the Sefrou Cherry Festival is held, featuring a parade with performing troupes, majorettes, bands and floats. The highlight of the event is the Cherry Queen, who hands out samples of the region's delicious produce.

Morocco has many Roman settlement remains, including major sites and smaller ones. Volubilis, the most famous and best preserved, is situated in the fertile plains of the Saïss Valley. Established in the third century BC, the city benefited from the area's agricultural richness, supported by the same alluvial soils that nourish modern-day Meknes and Fes. Volubilis became a thriving centre of trade and agriculture under Roman rule, producing olive oil, grain and other goods that were exported throughout the empire.
Visiting Volubilis is a step back in time. Standing at the city's gate, we gaze down at the remains of what was once a mighty city. As fans of historical epics will appreciate, Danny had his 'Gladiator' moment, running his fingers through the shrubs that lined the road toward the main gate and feeling like Maximus. But instead of armour and a Roman gladius (sword), he wore a loose linen shirt, a cap and a camera on his hip.

Surrounded by the Middle Atlas mountains, Fes was founded in the eighth century and became a major centre of Islamic culture and learning.
Its mediaeval medina, Fes el Bali, is a UNESCO World Heritage site, famous for its intricate architecture, narrow streets and ancient tanneries, reflecting the city's long-standing artisanal traditions. Under the Marinid dynasty, between the thirteenth and fifteenth centuries, Fes carried the title of Morocco's capital. The architecture of Fes, particularly the Marinid Tombs, reflects their dedication to scholarship and art. The hilltop site is modest, but these fourteenth-century mausoleums are distinguished by their graceful, intricately tiled façades and elegant, pointed arches. Like the young couple sat on a wall, we gazed out over the tan and ochre buildings to the green rolling hillsides beyond and were happy we made the steep walk up the hill.

LAKES & RIVERS

1 EL WAHDA DAM

Morocco's largest reservoir. The turquoise lake provides essential irrigation to the surrounding area, with olive and fig trees dotting the landscape. A small, natural harbour offered a fantastic spot for swimming and we joined local boys diving joyfully from the banks.
The reservoir attracts herons and other migratory birds. Boats are available to charter and a couple of hours on the lake shouldn't cost more than 100dh – negotiate first.
From Ourtzagh Bridge, head W on R419 for 6.5km; turn L down second dirt track after red house; turn R on to track and follow for 1.2km to parking spot (34.5525,-5.0045).

3 mins, 34.5517, -5.0044

2 BARRAGE SIDI CHAHED

Built on Oued Mikkes, a tributary of Oued Sebou, the reservoir's turquoise waters stretch into the distance, flanked by rolling hills and olive groves. Entry into the water is gradual and shallow for at least 40m from the beach, ideal for children to play safely. The surrounding area is home to bird species such as herons and kingfishers. A few stalls offered snacks and drinks. We bought freshly caught fish directly from a local fisherman and then paid a nearby stallholder to cook the fish with onions, tomatoes and cumin – delicious. Boat rides are available; negotiate the price first. From Fes, take Boulevard Mohamed VI to P1/N4/N6 for 5.5km; follow N4 for 33km; at sign for Jet-Dream turn L onto Rte de Sidi Chahed for 3km to park by lakeside.

2 mins, 34.0661, -5.3245

3 AOUINT RAGRAGUE

Also known as Dayet Aoua, this small lake is a popular spot among locals for picnicking, birdwatching and leisurely walks along its shores. Deep enough to swim, the lake's calm waters reflected the surrounding mountains and cedar and oak forests. Walk downstream from the lake to find shady areas to rest and paddle among the water reeds. Look out for coots, grey herons, storks and little grebes. Close to the lake was a pure spring where visitors filled their water bottles. From Sefrou, head E on R504 for 3km; turn R to stay on R504 for 1.4km; turn R on to P5033 for 6.1km; turn L down unmarked road and take first R after 500m; follow road for 1.4km and take the L fork for 260m; park (33.7792, -4.7311) and walk down the hill for 200m to the lake.

2 mins, 33.7800, -4.7319

4 BARRAGE ALLAL EL FASSI

A vast, uncut sapphire amid the lush and rugged green hills. Built in the 1980s, the 100m-deep reservoir plays a crucial role in supporting agriculture and supplying electricity to the region. Named after a notable Moroccan nationalist, poet and political leader, the dam commemorates his significant contributions to Morocco's fight for independence from French colonial rule. Locals enjoy the lake for swimming, fishing and pleasure boating and visitors can walk down to one of the natural beaches while taking in the mesmerising views from above. We parked in the small village of Tifratine and descended the hillside to discover this beautiful river beach, perfect for swimming or wild camping. Having pre-arranged a boat through Terre de Traces Ecolodge (Bougzine +212 622-298096) to take us to some of the best swimming spots around the lake, we had a fantastic time diving from the boat and visited a natural spring. Be aware that the lake is up to 100m deep and banks can be muddy, so ensure your exit point before entering the water. From the village of Tifratine, walk N into the olive grove until you meet a narrow path, which descends towards the lake for 1.5km; turn R at a gate near the bottom downwards towards the beach.

30 mins, 33.9219, -4.6703

5 BARRAGE ALLAL EL FASSI #2

Good spot for accessing the lake for swimming and boating. From Fes, follow N4, P5008 and P5031 for 44km; park by road (33.9276, -4.6654); follow path down to lake for 200m.

3 mins, 33.9233, -4.6640

6 BARRAGE ALLAL EL FASSI #3

Inland beach where groups of locals picnicked, swam and hired boats. A small stall served mint tea, coffee and snacks. Taxis were available from the car park and we hired one to take us back to our van in Tifratine. From Fes, follow N4, P5008 and P5031 for 42km to parking spot (33.9326, -4.6755); climb over wall and walk 50m down to the lake.

2 mins 33.9325, -4.6757

POOLS & WATERFALLS

7 SIDI HARAZEM

Designed in the 1960s by Jean-Francois Zebaco, this post-colonial modernist complex is a startling example of Brutalist Architecture. Fed by hot springs (33o), the magnificent swimming pool boasts a striking circular design and vast basin of sparkling, blue water. Above the pool, a second circular structure serves as a canopy, supported by a conical concrete pillar.

Only men and children are allowed to swim in the pool, although wives may watch if they are suitably covered. Women can enjoy the same spring-fed water in the smaller of the round pools and a traditionally shaped, rectangular, indoor pool. We found a mixed outdoor swimming pool to the south of the complex. Large parts of Sidi Harazem are in need of reconstruction and in 2017 a rehabilitation project was launched. Phase one is underway. Sidi Harazem Center, Sidi Harazem 30205
5 mins, 34.0278, -4.8847

8 CASCADES DE SEFROU

Powerful waterfall surrounded by woodland. The area is known for its rich flora, including olive and fig trees. A small pool constructed downstream offered a refreshing spot for swimming. Popular for picnics, especially on weekends and in summer, with snack stalls and a café. To enjoy a quieter experience, visit early mornings during the week or off-season. From Sefrou, drive along the Chemin de la Cascades as far as you can until you get to the car park (33.8282, -4.8484); carry on walking until you see the waterfall; descend steps.
5 mins, 33.8281, -4.8521

FORESTS, PARKS & GARDENS

9 BAB RMILA NATURAL PARK

Pine, eucalyptus, oak, carob and wild fig trees greeted us at the Bab Rmila Natural Park. We followed one of the mountaintop pathways, which wound around the dense forest, home to wild boar, hare, hedgehog and tortoise. Benches were strategically placed to offer rest and at the crest of a hill, we paused to appreciate the view of the mountains before us. The air was filled with the song of partridges, storks and wild pigeons. The forest is a thriving ecosystem, alive with ants, grasshoppers, bees and beetles. From Moulay Idriss Zerhoun, follow P7401 for 8km until you see parking spot on your L (34.0336, -5.4989); walk across road and walk up steps to picnic area and start of trails.
2 mins, 34.0335, -5.4992

10 JNAN SBIL GARDENS, FES

Jardin Jnan Sbil, often referred to as Fes's green lung, is a nineteenth-century garden nestled between the old medina and the former Jewish quarter. Featuring intricately tiled water gardens adorned with roses and soothing fountains, you can stroll beneath towering palms and poplar trees, circling the pond to see the ancient waterwheel. For refreshments, Café Restaurant La Noria offers mint tea, while Mezzanine, a rooftop lounge, has scenic

views of the garden. With more than 3,000 plant species, Jnan Sbil is a tranquil escape and perfect for relaxation amid Fes's lively atmosphere. Closed on Mondays. Free entry. Ave Moulay Hassan, Fes.

2 mins, 34.0595, -4.9882

VIEWPOINTS

11 BARRAGE SIDI CHAHED LOOKOUT POINT

Panoramic stopping point with a view of the lake. We enjoyed freshly squeezed orange juice and bought two bottles of freshly picked pickled capers and had a friendly chat with stall holders. From Fes, take Boulevard Mohamed VI to P1/N4/N6 for 5.5km; follow N4 for 33km until you see stalls on R.

1 min, 34.0483, -5.3217

ANCIENT

12 KASBAH OF AMARGOU

The walls and towers of the medieval Kasbah of Amergou remain virtually intact and there was evidence of reconstruction work on arches and walls. Although there is no roof, we could still explore rooms and around turrets to get a sense of the layout. The fortress is believed to have been built as part of the defences of the Almoravid Empire in the eleventh or twelfth centuries against northern tribal rebellions. In addition to the wonders of the kasbah, the high vantage point offers incredible views over the valley, mountains and El Wahda Dam below. From Moulay Bouchta, follow the steep, unnamed road N for 3km to the parking spot (34.5019, -5.1294) beneath the kasbah; follow path uphill for 400m; gate is on the LH side of the building.

15 mins, 34.5034, -5.1289

13 VOLUBILIS

Volubilis is an ancient Roman city near Meknes and one of Morocco's most captivating archaeological sites. Once a vibrant centre of the Roman Empire, it features remarkably preserved ruins including majestic basilicas, grand arches and intricate mosaics that reveal the grandeur of Roman life in north Africa. These mosaics vividly depict scenes from Roman mythology and daily life, while the Triumphal Arch of Caracalla stands as a striking landmark, framed by mountains, olive groves and small Amazigh villages. Even after 2,000 years, the city's structure remains impressive, a testament to Roman engineering, but also thanks to its designation as a UNESCO World Heritage Site in 1997. The silent ruins tell stories of a once-bustling city where commerce, culture and religion intertwined. Covering 20 hectares, ongoing excavations reveal new historical layers, including a Muslim settlement from the seventh or eighth century. Signage was minimal, but a map, historical details and ticket prices are available on their website. Arrive early to fully appreciate the huge site and have your Maximus Decimus Meridius moment to yourself. From the roundabout at Moulay Idriss Zerhoun Rd/P7014 take the first exit on to N13; after 1.9km turn L on to Rte de Volubilis for 800m. sitedevolubilis.org

5 mins, 34.0719, -5.55233

14 HAROUNE AQUEDUCT

Although it looks old and Roman, the Haroune Aqueduct was built in the twentieth century. Spanning a river below, the aqueduct is surrounded by steep hillsides adorned with wild olives, yellow mustard and orange marigolds. The majestic arches amplified the sound of a nearby waterfall. Butterflies fluttered around and children gathered as school let out.
The natural beauty surrounding the aqueduct, coupled with human ingenuity, is awe-inspiring. From the centre of the village of Moulay Idriss Zerhoun, head E on P7014 for 1.3km; aqueduct is on your R; walk over rocks to aqueduct

2 mins, 34.0599, -5.5080

15 PRISON DE KARA

Constructed in the early eighteenth century under the rule of Sultan Ismail bin Sharif, the Kara Prison, also known as Habs Qara, is a remarkable underground structure in Meknes. The prison lacks conventional doors and bars, yet it is infamous for having never allowed a prisoner to escape. Extending for miles underground, the complex labyrinth was built to deter escapes. Some sources claim they reach the city of Taza, more than a hundred miles away. Nowadays, a section of the former penitentiary is accessible to visitors, though the true scale, and purpose, of the prison remain a mystery. Opening times: 10am–5pm.

4 mins, 33.8911, -5.56462

16 ROYAL STABLES OF MEKNES

Constructed during the reign of Sultan Moulay Ismail in the seventeenth century, this impressive edifice proclaimed as one of the largest and most impressive horse stables of its time. While local lore states that the Sultan kept 12,000 horses here, the truth is that this was never a stable. According to the website, Atlas Obscura, the site was, in fact, a vast granary storing grain for the Sultan's horses and the city's inhabitants. The actual stables were located about 600m southeast of the granary. Despite this, the Royal Stables or Granary, is an architectural marvel, worthy

of its place on the UNESCO World Heritage List. Open daily from 9am-noon and from 3pm-6:30pm.

5 mins, 33.8808, -5.5571

17 MARINID TOMBS

Perched on a hilltop overlooking the medina of Fes, the dead look down upon the living. No zombies here, though; rather monumental tombs that served as a royal necropolis for the Marinid dynasty, which ruled Morocco from the late thirteenth to mid-fifteenth centuries. The Marinids captured Fes in 1250 and later, in 1276, established Fes el-Jdid as their administrative capital. They chose this northern hilltop to build a fortified palace complex, known as al-Qula, featuring a mosque and bathhouse. Over time, this site developed into the royal necropolis, with tombs dating back to the fourteenth century, including two tall mausoleums and a smaller domed structure. Today, fragments of carved stucco and inscriptions are still visible amid the ruins, and the site—encircled by the Bab Guissa Cemetery—offers a popular sunset vantage point. From here, the valley below transforms into a patchwork quilt of Fes's ancient urban fabric. Free entry. From the Bab Guisa gate into the old city, head NW for 150m toward the roundabout; turn L at the roundabout and then turn immediately R on to the Av des Mérinides; follow this road for 1.5km before turning L into the tombs.

5 mins, 34.0698, -4.9795

18 BAZINA DU GOUR

This archaeological site is believed to be a funerary monument. Experts have dated the curious circular stone construction between the fourth and second centuries BC. We circumnavigated and climbed to the top of the mound, imagining what funerals might have looked like over 2,000 years ago, respectful at the thought. From Bouderbala, head NW on P7048 for 3.3km; turn R onto P7067 for 1.7km; turn R on to P7050 for 750m; turn R down unmarked road for 150m.

3 mins, 33.8506, -5.3085

19 BHALIL CASTLE

Situated above a small hamlet, Bhalil Castle dates to the seventeenth century and was constructed by the Alaouite dynasty to strengthen the region's strategic defences. Today, it stands as a ruin, with only a few rooms and corridors left intact yet the panoramic views of the valleys and distant mountains are in sparkling condition. The castle's crumbling condition sharply contrasted with the renowned troglodyte homes of the village, which were carved into the hillside. However, these are people's houses and you can't just knock and ask to have a look around. You will need a guide from the village who will take you to the houses where the residents are happy to receive visitors. Bhalil Castle is reached from Sefrou along a series of unnamed roads and tracks, use GPS software to follow the route – not suitable for long vehicles.

15 mins, 33.8549, -4.9040

CAFÉS & EATERIES

20 CAFÉ VUE PANORAMIQUE

Basic café and snack bar with superb views over El Wahda Dam. Directions as for El Wahda Dam, but carry on W along R419 for 550m after turnoff.

34.5540, -5.0106 £

21 CAFÉ CLOCK

Named after the centuries-old water clock that occupies the wall facing the Bou Inania Madrasa, Café Clock dishes up excellent food including camel burgers. A percentage of the price of every camel burger sold goes directly to a local cause, including Fez Medina Children's Library, Friends of Fez Orphans and the Morocco International Women's Association. Also hosts art exhibitions, live music and cookery classes. Open 9am-11pm daily. 7 Derb El Magana, Talaaa Kbira, Fes. +212 535-637855.

34.0622, -4.9830 ££

PLACES TO STAY

22 DAR LALA ZHOUR

Homestay in a traditional Rif mountain village where we were welcomed as part of the family and invited to share in the life of the local people: we even took part in a Moroccan wedding. Group or family rooms with shared bathrooms decorated with traditional crafts. A terrace in one of the rooms offered superb views over Ouergha Valley and Oued Ouergha. Our hosts provided home-grown and locally sourced food. There are opportunities a-plenty to hike or bike around Sidi Masoud mountain and classes are organised to learn pottery from local craftspeople. Workshops in bread-making, weaving and yoga also available. From Ourtzagh Bridge, head NE on R408 for 1.8km; turn R, by wooden kiosk (34.54273, -4.93740) up narrow winding dirt track for 5.5km – gets a bit tight and steep in places, so not advisable for motorhomes. Dar Lala Zhour, Onsar Village, Ourtzagh, Taounate, 34044 taounate4ecotourisme.org +212 663-844694

34.5176, -4.9284 £

17

17

23 CAMPING ZERHOUN BELLE VUE

Pretty campsite with spacious pitches among olive trees and geraniums. Ethereal, misty morning views over the valley. Order food in advance. From Moulay Idriss Zerhoun, follow N13 for 10km; turn L on to P7008 for 170m. R. Moulay Moustapha El Hamdouchi. +212 663-569856

34.0153, -5.5623 £

24 ECOFERME D'HÔTES LES RACINES

This eco-friendly guest farm emphasises sustainable living and organic agriculture. The farm uses natural materials for its buildings and practices energy and water conservation. Rooted in the community, the farm organises activities such as hiking and workshops on traditional farming. From Meknes, take the A2 towards Fes; after 28km take R716 N towards Ain Taoujdate; after 8km turn R immediately after footbal pitch on L, follow road to L and then R under railway; bears R and then L for 20m; turn R at T-junction; after 500m track turns R round field; turn L at fork and follow track for 2km to the farm. +212 600-087605

33.9311, -5.1912 £

25 HOTEL SIDI HARAZEM

Beyond retro. Hotel Sidi Harazem enjoys a prime location with views over the Brutalist architecture of Sidi Harazem Thermal Pools. All food ingredients are sourced from the local daily market. Passive cooling systems provide eco-friendly alternatives to air conditioning. Sidi Harazem Center, Sidi Harazem 30205. hotel-sidiharazem.com +212 535-690135

34.0273, -4.8828 ££

26 TERRE DE TRACES ECOLODGE

A unique retreat that blends comfort with sustainability; the lodge uses traditional Amazigh architecture and locally sourced materials. Environmental impact is minimised by operating on eco-friendly principles, utilising solar energy for heating and electricity, along with a water recycling system. The lodge featured three swimming pools, including a whopping great irrigation pool (75x45m), where we swam and paddle boarded, and an ice pool for Wim Hof aficionados. A yoga and wellness room was also available. Organic gardens supplied fresh produce for the restaurant, which served authentic and delicious Moroccan cuisine. Enjoy nature-based activities such as hikes, birdwatching and horseback riding. The lodge supports the surrounding community by employing staff from the area and using traditional building methods. Available for group holidays upon negotiation and will arrange airport transfers. Highly recommended. Douar Boughioul

Commune Rurale De Aghbalou Aqorar 30000, Sefrou 30000. terredetraces.com +212 661-158241
33.9236, -4.8087 £££

27 AUBERGE AMAZIGH

Overlooking the Allal el Fassi reservoir and surrounding cedar forests. Features traditionally designed, simple yet comfortable rooms, some equipped with private bathrooms. The auberge conserves water, minimises waste and serves traditional Moroccan cuisine. Douar Aït Ayoub Dam Allal el Fassi, Sefrou 31000. aubergeamazigh.com +212 636-225207
33.9291, -4.6820 £

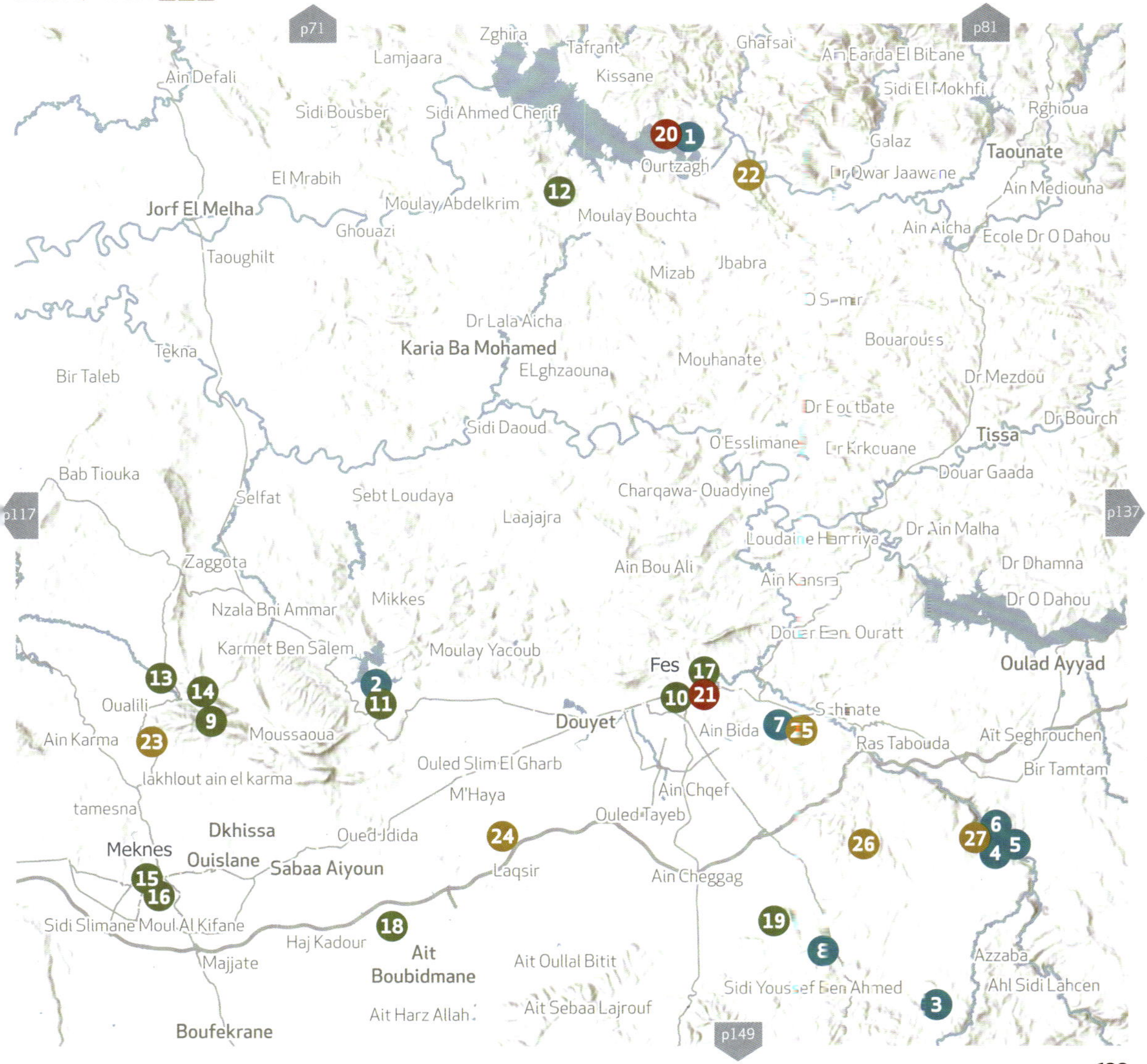

p71
p81
p117
p137
p149

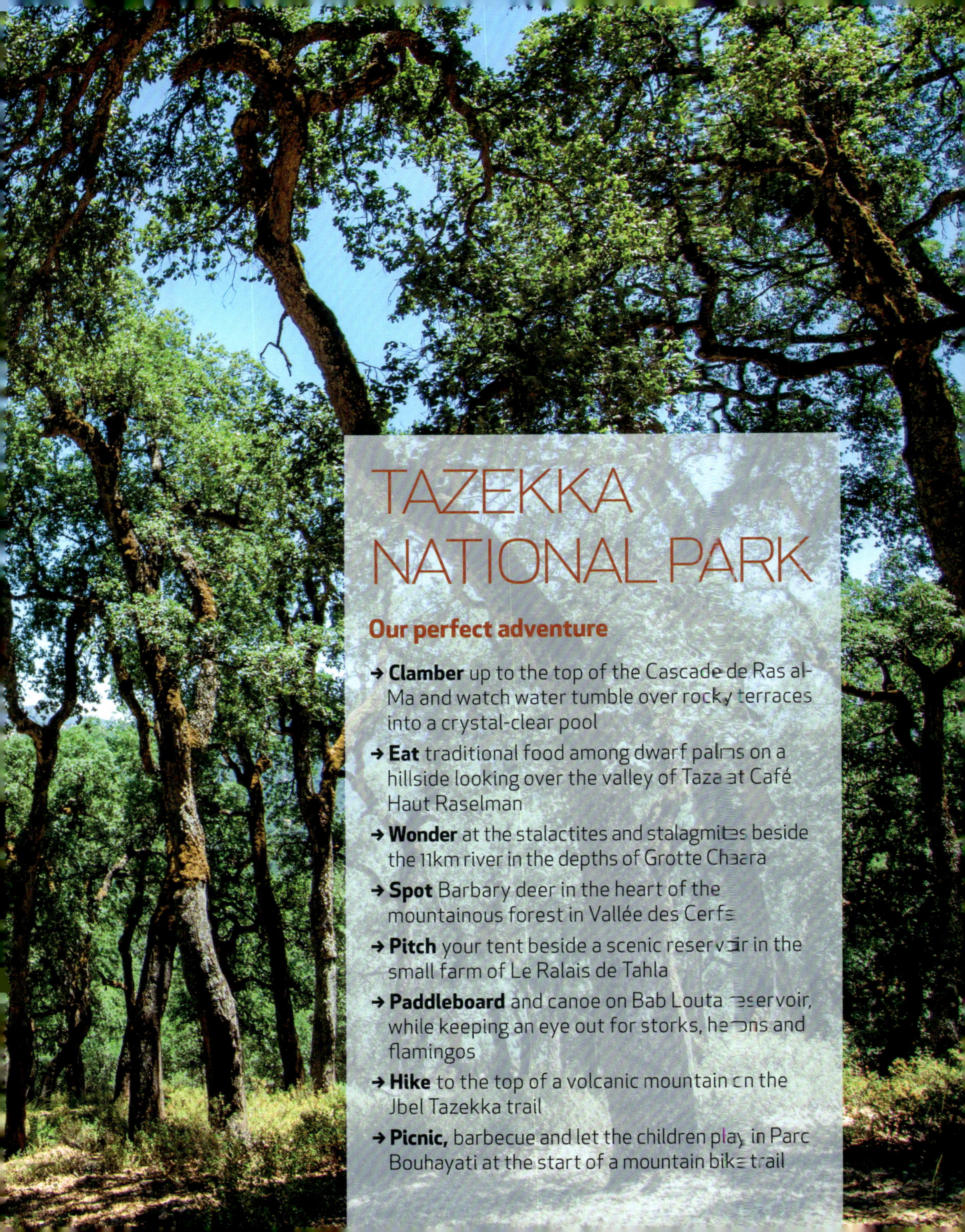

TAZEKKA NATIONAL PARK

Our perfect adventure

- → **Clamber** up to the top of the Cascade de Ras al-Ma and watch water tumble over rocky terraces into a crystal-clear pool
- → **Eat** traditional food among dwarf palms on a hillside looking over the valley of Taza at Café Haut Raselman
- → **Wonder** at the stalactites and stalagmites beside the 11km river in the depths of Grotte Chaara
- → **Spot** Barbary deer in the heart of the mountainous forest in Vallée des Cerfs
- → **Pitch** your tent beside a scenic reservoir in the small farm of Le Ralais de Tahla
- → **Paddleboard** and canoe on Bab Louta reservoir, while keeping an eye out for storks, herons and flamingos
- → **Hike** to the top of a volcanic mountain on the Jbel Tazekka trail
- → **Picnic,** barbecue and let the children play in Parc Bouhayati at the start of a mountain bike trail

3

3

4

'The earth opens
and welcomes you
One day, your beloved will rediscover
your legendary smile.'

Abdellatif Laâbi, The Earth Opens and Welcomes You

The land that international tourism forgot, watched over by a 1,980m-high Jbel Tazekka. The few visitors we meet are locals, cooking tagines in the forest in the same earthenware pots their Amazigh ancestors used 12 centuries ago. Located in the northernmost tip of the Middle Atlas mountain range, Tazekka is a wonderful example of the wild attractions Morocco offers for nature enthusiasts and adventurers alike. Established in 1950 under the French protectorate, the park was created to protect the cedar forests surrounding the volcanic mountain, Jbel Tazekka, from destruction by logging.

Mediterranean forests of holm and cork oak in the lower regions provide habitats to Barbary deer, wild boar, red fox, owls and eagles and are dense with rosemary, juniper and wild lavender. Higher in the mountains, alpine meadows and grasslands dominate. River valleys and gorges have been carved by watercourses, such as Oued Zireg, and attract amphibians, reptiles and migratory birds, making the park especially appealing to bird watchers.

Respectful tourism is encouraged and enabled by clearly marked picnic areas furnished with wooden tables and benches. We were invited to join a meal by a family from El Menzel and spent a happy hour eating homemade bread, rice and salad and drinking mint tea, switching between shared languages to learn about each other's lives and cultures. Trekking is supported in the park, with several clearly marked routes of varying lengths, including a hike to the top of the volcanic mountain Jbel Tazekka. Mountain biking is also possible, with routes leaving one of the picnic areas.

Adjacent to the national park, the turquoise Barrage Bab Louta is part of the wider ecosystem and where birdlife thrives, including migratory birds such as storks and herons. Popular water sports include kayaking, canoeing and paddle boarding, which can be organised through local groups or the campsite and hostel Relais de Talha, where we parked our van for a couple of nights.
Wild camping is permitted here and in the national park, if care is taken of the natural environment. The official campsite in Bab Boudir is due to reopen in 2025.

13

LAKES & RIVERS

1 CASCADE DE RAS AL-MA

A graceful cascade, where crystal-clear water tumbles down rocky terraces before gathering in a pool below. The falls are modest in height but possess a gentle, soothing charm. Water flows over mossy rocks, creating a delicate mist that nourishes the surrounding vegetation. Best between October & March. From Café Watani, turn L and walk 30m until road widens; turn L down small narrow path, which turns R and then bears L up hill for 500m until you reach waterfall.

15 mins, 34.1508, -4.0079

2 BARRAGE BAB LOUTA #1

Small shallow bay, perfect for families to take a dip. From Taza, head S on R507 and P5420 for 70km to parking spot (34.0159, -4.3273); walk 100m downhill to lake.

2 mins, 34.0152, -4.3274

3 BARRAGE BAB LOUTA #2

Ravishing spot for plotting up or swimming in the reservoir. From Taza, head S on R507 and P5420 for 66km; turn off down unmarked track on R to parking (34.0040, -4.3137); follow path for 500m down to lake.

10 mins, 34.0015, -4.3162

CAVES & HIKES

4 GROTTE FRIOUATO

One of the country's largest and most fascinating cave systems with deep chambers and intricate limestone formations. The cave descends more than 270m into a captivating underground world of stalactites and stalagmites. At the time of writing, Grotte Friouato was under reconstruction to improve accessibility and safety for visitors. Contact Aziz Ramouni at Tazekka National Park (+212 661-613929) to check if it is open before visiting. From Taza take R507 for 17.7km to fork; turn left onto P5420 for 17km; turn right on to Route Grotte Friouato for 1km.

20 mins, 34.1047, -4.0725

5 CEDAR TRAIL

The longest of Tazekka's trails takes you through the magnificent cedar forest and deer reserve and delivers panoramic views over the surrounding landscape and to the Rif and Middle Atlas Mountains. Trail distance is 17.3km so allow about 4.5 hours. From Taza, head S on R507 and P5420 for 33km; green sign and parking spot on L.

300 mins, 34.0653, -4.1273 

6

6

8

6 GROTTE CHAARA

Known as the Red Cave or Ifri Azoughar by the Amazigh people, Grotte Chaara encloses an 11km underground river. Our friend, Houssam Elwafi, told us about his experience: 'The hike from the parking spot to the cave was about 2km and we saw no signs. Out of nowhere, a small hole appeared in the forest – the entrance. We had to bend to get in and use a rope, then a ladder to descend five metres. As we hiked in the cave, it got darker and darker and the level of the water rose. We didn't need special equipment, apart from a helmet to protect the head and a headlamp. The experience was exciting. The air was very dry at the entrance and became more humid the deeper we went. The geological formations were incredible. Stalactites and stalagmites are abundant and there are fossils.' A highly recommended visit, which we suggest doing with an experienced guide, as there is no signage and it is extremely difficult to find. Official tour guide Hakim Bouhlala (+212 656-0425073) has 20 years' guiding experience. Turn off the P5411 (34.0334, -4.1570) and follow track for 5km to Mosquée de Tabhirte; walk through fields to cave.

30 mins 33.9559, -4.2461

7 ZEEN OAK TRAIL

This hike passes through Zeen oak forest and near Lakhal Wadi Gorge. Viewpoint over the Tazekka massif and the agricultural terraces of Beni Senane. Trail distance is 4.6km so allow about 1.5 hours. From Taza, head S on R507 and P5420 for 36km; green sign on R marks the start of the trail and parking.

90 mins, 34.0577, -4.1598

8 JBEL TAZEKKA TRAIL

Hike up to the top of the Tazekka (volcanic) Mountain following this trail, with a viewpoint halfway. Allow at least two hours to hike the 6km to the top and two hours back. From Taza, head S on R507 and P5420 for 38km; turn R on to track (34.0518, -4.1672) and park where you can, then follow the trail.

240 mins, 34.0519, -4.1657

9 JBEL BOULHADI TRAIL

Starting from behind the swimming pool at Bab Boudir, follow the track upwards. The trail is gentle at first, through cedar trees, but gets more challenging as you climb higher, with rocky outcrops and steeper inclines. Along the way, you will pass through areas of sparse vegetation and the trail gets rockier and narrower towards the top, but you are rewarded with panoramic vistas over the sweeping landscape from 1,835m above sea level. From behind the swimming pool at Bab Boudir (34.0687, -4.1187) follow the trail upwards.

100 mins, 34.0642, -4.1178

PICNIC & PLAYGROUND AREAS

10 SITE RÉCRÉATIF VALLÉE DES OISEAUX

Well-shaded picnic area and a great for a family lunch stop. From Taza, head S on R507 for 18km; parking spot on L as road doubles back (34.1296, -4.0311).

1 min, 34.1290, -4.0321

11 PARC BOUHAYATI

Picnic area with benches, tables, a barbecue pit and small children's playground. Start of the 'Rando-VTT' mountain bike trail, with options for 8-28km rides, which can also be walked. From Taza, head S on R507 and P5420 for 27km; park on R

1 mins, 34.0941, -4.0985

12 VALLÉE DES CERFS

We followed a rabbit path into the woods and found a picnic area that led into a forest of tall shady cork oaks, carpeted with ferns, grasses, sage leaves and rock roses. A magnificent location for a break in the heart of the mountainous forest, with generous tree cover to shelter from the heat of the sun. Watch out for Barbary deer. Toilets and café sometimes open, sometimes closed. From Taza, head S on R507 and P5420 for 42km; the parking spot is on L.

5 mins, 34.0462, -4.1861

VIEWPOINT

13 BARRAGE BAB LOUTA OVERLOOK

Lovely spot to park up and gaze out over the turquoise waters of the Bab Louta Lake, spreading to the green hills of the Tazekka National Park. The dam was built for irrigation and flood control but is now a scenic backdrop for water sports such as kayaking, canoeing and stand up paddleboarding. Picturesque, the lake is surrounded by mastic bushes and wild lavender and is visited by storks, herons and egrets during their migration seasons. Black-winged stilts and yellow-legged gulls also stop over at the lake's shores. During winter months, species such as Eurasian spoonbills and greater flamingos also make an appearance. Apparently, fishing is allowed sometimes, although we saw many signs forbidding the practice. From Taza, head S on R507 and P5420 for 69km to parking on L.

3 mins, 34.0101, -4.3223

14 VUE PANORAMIQUE SUR BOUIBLANE

Magnificent mountain views across the valley. Well worth the 'Wow' stop. From Taza, head S on R507 and P5420 for 37km; park on L

1 min, 34.0543, -4.1660

CAFÉS & EATERIES

15 CAFÉ WATANI

Stop-off near Ras al-Ma serving a variety of Moroccan fare. There is a seasonal waterfall and pool round the side of Café Watani. 4XXV+63Q, S311, Rass El Ma.

34.1480, -4.0074

16 CAFÉ PANORAMA

Roadside café with friendly staff that sells nuts and locally produced honey. The best place to sit is up on the hillside to enjoy a 360-degree view and an immense vista of Taza valley and mountains. Tables and chairs are set among dwarf fan palms, adding to the magical ambience. Mint tea and local dishes available. From Taza, head S on R507 for 12km; parking spot on L (34.1446, -4.0139); walk along road for 100m to café on R.

34.1438, -4.0137

PLACES TO STAY

17 LE RELAIS DE TAHLA

This small farm offers great views of the turquoise Barrage Bab Louta reservoir. You'll find an enclosure with poultry, including some peacocks and a vegetable garden. Guests can choose from three simple rooms or pitch tents and park campervans. There are shaded spots for eating outside. The farm provides kayaks for exploring the reservoir and can organise guided trips to a nearby cave. Amin, the owner, is friendly and speaks some English. From Taza, head S on R507 and P5420 for 65km; campsite on L. 35300 Parc National de Tazekka. +212 644-021395

34.0008, -4.3082

17

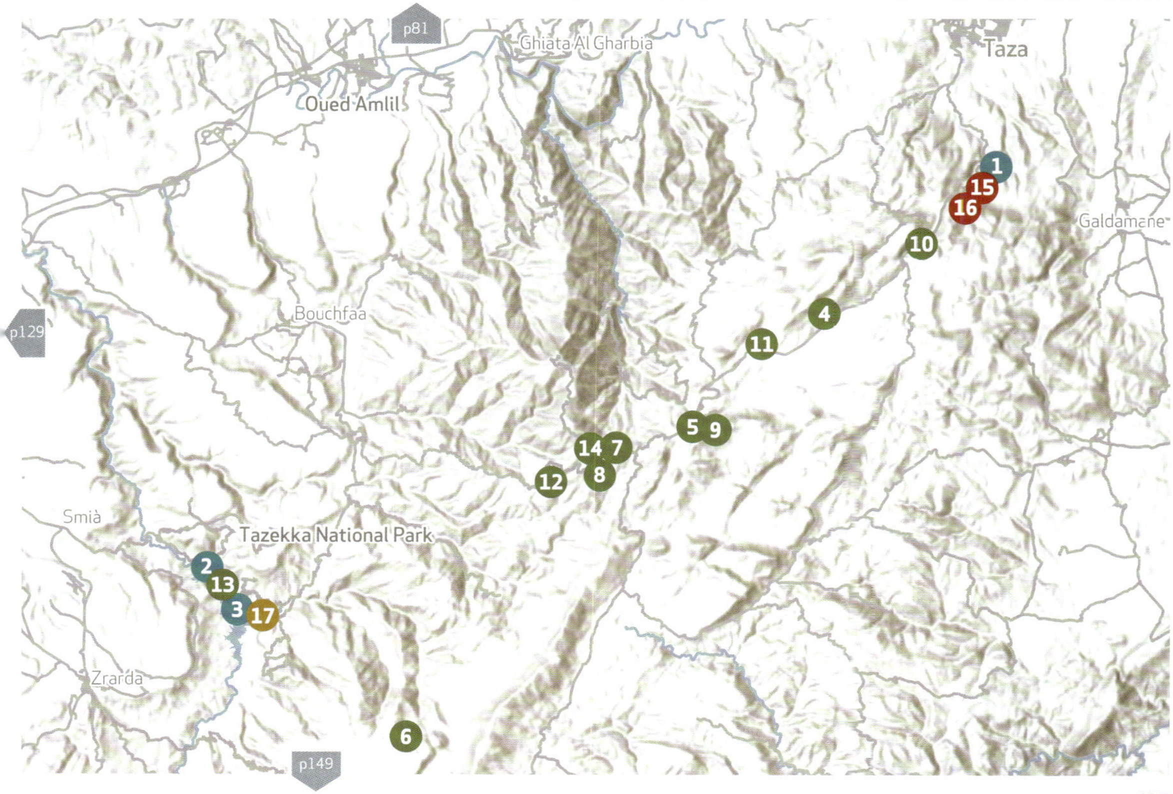

p81
Ghiata Al Gharbia
Taza
Oued Amlil
1
15
16
Galdamane
10
p129
Bouchfaa
4
11
5
9
14
7
8
12
Smià
Tazekka National Park
2
13
3
17
Zrarda
6
p149

AZROU, IFRANE & BOULEMAN

Our perfect adventure

- → **Gaze** up at the huge ancient cedar trees in the Cèdre Gouraud Forest while macaque monkeys jump around
- → **Enjoy** a range of delicious goats cheese from the Ferme de Fromage Chèvre
- → **Sleep** beneath mature cherry trees at laid-back Camping Amazigh
- → **Picnic** with friendly families and have a dip in Lac Zerrouka
- → **Re-energise** beneath the powerful Skoura M'Daz waterfalls, as they explode from oleander-covered hillsides
- → **Delight** in pure organic mountain honey from the honey man in Skoura
- → **Swing** like monkeys from trees, ropes and zip lines at Atlas Parc Adventure
- → **Wake** up to incredible views and lovely gardens in Gîte Auberge Zarwale Écobio

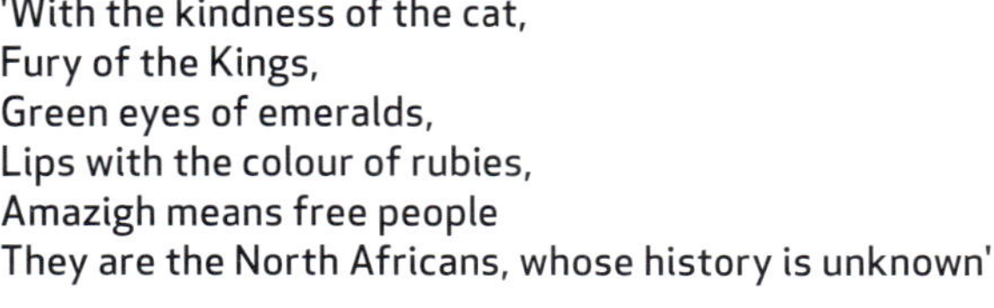

'With the kindness of the cat,
Fury of the Kings,
Green eyes of emeralds,
Lips with the colour of rubies,
Amazigh means free people
They are the North Africans, whose history is unknown'

Youssef Riadi, Moroccan Beauty

Water, trees and rocks define the landscape of Azrou. The Tamazight word azro means 'rock' and refers to a large outcrop in the city, marking the gateway to the Middle Atlas Mountains. For nature lovers, the Cèdre Gouraud is the main attraction, featuring ancient towering cedar trees. The forest is home to a friendly group of Barbary macaques; fearless locals allow the monkeys to climb on their shoulders. Nearby Ifrane is often called 'Little Switzerland' for its Alpine-style architecture and snowy winters. We see storks nesting on mosque minarets, telegraph poles and houses – often three or four nests per roof. The town of Ifrane, established by the French in the 1930s as a colonial hill station, was designed as a retreat from Morocco's hot summers. Ifrane's geology, characterised by volcanic rocks and limestone, contributes to its lush greenery and natural springs. The town is known for its well-maintained parks, which offer a picturesque contrast to Azrou's rugged aesthetic. As we stroll around Lake Zerrouka, we receive greetings and offers of tea or tagines from families relaxing on blankets.

Night began to fall as we drove along winding mountain roads to Skoura M'Daz in search of its three famous waterfalls. The longest journey ended with a buttock-clenching drive up a narrow track to Skoura Gîte. Tired and hungry, we vowed never to drive after sunset again. The morning revealed one of the waterfalls cascading nonchalantly into the garden. A 12km trek with a group of independent women from Casablanca, aged 40 to 70, restored our frayed nerves. We discovered more waterfalls, wild apricots, freshwater springs and a honey seller. Escaping the heat, we dove into a freshwater pool where young boys respectfully vacated the water while the fully dressed women waded in.

More hair-raising mountain roads led to Immouzer Marmouche, a small town with waterfalls, hot springs, an ancient kasbah and a museum celebrating the local role in the fight for liberation from French colonisation. We watched football in a café with the locals and delighted in discovering Lac Tanda, a secret watery grotto that appears on no maps.

FORESTS

1 AZROU CEDAR FOREST

Renowned for its majestic cedar trees, particularly the ancient Atlas cedar (cedrus atlantica), some of which are over 800 years old, this forest stands as a testament to the region's natural heritage. The landscape lies at an altitude of 1,500-2,000m above sea level, For centuries, the region has been home to Amazigh communities, who maintain a deep connection to the land and its traditions. The forest is also a haven for the endangered Barbary macaques (Macaca sylvanus). Once common throughout north Africa, they are now confined to specific pockets of the Atlas Mountains. At the forest's edge, we observed several monkeys, including a mother caring for her baby. It's important to resist the temptation to feed them. Feeding bread or other human food can lead to health problems like diabetes and aggression, and can interfere with their natural instincts to forage. The forest also offers scenic hiking trails, ideal for birdwatching and exploring the rich biodiversity of this unique region. From Ifrane, head SW on P24/N8 for 15km; continue on P21/N13 for 5.8km; turn R onto P7217; park where you can – several clearings suitable for picnics.

5 mins, 33.4174, -5.1865

2 ATLAS PARC ADVENTURE

Blending seamlessly into the cedar trees, Atlas Parc Adventure offers thrilling outdoor activities set amid the scenic beauty of the Middle Atlas Mountains. Kids will enjoy zip-lining, rope courses and climbing challenges designed for all ages and skill levels. The park emphasises safety and fun, with professional guides and equipment. Great fun for your little simians. Directions as for the Eco-Museum, but follow road for 450m; park is on your L; park where you can.
atlasparcaventure.com +212 666-558432

2 mins, 33.4200, -5.1724 ££

3 KHARZOUZA VIEWPOINT

Enjoy panoramic views of Azrou and the Cèdre Gouraud from the Kharzouza viewpoint. From Ifrane, head SW on P24/N8 for 14.3km; continue to P21/N13 for 1.3km; turn R on to P7215 for 5km; park in clearing on right (33.40679, -5.23087); walk NE past school buildings for 750m; bear L for 200m and climb rocks to viewpoint; from here follow steepish trail up to Les Falaises.

10 mins, 33.4137, -5.2272

4 LES FALAISES, AZROU

We trekked to the summit of Les Falaises National Park in the Azrou Cedar Forest. After a long, sweaty ascent beneath the canopy of towering cedars, we were rewarded with breathtaking views of the widespread forest of Ifrane National Park and the town of Azrou from the top of the cliffs. Directions #1: from Ifrane, head SW on P24/N8 for 14.3km; continue to P21/N13 for 1.3km; turn R on to P7215 for 4.9km; after 100m, park in clearing on R (33.40679, -5.23087); walk back up to P7215 and follow steep rabbit paths SE to summit. Alternatively, there's a longer path near Kharzouza Viewpoint marked on satellite GPS (33.4132, -5.2246). Directions #2: from Ifrane, head SW on P24/N8 for 13km; continue to P21/N13 for 5.8 km; turn R on to P7217 after 4.1km park on L opposite small track (33.3993, -5.2104); follow track W for 1.3km and bear sharp R along track for 900m to viewpoint.

60 mins, 33.4031, -5.2271

5 RÉSERVE NATURELLE DE CÈDRES, AZROU

A group of the most ancient Atlas cedar (cedrus atlantica) in the forest grow here and are reputedly 1,000 years old. A wide variety of walks through the forest are available in this area. Some stalls have been set up, offering snacks and drinks. Barbary macaques heavily populate this region. Once again, don't feed the monkeys. From Ifrane head SW on P24/N8 for 15km; continue to P21/N13 for 4km; park on R.

2 mins, 33.4314, -5.1773

LAKES

6 LAC ZERROUKA

A long lake surrounded by rushes stretched out before us. We joined families who had brought blankets and set up small barbecues for their picnics. From the eldest grandparent to the youngest child, everyone sat together to enjoy hearty tagines and salads, finished off with cups of sweet mint tea or homemade lemonade. Across the middle of the lake, a stone walkway extends, perfect for diving or even just dangling feet in the water. At one end of the lake, a grove of ancient oaks provided a welcome refuge from the sun, offering shade for afternoon snoozes. Coots glided by with their fluffy chicks paddling languidly in search of crumbs. As we strolled around the lake, we were greeted with warm smiles and, upon returning the gestures, kind families offered us tea and homemade cakes. A nearby flat stretch of grass served as a makeshift pitch where children chased after a football, the sounds of laughter echoing across the waters. From Ifrane, head N on N8 for 1.5km; turn R down unmarked track for 500m and park by lake

3 mins, 33.5431 -5.0958.

7 DAYET AL AMIRA

A small reservoir nestled among low, tree-covered hills. Olive groves lined one side, while families picnicked under the scattered shade. Children swam and dived from the low dam. The cool, clear water reflected the peaceful atmosphere as a gentle breeze rustled through the trees. Accessible via a narrow, rocky lane that wound around the lake's shallow parts – drivers of motorhomes should park by Café Dayet Al-Amira and walk round. On a Sunday afternoon, the vibe was relaxed and family-oriented, with cows grazing nearby and the smell of kebabs filling the air. From Café Dayet Al-Amira (33.6446, -4.9705), drive 400m SE on P5016 then turn L on to dirt track; after 300m turn R and follow track for 550m; park on hill overlooking lake.

2 mins, 33.6493, -4.9671

8 DAYET IFFER

Almost perfectly circular lake surrounded by woods of Aleppo pine. On a sweltering hot Sunday afternoon, children jumped in from a tiny beach, surrounded by swathes of water lilies that flowered around the edges of the lake. Locals claim that the lake had been formed in a crater and that it has never dried out. Slightly muddy as you enter with a shelf into deeper water. In the middle, you can feel the welcome cool water of the underwater springs. A family offered us a glass of tea, which we gratefully accepted, offering biscuits in return. From Sefrou, head S on N4 for 23km; bear R on to P5016 for 6.2km; turn L on to Circuit Touristique des Lacs/P7237; after 280m turn L by sign with Arabic writing; continue for 1.5 km down bumpy track to parking spot (33.6034, -4.9065); walk downhill for 300m to lake.

5 mins, 33.6055, -4.9073

WATERFALLS

9 SKOURA M'DAZ WATERFALL (TOP)

First of three impressive waterfalls. The cascade is surrounded by a lush carpet of greenery and oleander bushes, nourished by the year-round flow of water. The top of the first waterfall combines the excitement of witnessing the water's mountain exit and impressive views over the village of Skoura M'Daz to the valley beyond. From Skoura M'Daz, head E on P5109 for 2.1km; turn right for 650m and park by café on R (33.51551, -4.53666); walk 10m; follow the path behind the cafe towards a building; turn L round back of building; follow path towards cliff and you'll arrive at top of waterfall.

5 mins, 33.5161, -4.5380

10 SKOURA M'DAZ WATERFALL (BOTTOM)

Water cascades down the green cliffside like Rapunzel's hair, with tendrils separating out over rocky shelves before reuniting in the pools at the bottom. There are shady areas to sit and dip your feet in the river or picnic. The second waterfall is a hundred metres to the right of the first and can be seen from the road leading south from Skoura M'Daz. The third culminates in the garden of Skoura Gîte. Directions as for Skoura M'Daz waterfall (top), but a few metres past the café there is a right turn on the path leading downhill, follow the zigzag path all the way to the pools at bottom of the waterfall.

15 mins, 33.5169, -4.5383

11 CASCADE D'IMOUZZER MARMOUCHA

Nestled beneath the town, the waterfall cascades down limestone cliffs into a natural rocky amphitheatre. Concrete steps and stone pathways wind through cedar and oak trees, leading to a platform with stone benches, allowing visitors to get close while preserving the wild beauty. The seating area, adorned with graffiti naming local groups, hints at possible musical performances. Historically significant to local Amazigh communities, the waterfall is most powerful outside summer, when it builds to a cascading crescendo. The 175 steps down offer spectacular views as the water tumbles into a pool and flows onward through the valley. From the roundabout at Imouzzer Marmoucha head S on P5115 for 500m and park on your right (33.4666, -4.2948); descend 175 steps of Sent. de la Cascade to waterfall.

3 mins, 33.4671, -4.2953

12 LAC TANDA

Magical secret grotto with an idyllic round blue pool and cascade, hidden downstream of the Cascade d'Imouzzer Marmoucha. There are several means of access, but all involve scrambling down some steep rocks and there is no set path. Start at Cascade d'Imouzzer Marmoucha and follow the river downstream. Not visible or navigable using GPS navigation, so ask one of the local kids to show you the way.

10 mins, 33.4647, -4.2998

NATURAL SPRINGS

13 AIN TIOUMLILINE

Water source popular among locals to fill water tanks and bottles. Always purify unless you are used to Moroccan microbes. Directions as for Kharzouza viewpoint but park on R on P7215 after 2.1km; water source on L.

2 mins, 33.4143, -5.2081

14 SKOURA M'DAZ SPRING

En route between Skoura M'Daz and Immouzer Marmoucha we found a roadside freshwater spring and enjoyed magnificent panoramic views. For experienced speleologists, the source is surrounded by caves.

1 min, 33.5208, -4.5046

15 HOT SPRINGS SKHOUNAT

Wallowing in a hot spring during the heat of the day was surprisingly refreshing. The low-ceilinged spring was supported by intricately tiled pillars with a couple of small windows letting in natural light. A strict timetable is observed for the use of the springs: men 7am – 11am and 3pm – 7pm; women 11am – 3pm. The water is warm as it originates from the hot spring, supplemented by another tributary. If you walk past the building, you will discover a small natural pool, perfect for another refreshing dip. Children have ingeniously constructed a small weir along the river, adding to the charm of the setting. From Aït Makhlouf, head W on N4 towards P5049 for 1km; turn R on to P5049 for 4.2km; turn R down road for 220m to parking spot on L (33.4482, -4.3409); follow path for 500m around the hillside to the hot springs

10 mins, 33.4491, -4.3389 ££

16 RAS EL AIN

Water springs used by locals. Always purify unless you are used to Moroccan microbes. From Poste Maroc in Imouzzer Marmoucha head NE on P5115 for 1.3km; take a sharp right for 450m; turn R and after 350m the springs will be on your R.

2 mins, 33.4729, -4.2790

17 SOURCE D'EAU TADOUT

Crystal-clear water cascades from a spring where weary hikers refill their drinking bottles. A few metres on, this refreshing liquid gathers itself into a river that enterprising locals have dammed to make a rectangular pool where youngsters jump and swim, competing with each other to perform the most extravagant and acrobatic dives. Older Moroccan ladies enter fully clothed, unable to resist the temptation of a cooling dip. As we leave, they point out that the boys are now returning to the pool, having respectfully vacated the water while we swam. From Skoura M'Daz take P5109 for 3.5km until there is a fork; take the R fork for 450m and park by the first water source (33.5123, -4.5214); follow the path W and you will find the weir.

5 mins, 33.5125, -4.5251

15

17

18

18

17

ROAD TRIP

18 SKOURA M'DAZ - IMOUZZER MARMOUCHA

From the moment we left Skoura M'Daz, we encountered palm groves that provided a stark contrast to the arid surroundings. Ascending further into the mountainous region, the dramatic walls of rock loomed above us, creating a breathtaking backdrop. The route featured diverse vegetation, including oaks and Aleppo pines that clung to mountain slopes. The road was quite challenging and narrow in places, with sharp turns that demanded caution. Some stretches were barely a road. As we drew closer to Imouzzer Marmoucha, we noticed a shift in the landscape; the earth took on a vibrant orange hue and the fields became more cultivated. Much of the terrain remained rocky, peppered with hardy, resilient plants.

- Start/finish: Skoura > Immouzer
- Distance:67km
- Roads: P5109 and N29 (33.6608, -4.4325)
- Scenic stop-offs: Skoura M'Daz spring

ANCIENT

19 KASBAH AGHARM AMKRAN

Over 800 years old, according to locals, this partially ruined fortress at Aït Bazza once served as a bustling trading hub where Jews and Muslims conducted commerce. Abandoned in 1900 due to water shortages and illness, many of its towers and thick earthen walls are still visible. Each year, descendants of former inhabitants hold a festival here. The kasbah's sturdy construction has endured despite ongoing neglect. Visitors can see the cultivated valley below, dotted with 12 small hamlets where the kasbah's former residents relocated to be closer to trade routes. From the roundabout at Imouzzer Marmoucha head SE on P5115 for 6km; turn L on to N4 for 2km; turn L by Aït Tobacco shop for 2.7km; turn R and after 650m turn uphill to track on L (33.4111, -4.2873) and follow to kasbah for 850m.

3 mins, 33.4115, -4.2836

CULTURAL HOTSPOTS

20 CEDAR FOREST ECO-MUSEUM

The eco-museum showcases the natural and cultural heritage of the Middle Atlas region. Visitors w ill find exhibits on local flora and fauna, traditional Berber crafts and the unique cedar forest ecosystem. The museum offers educational programs and guided tours, highlighting sustainable practices and conservation efforts. Interactive displays and workshops provide hands-on experiences, allowing visitors to learn about the region's biodiversity and cultural traditions. Additionally, the eco-museum features scenic walking trails and a café serving local cuisine. Check the website for opening times. From Ifrane, head SW on P24/N8 for 15km; continue to P21/N13 for 6km; turn L after crossroads and the museum is on L. maisondelacedraie.ma

1 min, 33.4194, -5.1774

21 ESPACE DE LA MÉMOIRE

The Espace de la Mémoire Historique de la Résistance et de la Libération is dedicated to local history, particularly the resistance against the French occupation. In the garden, there's a lorry used in the fight against the French, who locked away opponents in a prison opposite the administrative building. This now houses exhibits, including photos of Morocco's sultans and documents detailing resistance efforts. Displays include resistance tools such as homemade bombs, bullets and traditional army clothing. A room showcases local artisanal tools and traditional women's clothing. The museum features a library, meeting room and computer facilities for local use. Enthusiastic staff are available to describe and explain the exhibits. From Poste Maroc in Imouzzer Marmoucha, head NE on P5115 for 230m; museum is on L; park outside.

1 min, 33.4726, -4.2927

19

CAFÉS & EATERIES

22 FERME DE FROMAGE

Drawing from the Amazigh centuries old tradition of goat farming, the farm was founded to safeguard this heritage while championing sustainable agriculture. It integrates traditional methods with contemporary techniques to craft high-quality cheese. Customers can select from fresh, medium and aged varieties. We left with goat cheese, camembert and local honey. From Azrou, head SE on P24/N13/N8 for 650m; turn L on to P24/N8 for 2.6 km; turn R and after 1km the track leading to the cheese shop is on your R. +212 661-423898

33.4402, -5.1712 £

23 HONEY SELLER SKOURA

Only the wooden beehive trays piled up outside the house of Mustafa, the honey seller, advertise his trade. The honey, from beehives high up in the mountains, comes in two qualities: one from bees exclusively fed on the ammi visnaga or boushnika plant, whose seed heads are also a source of natural toothpicks. This honey is dark, rich and strong. The other honey is from bees that feed on three separate herbs and is lighter and slightly cheaper. This is connoisseurs' honey. GF46+H4, Caïd Bou Malla. From Skoura Gîte climb steps and turn slightly R; follow the path downhill; turn L at intersection; follow the path until it turns L up the mountain; turn R uphill at the big rocks; turn L at the aqueduct and house is on the L. +212 673-028440

33.5061, -4.5393 ££

24 MOULIN TRADITIONEL OUBABA

Simple café serving traditional food and drinks, including some juices. Fantastic views over the valley. From the Gasoil station in Skoura M'Daz, head E on P5109 for 3km; café is on R, just before fork in road. +212 621-760571

33.5155, -4.5368 £

PLACES TO STAY

25 AZROU CEDAR FOREST REST AREA

Picturesque wild camping spot at the edge of the cedar forest. No facilities. From Ifrane, head SW on P24/N8 for 14km; continue on to P21/N13; after 7.5km your destination will be on the R.

33.4063, -5.1854

26 CAMPING AMAZIGH

Relaxed family-friendly campsite with informal pitches set beneath the shade of mature cherry trees. Good showers and facilities, including electricity and a restaurant. Azrou town and the cedar forest are easily accessible. Reasonable prices. Recommended. From Azrou, head E on P24/N13/N8 towards for 1.5km; turn L on to P24/N8 for 2.8km; campsite is on R just before the road curves L. N8 km 5 route d'Ifrane. Azrou Ougmes, 53100. camping-amazigh.com +212 535-560725

33.4496, -5.1703 £

27 FERME D'HÔTE LAANOUCER

We had a great time on the farm, only 50km south of Fes. Superb swimming pool surrounded by apple orchards. Local activities included horseback riding and hiking. KM25 Route de Boulemane, Sefrou 31000. +212 667-177253

33.6250, -4.8684 £

28 SKOURA GÎTE

One of the Tadout waterfalls cascades into a corner of the garden. The gîte has a long grass lawn, with a lower terrace set aside for tents. Good Moroccan food. The journey up to the gîte was challenging in a van due to the narrow, rocky track. Douar Tikhzanine Skoura M'Daz, 33352. From the Gasoil station in Skoura M'Daz, head S on P5109 for 450m; take a sharp R along the narrow unnamed track for 1km bearing L just before the gîte. skouragite.com +212 645-037943

33.5064, -4.5416 ££

29 GÎTE AUBERGE ZARWALE ÉCOBIO

Reconstructed with traditional materials, the hotel features an organic kitchen garden. Workshops in yoga and massage, utilising natural plants, along with cooking classes where guests can learn to prepare couscous and other traditional dishes. Fatima and Ahmed are excellent hosts and can arrange both short and long treks to waterfalls, valleys and mountain summits. Lovely garden with breathtaking views. Imouzzer Marmoucha, 33152 Morocco. From the roundabout at Imouzzer Marmoucha, head S on P5115 for 1.6km; the gîte is on your right just after the bend. +212 621-507972

33.4574, -4.2948 £

26

28

27

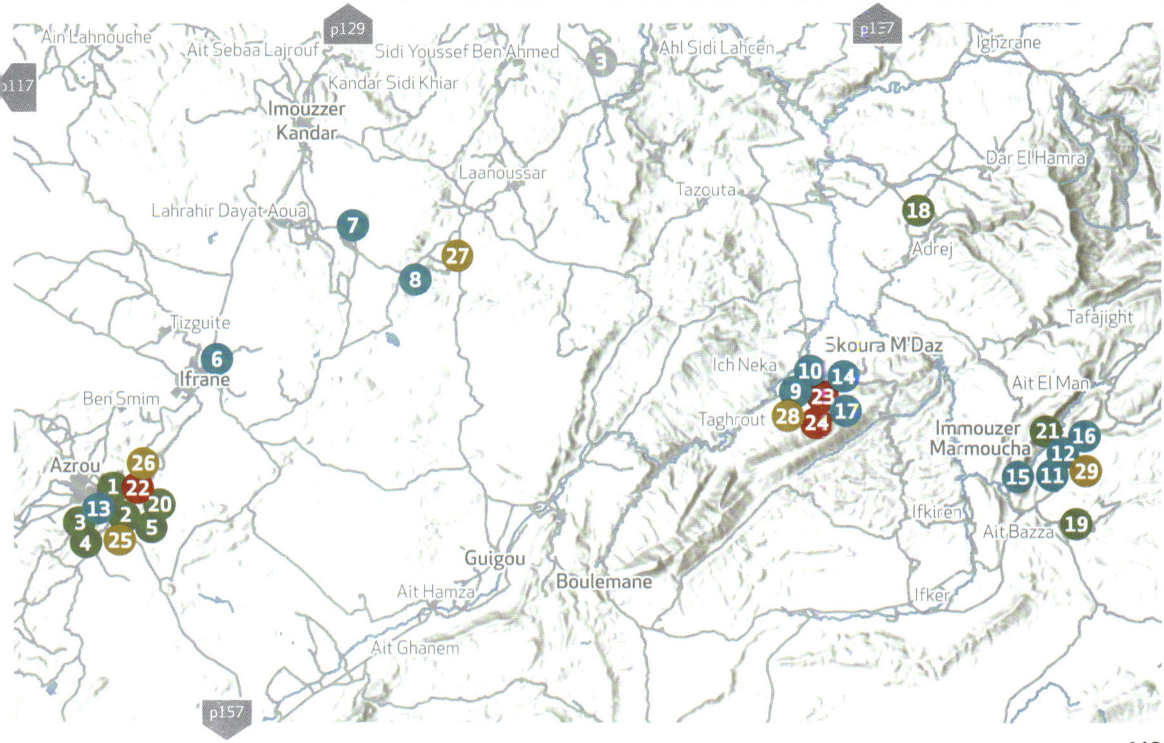

2

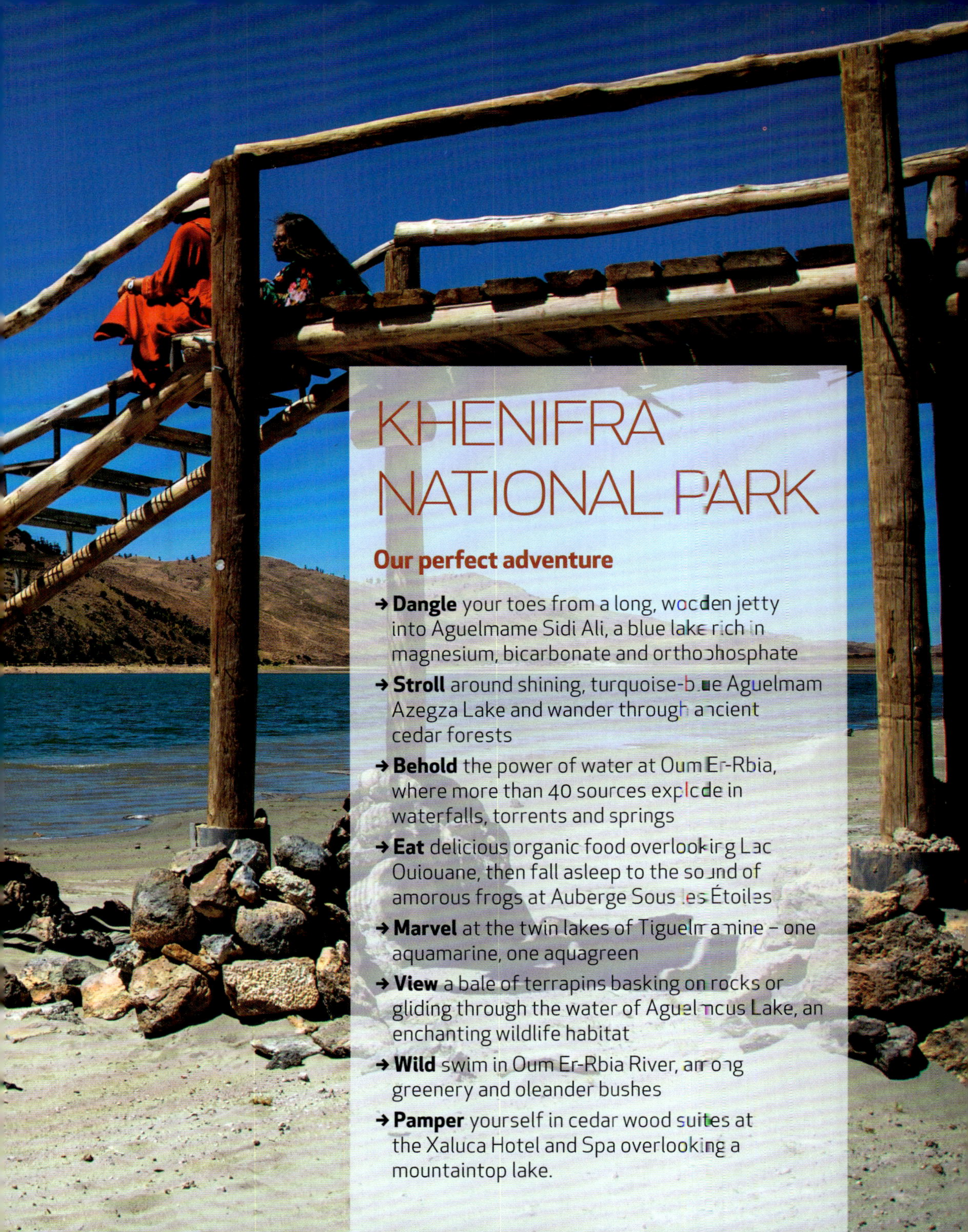

KHENIFRA NATIONAL PARK

Our perfect adventure

- → **Dangle** your toes from a long, wooden jetty into Aguelmame Sidi Ali, a blue lake rich in magnesium, bicarbonate and orthophosphate
- → **Stroll** around shining, turquoise-blue Aguelmam Azegza Lake and wander through ancient cedar forests
- → **Behold** the power of water at Oum Er-Rbia, where more than 40 sources explode in waterfalls, torrents and springs
- → **Eat** delicious organic food overlooking Lac Ouiouane, then fall asleep to the sound of amorous frogs at Auberge Sous les Étoiles
- → **Marvel** at the twin lakes of Tiguelmamine – one aquamarine, one aquagreen
- → **View** a bale of terrapins basking on rocks or gliding through the water of Aguelmous Lake, an enchanting wildlife habitat
- → **Wild** swim in Oum Er-Rbia River, among greenery and oleander bushes
- → **Pamper** yourself in cedar wood suites at the Xaluca Hotel and Spa overlooking a mountaintop lake.

**'I don't like the mountains
that reach closer to the sky of speech. I like the paths
that lead secretly to the heart, pull
the soul back to its retraced steps, and take me
to the limits of the earth.'**

Hassan El Ouazzani, Elegy for Love

Khenifra National Park, spread out among the Middle Atlas Mountains, offers a peaceful retreat into nature. Established in 2008, this 842km^2 park is a sanctuary for flora and fauna and a haven for wilderness seekers. The park is famous for its lakes and rivers: Lake Aguelmam Azegza, a sparkling gem surrounded by dense cedar and oak forests, is a priceless spot teeming with birdlife and amphibians. As night falls, the lake comes alive with the sounds of locals drumming and playing music, adding to the enchanting atmosphere; Lake Aguelmame Sidi Ali offers a more secluded experience, with a hotel and spa on one side and wild camping on the other. This lake invites you to swim or fish from a long, picturesque, wooden jetty, perfect for those seeking a peaceful refuge.

Khenifra's rivers, including the Oum Er-Rbia – one of Morocco's longest – add to the park's charm. These rivers are lifelines for wildlife, nurturing vegetation along their banks. We visit the Oum Er-Rbia's springs: the powerful falls and rushing streams cannot fail to impress. We head downstream and discover a spot where tributaries converge. Peering over a low cliff, we spot a pool where the fast-flowing river bends around a rocky promontory. The green water shimmers in the morning light and we cannot resist the call of a cheeky dip. Scrambling down the rocks, we reach the river's edge, quickly shedding our clothes to slip into the cold, fresh mountain water.

Khenifra National Park is also home to vast cedar forests, where ancient trees create a dense canopy sheltering a rich variety of plants. The park's flora shifts with the seasons, offering a vibrant display, especially in spring when colourful wildflowers blanket the forest floor. Lake Aguelmous proves elusive, so we enlist the expertise of local boys on bicycles who lead the way. 'You can't swim there,' they tell us but are unable to explain why. The reason becomes clear when an abundance of terrapins swim towards the bank where we are standing. Untroubled, we leave the water to them and head to a nearby campsite with a pool.

LAKES & RIVERS

1 AGUELMAME TIFOUNASSINE

Located in the Ifrane National Park, this seasonal lake is named after the Amazigh phrase meaning 'Lake of Cows'; when we visited, sheep abounded. A peaceful area to walk around. Water evaporates in summer. From Lac Aguelmame Sidi Ali, head SW for 2.8km; turn R on to N13 for 12km; take sharp L for 1.2km; turn L for 2.1km; park near lake.

5 mins, 33.1550, -5.0953

2 LAKE AGUELMAME SIDI ALI

Blue lake rich in magnesium, bicarbonate and orthophosphate, 2,100m high in the Middle Atlas Mountains. The low surrounding hills are covered with cedars and junipers, home to macaque monkeys. We saw tents on one side of the lake and the luxurious Xaluca Hotel and Spa on the other. In the evening, a few families came to picnic, paddle and swim, while Amazigh shepherds from the Aït Mgild tribe brought their flocks to drink. A long, wooden jetty leads from the road to a pontoon where people dangled their toes or paddled in the water. From Azrou head E on P24/N13/N8 for 52km; turn L for 1.2km and follow road for 2.7km where you will see a long, jetty in front of Xaluca Hotel.

5 mins, 33.0744, -4.9954

3 AGUELMOUS LAKE

Aguelmous Lake is a lesser-known yet captivating spot situated within Timnay Agro-ecological Park. The lake is home to an ancient tumulus that hints at the region's historical or ceremonial significance. An empty brick building with a turret on the opposite side of the lake provokes further questions.
A unique feature was its population of terrapins; hundreds can be seen basking on rocks or gliding through the water, their heads raised inquisitively. From Ksar Timnay Hotel, walk along the signposted path for 500m.

5 mins, 32.7526, -4.9103

4 TIGUELMAMINE LAKE

Two lakes of different colours – aquamarine and aqua green. We found a spot on the hillside to sit and see both circular lakes. When bored of being mesmerised by one lake, turn your head ever so slightly and be mesmerised by the other and so on and so forth. Other than the occasional family cooking up a tagine or a few fishermen, the place was deserted. From Khénifra, head SE on P7306 for 41km; to parking spot (32.9100, -5.3312); the track from here to the lake is pretty rough and narrow in places. If you run into another car, you'll struggle to pass each other, so we advise walking down to lake.

25 mins, 32.9040, -5.3421

7

8

5

5 AGUELMAM AZEGZA LAKE

Surrounded by cedar woods and only 30km from Khenifra, this shining, turquoise-blue lake is the stuff dreams are made of, especially when it's roasting hot. The lake, formed by glacial activity, is located at an altitude of roughly 1,600m and provides a unique habitat for all manner of flora and fauna. However, the large car park and walkway lined with tagine and mint stalls are a testament to how popular the place must be in summer. The walk to the lake from the car park was longer than anticipated and we almost had the place to ourselves, bar a few fishermen around the water. A man playing guitar created a calm atmosphere. The lake hosts the annual International Ice Swimming Association Championships. From Khenifra, head E on P7306 for 22km; slight L on to P7311 signposted Aguelmam for 7km; after 350, car park is on your L (32.9802, -5.4596); walk 350m down path to lake.

15 mins, 32.9722, -5.4454

6 OUM ER-RBIA SOURCES

Situated within the Aguelmam Azegza National Park, more than forty sources of the Oum Er-Rbia River explode in waterfalls, torrents and springs. The sheer volume of water is quite incredible, although the biggest waterfall only has water from October to March. Enterprising locals have built wooden platforms to offer the many Moroccan summer tourists tea and tagine. There appeared to be a disproportionate number of public toilets on offer – maybe it's all the running water. If you want to take a hike up to the top of Jbel Khdoud, there is a path clearly marked with white stones (33.0524, -5.4137), about an hour's hike each way. From Khenifra head E on P7306 for 21km; slight L on to P7311 signposted Aguelmam for 5.2km; turn L to stay on P7311 for 17km; car park is on R as you enter village (33.0535, -5.4147); follow path up the cascades for 400m.

10 mins, 33.0519, -5.4120

7 OUM ER-RBIA RIVER

Just a kilometre away from the Oum Rbia waterfalls, we find a great spot by the river among the greenery and oleander bushes. A burnt patch of ground indicates that we are not the first visitors. Sheltered from the strong current by a small promontory, we take a careful dip, indulging in the freshness of the cold water. Directions as for Oum Er-Rbia Sources, but park by P7311, 1km NW of the falls (33.0544, -5.4242); turn L down the side of the car park and follow the zigzag path downwards towards the river; near the cliff edge near the river, turn L and scramble down the rocks to the river.

5 mins, 33.0558, -5.4247

8 LAC OUIOUANE

Surrounded by lush woods of holm oak, this picturesque lake sits at an altitude of 1,800m. Frequent frog calls echo across the water. A popular spot for picnics and relaxation. Not suitable for swimming. Great circular walk around the lake. Directions as for Oum Er-Rbia Sources, but continue on P7311 for 13.5km until you see the lake on your R; follow path down to lake for 100m.

2 mins, 33.1305, -5.3448

PLACES TO STAY

9 XALUCA HOTEL AND SPA

Combines luxury with sustainability. The large cedarwood suites, designed to resemble a Swiss chalet, are crafted from locally sourced wood, highlighting the hotel's commitment to eco-friendly practices. Spacious walk-in showers and bedrooms offer spectacular lake views. An indoor swimming pool, with its warm water and starry overhead view, feels like a flotation tank. On a hill next to the hotel, a swing chair and jacuzzi offer the ultimate luxury in nature. Guests can enjoy the gym, saunas and massages. The food is excellent. Vegetarians should call ahead. Directions as for Lake Aguelmame Sidi Al..

xaluca.com +212 673-243020

33.0301, -4.9939 £££

9

11

10 LAKE AGUELMAME SIDI ALI

Big space for campervans and motorhomes by the lake. No facilities. Directions as for Lake Aguelmame Sidi Ali, but turn down track 1.2km after you exit the N13

33.0725, -5.0061

11 KSAR TIMNAY HOTEL

Shady two-hectare campsite with large pitches, a swimming pool and a decent restaurant. In the hotel there are 120 beds in comfortable suites. Nearby, a 50-hectare Timnay Agro-ecological Park showcases a fish lake, archaeological sites, diverse fauna and 30,000 trees. Activities include hiking and mule treks. From Zaida, head SE on N13 for 8km; Ksar Timnay is on your L; Route National 13, entre Zaïda et, Midelt 54350. ksar-timnay.com +212 535-360188

32.7515, -4.9190

12 GÎTE D'ÉTAPE RAHHAOUI

Spacious dining terrace with great views over the Oum Er-Rbia Cascades. Clean rooms, some en suite. Friendly and welcoming. Good food available – call ahead for a special diet. Free airport transfers from Fes. Local area information and trekking guides available. Aït Bouzzaouite, Oyoun Oum Rabia, 54450. Directions as for Oum Er-Rbia Sources but continue for 350m along P7311; take sharp turn R and drive up narrow dirt track; after 170m there will be a flat parking area on the R (33.054725, -5.414393), you will need to pay a small fee for this when you leave; continue for on foot along path for 70m to Gîte d'étape Rahhaoui. +212 614-374152

33.0539, -5.4140

13 AUBERGE SOUS LES ÉTOILES

Delicious organic food including some of the best vegetarian dishes we ate in Morocco. Wood-built family rooms at the top of the hotel have one glass wall to give the full view of the valley and lake and are big enough to accommodate a dining table, fridge and sofa, making this a great destination for long stays. Two terraces overlook Lac Ouiouane and an indoor dining room and wood-burning stoves provide heat for the winter months. You'll feel like you're in the Swiss Alps. One of our favourite accommodation stops. Highly recommended. Directions as for Lac Ouiouane, Auberge Sous les Étoiles is on your L. +212 666-974622

33.1324, -5.3466

8

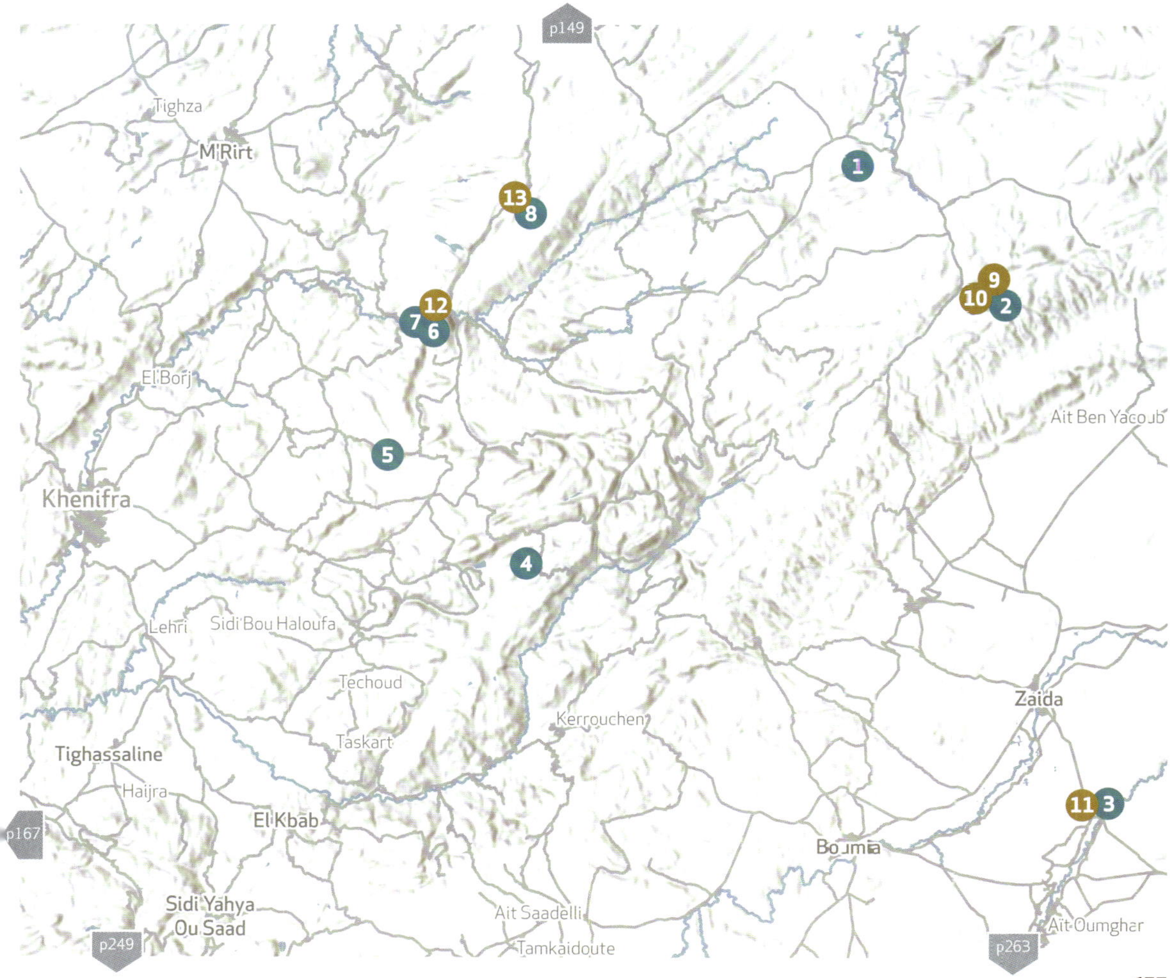

p149

Tighza
M'Rirt
1
13
8
9
10
2
12
7
6
El Borj
Ait Ben Yacoub
5
Khenifra
4
Lehri
Sidi Bou Haloufa
Techoud
Zaida
Kerrouchen
Taskart
Tighassaline
Haijra
11
3
p167
El Kbab
Boumia
Sidi Yahya Ou Saad
Ait Saadelli
Aït Oumghar
p249
Tamkaidoute
p263

CASABLANCA TO SAFI

Our perfect adventure

- → **Catch** a wave or a wipeout at Dar Bouazza's Jack Beach. Surf's Up
- → **Deepen** your understanding of diverse cultures at Hassan II Mosque, one of the only Moroccan mosques accessible to non-Muslims
- → **Wild** camp on the sands and under the stars on Plage Sidi Moussa
- → **Frolic** among the flamingos and their feathery friends at Sidi Moussa Lagoon
- → **Watch** the scintillating sunset from the ramparts of the well-preserved Kasbah Oualidia
- → **Meditate** for a moment or more in the salt-sprayed hollows of Grotte Oualidia
- → **Climb** the staircase to nowhere on the mysterious Sidi Chachkal
- → **Sit** in silent solitude on the remote, pink sands of Baaliten beach

3

4

5

'I am like a grasshopper, jumping from place to place, never knowing where we will end up.'

Mohamed Choukri, For Bread Alone

Founded by Amazigh tribes in the seventh century and later developed under French colonial rule in the early twentieth century, Casablanca is Morocco's largest city; a bustling metropolis blending modernity and tradition. Featuring architectural landmarks such as the Hassan II Mosque, one of the largest mosques in the world and the art deco buildings in the city centre. The city gained international fame from the 1942 film Casablanca, which romanticised its wartime intrigue: 'Here's looking at you kid.'

The stretch of coastline between the towns of El Jadida and Safi is home to nature reserves such as Oualidia Lagoon and Sidi Moussa's wetlands. Scores of migratory birds use this coast and its pockets of calm waters as rest stops on the northern avian highway. Take a drive along this coastline during Spring or Autumn and you might catch a glimpse of flocks of migrating birds on their journey between Spain and southern Africa, making the area a premier birdwatching destination. Although the main attractions are undoubtedly the bright-pink flamingos, storks are a common sight, flying north in long, white lines as they head to roosts in Fes, Rabat and beyond, clacking to their heart's content.

Rolling into the seaside town of Oualidia on the CTM bus, a spectacular scene unfolds before me; a long, thin lagoon snakes along the coastline, fed by a small channel leading to the sea at the southern end of town. The sky is set ablaze by the setting sun, casting vibrant colours on to the waters of the Atlantic and the saltwater lagoon. I walked through scrubland and emerged through the gates of Kasbah Oualidia, an ancient fort perched atop the headland, keeping watch over the surrounding landscape. Fishing boats and tourist crafts navigate the lagoon and return from the wider seas.

Wild and beautiful beaches abound around the town of Safi, a major port in the region and home to purportedly the world's largest tagine pot – it has to be seen to be believed. Sidi Chachkal is the most accessible beach in the area, its southern headland crowned by the majestic Cap Bedouza Lighthouse. Further south is a group of three beaches: Baaliten is for intrepid adventurers, only accessible via a scramble down a steep cliff. Lalla Fatna is slightly more developed, with a Tarmacked road leading all the way to the beach; yet its pink sands remain irresistible. Sidi Boudala is also a popular spot among fishermen and a great place to watch the sunset. All are worth a visit.

6

BEACHES & SURFING

1 JACK BEACH DAR BOUAZZA

The surf culture in Dar Bouazza is everywhere. There's no shortage of surf schools or places to eat and drink while waiting for the tide to drop. Jack Beach is a prime spot with consistent surf year-round, thanks to its exposed beach break. Offshore winds from the south-east and clean groundswells from the north-west create optimal conditions. The waves break both left and right, and the beach is rarely crowded, even during prime surf conditions. Winter, particularly December, offers the most consistent clean waves. Take the R320 for 20km out of Casablanca before turning R at the roundabout on to the P3012. Follow this road for 9km and the beach will be on your R.

4 mins, 33.5243, -7.8410

2 SIDI ABED

Hiding behind the small town of Sidi Abed lies a secluded stretch of sand, curving off to the south like a shepherd's crook, culminating in a rocky promontory. A young family was eating a tagine, while a young boy waded out into the sea, net in hand, on the hunt for mussels. Grassy dunes fringe the sands, sloping gently down to the water's edge, from which a disturbed seabird will sometimes soar into the skies. From Oualidia, take the R301 NE for 48km, take a L off the main road at the Station Afriquia petrol station just before entering the village of Sidi Abed; parking (33.0476, -8.6883) will be on your L; walk straight down the road off the R301 over the dunes and onto the beach.

2 mins, 33.0474, -8.6917

3 PLAGE ET RÉSERVE D'AL HARCHANE

Hidden behind wetlands, farmland and tall dunes lies Al Harchane, a steeply sloping beach popular with locals and families. Children happily splashed in the waves while their parents watched on like hawks. Take the R301 for 45km N from Oualidia; turn L off the main road onto the Harchane Beach Road; a track leads all the way down to the parking (33.0295, -8.7048).

2 mins, 33.0296, -8.7060

4 SIDI BELKHEIR BEACH

The track through the wetlands to the beach is flanked by bushes of sea lavender, while black-necked stilts with impossibly long and brittle legs soar above, their calls a consistent chorus and companion. Huge plumes of water shot into the air above the double cove, produced by waves smashing into the headland at the southern end of the beach. From El Jadida, head S on R301 for 34km; turn R by the TotalEnergies petrol station (32.9957, -8.7274) on to the track through the wetlands until you come to the dune; parking on R (32.9979, -8.7383) walk over dune to beach.

5 mins, 32.9971, -8.7412

5 HEYRASH BEACH

Unknown to the tourist hordes and even to some locals, this small stretch of golden sand, hidden by a headland, is an ideal retreat for a secluded swim. Directions as for Sidi Belkheir Beach; but once on beach, turn R and walk over the headland to Heyrash Beach.

10 mins, 33.0025, -8.7338

6 PLAGE SIDI MOUSSA

On the southern side of the Sidi Moussa Lagoon, Sidi Moussa Beach extends itself, lazily and gently, down towards the waiting arms of the waves. A fisherman cast his line out repeatedly, yet either the fish were wise to his tricks, or his tricks were not good enough in the first place, as his efforts yielded nothing. Curving away to the north, the sea has forged a channel over countless years to create saltwater wetlands. Turn off the R301 (32.9661, -8.7585) on to the Sidi Moussa access road (sandy track) and follow to the parking spot (32.9740, -8.7591).

5 mins, 32.9785, -8.7578

8

9

7

7 PLAGE SABLE D'OR OULAD GHANEM

Hidden behind farmland and vast sand dunes, lay the golden expanse of Sable d'Or. This must be a synonym for solitude because I had this beach to myself. The only sound, other than the waves, was the crunch of mussel shells under my feet, evidence that locals pulled food and a living from these shores. Turn off the R301 (32.8399, -8.8941) on to the farm track and follow until you reach the sand dune and the two silver tree stumps by the parking spot (32.8423, -8.8963).

3 mins, 32.8340, -8.9103

8

8 PLAGE OUALIDIA

Bordered by the lagoon on one side and the headland on the other, this beach was a perfect spot for a swim. Families frolicked together in the clear water while paddleboarders glided up and down the canals. On the northern end of the beach lay the royal palace of King Mohammed V: once a grand, opulent home, now a ruin. Unfortunately, entry to and taking photos of the palace was forbidden, with the building itself ringed by a fence, police and members of the auxiliary forces. Herons and marsh birds lined the canals leading out to the beach, picking their way along the shore looking for tasty treats. On the northern edge of the beach, the golden sands gave way to sharp rocky cliffs pierced through with caves and arches, which were begging to be explored. Be aware that due to the canals and the nearby lagoon, this beach floods at high tide, so don't get caught with your towels down. Turn off the R301 at the roundabout (32.7343, -9.0335); follow the road down to the beach parking (32.7313, -9.0469); walk on the road N out of the parking area before taking a L at Club Dream Surf and heading out on to the boardwalk and down by the sea.

5 mins, 32.7362, -9.0431

9 LA GRANDE PLAGE

Just around the headland from Plage Oualidia is La Grande Plage. Although lacking the channels and lagoon of its beach brother, La Grande Plage was beautiful in the more traditional sense. Its curving coves are easy on the eye as the sun warms your soul, while waves crashed against the rocky headlands at either end of the beach, sending up huge spurts of water into the salty air. Turn off the R301 at the roundabout (32.7343, -9.0335); follow the road down to the beach parking spot (32.7313, -9.0469); walk on the road N out of the parking area and take a L at the entry to the beach (32.7330, -9.0457).

3 mins, 32.7331, -9.0465

10 SIDI CHACHKAL BEACH

The beach gave the impression of being half-finished, with a solitary staircase snugly embedded in the sand, leading up to and down from nowhere. A half-built promenade stretched along the beach, its walkway periodically covered by sand, rendering the staircases and ramps leading to the beach useless as they were now buried up to the promenade's edge. Despite its incomplete state, the beach was popular with fishermen, whose numerous poles stuck up like leafless tree trunks. The crystal-clear water and a sheltered area at the southern end of the beach formed a natural pool, ideal for swimming. However, the

10

10

waves can be strong, with many underwater rocks posing potential hazards. Take the R301 S from Oualidia for 30km through the town of El Bedouza and the lighthouse on the headland; follow along the coast until reaching the parking outside Café Le Phare (32.5449, -9.2763); walk down stairs from clifftop. Alternatively turn L on to the beach access road (32.5364, -9.2775) and park by the beach (32.5460, -9.2790).
5 mins, 32.5629, -9.2552

11 BAALITEN BEACH

If you're looking for a secluded spot for a solitary swim, this is the place for you. Tucked away behind a pair of cliffs lies the pink jewel that is Baaliten beach. The clear water of the wave tops sparkled in the sunlight when viewed from the clifftop and the only other visitors to the beach were seagulls. This beach was only accessible by two steep paths down the cliffside starting at the red and yellow coloured section of the cliffs. Follow the trail down to the beach for an isolated and peaceful experience. Take the R301 N from Safi for 14km and turn L at the sign for Lalla Fatna Beach (32.4010, -9.2508); then take first R on to track; follow the road until reaching the auberge on the left where you can park (32.4073, -9.2518); walk 10 mins along the cliffs by the camel pastures to the descent points – 20 minute walk to the bottom of the cliff – two potential routes starting at the yellow and red sections of cliff; yellow is more difficult (32.4186, -9.2465) red easier (32.4193, -9.2464).
10 mins, 32.4148, -9.2497

12 LALLA FATNA BEACH

Although this was possibly the most developed beach in the area, in that it had a lifeguard station, Lalla Fatna was one of my favourite swims in the area. Made distinctive by its pink sand, it was popular with local families and young boys, who threw themselves headlong into the waves, roaring with delight. Meanwhile, a young couple took a romantic stroll along the shore. The water was delicious and refreshing, the perfect antidote to a long day of hitchhiking. Be careful not to swim too far away from the lifeguard station as the waves here are powerful with a strong pullback. The beach is steep and, as the lifeguards explained, while posing for a photo like Moroccan Baywatch, it can be difficult to get out once you've got in. Take the R301 N from Safi for 14km; turn L at the sign for Lalla Fatna Beach (32.4010, -9.2508); then take the first L and follow the paved road down to the beach and parking spot (32.3965, -9.2625).
2 mins, 32.3983, -9.2620

11

12

13 SIDI BOUDALA BEACH

This beach was accessible by aroad or by a hike over the rocks from Lalla Fatna Beach. This hike was difficult and a scramble in some places. The tracks I followed were little more than goat paths, and I followed faint footprints in the sand over bushes and rocks until I reached my prize. Sidi Boudala consists of two coves separated by a rock barrier, which jutted out from the cliff. The northern cove was empty when I arrived apart from a couple of boys who chased each other in circles on the sand. Its southern counterpart was used by Moroccan tourists and fishermen with tents set up against the cliff. Many of the beachgoers carried bottles of mud from a nearby spring, supposedly good for the skin, which they rubbed liberally over their faces and bodies. The exit from the beach was a steep climb up the cliffs on a rough-hewn path. From Ait Torkin, head NE on R301 for 2km to parking spot on L (32.3886, -9.2690); follow the path and steps down to the beach; or hike over the rocks from Lalla Fatna.

15 mins, 32.3917, -9.2688,

14 LES GROTTES DE OUALIDIA

A concealed treasure, only accessible by narrow passageways hidden in the rock. Two tiny, secluded caves within the cliffs were expanded in the eighteenth century by the army to spy on Portuguese naval movements. It was a great place to reflect and meditate. The sharp contrast between the darkness of the cave and the brightness of the sea and sun forced me to focus on the hypnotising power of the waves. After five minutes there it felt like waking up refreshed from a 20-minute nap. The guardian will expect a donation. From the roundabout at the centre of Oualidia (32.7342, -9.0333) take the exit down the hill towards the lagoon for 1km before turning L on to Boulevard Tarik Ibn Ziyad; follow it for 550m and then turn R by La Citronnelle guest house; follow this road for 90m until you emerge on to a large parking area (32.7285, -9.0502); walk out of the parking on the path at the far southern end and head in the direction of the military watchtower; from there you will be able to see two parasols, the one 200m to the S is the guardian's parasol; walk along the cliffs to reach it.

20 mins, 32.7274, -9.0547

LAKES & RIVERS

15 SIDI MOUSSA LAGOON

Deep-blue channels carve their way through the sands, shaping the landscape with a blend of softness and strength. While the powerful Atlantic waves of Plage Sidi Moussa challenge inexperienced swimmers, these calm, shallow channels are ideal for children.

In the cliffs above the rocks are perforated with holes from rain or, perhaps, ancient tides. Sheep grazed peacefully on islands within the wetlands, naturally protected and kept in place by the surrounding waters. Seabirds soared overhead, their mournful cries echoing across the expanse, while a flock of flamingos noisily descended, seeking refuge from the scorching African interior. Turn off the R301 at the red-roofed barn (32.9750, -8.7461); and park on the open space next to it. Walk out across the rocks to the viewpoint.

7 mins, 32.9759, -8.7457

16 OUALIDIA LAGOON

The sunset across the lagoon was magical. The sun painted the water orange, as fishing craft chugged back and forth across its surface and a flamingo made its noisy landing among the small waves. This colouring extended to the sea and soon the whole landscape was bathed in a gorgeous glow. Oualidia and its lagoon is a top destination for birdwatching, as Morocco lies along the western Mediterranean migration route between Europe and Africa. In the spring and autumn, more than 400 species, including flamingos, egrets, stilts and storks can be spotted here. Even during the off-season, it's possible to catch a glimpse of a flock of flamingos in the marshes and wetlands. This was Danny's favourite sunset spot of the entire trip. Turn off the R301 at the sign for the La Sultana and follow the track down to the parking spot (32.7417, -9.0258); walk along the path down to the lagoon, turning L at the first fork and R at the second; walk all the way along the lagoon shore to Plage Oualidia.

7 mins, 32.7511, -9.0223

FORESTS, PARKS & GARDENS

17 BOUSKOURA FOREST

A peaceful retreat for nature enthusiasts, families, and sports enthusiasts alike, this is Casablanca's green lung. Populated with eucalyptus trees, this 3,000-acre wooded area features nature trails and picnic spots.

15

18

19

20

21

A popular 7.6km loop trail runs through the forest, perfect for jogging and leisurely walks. Facilities include pedestrian and bicycle tracks, children's play areas, well-signposted paths and food stalls. From Casablanca, head S on R135 for 8.5km; turn R on to the P3020 (dirt road) for 3km until you reach the forest; park where you can.

5 mins, 33.4633, -7.5797

CULTURAL HOTSPOTS

18 HASSAN II MOSQUE

The Hassan II Mosque in Casablanca is one of the few mosques in Morocco open to non-Muslims. Renowned for its intricate architecture and a prayer hall that can accommodate up to 25,000 worshippers, this is the second-largest functioning mosque in Africa. Standing at 210m, its minaret is the world's second tallest. Book a guided tour to enter and you must have shoulders and knees covered. This seaside mosque offers a stunning location for visitors. Open year-round (check the website for opening hours). Boulevard de la Corniche, 20000 Casablanca. Fmh2.ma

3 mins, 33.6081, -7.6325

19 CINEMA RIALTO

Established in the 1930s, the Art Deco cinema boasts striking geometric patterns and ornate designs. Step into a bygone era, where the allure of film meets architectural beauty. Showing a mix of classic and contemporary films, Cinema Rialto invites cinephiles to sit back and enjoy the film. Play It, Sam. 20 Rue Mohamed El Quorri 20000, Casablanca +212 634-750983

2 mins, 33.5944, -7.6145

ANCIENT

20 PORTUGUESE CISTERNS

A UNESCO World Heritage Site, the cistern was built in 1514 as part of the Citadel, the first permanent Portuguese structure. Its initial purpose is unclear but may have served as an armoury, barracks or granary before being converted into a cistern in 1541. Built in the manueline gothic style with five rows of stone pillars, it has a central opening for collecting rainwater. Water, water everywhere. Rue Hachmi Bahbah, El Jadida. cite-portugaise.com

3 mins, 33.2567, -8.5028

21 KASBAH OUALIDIA

The ramparts of Kasbah Oualidia are remarkably well-preserved and are free to enter. Built in 1634 for Sultan El Oualid, for whom the town was named, it was the ideal location to watch the sun disappear over the horizon, reflected on the waters of Plage Oualidia and the saltwater lagoon. From the roundabout at the centre of Oualidia (32.7342, -9.0333), follow the R301 N; go straight ahead at the next roundabout at the sign for the Taxi Collectif; from the parking spot (32.7362, -9.0297), walk towards the mosque and the kasbah will be on your L.

2 mins, 32.7369, -9.0317

CAFÉS & EATERIES

22 THE FISHERMAN'S PARASOL

On a headland down the coast from Oualidia, where the auxiliaries had a lookout tower, a solitary parasol, table and chair sticks among the rocks. It didn't look like much but I ate some of the best fish I had in Morocco: a full plate of prawns with garlic and parsley, two grilled dorados, which the fisherman had caught from the rocks, with salad tea and bread came to 150dh. An absolute bargain. Directions as for Les Grottes Oualidia; head for the first parasol.

32.7292, -9.0531

23 CAFÉ RESTAURANT LES FRERES

In the heart of Oualidia and overlooking the centre of town and the lagoon beyond, this cosy restaurant is a great spot to observe the comings and goings of the Oualidians while tucking into a variety of Moroccan delicacies. Parking available in nearby streets.

32.7340, -9.0332

24 RESTAURANT LA TRATTORIA

Originally opened by an Italian family, the restaurant has been taken over by a Moroccan, who has traditionalised the menu, while keeping some Italian flair. Delicious seafood and live music on the weekends. From Safi's Old Medina, take the Route du Port north for 280m before turning R at the roundabout. Follow Av. El Raqib Ben Slimane for 550m and the restaurant is on the R. Parking available on-site

32.3040, -9.2416

25 'SAFI CAFÉ'

Unlisted on Google Maps and without a name over the door, these small eateries are ubiquitous throughout Morocco, recognisable by their enormous steel stewing pots that can't fail to attract the eye. Although it may not look like much, they serve up a hearty stew to fill your belly and heart with contentment. Cheap and cheerful and very authentic. Park on the corniche. From Safi Corniche, turn right on Derb Sidi Shahri and walk to the end of the alley. The café will be on your left before you reach the main market road.

32.2936, -9.2432

PLACES TO STAY

26 CAMPING L'OCEAN BLUE

The family-run campsite is calm and divided into spacious pitches separated by trees. At the entrance, you'll find a small seaside café and reception offering bread in the mornings. Basic bungalows accommodating two to four people are available for rent. The final approach to the campsite is a dirt road, but it's accessible for all cars and vans. Open year-round. +212 660-911922

33.7376, -7.3236 £

27 SIDI MOUSSA CAMPER PARK

Park your campervan overnight. See Sidi Moussa.

32.9740, -8.7591 £

28 DAR DOUKKALA

A cosy, family-run guest house with a homely vibe. A tasty Moroccan breakfast is available for a small fee and can be eaten on the rooftop terrace overlooking the lagoon. Turn off the R301 (32.7415, -9.0233) near the pharmacy; Dar Doukkala is the second building on the R. +212 634-196520

32.7410, -9.0227 ££

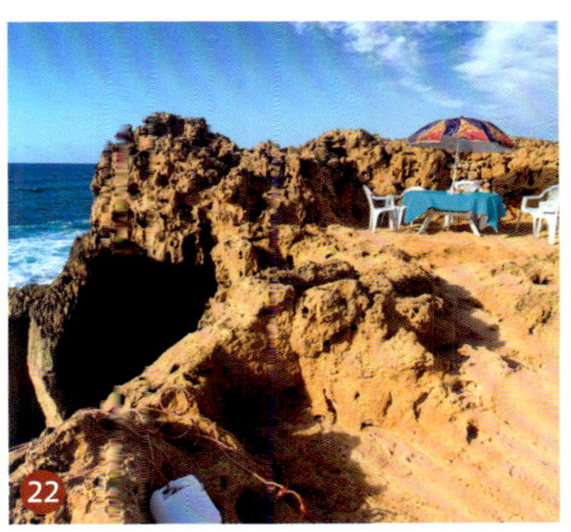

22

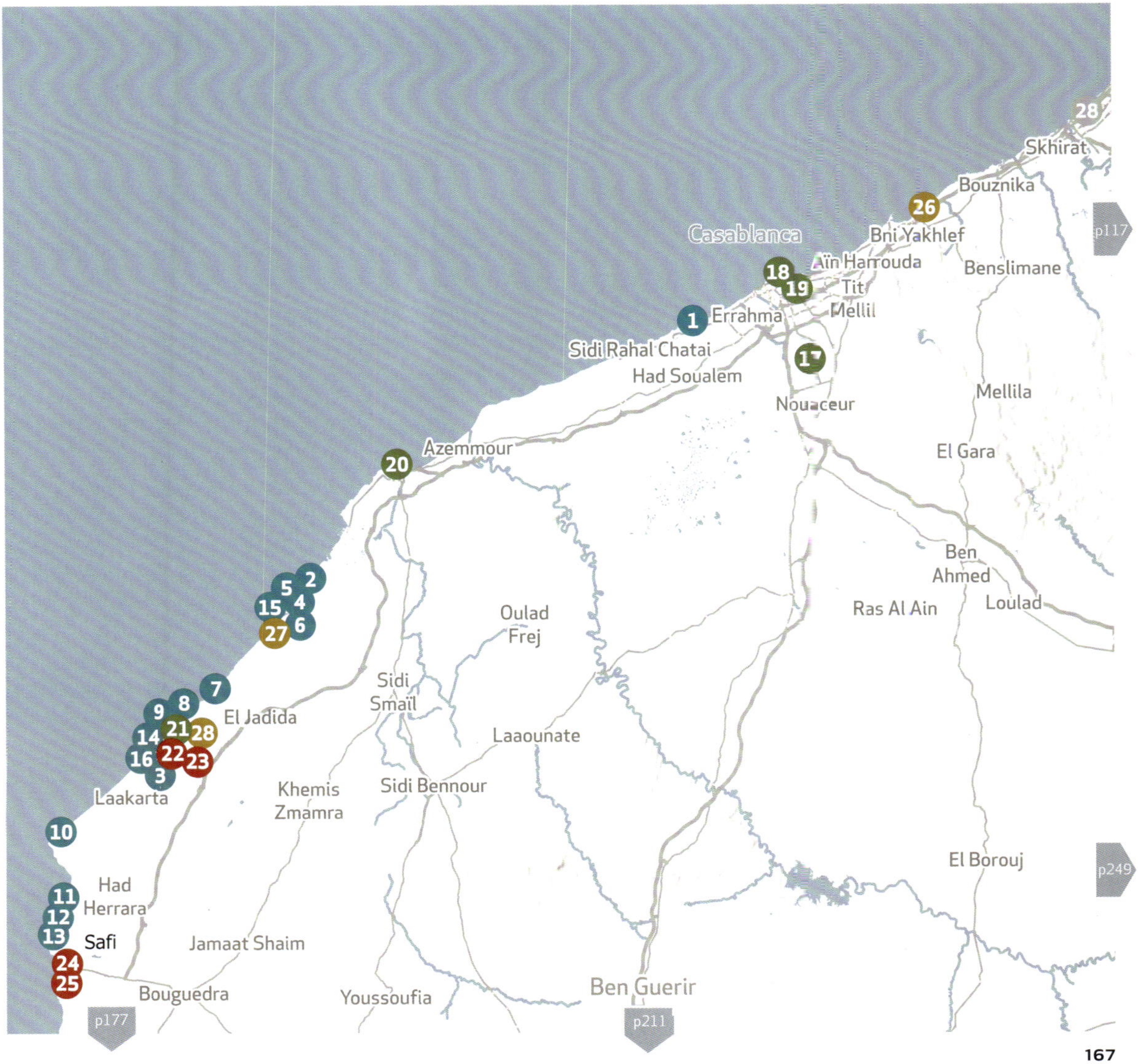
28
Skhirat
Bouznika
26
Casablanca
Bni Yakhlef
p117
Aïn Harrouda
Benslimane
18
19
Tit Mellil
1
Errahma
Sidi Rahal Chatai
Had Soualem
17
Nouaceur
Mellila
Azemmour
20
El Gara
Ben Ahmed
Loulad
Ras Al Ain
Oulad Frej
2
5
15
4
6
27
7
Sidi Smaïl
9
8
El Jadida
21
28
14
Laaounate
16
22
23
3
Laakarta
Khemis Zmamra
Sidi Bennour
10
El Borouj
p249
Had Herrara
11
12
13
Safi
Jamaat Shaim
24
25
Bouguedra
Youssoufia
Ben Guerir
p177
p211

5

AROUND ESSAOUIRA

Our perfect adventure

- **Imagine** yourself a part of the World of Ice and Fire, as you walk through iconic Game of Thrones backdrops in Essaouira
- **Relive** the 60s with a drink and dinner in the Jimi Hendrix Café
- **Wave** or windsurf across the rippling waters of Mogador bay
- **Relax** surrounded by art in Essaouira's Chill Art Hostel
- **Taste** tradition in the Souk el Had du Drâa market, which even Moroccans visit for a reminder of authenticity
- **Swim** in the calm waters of Sidi Bhaibah, followed by some fresh and tasty grilled sardines on the beachfront.
- **Climb** into the natural stone tower of Borj El Baroud, surrounded by the waves; only at low tide though
- **Stand** amid the ruins of antiquity in the shell of the Dar Sultan Palace in Diabat.

1

2

4

'Travelling – it gives you a home in a thousand strange places, then leaves you a stranger in your own land.'

Ibn Battuta

Essaouira's harbour is protected against strong marine winds by the island of Mogador. The coastline to the north and south of the port is prime waterfront property for windsurfers who harness these Atlantic winds and put them to good use. The coast to the north of Essaouira is full of golden-sandy gems that have remained hidden from tourist treasure hunters. Essaouira has been a significant trading post since it was established in the fifth century BC. However, archaeological research shows that the town has been occupied since prehistoric times. Various European countries attempted to conquer Essaouira in the sixteenth century, but it remained a key port for exports and pirate activity. The town flourished with a significant Jewish population until trade changes and geopolitical events led to their exodus. In modern times, Essaouira became a cultural and cinematic hub, known for its atmospheric medina and historic significance, captured in Orson Welles' Othello and HBO's Game of Thrones. Since the 1960s and Jimi Hendrix's 11-day visit in 1969, Essaouira has become a hippy hangout and is the end of the unofficial 'surfer's trail' from Agadir.

Essaouira's old city and souk are a swirl of contrasts, as tourists with open eyes and eager minds take in their surroundings, while its inhabitants carry on with their daily lives. Every year the city is swelled by thousands of Moroccan and foreign tourists for the Moga Essaouira Festival, the biggest Gnawa (traditional Moroccan folk music) festival in the world. People camp on the beach and on rooftops to take in this incredible cultural event. The city has a laid-back and welcoming atmosphere and is the perfect starting point to explore the wilder places in the area.

Doing just that, a round-the-houses, four-stage taxi ride took me out to the furthest reaches of my beach-hopping expedition. Starting at Plage Sidi Abdellah Ben Battach, where shoals of blue fishing craft sit at anchor, taking a moment's rest from the day's catch, I made my way back south. Hiking over the cliffs towards Bir Sidi Salah, I passed mosques clinging to the hillside and abandoned houses that piqued my curiosity, begging further exploration. What the beaches in this area lacked in amenities such as toilets and cafés, they more than made up for with their untamed and untouched natural beauty. Your sole companions on Bir Sidi Salah are likely to be seabirds, migrating storks and maybe an occasional wandering goat. However, if you need to fill your belly, the beachside cafés at Sidi Bhaibah do a platter of sardines, fresh from the sea and freshly grilled, which will have fish eaters salivating in seconds.

BEACHES

1 PLAGE ASSAFI

Long, golden stretch of sand beneath big dunes just north of the medina in Essaouira. Enjoy exploring the rock pools beneath the northern tip of the medina. The beach stretches for miles, so great for long, early, wild and uninhabited walks. Watch out for the tide, which comes in quickly. In Essaouira, walk N along Av. Al Aqaba until you reach the edge of town; head L towards the sea.

8 mins, 31.5343, -9.7460

2 PLAGE TAGHARTE

A sweeping curve of gold between Essaouira and the sea, a hot-spot for wind and kitesurfers. Strong waves blow in off the Atlantic and the bay reduces the power of the waves, making it a great place for beginner surfers. I spent two days out on the water with a surfboard rented from NaneaKite and enjoyed myself no end. In Essaouira, head to the big beach.

5 mins, 31.5011, -9.7641

3 ESSAOUIRA TIDE POOLS

Essaouira's tide pools are dark and rocky and offer exceptional views of the old city's ramparts and port, which provided the backdrop to Astapor in Game of Thrones. The tide pools are best explored at low tide, so be sure to check the tide table. Sublime sunsets can be enjoyed from the beach. The rocks were slippery, so wear shoes with good grip. From Place Moulay Hassan, walk E towards the sea overlooking the beach, the tide pools, the port and the ramparts.

3 mins, 31.5112, -9.7728

4 ESSAOUIRA SAND DUNES

I went for a coastal walk one morning and got a bit lost. Determined not to retrace my steps, I took a long, arduous trek through the sand dunes and up into the hills. Completely pointless, but made for a highly enjoyable and unforgettable morning. Luckily, I took lots of water and a compass. In Essaouira, walk N along Av. Al Aqaba until you reach the edge of town; follow the road NE for 1.6km keeping the big dunes on your L until you reach the water treatment plant; turn R and follow path alongside water plant for 600m; head roughly S (use your compass) up through the dunes heading towards the red-and-white communications tower on the hill until you reach the viewpoint overlooking Essaouira; I hitchhiked back to town.

180 mins, 31.5273, -9.7269

5 PLAGE SIDI ABDELLAH BEN BATTACH

A scimitar's curve of beach stretches gracefully into the distance, with waves tracing white lines across the blue canvas of the sea. On the headland, a small, faded, white mosque stands, having protected the souls of the fishing boats and their crews anchored in the tiny bay below. Hidden, isolated and only accessible via a single sandy path leading down from the main road. Not a soul in sight apart from a lonely man in a beige hoodie sitting on the rocks, contemplating the mysteries of life. Take the R301 N from Essaouira for 45km before turning left towards the sea just after the village of Rabza; follow track for 1km; at junction at base

of cliff continue straight into the village and turn L towards the mosque; parking spot on L (31.8548, -9.5252); walk towards the sea and 50m to the L of the mosque is a small path leading down to the beach and the rocks below.

2 mins, 31.8522, -9.5252

6 BIR SIDI SALAH

A windswept expanse of golden sands, Bir Sidi Salah was more popular with birds than with locals or tourists. Vast flocks of seagulls asserted their dominance over the beach and lines of storks beat their way northwards overhead on their avian highway. The sands offered a gentle and gradual entry into the water, but beware powerful Atlantic waves. Take the R301 N from Essaouira for 40km before turning L towards the sea in the hamlet of Bir Sidi Salah just after the Gannour Hassan Villa; follow the sandy track for two minutes where you will reach an open space where you can park (31.8107, -9.5569); walk down path to your R to the sand dunes; beach is on R.

8 mins, 31.8167, -9.5585

7 SIDI BHAIBAH

Blue fishing boats clustered at the northern end of the beach while their brethren comb the waters further out to sea. According to locals, this beach was the best place to swim in the area as it was in a bay, which makes the water 'like a swimming pool'. The proximity of two cafés close to those boats could mean only one thing, fresh fish – Espace Bhaibah. Perfect for a family day out to the beach from Essaouira. Turn off the R301 (31.7947, -9.5647) and follow all the way down to the beach. Park here (31.7979, -9.5810) – don't park on the beach, you will get stuck and have to be pushed out.

2 mins, 31.7961, -9.5821

8 PLAGE DU SOLEIL

Before heading to this beach I was repeatedly warned there was nothing there. To some, this could be a discouragement. But for me, it was music to my ears. However, after jumping out of my hitched ride, I saw just how right they were. No paths led to the beach and I was forced to go cross country. Once on the sands, I felt like I'd been dropped 200km further south in the Sahara. Drifts and dunes rose over head height, sand sprayed off them by the force of the wind. The sun was starting to set in front of me, carving a golden path through the water and the sands hissed around me. This was the perfect place to disconnect. There was, however, a strange structure on the beach, what seemed to be a wooden frame for a tent, but only one foot high. Go and have a look, maybe it's still there. Take the R301 N for 29km from Essaouira; turn L off the main road on to a sandy track to the parking (31.7354, -9.6249), just before the Maison d'Hôtes Dar El Janoub; walk down the driveway to an auberge before cutting across a field with a barely visible path, make sure you ask if it's OK before doing this if you see anyone as it is private property, but backs on to the public property of the beach.

7 mins, 31.7390, -9.6296

9 BORJ EL BAROUD

A counterpoint to the man-made buildings on Mogador island, the natural stone tower of Borj El Baroud rose proudly from the waves. Visible only from a distance at high tide, at low tide the water receded enough that I could walk out to the tower and climb its rocky parapets. From Diabat, head north for 270m; turn L for 450m to parking spot (31.4843, -9.7693); follow the path out of the car park towards the sea, keeping Mogador island in front of you; once you hit the sea, you can't miss the tower.

10 mins, 31.4889, -9.7756

SURFING

10 NANEAKITE SURF SCHOOL

NaneaKite is a water sports school that offers kitesurf lessons, surf lessons and wing foil. They also make and sell jackets made from recycled kite sails. Possibly the friendliest surf school in Essaouira. Rue Abdari, Essaouira 44000. naneakite.com +212 601-297087

5 mins, 31.5011, -9.7617

11 ORD OMAR

Within sight of Borj el Baroud and Mogador island was a small nondescript beach, where golden sands were whipped into a fury by the winds howling off the Atlantic. With great winds came seven windsurfers. It was a pleasure to watch as the magnificent seven soared and flipped their way up and over the waves.
A local windsurfing school was also there with its students teaching them the basics before heading out into the surf. If you feel like flying, this is the place for you. Walk 2 mins S from Borj El Baroud.

8 mins, 31.4791, -9.7767

ANCIENT

12 ESSAOUIRA RAMPARTS & MEDINA

Constructed in the 1760s by French military architect Théodore Cornut, these city walls were designed to protect the port from raiders. The ramparts served as a backdrop for the third series of Game of Thrones, representing the slave trader city of Astapor. At one end lies the Skala du Port, which marks the entrance to the fishing port, while at the other end stands

the Skala de la Ville, adorned with 19 bronze cannons along the sea wall, providing an ideal vantage point to watch the sunset. Formerly known as Mogador, the Medina of Essaouira is a UNESCO World Heritage site. As I wandered through the narrow alleyways flanked by tall, whitewashed buildings, I enjoyed the delightful twists and turns laid out on a French-inspired grid design (Es-Saouira translates to 'beautifully designed').

6 mins, 31.5152, -9.7720

13 DAR SULTAN PALACE

With its long-guarded interiors exposed to the elements and prying eyes, the Dar Sultan Palace at Diabat is a symbol of broken power and a testament to time's tenacity. Centuries of sand have piled up against the walls, providing access to the parapets, an entry unplanned by the original architects. The four lengths of stone bastions, punctured at each corner by guard towers, surround the palace interior, with a large central building encircled by smaller servant's quarters. Rather than the once elegant stairs, a rocky slope leads to the top floor of the palace, where the coloured tiles and mosaics of the richly decorated floors were still visible. Graceful stone arches on three sides gave views of Essaouira in the north, the Borj El Baroud natural stone tower in the sea to the west and the village of Diabat to the south. This must have once been a tranquil place to take in the surrounding scenery and watch the sunset over the bay in the evening. Now its ceilings are the sky and strong winds sling sprays of sand across its faded majesty. Take the turn off on the S bank of the river (31.4827, -9.7659) and follow for 2 mins past the ruins to reach the parking at the end of the road.

2 mins, 31.4835, -9.7687

MARKETS

14 JOUTYA MARKET

Essaouira's lively Sunday flea market, offers up an intriguing variety of items – from bicycles and handcrafted jewellery to sculptures made from repurposed materials. Beauty really can blossom from the most unexpected of places. A lot of junk is on display and we nosed around some architectural salvage yards; a typical Sunday activity. Afterwards, we set off to explore artists' workshops located in the same area to soak up some local culture. Joutiya is derived from the French word jeter (to throw away or discard). Head to the industrial quarter, in the north of the city. The market extends from Avenue Mohamed Akkad all the way to Moulay Hicham Avenue.

4 mins, 31.5235, -9.7562

15 SOUK EL HAD DU DRÂA

Even Moroccans from the big cities visit this market for a 'taste of Moroccan tradition'. Every Sunday, vendors start arriving at 3am to claim their spots and at 5am the real business of the day begins, slaughtering and butchering animals. Camels, cows, fish and more find their end here, before being displayed in varied states of dismemberment on stalls. Decapitated cows' heads stare at you from countertops, while you dodge their detached feet, hanging from the hut gables. This was not just a carnivorous affair; walls of onions lined the paths between pitches, flanked by fields of plucked pumpkins, swathes of red and green chillies spilt from split bags. The blare of their bright colours was only outdone by the calls of the merchants shouting the price of their wares in a machine-gun staccato. This market is an assault on the senses, with smells, sights and sounds clambering over each other for the greatest portion of your attention. If you're hungry, charcoal grill stations are set up near the meat section and you can buy meat or fish for the cooks to prepare for you for a reasonable price. Late risers beware: get here early, as by 11am, it is largely done for the day. From Essaouira, follow R207 and N1 for 27.6km; turn on to the P2209 just before you reach the town of Had Drâa. Park where you can.

2 mins, 31.5792, -9.5375

16 IDA OUGOURD

A trip to a rural market offers a glimpse into rural Moroccan life. If your visit to Essaouira didn't align with the Sunday market at Had Drâa, the midweek alternative is Ida Ougourd, which takes place every Wednesday. A sprawling open area for fruits and vegetables lay in front of the mosque and animals are traded in a secured square. Vendors begin arriving at 5am, with the busiest livestock trading occurring in the early mornings. Despite the early start, the market remains lively until 10am, when the action begins to wind down. The meat section is a halal abattoir, where goat and cow legs hang alongside bloody carcasses, a sight best avoided for the faint-hearted.
Commune Rurale Agerd.

5 mins, 31.4252, -9.6362

17 COOPERATIVE D'ARGAN MARJANA

Dedicated to producing high-quality argan oil through sustainable practices and empowering local women by providing fair wages.
The co-operative promotes traditional methods and environmental conservation.
Visitors are welcome to join in.
R207, Essaouira 44000.
coopmarjana.com +212 670-877943

3 mins, 31.5206, -9.6302

14

19

22

24

26

CULTURAL HOTSPOTS

18 MUSÉE MOHAMMED BEN ABDELLAH

A small museum in the heart of the medina. Housed in an 1800s colonial house with an impressive stairway and ceiling, it displays old photography, utensils found from prehistoric ages, musical instruments, old photography of Essaouira, jewellery and some armoury. The musical instruments are the most interesting artefacts on display. The signs are in Arabic and French so have your Google Translate app at the ready. Rue Laalouj, Essaouira. +212 524-475300

3 mins, 31.5139, -9.7713 £

19 BAYT DAKIRA

The Bayt Dakira Museum in Essaouira offers a captivating insight into the region's Jewish heritage. Located in an historical building, it showcases artefacts, documents, and exhibits that celebrate the cultural contributions of the Jewish community to Moroccan history. Visitors can explore the rich tapestry of traditions and stories within this unique space. Entry free. Rue Ziry Ibn Atiyah, Essaouira. +212 524-663587

5 mins, 31.5133, -9.7711 £

CAFÉS & EATERIES

20 LE VAL D'ARGAN

On a sunny afternoon we enjoyed a glass of refreshing organic rosé wine beside a vineyard just 30 minutes from Essaouira. Contrary to popular belief, Morocco boasts a thriving winemaking tradition, producing about 40 million bottles annually, making it Africa's second-largest exporter. Though most vineyards are situated in the north, Val d'Argan, the southernmost winery, offers unique flavours primarily derived from Rhône Valley grape varieties. We took a tour that included a visit to the production area and a stroll through the irrigated vineyard. The restaurant is open on Sundays for lunch and a dip in the pool. Rooms are available in the guesthouse. Email in advance to reserve your wine-tasting session. +212 660-279024 d.valdargan@gmail.com

31.5373, -9.5457 ££

21 SAÏD'S PLACE

Located in the heart of the Medina of Essaouira, this hole-in-the-wall establishment serves delicious bean and lentil stews with chicken, lamb and beef. Frequented almost exclusively by locals, seating is available on the ground floor and on a platform accessible only by steep wooden steps. It lacks an official name and an entry on Google Maps. From the Bab Marrakech, walk 400m down Rue Mohamed El Qorry, before turning L on to Rue Khabdazine; walk down the alley for 30m and it will be the first eatery on your R, opposite Chez Omar.

31.5135, -9.7679 £

22 ESSAOUIRA FISH MARKET

Heading out of the old medina, make your way to the port and the fish stalls, where fishermen flog the day's catch. I bought a kilo of sardines with some fellow travellers and paid 100dh (£10) for a kilo, which a local grill stall cooked with garlic, lemon and parsley. Each one hit the spot. From Place Moulay Hassan head S for 100m through Bab El Marsa and you will emerge into the port.

31.5097, -9.7734

23 ESPACE BHAIBAH

I ordered fish and was served 12 of the biggest, juiciest and freshest sardines I had ever eaten, alongside salad, bread and mint tea for only 50dh. Directions as for Sidi Bhaibah.

31.7984, -9.5818 £

24 JIMI HENDRIX CAFÉ

A charming, laid-back spot steeped in musical history and local culture. Named after the legend who visited the area in late 1969, the café exudes a bohemian vibe that attracts tourists and locals alike. Located near the beach, visitors can enjoy mint tea, coffee and traditional cuisine while soaking in the eclectic decor inspired by Hendrix's era. Walls are adorned with photos and Hendrix memorabilia, making it a nostalgic haven for fans. Whether you're a Hendrix enthusiast or simply looking for a unique place to unwind, the café provides a blend of music, history and Moroccan hospitality. The owner has run the café for over 30 years and was living in the town of Diabat when Hendrix visited, although he was too young to remember. A popular rumour is that the Dar Sultan Palace in the sand dunes of Diabat was the inspiration for his Castles Made of Sand. However, it was released in 1967, before his visit to Morocco, disproving the legend. At the N end of the village of Diabat +212 628-443878

31.4805, -9.7659 £

PLACES TO STAY

25 RIAD KAFILA

Traditional riad bordering the sea wall and overlooking the rocky beachscape of the northwest corner of Essaouira. Three floors and a rooftop terrace where we enjoyed a hearty Moroccan breakfast. 4bis Rue Yemen, Essaouira 44000. riadkafila.com +212 524-783275

31.5151, -9.7711 ££

26 CHILL ART HOSTEL

This hostel in the heart of Essaouira's medina is the perfect accommodation for budget travellers. With every conceivable surface covered in art installations by local artists, this is a backstreet hidden gem. The owner and manager, Nadia, is hospitable and friendly. Dorms or private rooms are available. Healthy breakfasts and daily tea sessions at 6pm to help those at the hostel forge new connections. 21 Rue Abderrahman Eddakhil, Essaouira 44000. +212 524-473724

31.5146, -9.7707 £

27 CAMPING DES OLIVIERS

Just 24km from Essaouira, this lovely campsite offers clean showers and toilets, a swimming pool, spacious kids' playground and tagines to order. Accessible facilities for motorhomes and camping vehicles. Souk el Had du Drâa is 6km down the road. BP 13 Centre Ounagha (Ounara) Province d'Essaouira +212 613-954382

31.5327, -9.5469 £

28 LA FROMAGERIE

A charming hotel and restaurant set amid tranquil gardens and olive groves, blending rustic elegance, modern comfort and commitment to sustainability and eco-friendly practices. The architecture reflects traditional Moroccan design with whitewashed walls, arched doorways and terracotta accents. A cute outdoor pool is surrounded by lush greenery. The gardens are filled with fragrant herbs, fruit trees and flowering plants, offering shaded corners to unwind. La Fromagerie was once a farmhouse, now transformed into a boutique guesthouse by Jaques (Abdel) who speaks very good English, French and Arabic. The guesthouse embraces a farm-to-table philosophy, using organic, locally sourced ingredients, many of which are grown on the property. Cheese production also follows traditional, sustainable methods and a cheese-making experience is offered to visitors. Cimetière Douar Laarab, 44000 +212 607-250751

31.5130, -9.6996 £££

29 DOMAINE DE L'ARGANERAIE

The gardens at Domaine de l'Arganeraie provided a tranquil retreat. The enormous, heated swimming pool was an absolute treat. The three-hectare garden featured ancient argan trees, palm trees and bougainvillaea, along with a pétanque court and table tennis. We enjoyed delicious meals and poolside breakfasts, all made from seasonal and local ingredients. Imintagant-El, Ghazoua 44000. essaouira-riads.com +212 661-508013

31.4365, -9.7440 £££

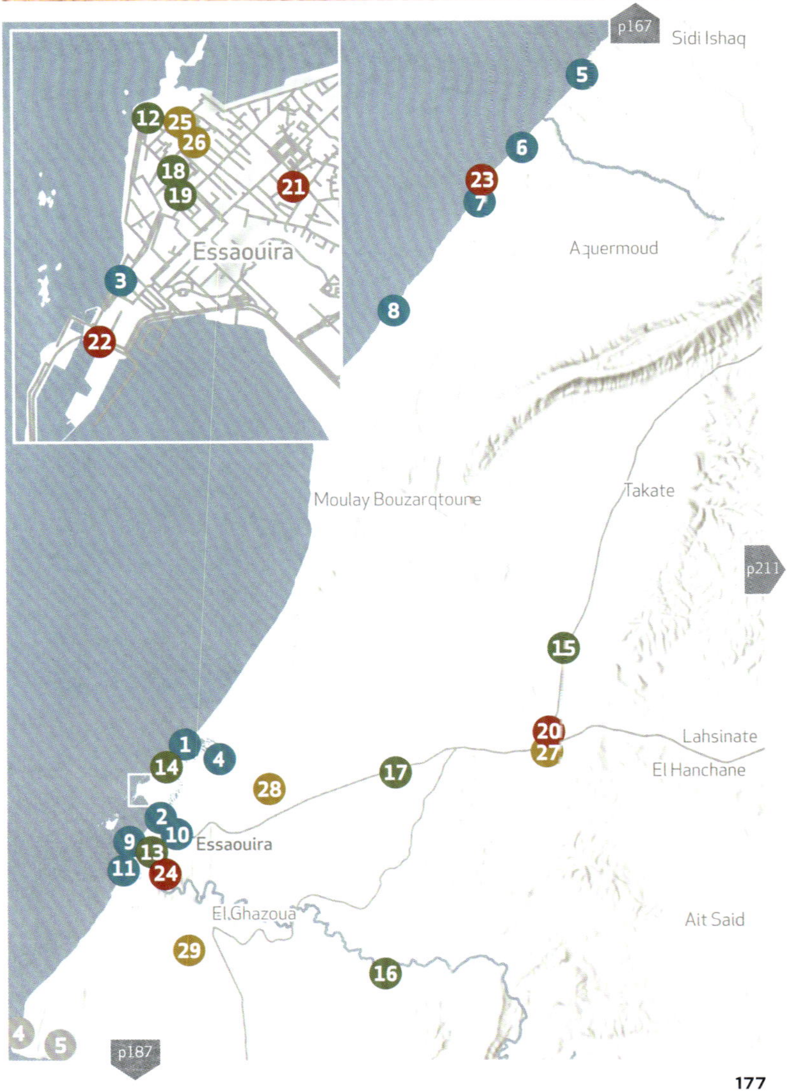

15

SIDI KAOUKI TO IMSOUANE

Our perfect adventure

- → **Sun** yourself on the solitary Sahara-esque shores of Cap Sim
- → **Gallop** along the sands at Sidi Kaouki Beach, or soar high above the waves as you windsurf
- → **Feel** the power of the waves wash over your tingling skin at Sidi M'Barek
- → **Stroll** in solitude along the wide, sun-kissed shores at Plage Tafedna
- → **Enjoy** your home-from-home with the incredible hospitality of Authentic Moroccan Homestay
- → **Catch** the moment in the sparkling, blue waters of the Fisherman's Cove
- → **Ride** the best waves of your life at long smooth breaks at The Bay, or test yourself on the tougher waters of Cathedral
- → **Watch** the sunset beyond the surfers from Imsouane Panorama

1

3

3

'You cannot stop the wave, but you can learn to ride it...'

Graffiti in Imsouane, artist unknown

Sidi Kaouki and its long beach is one of the highlights on the surfer's trail. Great surfing conditions in the spring season and strong winds in summer make it a hot-spot for wind and wave surfers alike. Tiring stuff. I awoke from an ancient slumber to the sound of 30 horses charging towards me at full pace along the beach; their riders appeared to be dressed in chainmail armour and pointed helmets, brandishing curved swords. My instinct was to draw my sword, run and hide, lock away my treasures and defend my non-existent daughters. I rubbed my sleepy eyes. On closer inspection, this band of would-be warriors were dressed in shorts, T-shirts and sunglasses and were merely out on a gallop from the local riding school, intent on pleasure, not plunder. I got my camera out instead.

If you're searching for hidden beaches, this stretch of coast will be your next stop. Around the hamlet of Timizguida Ouftas, unblemished beaches offer themselves exclusively, basking in the sun, waves kissing their golden shores. Plage Tabayat sits beneath the village at the base of a cliff. An ancient and forgotten mosque guards the passage to the beach; it's been here for over 600 years, that's all anybody knows. Hidden in the cliffs is a small cave, where you can view the rolling waves from above, maybe with a glass of mint tea and some sweet treats. Surf schools occasionally visit Tabayat in preparation for the bigger waves at Imsouane. Over the headland are the sparkling, blue waters of Imarditzen Beach, 'the Fisherman's Cove'. The water here is crystal clear and great for a refreshing splash after a long hike. Locals performed backflips into the waves from a nearby rock as I watched in awe.

Imsouane is a hotspot for surfers on their pilgrimage to The Cathedral and The Bay. The town's reputation as a surfer's paradise is well-earned and well-deserved, tucked away beneath high cliffs and populated exclusively by those seeking the thrill and the ecstasy that only riding waves can offer.

SURFING

1 SIDI KAOUKI BEACH

If the wildness you seek in Morocco is the rush of adrenaline through your veins, then Sidi Kaouki Beach is the place for you. Popular with thrillseekers of every description, strong winds make it ideal for kitesurfers; gentle waves are great for surfers and wide sands are ideal for equestrian pursuits. Following an action-packed day, the scene was blessed by a gorgeous sunset, when local boys came out to kick a ball around in the face of the rising tide and against the glow of the setting sun. No card payment or ATM in this beach town, so bring a ready supply of dirhams. No direct taxi from the nearby towns of Essaouira or Smimou to Sidi Kaouki; even the Souk to Surf shuttle bus has stopped running routes to the beach town; your best bet is to catch a taxi or a bus to the Sidi Kaouki intersection (31.4070, -9.7154) then hitchhike down to the beach or book a direct taxi (10dh).

1 min, 31.3497, -9.7974

2 IMSOUANE - THE CATHEDRAL

The picturesque coastal village of Imsouane is the a highlight for surfers. Imsouane has something to offer every surfing enthusiast, but The Cathedral offers the more experienced surfer a varied and thrilling ride: a combination of beach break, reef and point break waves. This spot caters to surfers of all levels, from novices to seasoned riders, but when the waves start getting bigger, it's recommended that only experienced surfers take to the sea there.

The waves at The Cathedral are best ridden when the tide is low to medium, similar to The Bay. However, The Cathedral stands out with its ability to deliver both right and left-hand waves, creating diverse surfing opportunities. Waves can reach up to 1.5m, with the occasional barrel adding an extra thrill to the ride. Soft sand and rocks beneath the waves create smooth and manageable conditions, making If you're coming without a car, look at souktosurf.com, which runs reasonably priced shuttle buses all the way up the coast from Agadir to Essaouira and provides space for boards. Collective taxis don't go into Imsouane but drop you off on the P1000 leading down to the village. Taxis waiting there charge a premium for a short journey. If driving, continue on this road all the way into town. When entering the town, go straight down the main road for 150m before turning right at the T-junction. Follow this road for 200m then turn left at the T-junction and the parking will be 100m down the road on the right of the street (30.8432, -9.8210), motorhomes can be parked here. From the parking spot, there are paths down to the sand at the northern and southern ends of the beach.

2 mins, 30.8426, -9.8217

3 IMSOUANE - THE BAY

The Bay, known for its consistent and gentle right-hand point break waves, is ideal for beginner surfers looking to hone their skills. The waves here are best when the tide is low to medium, offering some of the longest rides on the African continent. I caught the longest wave of my life here and saw someone catch a wave from the opening of The bay a full three minutes into the beach. These long, smooth rides allow beginners to practise their technique and gain confidence. The Bay's waves peel softly over the sand, providing a forgiving environment that encourages improvement without the intimidation of larger,

4

4

5

more powerful waves. Gliding from one end of The bay to the other, surfers can enjoy the dramatic cliff-bound landscape and the exhilarating experience of riding one of the continent's most famous waves. The town itself has been undergoing some serious redevelopment, with sections of it being demolished due to illegal constructions. Imsouane's reputation as a surfer's hideaway is coming to an end but some of the magic remains. Get in there quick. For directions, see Imsouane – The Cathedral. Walk south along the boulevard, take the first L and first R and follow the road for 200m until reaching the roundabout. Turn L and then R at the EasyRide Surf Shop on to the beach path; 50m in front of you there will be stairs down to the beach.

5 mins, 30.8406, -9.8174

BEACHES & VIEWPOINTS

4 PLAGE CAP SIM

Someone stole a section of the Sahara, dropped it on the coast and rebranded it as the sands of Cap Sim. At least that was what I thought as I emerged from behind a rocky outcrop on the path from the village of Oussane. Below the lighthouse on the cliffs above, rolling sand dunes stretched out into the distance. Ringed by towering dunes, dust ripped off their crests by howling winds, the only sign of humanity on this windswept beach was a battered fisherman's hut emerging from the dunes and, a sight ubiquitous across Morocco, a man on a donkey. We had a long chat about life and Morocco and he left me with this gem: 'You need to breathe this country, this life, in. Open your eyes to it, let its sounds into your ears. Some people wouldn't know life if they accidentally pissed on it.' I hope you meet Ali if you come to Cap Sim. From Essaouira, follow N1, P2216 and P2201 for 20km; turn R opposite Mellow Beach House and continue for 2.8km to parking spot (31.3878, -9.8137); follow the path W out of town into the hills for 20 mins until you reach the dunes; on your L at the bottom of the dunes is Cap Sim.

25 mins, 31.3974, -9.8381

5 PLAGE TAGUENZA OVERLOOK

High cliffs overlook Plage Taguenza, a narrow stretch of golden sands set apart from Sidi Kaouki, frequented solely at this northmost point by those who seek solitude. To the south, gulls circled over the tiny huts of Taguenza, highlighting its fishy stock in trade. Directions as for Plage Cap Sim; turn L off the path from Oussane down to Cap Sim (31.3872, -9.8155).

12 mins, 31.3844, -9.8157

6 PLAGE TAGUENZA

Fisherman's huts mark out the beginnings of Taguenza beach, the iconic blue fishing craft pulled up onto the sands after a morning's work. Fish freshly caught smoke on wood fires, making my own stomach rumble louder than the engine of a boat pulling into the shore. Huge flocks had gathered on the now seagull-owned sand to take advantage of the men's hard work. Unlike the battle-hardened aviators of the British coastline, these gulls will not dive at you for a loosely held sandwich but instead soar into the sky en masse at your approach, creating an impressive yet fleeting spectacle. A lovely place for an evening stroll. From Sidi Kaouki, head N on P2201 for 2.2km before turning L at the first tarmacked road off the main road (31.3704, -9.7940); follow for 1.2km to parking spot near the auxiliary station (31.3721, -9.8054); walk N out of the car park towards the beach past the fishing huts.

2 mins, 31.3734, -9.8069

7 SIDI KAOUKI SECRET BEACH

A small sliver of pebble-strewn shore sits just up the coast from Sidi Kaouki. Unlike the most popular beach in this region, it's not frequented by horse riders or quad bikes. This is the beach for you if you want to be close to the centre of town but not have to lift your head every time a four-legged or four-wheeled adrenaline inducer thunders by. Walk N out of Sidi Kaouki past Chez Meryem and head along the beach for 1.5km until you see signs on the R for Les Mouettes et Les Dromadaires restaurant, park here (31.3558, -9.7980).

10 mins, 31.3628, -9.8018

8 AZRO PLAGE

There's a nice walk to be had all the way along Sidi Kaouki beach. Cresting the headland at the southern end, you'll see yet another eye-catching strand lying before you. Local men along the shoreline pull up mussels from the sea pools at high tide. Two young boys clad in neoprene and equipped with masks and baskets called to me from the rock pools below, but the wind ripped away their words. I gave a wave and a tap of the heart, the Moroccan gesture for peace and respect and they answered in kind before I continued my journey. Take the exit off the P2201 (31.3279, -9.7870) and follow the track until you reach the Bistro; park up there (31.3310, -9.7933) and facing the sea to your R there is a track leading to the S end of Sidi Kaouki Beach; on your left at the back of the parking area is a track leading to Azro Plage.

5 mins, 31.3277, -9.7938

9 PLAGE TAKOUCHET

Plage Takouchet has golden sands and is a popular destination for locals and tourists. Take a long stroll south alongside the powerful waves. From Essaouira, head S on P2201 for 15km; turn R at sign for PS/23 AGNG (31.2942, -9.7905); follow the track for 1.2km and park by beach (31.2894, -9.7966).

2 mins, 31.2865, -9.7965

10 CASCADES DE SIDI M'BAREK

The gentle Cascades de Sidi M'Barek make a great photogenic stop-off to take photos on the way down to the Sidi M'Barek Beach.

The green pools running down the cliffs to the beach are also the local watering hole for the donkeys, cows and goats, and Danny made friends with one very cute baby donkey. Directions as for Sidi M'Barek Beach.

20 mins, 31.2613, -9.8035

11 SIDI M'BAREK BEACH

At Sidi M'Barek Beach, powerful waves crashed against the shore. Approaching the small, sandy beach, excitement surged through me, balancing my sense of vulnerability as I faced nature's force. The waves roared with raw power. With trepidation, I picked my way through the large pebbles littering the beach. I felt invigorated as I dipped my toes into the cool Atlantic water. The waves enveloped me but I kept my feet firmly on the ground, respectful of nature's might, enjoying the tension between thrill and caution. Sidi M'barek left me feeling alive. Try it out for yourself. From Essaouira, head S on P2201 for 34km; park near signs for Cascades on your R (31.2663, -9.7957); follow the path downhill for 1km until you reach the waterfall; follow the path down the valley for another 500m until you reach the beach; walk back across the dunes to complete the circuit.

30 mins, 31.2635, -9.8065

12 PLAGE TAFEDNA

Tafedna is a one-donkey town with a single road leading in and out, yet before it lies the enormity of Plage Tafedna. Broad sands stretch in front of the small fishing village, like a runway with the seagulls who set upon it. Long, rolling waves sweep in from the Atlantic, lazily caressing the golden no man's land between earth and sea. Bisecting those sands lies a river whose waters nourish the hamlets and villages upon its bank, eventually finding their way back into the welcoming arms of the sea. Be very careful if you walk in these rivers. They may look inviting but some sections of sand will suck you in. Only a string of expletives and some slow movements got me free. If you choose to take a sunset stroll along the beach, make sure you have sorted your dinner beforehand, as the cafés close around 9pm. There is space to park motorhomes by the beach (see parking co-ordinates). The beach has access ramps, although they can get covered by sand. Take the N1 north from Tamanar for 20km, turning L onto the P2226in the town of Ida Ou Aazza by the small supermarket; follow this road for 14km until reaching the sea and parking spot (31.0947, -9.8191).

2 mins, 31.0954, -9.8219

13 PLAGE TABAYAT OVERLOOK

A panoramic viewpoint and, tucked away beneath an outcrop of rock, a hidden cave. A secluded spot to shelter from the sun and wind as my guide lit a fire and brewed up some mint tea, with a view of the beach and waves below. This spot is difficult to find; I went with a guide called Mohamed from Authentic Moroccan Homestay; park at (31.0033, -9.7999), then turn off the RP2201 (31.0139, -9.8015); follow rough path along the RH side of a small gorge until you reach a promontory; below that promontory, accessible by small ledge is the cave.

20 mins, 31.0153, -9.8062

14 PLAGE TABAYAT

Gorgeous and isolated beaches abound in this region and hikes beckon from every direction. One such beach is Tabayat, directly below the hamlet of Timizguida Ouftas, at the base of a high cliff. Trudging down the long cliffside trail to the beach, the vast expanse of the sea stretched out below us, a blanket covering the earth. Sunlight danced off the waves like errant sparks of nature's fire, lighting my path down the cliffside. After many slips and slides, salutations and salaams to passing fishermen: a broad expanse of sea and sand appeared, complete with donkeys, dogs and downright dazzling views. Crowning a crest above the beach lay the coastguard tower, next to a series of small walls and squat green mosque. My guide, Mohamed (Authentic Moroccan Homestay), in the village, told me that it had been established over 600 years ago: 'I have tried to find out more about it but records on this time for this area are so hard to find.' A day at the beach turns into a history lesson. The past can keep a strong hold on its stories, until they fade and become secrets. Park in Timizguida Ouftas (31.0035, -9.8005), head NW on P2201 towards P2236 for 2km; turn L down path (31.0063, -9.8003) and follow the path down, many twists and turns but the path is fairly well marked.

30 mins, 30.9962, -9.8122

15 FISHERMAN'S COVE

After a 45-minute trek over the headland from Plage Tabayat, past farting goats and deep crevices left by the Marrakech earthquake, we reached our goal. Nestled into a curve of the cliff is a sapphire; a cove with sparkling, blue waters; its shores crowded with fisherman's huts like eager seabirds itching to get into the water and pull out a struggling fish.
After a short scramble down the cliff through rows of blue fishing boats, we emerged on to baking-hot sands. With no hesitation, we threw ourselves into the water, rinsing off the sweat of the midday hike. Stefan and Mohamed from Authentic Moroccan Homestay,

11

11

13

14

14

15

16

joined me. Be aware that this is a working beach and be respectful of local customs, particularly regarding dress. This is a very isolated area and not exposed to many tourists. From Timizguida Ouftas, head SE on P2201 for 4.5km; turn R (30.9556, -9.8021) and follow road for 4.7km to parking (30.9553, -9.8222); path down to beach is on L.

6 mins, 30.9548, -9.8211

16 IMSOUANE PANORAMA

If you're on your way into Imsouane, take a moment to stop and look out upon the town you are about to descend into. Admire the beautiful curves of the waves as they wash into the shore. Get excited for all the waves you are going to ride. Embrace the times you're going to fall off. Alternatively, if you've already descended into the salty arms of Imsouane, make the journey up here just before sunset and prepare to be amazed. You can get a taxi up to the viewpoint, or walk and try to hitch a lift. If driving to town, turn off N1 from Assaka at p1000. Follow road for 4.5km and viewpoint will be on your L.

1 min, 30.8350, -9.8002

CAFÉS & EATERIES

17 RESTAURANT ABOUDRAR

A cosy beachside eatery on Plage Tafedna with an array of delicious stews on offer, but their specialty is grilled fish, fresh from the sea only 100m away.

31.0954, -9.8208 £

18 IMSOUANE PORT CAFÉS

At the very tip of the headland lies the port, where for hundreds of years, fish have been unloaded from boats onto the shore, ready for gutting and grilling. There are several restaurants to choose from, all serving very fresh fish. I recommend you go to the cafés right at the very end, near the lighthouse, so you can have a sea view while you eat. I had prawns, grilled calamari and homemade fries, drizzled in lime juice while watching the surfers. Perfection. Walk south along the boulevard for 200m until reaching the roundabout. Turn R and follow the road into the port for 300m.

30.8382, -9.8215 £

PLACES TO STAY

19 DAR IZIKI

This classically painted blue and white hostel is set just two minutes back from the beach and comes with a swimming pool, indoor and outdoor lounge rooms with board games, books and Wi-Fi. A nice taste of luxury for the budget traveller. Breakfast and a delicious dinner are available. Parking on site.
dariziki.com +212 648-646055

31.3550, -9.7947 £

20 WINDY KAOUKI

A stylishly designed boutique hotel set just back from the beach. Delicious menu blending traditional Moroccan dishes and touches of Italian flair. Complete with a pool to refresh yourself during the heat of the waves and a rooftop terrace offering wide vistas over the the waves.

31.3569, -9.7961 ££

21 AUTHENTIC MOROCCAN HOMESTAY

Mohamed has built this business, stone by stone over the past ten years, alongside his sister, Aicha, (one of the best chefs I've ever met), and Stefan, a German who visited over 10 years ago and fell so much in love with the place that he decided to help with the business. This is a family home and amenities are basic, as Mohamed stated: 'Don't come here expecting luxury. But if you make a mistake, I will give you your money back.' They can organise hikes, day trips, cooking classes and more. Staying here was one of the highlights of my time in Morocco.
moroccan-homestay.com +212 629-891572

31.0015, -9.7989 ££

22 OLAS SURF HOUSE

A reasonably priced hostel, five minutes walk from The Bay with clean rooms, showers and cooking facilities on each floor. The highlight is the rooftop terrace with cushions and sofas overlooking the Cathedral Beach to watch the sunset. Their surf shop offers guests a 20% discount on surf rentals. olassurfmorocco.com +212 666-573754

30.8442, -9.8179 ££

15

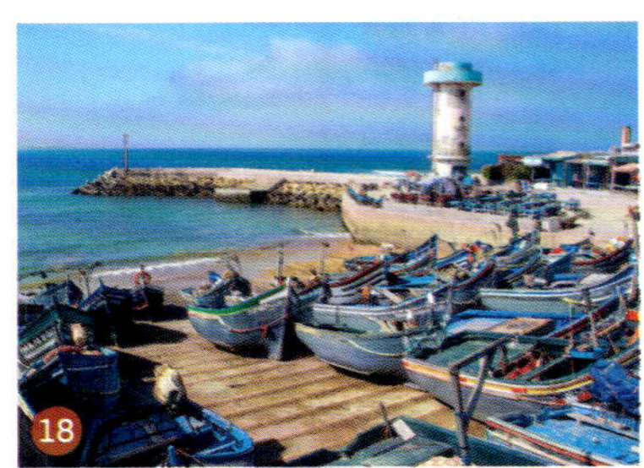

18

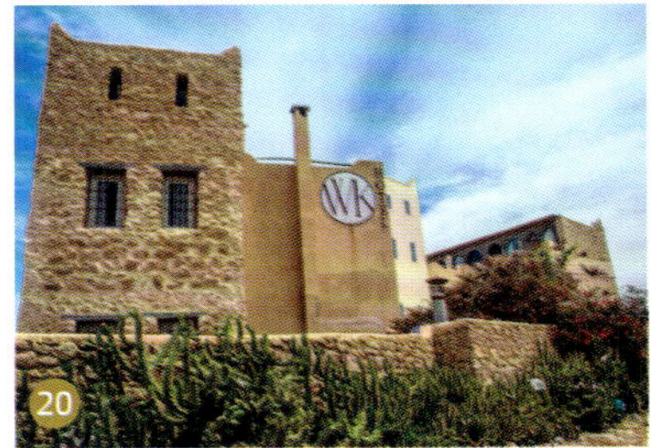

20

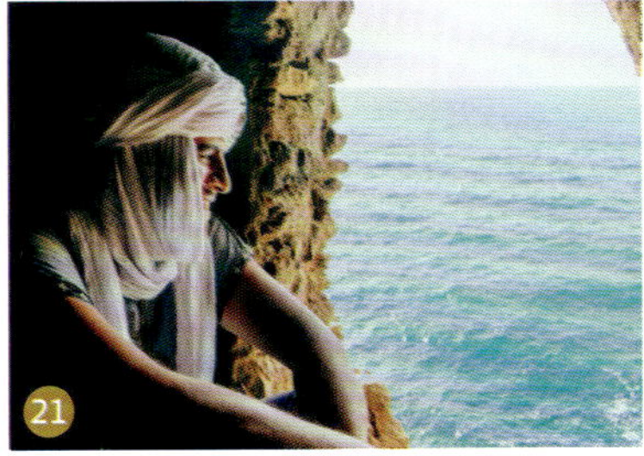

21

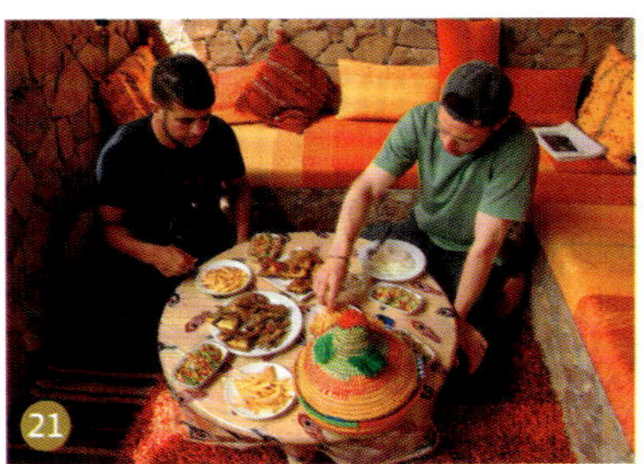

21

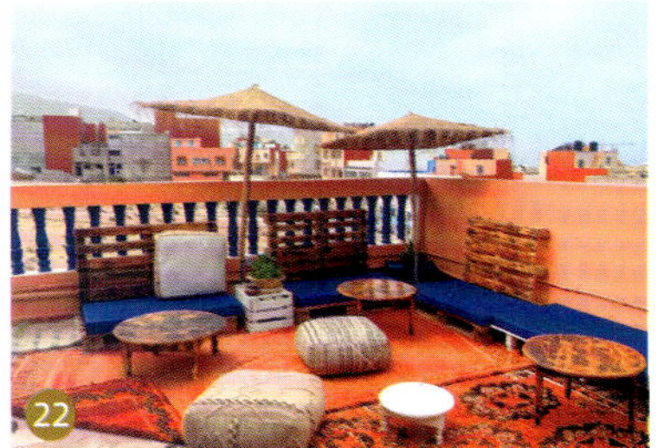

22

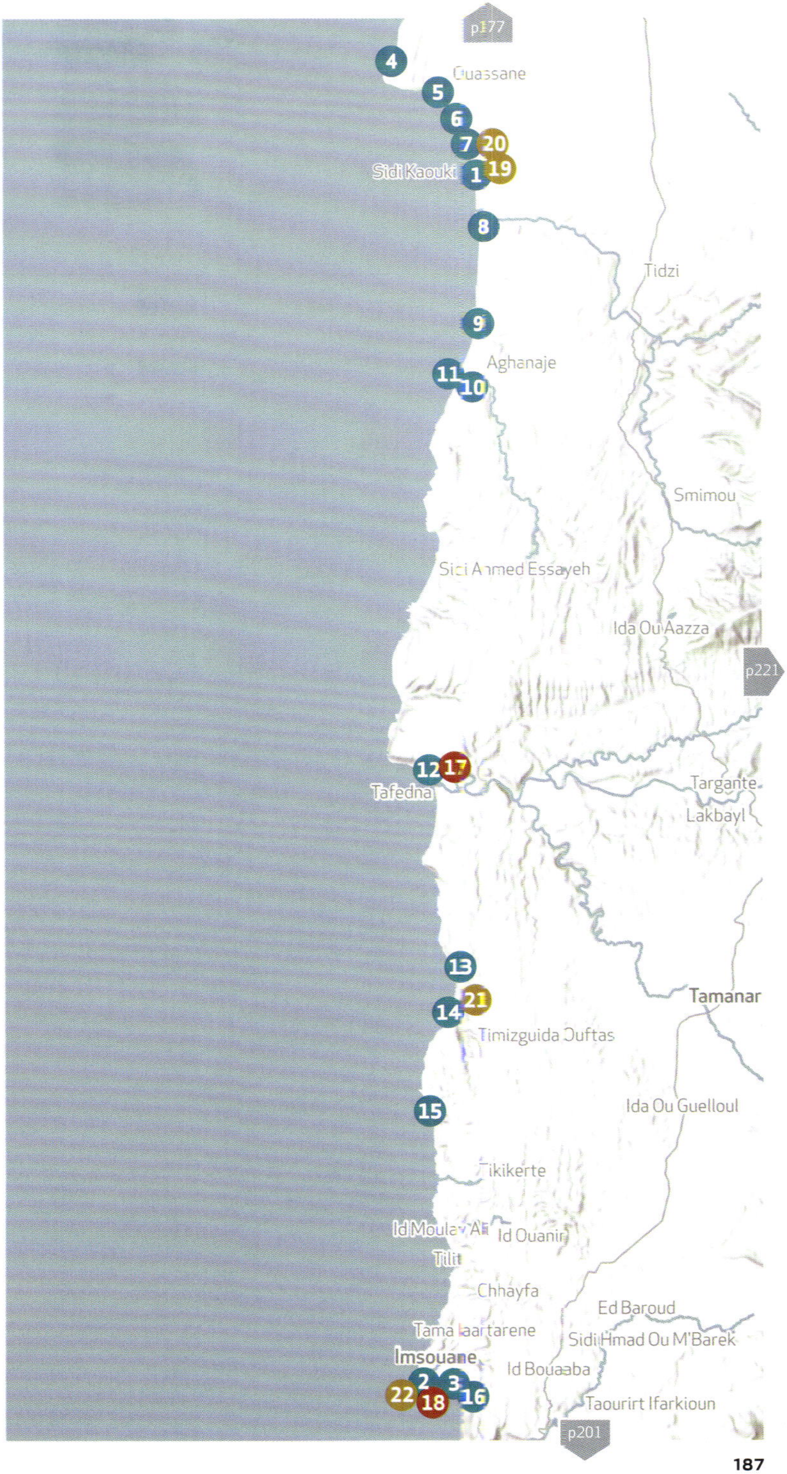
p177
4
Ouassane
5
6
7
20
Sidi Kaouki
1
19
8
Tidzi
9
Aghanaje
11
10
Smimou
Sidi Ahmed Essayeh
Ida Ou Aazza
p221
12
17
Tafedna
Targante
Lakbayl
13
21
14
Tamanar
Timizguida Ouftas
15
Ida Ou Guelloul
Tikikerte
Id Moulay Ali
Id Ouanir
Tilit
Chhayfa
Ed Baroud
Sidi Hmad Ou M'Barek
Imsouane
Id Bouaaba
2
3
22
18
16
Taourirt Ifarkioun
p201

AROUND AGADIR & TAGHAZOUT

Our perfect adventure

- **Leap** into the welcoming embrace of the waves in Tiguert's secret jump spots
- **Pamper** yourself in a river fish spa in the aptly named Paradise Valley, then take a leap of faith at the jump spots upriver
- **Forget** the 7:56 to London Bridge; we're going on a hike to Lake Al Marouani
- **Talk** to the animals at Smili's Farm, where nature comes alive
- **Assail** your senses with a mountain walk to Cave Win Timdwin
- **Catch** a wave or three on Taghazout's surf-haven beaches
- **Join** a host of surfing legends who have taken to the waves at the world-famous Anchor Point
- **Sample** authenticity at the Paradis Nomade Maison d'hôtes Agadir. Fill yourself with delicious food, and insights into Moroccan style and architecture

2

3

4

'...those who needed a boat became, themselves, a ship.'

Driss Mesnaoui

Founded in the 16th century by the Portuguese, Agadir quickly became a prosperous trading post, especially in sugar and spice and all things nice. In 1960, an earthquake destroyed most of the city, leading to its reconstruction as a tourist resort. If you want sun, surf and sand, this is the place for you. However, you don't have to look far to discover quieter surfing beaches, mountains, ruins and paths less trodden.

The coastline around Agadir is the heartland of Morocco's surf scene. Tamri and Moknari are surfing paradises, but Tamraght and Taghazout are the big-name draws for surfers around the world. Beaches like Panorama, Mystery and Anchor Point provide breaks and sets that will have surfers of all calibres salivating and desperate to get out among the swell. If wave surfing isn't your cup of mint tea, try sandboarding in the Timlalin Dunes north of Taghazout. Paradise Valley is also a must-visit, with hikes, river pools and jump spots to wet everyone's appetites.

An hour's drive east took us to the beginning of the Atlas Mountains where we hiked to Lake Al Marouani from the tiny settlement of Tizgui n Chorfa. Palm trees cling to the side of the mountain and houses blend in with the red clay. Birds sing and a melodic rivulet trickles nearby. Enchanted, we followed a river lined with oleanders where a donkey's mournful bray cracked through the silence. A woman in traditional red-and-gold embroidered dress emerged from between the trees carrying a large bundle of thyme, oregano and mint. She smiled open-heartedly and offered us a sprig of herbs. Finally, we reached a small waterhole. Gazing at this ancient pool gave us a sense of our own brief existence. We were definitely not on Platform Three waiting for the 7:45 to London Bridge.

Arriving at the Amazigh village of Imouzzer Ida Ou Tanane, we find the food stalls closed due to Ramadan. A local man brings us harira soup and dates (traditionally eaten to break the fast after sundown) from his own house. M'barek refuses money, saying: 'Ce n'est pas pour argent. C'est du coeur.' (It's not for money. It's from the heart). A recurring motif on our travels through Morocco.

BEACHES

1 TIGUERT SECRET BEACH

Hidden between two jutting cliffs, this secret gem is an inlet of cool calm in the roaring heat of the day. Over the millennia, wind and waves have carved the northern cliff into a series of pillars, whose presence lends the wild beach a manmade quality. Only accessible by a path lined with cacti and palm trees, which came to an abrupt halt 2m above the sand. Helpfully, a rope was provided, allowing me to scramble down. From Taghazout, head W on N1 for 15.5km to parking spot on R; from the parking spot (30.6291, -9.8397), take the RH path by the side of the motorway; cross the storm drain and then turn L down towards the beach; follow the path down for 100m until reaching a small cliff about 1.5m high; there should be a rope attached for you to climb down.

10 mins, 30.6282, -9.8413

2 PLAGE MOKNARI

Golden sands are a characteristic of the coastline north of Agadir. Plage Moknari is no different. The winds off the Atlantic have piled a vast drift of sand up against the cliffs at the southeastern end of the beach, on which two puppies were playing in the sunset. After a quick tussle, they traced their footprints down the sand drift and back towards the fisherman's hut with its fishnet fencing, probably for a fish supper. Although there were many great beaches for surfing in this area, this was not one of them. The waves were gentler here, making it a great place to swim and then sit back, relax and take in the view. From Taghazout, head W on N1 for 15km to the small hamlet of Moknari; directly opposite is the turn-off and parking for Plage Moknari (30.6233, -9.8156); walk towards the cliffs, to your L there is a path down to the beach 2m below you.

2 mins, 30.6233, -9.8166

3 PLAGE AMSNAS

Below red-veined cliffs topped with the ruins of a fisherman's hut lie the dark-yellow sands of Amsnas. Pebbles have dug themselves into the sand, creating a textured pattern to the beach's otherwise smooth surface. The entry into the water is gentle and the beach is isolated from the outside world, even though it sits not far from the busy N1 coastal highway. From Taghazout, head W on N1 for 14km; after crossing the dried out riverbed that leads on to Palm Beach, turn L off the highway before reaching Moknari on to the sandy beach path; park on cliff top overlooking the beach (30.6192, -9.8084); walk down the rocks on the RH side of the beach down on to the sands.

2 mins, 30.6189, -9.8085

4 PALM BEACH

At the mouth of a dry riverbed lies a small beach, flanked by the remnants of ancient riverbanks. Standing sentinel on these same escarpments are the palm trees that give this beach its name. Sandpipers strut and stroll along the seafront and a ramshackle fisherman's hut is tucked away on the southern bank. The equipment of his trade – nets, floats and ropes – dried in the sun. Walking south over the rocks, you will find a tucked away rocky cove where the sea crashes over rocks smoothed to a bright sheen over countless centuries. From Taghazout, head W on N1 for 13km; turn L (30.6168, -9.8037) for 200m down dirt track and park where you can (30.6166, -9.8[illegible]46).

2 mins, 30.6155, -9.8034

SURFING

5 PLAGE TAMRI

Between the legendary surfing spots of Taghazout and Imsouane lies the little-known, pristine surfing hub at Plage Tamri. Complete with a rivermouth and viewpoint set on the cliff above the beach, this is a place for surfers and observers alike. Renowned for its consistent and powerful waves, Tamri is free from the overcrowding of other nearby breaks. Suitable for intermediate to advanced surfers;

5

5

8

7

both left- and right-hand breaks make the surf a bit messy, forcing surfers to keep their wits about them. Known for its reliable surf conditions, especially during the winter months. The scenic mountain backdrop and the authentic, laid-back vibe of the local village add to the charm. From Tamri, head SW on N1 for 4km; park on R by the viewpoint (30.7088, -9.8589); via steep cliff from Mirador; at the northern end of the parking there is a rocky path down the cliff to the beach.

2 mins, 30.7106, -9.8584

6 PLAGE AGHROUD

Small waves with a right-to-left break make this beach a hot-spot for local surf schools to train their latest recruits. This mile-long beach is also ideal for an evening stroll, soothed by the sound of the crashing waves. Perched above the beach is a cluster of guest and surf houses, painted every colour of the rainbow. Despite their multi-coloured brilliance, the twinkle of spray flying from rolling waves will always win the battle for your attention. From Taghazout, head N on N1 for 10km, passing through the Colour Village opposite Arhoud Village; 200m past school on your L there is a turn off on to a dusty track and a section of open ground. Park where you can (30.6091, -9.7824).

2 mins, 30.6075, -9.7820

6

7 MADRABA BEACH

Also known as ' Mystery Beach', the 20-minute walk out of Taghazout and lack of facilities meant that there were less surfers and beach dwellers, plus lots of parked-up hippy buses. If you aren't a surfer, this is an incredible place for a sunset, so it's worth the walk. Beach will disappear altogether at high tide. Drive or walk 1km N out of Taghazout taking the left fork in the road to Anchor Point; turn L into the parking area (30.5460, -9.7263); walk over rocks on R to beach.

5 mins, 30.5478, -9.7290

8 ANCHOR POINT

If you don't need lessons and you know all the lingo, this is the place for you: where the serious surfers hang out. Anchor Point is a world-renowned spot that draws surfers from around the globe. Known for its exceptional right-hand point break, long, powerful rides can extend for hundreds of metres. Beyond the waves, a backdrop of rugged cliffs and the panoramic view of the Atlantic Ocean adds to its allure. Directions as for Madraba Beach, but from the parking, walk out to the L and along the rocks.

2 mins, 30.5453, -9.7269

9 TAGHAZOUT BEACH

The village and beaches of Taghazout are a celebrated destination for international surfers. Expect a relaxed, welcoming and inclusive vibe, the ideal place to immerse yourself in Moroccan surf culture. Whether you're just starting or looking for a mellow day on the waves, Taghazout Beach provides an unforgettable surfing experience. With its sandy bottom and softer waves, it's perfect for beginners looking to build their confidence and skills. Surf shops, cafés and accommodation are all just a short walk away. From the parking spot (30.5439, -9.7062), walk across the road, past the shops and on to the beach.

3 mins, 30.5436, -9.7095

10 PANORAMA BEACH

Panorama Beach offers an idyllic setting for surfers with a long stretch of golden sand and a laid-back atmosphere. Ideal for surfers of all levels, with consistent and manageable waves. Beginners can enjoy the gentle whitewater near the shore, while more experienced surfers can venture out to catch the larger sets. Situated a few minutes south of Taghazout, Panorama Beach is known for its beginner-friendly conditions and scenic beauty. The wide, open beach provides plenty of space for surfers to spread out and enjoy the waves without feeling crowded. Non-surfers are welcome. Directions as for Taghazout Beach, but turn L and take the corniche walkway down to the beach.

3 mins, 30.5422 -9.7053

CLIFF JUMPING

11 PARADISE VALLEY JUMPS

For the thrill-seekers who need a bit more than a dip in cold water to make them feel alive, Paradise Valley provides a natural pool further up the river with 8m and 10m jump spots. My travelling companion shocked everyone by doing not one but two perfect backflips off the second-highest jump spot. His applause was well-earned. Directions as for Paradise Valley Family Pool, from there either follow the riverbed until you reach the pool, which

will involve some jumping and scrambling over rocks, or take the path over the cliffs on the RH side of the family pool starting at (30.5882, -9.5274).

60 mins, 30.5892, -9.5186

12 TIGUERT SECRET JUMP SPOT

A great spot for a quick mid-trip secret cliff jump. I only found it because I spotted some local boys jumping into the sea as I walked past. This is a single-use place, dedicated to adrenaline-fuelled thrill-seeking, with no comfy areas among the sharp rocks to lay towels down for an afternoon. For jumping, for diving, even for backflipping, if you have the skill. The jump is about two metres; be sure to always watch a local jump first. From Taghazout, head W on N1 for 17km; turn off towards the sea when you see the sign for Les Grottes du Cap Ghir (30.6257, -9.8544).

3 mins, 30.6253, -9.8533

LAKES & RIVERS

13 PARADISE VALLEY FAMILY POOL

Whether you like walks, cafés, wild river fish foot spas, hikes, wild swimming or cliff jumping, Paradise Valley has something for you. Enjoy the dramatic mountain landscape surrounded by palm trees and the gentle hiss of the Tamraght River as it laps around your ankles. The pool has a deeper and a shallower section, great for families with young children to swim and enjoy the day. From Tamraght, follow the P1001 for 27km to parking spot (30.5887, -9.5311); exit by the path at back and follow round the side of the mountain until you reach a junction, one path taking you down to the river and one up the mountain; follow the path down to the river for cafes and fish foot spas where you can get fed and pampered next to the river; follow the river round to your left for 15 mins until you reach a natural pool.

35 mins, 30.5883, -9.5273

14 TANIT CANYON OASIS

Natural pool with lots of lillies at the bottom of the monumental Tanit Canyon. Inhabited by frogs and surrounded by huge forests of palm trees and oleander bushes. The P1004 road can be challenging in places and not for the faint-hearted. From Idmine, head E on P1004 for 18km to parking spot (30.5683, -9.4343); scramble down steep hillside to water, crossing several viaducts and streams.

10 mins, 30.5676, -9.4352

15 CAVE WIN TIMDWIN AND POOL

Cave Win Timdwin is home to one of Africa's largest caves and the region's largest groundwater reserve. The entrance to the cave is a long, dark tunnel reminiscent of the boulder scene in Raiders of the Lost Ark. Rocks in the cave have created the shape of a minaret. The tunnel extended for about 25m before we met a locked gate. Although the rest of the cave was closed to the public, the surrounding area offered fabulous views of the valley and mountains. Directly in front of the cave sat a 10m2 square pool fed by water trickling from the cave. An invitation for a glorious mountaintop swim was impossible to ignore on this hot day. From Tizgui n Chorfa, head S for 400m; turn left for 950m; slight R and park by the locked gate and building after 1.9km (30.6752, -9.3397); follow the undulating path for 1.2km to the pool and entrance of the cave.

15 mins, 30.6804, -9.3447

16 LAKE AL MAROUANI

A well-kept secret in an extremely secluded spot, tucked away in the High Atlas Mountains. The lake is fed by a 12m waterfall that cascades in a shower of sparkles down the hillsides. The cliffs around the lake are made of ancient sandstone and limestone, worn down over time to create the rugged landscape. Shrubs and small trees grow around the pool in unlikely places, clinging to the rocks. The plants here, like juniper and wild rosemary, are tough, well adapted to the challenging environment. Meanwhile, floating in the lake, with the cliffs rising on all sides and the sound of the waterfall

15

17

18

in our ears, everything else fell away. A moment of complete stillness between the water and the open sky. No facilities for miles, so bring plenty of water and something to eat if you plan to stay a while. Wear sturdy shoes. From the N side of the village of Tizgui n Chorfa, follow the road which becomes a track and crosses the river and is signposted by many, many cairns for 5km. Park near Gîte Meriem (30.6701, -9.3497). Allow 5-6hrs for the return journey.
180 mins, 30.7005, -9.3509

17 CASCADE IMOUZZER

An incredible deep-green pool surrounded by Gaudí-esque rock formations, similar to wet-sand dribbled sandcastles. Water doesn't so much cascade as drip down from the many plants that flow like green hair. Arriving in the early evening during Ramadan we found all the shops and restaurants closed in readiness for iftar. Villagers asked us for toys for the children; luckily, we'd bought a bag of art supplies. No guide required. From Imouzzer des Ida Outanane, head S on Rte du Brg Prince Moulay Abdellah/P1000 for 3km and park just before the bridge (30.6789, -9.4839); walk over the bridge and head R past the stalls to the cascade.
5 mins, 30.6775, -9.4791 

ADVENTURES

18 TIMLALIN DUNES

Rolling waves of sand that looked to have been lifted directly from the heart of the Sahara and dropped on the coast. Trudging up the sandy crests with the sea to my left was beautiful, but a serious calf workout. Best done at sunset, rather than in the heat of the day; the dying light serving as a sumptuous backdrop. As you race down the sand on a sandboard (repurposed surfboard), a word of advice: keep your weight on the back foot and don't get off the board until it has fully come to a stop. No matter how slow you think it's moving, you'll eat sand in front of a watching crowd... I should know.
The descent was an absolute blast, but the walk back up through the cloying and shifting sand was tough. From Assaka, head SW on N1 for 13.5km; turn off R (30.7642, -9.8219) and follow road to parking spot for 600m (30.7621, -9.8279).
20 mins, 30.7656, -9.8281 

19 TAGHAZOUT SKATE PARK

A true feeling of community abounded in this well-maintained skatepark. Locals mix with tourists, weaving in and out of each other across the pristine hard-topped and beautifully painted skate park. United by their love of their sports, skaters and rollerbladers rose into the air, against the backdropof the setting sun.
If you've got the skills, swap a surfboard for

a skateboard. If not, sit back and enjoy the show. Walk up the path through the cliffs opposite the Surf Times surf house by the abandoned hut.

15 mins, 30.5480, -9.7133

FORESTS, PARKS & GARDENS

20 LA PALMERAIE DE TADRINE

We discovered a small watering hole where a group of young boys were diving and jumping ever more flamboyantly into the waters of the Oued Tadrine. Crossing the river into La Palmeraie de Tadrine, we found small fields of sweetcorn and banana groves. Young men tended the crops and had a friendly chat with us, and a grandmother carrying a bundle of fresh thyme kindly offered us a few sprigs. Some girls showed off their school French and we gave them pens and paper, soon finding ourselves surrounded by a much bigger crowd all with outstretched hands. Head to the W end of Ankrime to the parking spot (30.5545, -9.5846); follow the path for 150m down to the river; cross the river to explore the palmeraie.

2 mins, 30.5539, -9.5857

21 JARDIN OLHAO, AGADIR

Established in 1992 to commemorate the twinning of Agadir with the Portuguese town of Olhão. Covering several acres, this charming garden boasts flower beds, palm trees and meandering pathways that invite leisurely exploration. Discover a diverse array of flora, including fragrant herbs and colourful Mediterranean plants. Benches and gazebos are available for visitors to unwind, while children enjoyed the playground facilities. Free entry. Av. Président Kennedy, Agadir 80000.

2 mins, 30.4246, -9.5971

22 SOUSS-MASSA NATIONAL PARK

We took a late afternoon stroll alongside the mouth of the Oued Souss River towards the sea. Particularly at the weekend, expect to see families and groups having picnics by the river. You can also swim here but be sure to take mosquito repellent if you visit in the evening. The river was dry further upstream, but at high tide, the water reached quite far in. From the parking spot (30.3632, -9.5851) at the S end of Agadir, follow the path alongside the river towards the sea.

5 mins, 30.3637, -9.5925 

18

19

23 SMILI'S FARM

A tranquil oasis beside the arid Souss-Massa National Park, Smili's Farm was filled with lush greenery and numerous animals. Rows of palm and olive trees provided shade, while turkeys, cockerels and peacocks roamed freely.
The farm was also home to horses, sheep, donkeys, tiny ponies, goats and ducks – all of which delighted visiting schoolchildren and families. Meticulously maintained gardens, with aromatic bushes created a sensory experience. For a reasonable fee, families can enjoy a day at the swimming pool and a playground filled with swings, games, trampolines and seesaws. The farm also featured summer houses with sofas and tables, perfect for relaxing with tea, and a prayer space. Maryam, the farm's creator, envisioned a place where women and children could escape the pressures of daily life. The farm's thoughtful and accessible design, complete with tree ladders, roundabouts and tents filled with toys, reflected her desire to create a haven for relaxation and play. Though Smili's Farm didn't officially offer campervan accommodations, guests can stay upon special request. A villa is available for longer stays. Magnificent. 7FG5+VR5, Unnamed Road, Ihchach. +212 661-170500

1 min, 30.2771, -9.5403

VIEWPOINTS

24 LTAHT BEACH

Following the track down and to your right, hidden from the prying eyes of the world, were the winding, wind-carved halls of an ancient canyon. I strolled into its depths to indulge in some self-reflection amid its golden dusty walls, before continuing down the original path. Suddenly, the dunes and cliffs opened out onto the sea. Just like the wind, the sea had left its mark on these sandstone cliffs, but it had much more drastic results. A vast cove lay below the path's final viewpoint, the stone etched with gorgeous curves by the sea's harsh but loving fingers. Only accessible by boat. Directions as for Timlalin Dunes.

5 mins, canyon 30.7625, -9.8289
10mins,cove30.7622,-9.8296

25 TANIT CANYON

After driving for miles along the winding P1004 road on the way to Tanit Canyon, we stopped, arrested by the view. We were at the top of a very rocky world. From Idmine, head E on P1004 for 15km until you see somewhere to stop and enjoy the view.

1 min, 30.6522, -9.4030

23

23

25

CULTURAL HOTSPOTS

26 MUSÉE MÉMOIRES D'AGADIR

Set within the Jardin Olhão, displays include period photos that capture the beauty of the city, the Kasbah Agadir Oufellah and the extent of the damage caused by the terrible earthquake of 1960. An thought provoking museum in a beautiful park. Avenue Président Kennedy, Av. Des Forces Armees Royales, Agadir 80000.

1 min, 30.4248, -9.59840 £

CAFÉS & EATERIES

27 WINDY BAY

Beachfront restaurant serving Moroccan and international cuisine. Careful if you sit near the front as, when the waves get big, this is the splash zone. Also a co-working space for digital nomads. campsite.bio/windybay

30.5448, -9.7103

28 WORLD OF WAVES

Overlooking Taghazout Beach, this is a great place to watch the surfers glide in, or wipe out, while you dine on delicious dishes. Accommodation and surf rental are available. wow-surfhouse.com

30.5448, -9.7107

29 CHEZ MOHAMMED

Eclectic café serving mint tea, coffee and snacks. Ideal stop-off if you've been exploring Oued Tadrine or the palmeraie. HC37+GQ, Ankrime.

30.5545, -9.5848 £

30 PARADISE VALLEY RIVER CAFÉS

Looking for food and a chance to cool your feet off after a long walk? Paradise Valley has several riverside cafés serving an array of traditional food. Eat with your feet in the river and enjoy the surrounding scenery. Alternatively, some cafés offer a fish pedicure along with the food, so if you're feeling peckish and in the mood for a bit of natural pampering, these are the places for you. Directions as for Paradise Valley Family Pool, but find yourself a suitable café after first descending into the river valley.

30.5879, -9.5287 £

PLACES TO STAY

31 TIMLALIN DOMES

Timlalin Domes provides a unique, memorable and eco-friendly lodging experience, offering accommodations that go beyond the typical hotel stay with breathtaking views of the desert and ocean. Each dome spans 60m² and includes a king-size bed, an indoor seating area, a mini bar, a private bathroom and a terrace with sun loungers. Guests can relax and enjoy the views and swimming pool. Timlalin, Tamri 80502 - take the dirt road up the hill just opposite the quad bike station at Timlalin dunes. timlalindomes.com +212 703-189102

30.7607, -9.8201 £££

26

36

32 SURF HOUSE DESERT POINT

A laid-back family-run guest house, with your wonderful host Hicham, his amazing team of surf coaches and the many sheep and goats kept by local families. Perfect for solo travellers, groups and families. If you have an open mind, good vibes and want to experience local life, this is the place for you. Dorm and private rooms available. Free Wi-Fi. Directions as for Plage Moknari, but turn R off the N1 and follow the track up the hill for 200m. hicham.gssimi@gmail.com +212 611-833291

30.6239, -9.8149 £

33 MABIDI SURF HOUSE

Just off Taghazout's main drag, this is a wonderful place for travellers to rest their backpacks while they catch some waves and make some friends. Particularly good for travellers on a budget. Rooms and showers are clean and Mabidi's connections with a local surf hire shop attract discounts for guests. The rooftop terrace is a relaxed and friendly environment where you can look out over the waves and take in a beautiful sunset. mabidisurfmorocco.com +212 655-353018

30.5451, -9.7079 £

29

34 TEDDY PIRATE CO-LIVING

Located right behind Taghazout Beach, Teddy Pirate is a place for travellers and digital nomads to live and work. Offering mixed dorms, private rooms, delicious breakfasts and a sauna, this is co-living done in style. The interior is a gorgeous mix of Italian and Moroccan decor, with a large terrace for morning yoga and evening views of the sunset over the waves. Also available; surf lessons and camps, cooking classes and trips to local places of interest. Aftas 12, Taghazout, Durban, Taghazout 80200. +212 767-623125 teddypirate.com

30.5439, -9.7084 ££

35 CAMPING AOURIR

Rustic campsite 15km from Agadir just outside the village of Aourir. Great views towards the mountains and Paradise Valley. Pitches for tents, campervans and motorhomes. Swimming pool, restaurant and boules pitch available onsite. Walks and hikes can be recommended in the local area or guides organised for longer adventures. Management can help organise the extension of the three-month visa if you find you just can't leave. National Road P1001, 5km after Aourir on the Route to Imouzzer des Ida-Outanane, Aourir, Agadir 80750. camping-aourir.com +212 808-501653

30.4949, -9.6235 £

36 PARADIS NOMADE MAISON D'HÔTES

Set in the hills outside Agadir, this hotel offers a wonderful mix of comforts and traditional architecture. We stayed in one of the Berber suites, built and decorated in the traditional fashion, giving us a brief taste of Moroccan living. Speaking of tastes, they provided a delicious and hearty barbecue with meats, succulent olives and warm flatbreads, which left our stomachs feeling full and our hearts content. They also offer tours and space for motorhome parking. Le Paradis Nomade Douar Azrarag 80000 Agadir. paradis-nomade.com +212 671-121535

30.4755, -9.4657 £££

37 GÎTE MERIEM

Family-run Gîte Meriem is neat and tidy with chestnut-brown walls and a gorgeous entrance gate. Rooms were basic yet comfortable, each equipped with en suite facilities. Guests have access to a roof terrace with great views over the valley. We arrived late, yet were treated to hrira and tagine and parked our campervan outside. MMC2+278, Tizgui n Chorfa. +212 662-743481

30.6701, -9.3489 £

29

35

35

33

37

37

p187
Tamri
Tizgui
Taghazout
Amskroud
p311
Aourir
AGADIR
Drarga
Temsia
Lqliaa
p321

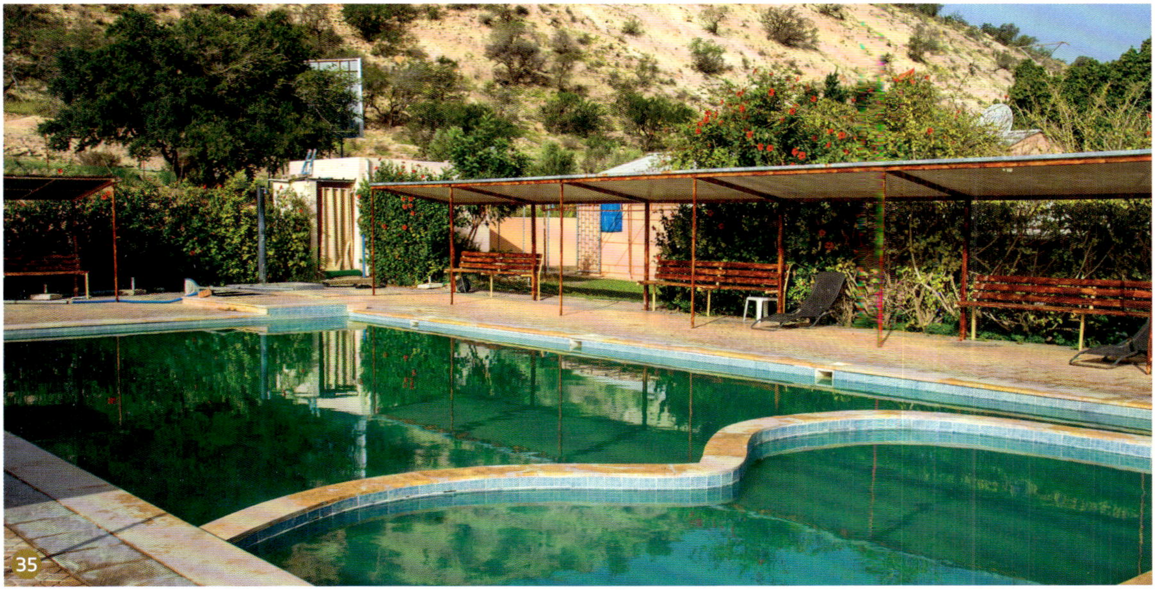

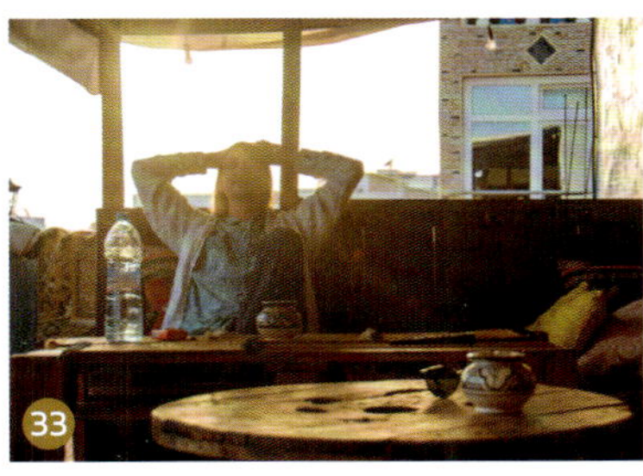

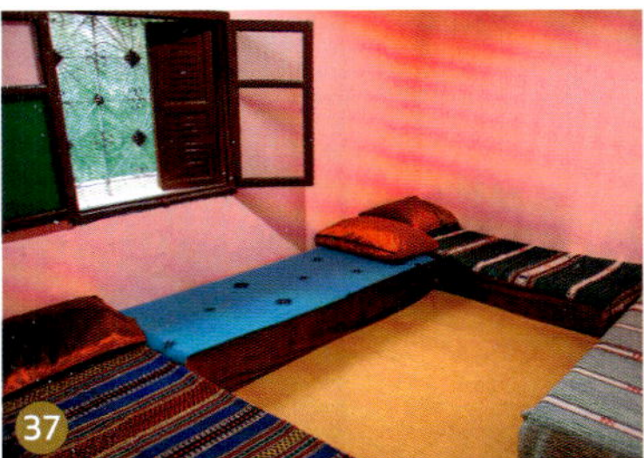

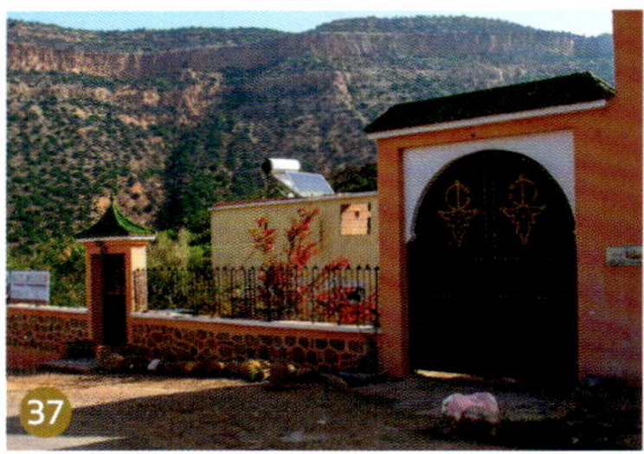

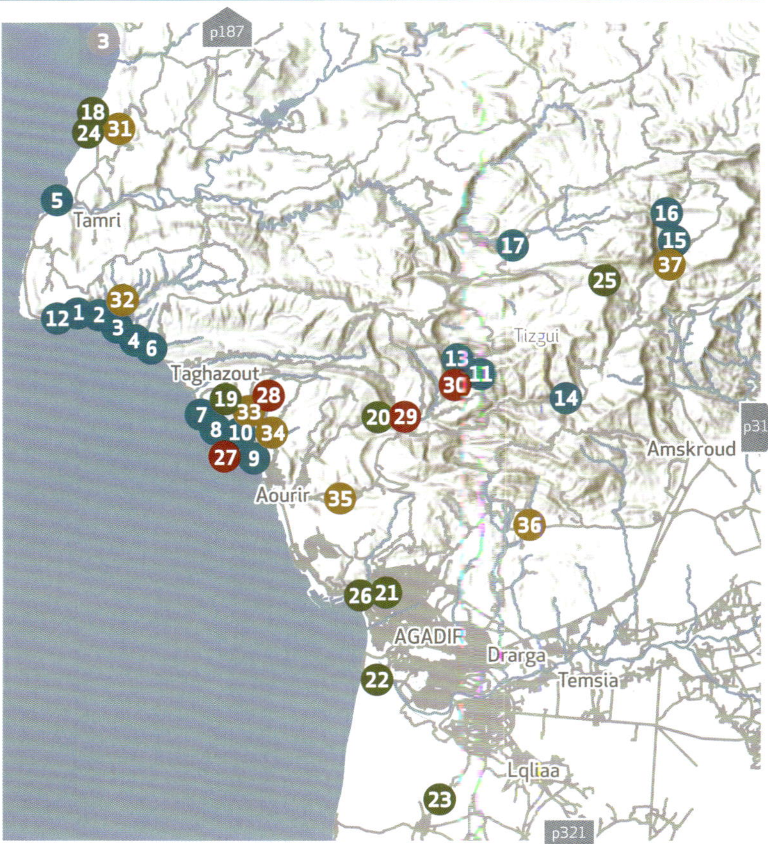

2

AROUND MARRAKECH

Our perfect adventure

- → **Buzz** around the Red City on a rented bicycle from Marrakech Green Wheels
- → **Spike** up your life – visit Cactus Thiemann, reputedly the largest cactus plantation in Africa
- → **Gaze** into the reflecting pool at Marrakech's Menara Gardens
- → **Listen** to enchanting tales at the World Storytelling Café
- → **Uncover** hidden wonders at Le Jardin Secret in Marrakech, where magic awaits in secluded gardens
- → **Marvel** at the enormous earthly sphere constructed entirely of bicycle parts in the Jardin Des Arts
- → **Embrace** the adventure of losing yourself in the winding maze of Marrakech's medina as you search for your riad
- → **Discover** the hidden legacy of the Saadian Tombs, where Marrakech's royal history whispers through ancient stones

1

2

4

**'Marrakech ought to be earned as a destination.
The journey is the preparation for the experience.
Reaching it too fast derides it, makes it a little less easy to understand.'**

Tahir Shah, Arabian Nights: A Caravan of Moroccan Dreams

The Almoravids arrived by camel from the Sahara via the High Atlas and established Marrakush (*Land of God*) as their capital in 1070, using it as a base to conquer the Maghreb and, eventually, Al-Andalus (Muslim Spain). Over the years, many notable figures have also ended up here: Crosby, Stills & Nash arrived by express train; Antoine de Saint-Exupéry flew in by mail plane; and in the 1930s, authors Gordon and Mary West passed through *By Bus To The Sahara*. The city offers lots of activities but also serves as a gateway to the region's many wonders, including road trips, mountain treks to Amazigh villages, waterfalls and long weekends in eco-lodges in the High Atlas. Only a three and a half hour flight from London-Marrakech serves as your enchanting entrance to exhilarating off-the-beaten-track adventures, no matter how you choose to get there or how long you plan to stay.

Marrakech's famous Jemaa el-Fnaa square was easy to find and its surrounding souks were even easier to get lost in. We were feeling adventurous and keen to explore the Red City beyond the food stalls, so we rented bikes from Marrakech Green Wheels, a bicycle shop offering bike rental and guided tours of the city's finest exotic gardens and ancient wonders. Equipped with water, snacks, GPS and a paper map, we went on the Marrakech Garden and Palmeraie Tour, taking in the UNESCO World Heritage Sites Menara Gardens and Le Jardin Secret, and Jardin Majorelle, to name a few. With its growing network of cycle lanes, navigating Marrakech by bike was pretty straightforward, though be prepared for unexpected traffic. Pedalling through the medina's narrow streets is a memory that will linger infinitely longer than the tagine you had for lunch.

As Morocco's ex-capital, Marrakech's legendary souk is a bustling centre of commerce and haggling, a vital part of the local culture. Stall owners seek the best prices for themselves, while visitors are expected to negotiate for better deals. This daily barter and banter can be fun and is an integral part of the Marrakech experience.

GARDENS

1 MENARA GARDENS

The UNESCO World Heritage Menara Gardens were established in the twelfth century by Almohad Caliph Abd al-Mu'min, who was instrumental in unifying the Maghreb and Al-Andalus under the Almohad rule. The gardens feature orchards of palm, olive and fruit trees, but the star attraction and centrepiece is the reflecting pool, overlooked by a large pavilion. According to the guide, the pool was used as a training facility for Almohad soldiers in preparation for swimming across the Mediterranean to Andalucía. Unfortunately, swimming is no longer permitted. Beyond their beauty, the gardens were designed with a sophisticated irrigation system that channels water from the nearby mountains, showcasing the advanced engineering techniques of the time. Open daily between 8am – 7pm. Free entry. Les Jardin De La, Marrakech 40000. Menara Gardens is a 45 mins walk or 15 mins cycle ride SE from Jemaa el-Fnaa.

31.6140, -8.0170

2 LE JARDIN SECRET

A restored Islamic garden dating to the Saadian Dynasty (1510-1659). Tucked away in the labyrinthine streets of Marrakech's ancient medina, the gardens feature intricate Moroccan architecture and a rooftop café that is the second-highest viewpoint in Marrakech. The scent of jasmine and orange blossom filled the air, transporting us to a bygone era. The garden is spacious, offering shaded areas and a small exhibition and gift shop. A nineteenth-century renovation added a touch of elegance, while subsequent owners left behind stories of scandal and mystery. After decades of abandonment, the property was rediscovered in 2008. Today, Le Jardin Secret invites visitors to explore its intricate archways, ornate mosaics and exotic gardens. Admission prices vary, with free entry for children under seven years old and discounted rates for locals and young adults. Rue Mouassine 121, Marrakech Medina. Le Jardin Secret is a 15-20 mins walk N through the medina from Jemaa el-Fnaa. lejardinsecretmarrakech.com

31.6306, -7.9895

All of Le Jardin Secret, except the tower, is accessible to visitors with physical disabilities. Visitors with disabilities and their carer have the right to free and priority access

3 CACTUS THIEMANN

Claimed to be the largest cactus plantation in Africa and established by Hans Thiemann, a German horticultural engineer with a passion for prickly plants. For over two decades,

4

4

4

6

5

Hans travelled the world to gather cacti seeds and other succulents. The plantation boasts an impressive array of cacti, ranging from towering monoliths reaching five metres tall to squat, round varieties such as the echinocactus grusonii, which resemble festive ornaments. During our visit, we enjoyed a refreshing lemonade at the café. The plantation also features a children's playground. Open from Wednesday to Saturday, between 10am and 5pm, with the last entrance at 4pm. Admission free for children under five, the plantation is closed annually in August. Km 10, Route de Casablanca, BP 735 Guéliz, Marrakech. 40 mins taxi ride N from Jemaa el-Fnaa. cactusthiemann.com
31.7150, -7.9914 ££

4 JARDIN MAJORELLE

An exquisite botanical garden created by French artist Jacques Majorelle in the 1920s and 1930s. The unique blend of Moorish and art deco architecture features vibrant blue and yellow buildings, intricate tile work and ornate details. Includes a vast array of plants from around the world, including cacti, succulents and tropical flowers. The garden's many nooks and crannies all burst with plants and exquisite fountains. Also home to the Majorelle and Yves Saint Laurent museums. Meanwhile, the Musée Berbère showcases the traditional crafts, art and culture of the Amazigh people. Book tickets in advance and arrive early to avoid queues. Rue Yves St Laurent, Marrakech 40090. 40 mins walk or 15 mins cycle NE from Jemaa el-Fnaa. jardinmajorelle.com
31.6426, -8.0036 £

5 JARDIN JNANE EL HARTI

Spanning over four hectares, landscaped gardens and vibrant flowers immersed us in nature. Meandering through pathways lined with palm and orange trees, cacti and exotic plants. JXJR+F54, Rue El Qadi Ayad, Marrakech 40000. Forty mins walk or 10 mins cycle ride from Jemaa el-Fnaa.
31.6299, -8.0101

6 MARRAKECH CYBER PARK

Established in the eighteenth century by Sultan Sidi Mohamed Bin Abdullah, the area became a public park in the early twentieth century. Includes a telecommunication museum, a rose garden and a reading corner. The park promotes environmental sustainability with composting, drip irrigation and solar energy initiatives. Open daily and a guardian near the gates will keep an eye on your bike, for a small fee. Boulevard Mohamed V, Marrakech 40000. 10 mins walk or 5 mins cycle ride NW from Jemaa el-Fnaa.
31.6265, -7.9959

7

9

9

9

10

10

8

7 KOUTOUBIA MOSQUE GARDENS

Also known as Lalla Hasna Park, the gardens are located near Jemaa el-Fnaa, beneath the towering minaret of the famous Koutoubia Mosque. Spanning two hectares, the gardens are a popular spot for locals and tourists, featuring neatly trimmed rose bushes, symmetrical walkways and shaded benches. A notable feature was the Koubba, the tomb of Lalla Zohra, who, according to legend, transforms into a dove at night. Park is open day and night. 10 mins walk or 5 mins cycle ride W from Jemaa el-Fnaa.

10 mins, 31.6232, -7.9949

8 HOUSE OF PHOTOGRAPHY

Morocco's history is showcased through a vast collection of photographs dating from the 1870s to the 1950s. The museum houses nearly 10,000 photos, with exhibits spread across two floors. Highlights include aerial photos by Marcelin Flandrin and everyday life shots by Gabriel Gillet. Panoramic views from the rooftop café and terrace. The museum is open daily. Under-15s free. Rue Ahl Fes, 46 Rue Bin Lafnadek, Marrakech 40030. 20 mins walk N through medina from Jemaa el-Fnaa. maisondelaphotographie.ma

20mins, 31.6319, -7.9842

9 JARDIN DES ARTS

An enchanting open-air art gallery featuring more than a dozen sculptures by artists inspired by the African continent. Situated at the heart of Marrakech, the garden offers a unique opportunity to admire artworks which convey an environmental message. The highlight is an enormous earthly sphere constructed entirely of bicycle parts: out of this world. Open 24 hours. 20 mins walk NW from Jemaa el-Fnaa.

20 mins, 31.6292, -8.0029

10 SAADIAN TOMBS

Steeped in mystery and history, the Saadian Tombs are a fascinating glimpse into Morocco's past. Built in the 16th century during the reign of Sultan Ahmad al-Mansur (1578–1603), the tombs were constructed to honour the Sultan's ancestors and showcase his wealth and power. The intricate tiles and ornate architecture transported us to a bygone era. As we wandered through the magnificent courtyards, we found the tombs of more than 200 Saadian sultans. Rue de La Kasbah, Marrakech 40000. 20 mins walk S through the medina from Jemaa el-Fnaa. saadiantombs.com

20 mins, 31.6170, -7.9890

11 MIAÂRA JEWISH CEMETERY

A well-maintained and historic site surrounded by high white walls and lined with ancient olive and cypress trees. First established in the 15th century, yet it is believed that Jews have been buried there since as early as the 12th century. The cemetery's 20,000 graves spread out in waves across the enclosed space, with the left corner dedicated to 6,000 children who died during a typhus epidemic in the 19th century. Small paths wend their way through the largely simple white headstones inscribed with Hebrew and Arabic script; some featured more intricate carvings and ornate designs. The site is studded with mausoleums of saints and venerated rabbis. The cemetery's unique architecture features concentric circles, divided into seperate sections for men, women and children,with the oldest graves at the centre and the graves of the particularly pious, judges and scholars of the city at the edges, believed to protect the rest of those buried there. Closed Saturday. Small entry fee. Av. Taoulat El Miara, Marrakech 45000. 20 mins walk SE from Jemaa el-Fnaa.

20 mins, 31.6199, -7.9802

No stairs and most lanes are wide and step-free. However some of the narrower lanes in the older sections of the cemetery may make access difficult.

ADVENTURE

12 MARRAKECH GREEN WHEELS

Bicycle tours and rentals. Offers city, palmeraie, desert and mountain tours. Promotes cycling for locals and tourists, creating jobs, offering training and empowering communities through sustainable transport and ecotourism initiatives. 240 Tariq Makhzen, Marrakech 40000. marrakechgreenwheels.com +212 611-768989

3 mins, 31.6132, -7.9865 £

CAFÉS

13 WORLD STORYTELLING CAFÉ

An enchanting café where local legends and myths are spun into tales that transport us to a world of mighty sultans and mythical creatures. The fusion of traditional Gnawa rhythms and modern melodies played by the café's resident musician brought the tales to life. Meat and vegan options, including camel burgers and falafel salads served with homemade chips and aioli. Yum. 23 Route Ahel-Fes, Marrakech 40000. 20 mins walk N from Jemaa el-Fnaa. worldstorytellingcafe.com

31.6317, -7.9850 £

14 CAFÉ CLOCK

We stepped into the mystical realm of Café Clock, where Morocco's tellers of ancient stories wove their magic, transporting us to a world of wonder and awe. As we sipped on a refreshing cup of mint tea, the sounds of the Sahara came alive through the tales of the storytellers. We came for the tea and stayed for the tales. Hosts cooking and baking classes; calligraphy lessons; jam sessions and live music. 224 Derb Chtouka, Kasbah, Marrakech. 25 mins walk S of Jemaa el-Fnaa.

31.6128, -7.9872 ££

PLACES TO STAY

15 HÔTEL RACINE

A European-style hotel is a ten-minute taxi ride from Jemaa el-Fnaa and 15 minutes from the airport, perfect for early-morning departures and late-night arrivals. Great views over the city from the rooftop pool. Accessible. Free Wi-Fi. Friendly and professional staff. Eco-friendly water practices and locally sourced food. Angle Rue Oum Errabia et, Rue Ibn Atya, Marrakech 40000. hotelracinemarrakech@gmail.com +212 5243-79223

31.6318, -8.0038 ££

16 RIAD DAR SOUKAINA

Charming riad on the edge of the medina. Bedrooms are named after Moroccan spices. Knock, knock. Cumin. 19&24, Quartier Riad Laarouss, Derb El Farrane, Marrakech Médina 40000. darsoukaina.morocco-ma.website +212 5243-76055

31.6341, -7.9898 ££

17 RIAD BOUSSA

Traditional guesthouse in the middle of the old town. Friendly and helpful staff. 192 Derb Dabachi, Derb Jdid, Marrakech 40040. riad-boussa.com +212 524-380823

31.6272, -7.9835 ££

18 CAMPING DAR BARI TARGA

Great campsite set among ancient olive trees just 30 minutes west of the Red City. Spacious pitches and modern shower facilities in rustic wooden buildings. A fully equipped kitchen and barbecue area meant we could cook up a storm, while the peaceful surroundings helped us relax and recharge. The French owner, Marc, greeted us with a warm welcome. A convenient stopover. Dar Bari, Piste Fléches Rouges de Douar Bari, Marrakech. darbaritarga@gmail.com +212 661-244151

31.6932, -8.2456 £

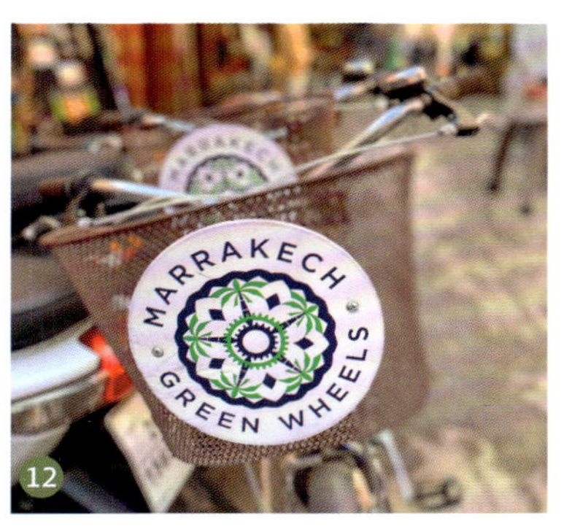

MARRAKECH
GREEN WHEELS
12

14

18

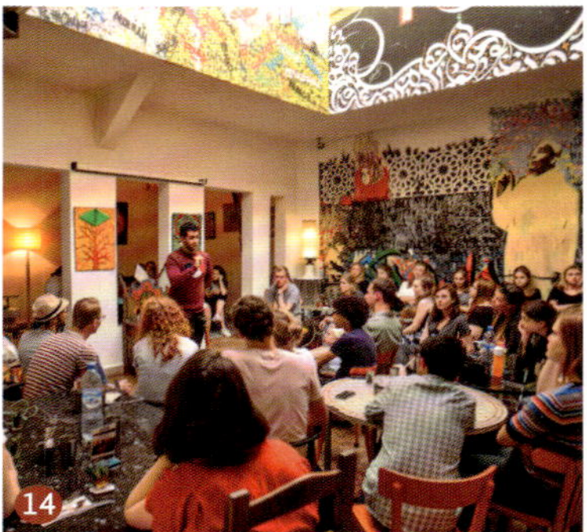

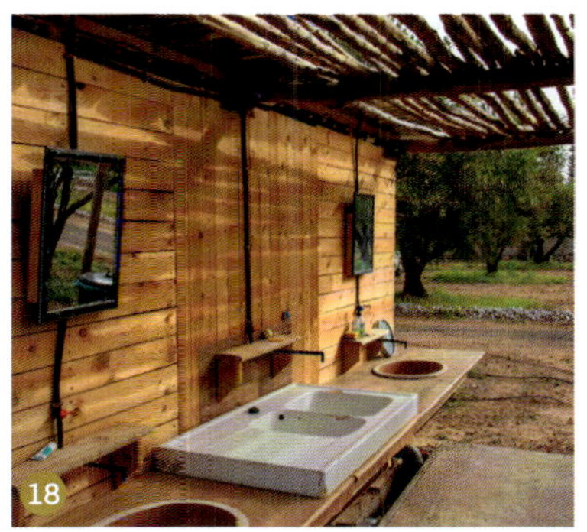

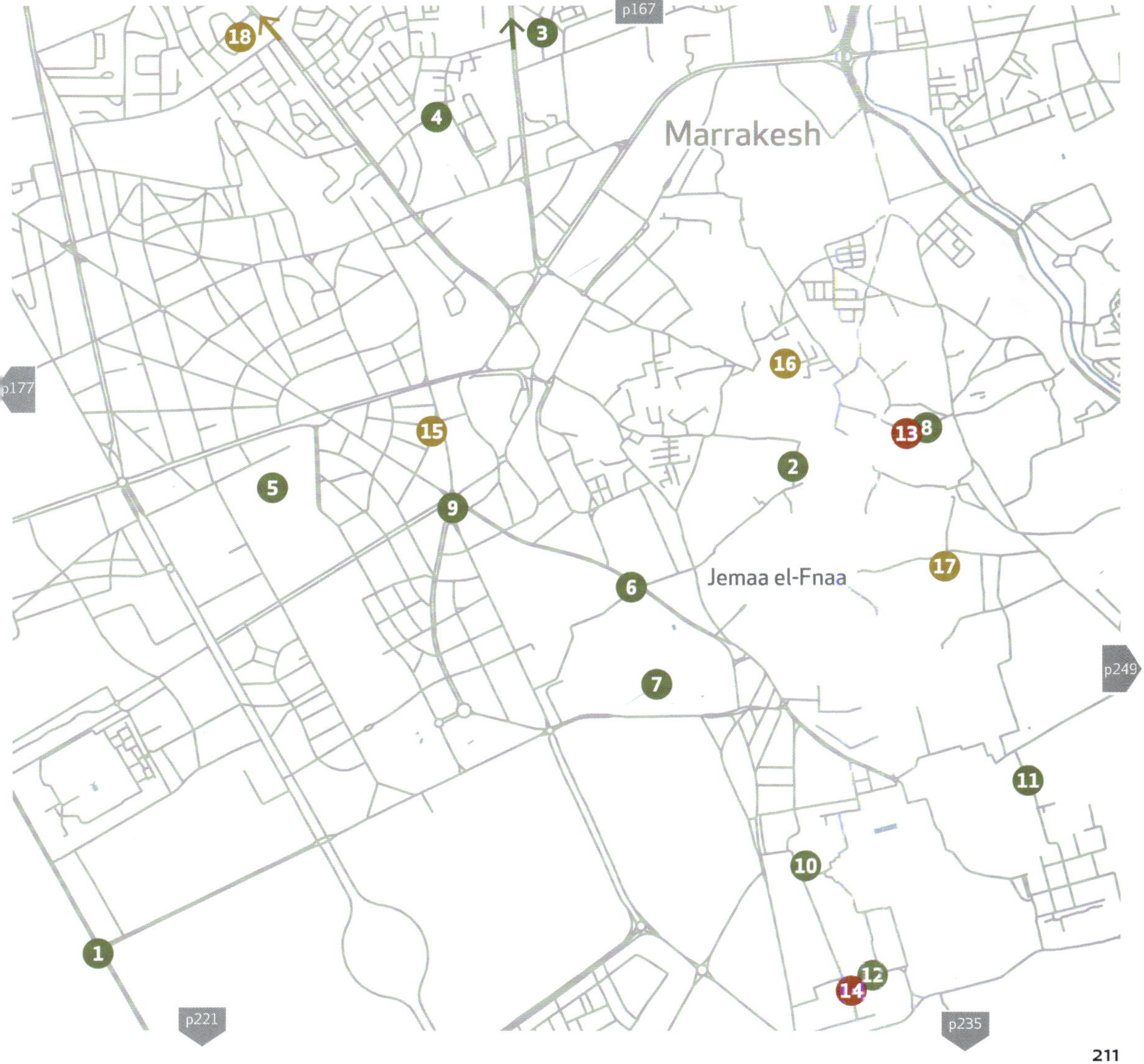
Marrakesh
Jemaa el-Fnaa
p167
p177
p249
p221
p235
1
2
3
4
5
6
7
8
9
10
11
12
13
14
15
16
17
18

7

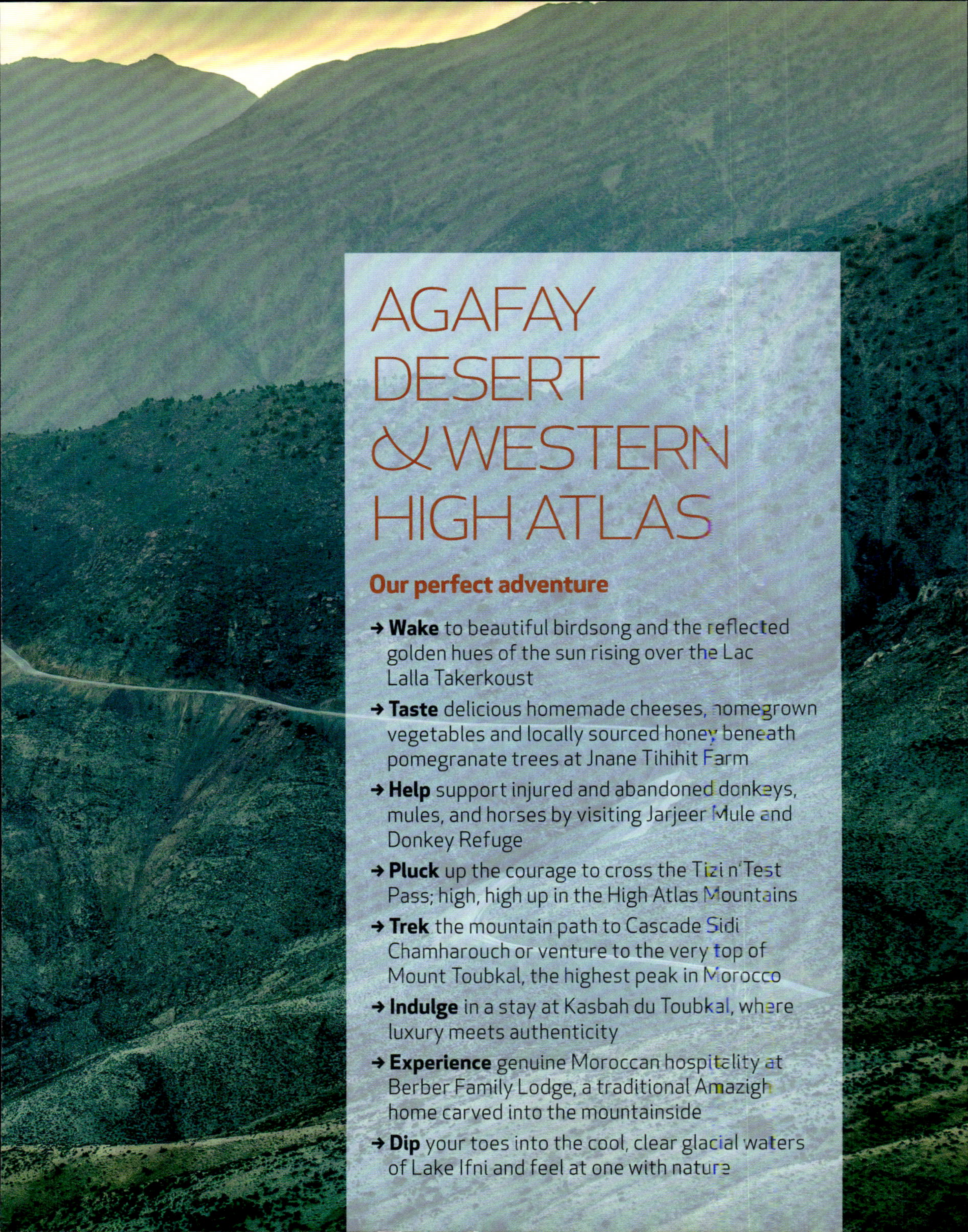

AGAFAY DESERT & WESTERN HIGH ATLAS

Our perfect adventure

- → **Wake** to beautiful birdsong and the reflected golden hues of the sun rising over the Lac Lalla Takerkoust
- → **Taste** delicious homemade cheeses, homegrown vegetables and locally sourced honey beneath pomegranate trees at Jnane Tihihit Farm
- → **Help** support injured and abandoned donkeys, mules, and horses by visiting Jarjeer Mule and Donkey Refuge
- → **Pluck** up the courage to cross the Tizi n'Test Pass; high, high up in the High Atlas Mountains
- → **Trek** the mountain path to Cascade Sidi Chamharouch or venture to the very top of Mount Toubkal, the highest peak in Morocco
- → **Indulge** in a stay at Kasbah du Toubkal, where luxury meets authenticity
- → **Experience** genuine Moroccan hospitality at Berber Family Lodge, a traditional Amazigh home carved into the mountainside
- → **Dip** your toes into the cool, clear glacial waters of Lake Ifni and feel at one with nature

2

3

17

'Whether it's a house, the stars or the desert, what makes them beautiful is invisible.'

Antoine de Saint-Exupéry, The Little Prince

The Agafay Desert and Lac Lalla Takerkoust offer distinct natural experiences, perfect for adventure, relaxation and cultural immersion. Unlike the sandy Sahara, Agafay is a rocky, arid landscape of rugged hills and barren expanses. Its stark beauty provides a unique desert experience. Visitors can explore the wild terrain on camel or horseback. During a stroll along a dry riverbed near our camp, we encountered a desert fox – all of us frozen before it darted away. For those seeking solitude, Agafay offers a peaceful connection with nature. The desert camps range from basic tents to luxurious setups, offering traditional Moroccan cuisine, stargazing and cultural performances under clear and expansive skies. Nearby, Lac Lalla Takerkoust contrasts with the desert's aridity. This man made reservoir on the N'fis River is a refreshing retreat, popular for water activities such as boating and fishing. The surrounding area, with the Atlas Mountains as a backdrop, is perfect for picnics and leisurely walks. Parking our campervan by the shore, we watch the sun set, casting a golden path across the water.

Donkeys are a common sight in Morocco; vital partners in transportation and agriculture. While some of these creatures are cherished and well cared for, many bear the burdens of neglect and mistreatment. Our journey takes us to the Jarjeer Mule and Donkey Refuge, a sanctuary established by a devoted British couple who have dedicated their lives to rescuing and rehabilitating these hardworking animals. Visiting the refuge is not just a cute encounter, it's an invitation to support animal welfare in Morocco.

At the heart of Western High Atlas stands Mount Toubkal, a sentinel of nature and the tallest peak in north Africa, reaching 4,167m. Toubkal beckons adventurers to explore its slopes and peaks. Imlil, an Amazigh village at its base, serves as a gateway for trekkers and connects remote communities. Connecting Marrakech and Taroudant, the Tizi n'Test Pass takes us high into the Atlas Mountains, while the road gets narrower and narrower.
At the summit, Hotel la Belle Vue provides a break from the relentless ascent; we enjoy a spontaneous party with fellow travellers – two French lovers on an old Italian motorbike and two Italian brothers who play the French horn. Night unveils a starry sky above and twinkling village lights below, while morning discloses a vast landscape, the lower mountain slopes reveal the Earth's millennia-old formations. An infinite plain stretches way beyond the horizon, bordered by meringue-shaped mountain ranges. What goes up, must come down; we all head our separate ways.

LAKES & RIVERS

1 LAC LALLA TAKERKOUST

Beneath the setting sun, the lake's calm waters reflected the golden hues of the sky and created a perfect picture. As the stars began to twinkle, a few locals arrived for an evening stroll but soon drifted off as the darkness fell. A campervan sat on a small promontory, its occupants settled in for the night, experiencing the magic of sleeping by the water's edge. The next morning, we woke to the sweet songs of birds and took a refreshing swim in the lake. This was the perfect time to enjoy the water. From Lalla Takerkoust head SW on P2024 for 1km; turn R and follow the track for 350m to the lakeside.

2 mins, 31.3479, -8.1303

2 BARRAGE OUIRGANE

A picturesque lake surrounded by the rugged peaks of the Atlas Mountains. We took a walk then pulled up a chair along the dam's edge to enjoy the waterside view and sumptuous sunset. From Ouirgane, head NE on N7 for 2.2km; turn sharp L for 1.4km; slight L and your parking spot (31.1798, -8.0819) will be on the R after 700m.

3 mins, 31.1813, -8.0852

3 CASCADE SIDI CHAMHAROUCH

Walking up the well-defined path towards the waterfall and the towering, snow-decorated peak of tremendous Toubkal, we couldn't fail to be impressed. We entered a world devoid of worries or Wi-Fi. Despite following the clearly defined donkey-poo trail, we were unable to pass the Poste de Gendarmerie Royale checkpoint without a registered guide. We paid 300dh (about £25, prices may vary) for two of us to tag along with another trekking party. At the Cascade Sidi Chamharouch, we climbed down to the river and had an exhilarating dunk in icy water, followed by sweet mint tea in Café Chamharouch. From here, you could continue the trek to the summit of Toubkal.

The waterfalls and the mountain views were well worth the fee and the effort. From the parking spot (31.1226, -7.9194), walk back towards Imlil and take first L on to the track (P2005 on Google maps) and past houses for 400m; then walk across scrubland for another 500m until the path starts zigzagging upwards; after about 600m you will see the checkpoint where you will need to show passports and confirm that you have a guide; climb the path for another 1.5km until you reach the falls.

60 mins, 31.0989, -7.9142

4 CASCADE IMLIL

White water cascaded from six metres over huge boulders and formed cold shallow pools where children paddled and played. A stall served tea, orange juice and tagines.
We watched local women drumming out traditional music. Can get busy, especially on a Sunday. Walk up from centre of Imlil past Kasbah du Toubkal; when you get to mosque, follow aqueduct all the way until water splits and there are some wooden boards over river; turn R to get to cascades.

10 mins, 31.1290, -7.9196

5 LAKE IFNI

Reaching the brow of the hill, we overlooked Lake Ifni, a giant blue opal shimmering beneath the barren rocks of the surrounding High Atlas Mountains. The scramble down to its edge was a bit daunting, with loose stones sliding beneath our feet. As we approached the water, fish surfaced curiously and swifts darted gracefully overhead. Tentatively, we dipped our toes in and were pleasantly surprised – it wasn't as cold as expected, despite the lake being fed by glacial melt from nearby peaks. At 800m long and about 50m deep, its size is impressive, cradled in this remote basin. Lying on our backs, gazing up at the vast expanse of Mr. Blue Sky, we felt alone together, completely in tune with nature. The tranquillity was broken only by the faint buzzing of bees, the occasional song of swifts and the distant bleat of a goat. Drive to top of Imhilene village where road ends and park outside Hussain's house for a small fee – he will also offer you mint tea; from parking (31.0189, -7.8655), follow winding path up to Lake Ifni with a 540m elevation gain.

150 mins, 31.0300, -7.8806

DESERT

6 AGAFAY DESERT

These vast, rocky empty plains lie 30km southwest of Marrakech. Known as a 'stone desert', it is markedly different from its southern Saharan cousin, characterised by rolling hills and expansive plateaus, ideal for camel and horse treks. An accessible retreat from the city, where you can appreciate the pollution-free star-studded night sky.
This wide, flat landscape, cut through by dry riverbeds and crisscrossed by scampering lizards and the occasional desert fox, contrasted sharply with the Toubkal mountain range. We don't recommend travelling into the desert on your own. For the best experience, stay in one of the camps offering a desert experience, such as Inara Camp. Follow R212 from Marrakech for 23km until reaching outskirts of desert near Aït Chekh and Nzala.

5 mins, 31.3935, -8.2111

6

8

ROADTRIP

7 TIZI N'TEST PASS

At an elevation of 2,093m, Tizi n'Test Pass is the second highest and longest mountain pass in Morocco. The road was constructed between 1926 and 1932 and connects Marrakech in the east with Taroudant in the west. The drive was an incredible experience, offering up-close views of the vast monoliths of the Western High Atlas. Leaving Taroudant, we began our ascent on one of the best roads in Morocco. As we climbed ever higher, the views became ever wider and more magnificent. There were occasional warnings of rockfalls, but we were in our element. However, as we soared upwards, the sun sank slowly downwards, the road narrowed and deteriorated, and our nerve began to fail. By the time we reached the pass, the sun had called it a day; we agreed this was one mountain that was more than high enough and sought refuge at Hotel la Belle Vue Hotel, where we watched the final throes of sunset over the mountains. This was probably one of the best decisions we have ever made. Our slower descent eastwards the following morning was equally as exhilarating and hair-raising.

- To/from: Taroudant > Marrakech
- Distance:300km
- Elevation: 2,093m
- Roads: N7
- Scenic stop-offs: Hotel la Belle Vue
- 30.8646, -8.3784

ANCIENT

8 TINMEL MOSQUE

Also known as the Grand Mosque of Tinmel, it was built in the 12th century and served as a religious centre for the Almohad Dynasty. Notable for its design, the mosque features intricate geometric patterns and exemplifies the beauty of Islamic architecture. Constructed primarily of local stone and adobe, walls glowed with a warm, earthy palette that co-ordinated with the surrounding mountains.
The Tinmel Mosque was significantly damaged during the 2023 Marrakech earthquake.
At the time of writing reconstruction works were well underway. XQMC+WJX, Tinmel
2 mins, 30.9849, -8.2280

ANIMAL SANCTUARY

9 JARJEER MULE AND DONKEY REFUGE

On the outskirts of Marrakech lies a remarkable story of compassion and dedication.
Octogenarian couple Charles Hantom and Susan Machin have spent over three decades rescuing horses, donkeys and mules that have been abandoned, injured, or mistreated.
The sanctuary's success is largely attributed to its collaboration with local villagers, who play a vital role in rescue efforts. Ayoub, a local, developed his own method of treating injured animals using traditional Amazigh splints and honey. The sanctuary receives individual donations from overseas, enabling them to continue their vital work. We visited the women-run café and enjoyed vegan chilli and veggie spaghetti bolognaise. Call in advance to arrange your visit. Susan was awarded an OBE for services to equine welfare in Morocco in 2024. Oumnass, Marrakech 40000, public transport: bus 45 from Sidi Mimoun, Marrakech, to Oumnass (6dh).
jarjeer.org +212 602-866013
1 min, 31.4190, -8.0848

CAFÉS & EATERIES

10 CAFÉ CHAMHAROUCH, MT TOUBKAL

Offering well-earned drinks on the way up Mount Toubkal. Also sells tagines, omelettes (made with tomato, onions and spices) and salads. The oft-asked question: 'Are you on your way up, or down?' Opposite Cascade Sidi Chamharouch. +212 626-062417
31.0979, -7.9124 £

11 JNANE TIHIHIT

A working farm owned and managed by a Belgian couple combining a mid-range hotel and restaurant. Stylish accommodation and delicious organic food of which 80% is sourced on-site, including cheese, milk and honey from local beehives. Fifteen rooms and family suites, a hammam and a small swimming pool fed from their own well, filtered with reeds and additionally used for irrigation. Offers children's activities, including donkey rides and toy house-building workshops using traditional brick-making techniques. Cookery classes are available for adults and children. We enjoyed a delicious lunch in the garden beneath olive, orange and pomegranate trees. 132, Derb Dekkak, Bab Doukkala, Marrakech. jnane-tihihit.com

31.3320, -8.16608 ££

PLACES TO STAY

12 CAPALDI HOTEL

The luxurious Capaldi Hotel is committed to promoting sustainable tourism practices, and features sustainable building methods, 200 solar panels and LED lighting throughout, as well as efficient irrigation systems to minimise water waste. The hotel's farm-to-table dining philosophy focuses on locally sourced, organic produce and supports farmers to promote sustainable agriculture. They also use locally sourced materials, including Bejmat, a traditional Moroccan material and stonework from previously unused land. Delectable en suite rooms and fabulous swimming pool. We explored the surrounding area with Ed, the friendly and knowledgeable owner of the hotel. Route d'Amizmiz km39 Lalla Takerkoust, 42202 Marrakech. thecapaldi.com +212 600-069900

31.3523, -8.1715 £££

13 ECO CAMP MOROCCO, OUIRGANE

A charming rustic retreat in the Azzaden Valley surrounded by oleander-filled gardens and the soothing sound of Mother Nature. Clean showers and homemade cuisine; a bowl or two of hrira soup, a boiled egg, olives and dates with homemade bread for dinner. As night fell, the melodic chirping of frogs and sounds of the nearby river lulled us into a peaceful slumber. Sunrise revealed a jaw-dropping view over the valley where pink and ochre houses blended in with the red and green trees. The helpful owner can arrange activities such as horse riding and treks. Track leading to the site was basic, but just about manageable in a campervan. Douar Torord, Azzaden Valley, Ouirgane Al Haouz. ecocamp.morocco@gmail.com +212 638-971988

31.1714, -8.0558 ££

13

14

14 INARA CAMP

A sanctuary from the scorching desert sun; complete with air-conditioned tents, delicious food, campfire, pool and a healthy serving of Moroccan hospitality. Staffed by locals and people from Saharan regions, who have extensive desert experience. The camp is the perfect option to experience the wildness of the desert by day and some creature comforts after the sun goes down. We enjoyed nightly shows of traditional Moroccan music and dancing, as well as fire-dancing performances. Do not attempt to drive to Inara Camp unless you have a 4x4. Transfers from Marrakech available. inaracamp.com +212 524-205070

31.3930, -8.2080 £££

15 GITE D'ETAPE CHEZ IMNIR

Tucked away in the village of Imnir, the gîte gave us a great welcome. Featuring nine comfortable, rustic rooms adorned with traditional Amazigh décor. We relaxed by the small swimming pool and enjoyed home-cooked food made with local ingredients and flavours. The gîte organises walks, including a four-hour trek to the twelfth-century Tinmel Mosque, a five-hour river and mountain excursion, and a tagine pot-crafting workshop. Talat N'Yaaqoub 42353, Morocco. gitechezimnir.com +212 623-565963

30.9869, -8.1824 ££

16 ISSOUGANES N TOUBKAL

Well-built, decorated and furnished. Delicious food was prepared on-site. The wide terrace overlooked rocky mountain peaks that contrasted with steps carved out of the mountains by the Amazigh people.

We scrambled down to the tiny village to be greeted by local children and watched a sheep being hand-sheared. There were no cars and no Wi-Fi, just the sounds of birds and the occasional bray of Steve the donkey. Treks can be organised with Karim, preferably in advance. Inform him of any special food preferences. Oussertek, Morocco – the road is reasonably Tarmacked but extremely steep with sharp hairpin bends; park by bend in the road at small, yellow sign LODGE (31.2022, -7.8999); walk down to the lodge along rabbit path. issouganes-n-toubkal.com +212 661-618236

31.2020, -7.8999 ££

17 HOTEL LA BELLE VUE, TIZI N'TEST PASS

Hotel la Belle Vue lived up to its name, with incredible mountain views from the very top of Tizi n'Test Pass. Hostel-style rooms with shared bathrooms and showers. Traditional Moroccan menu or use the kitchen to prepare your own. A hearty breakfast was provided by our lovely host, Mohammed. R203 Tizi n'Test. +212 629-674167

30.8608, -8.3769 £

18 KASBAH DU TOUBKAL, IMLIL

The village of Imlil plays host to a renowned eco-lodge, which blends luxury with authenticity. Originally a summer home for a local Caid in the early twentieth century, it was restored and transformed into a sustainable retreat, employing local staff and incorporating solar energy and water recycling. Guests can enjoy incredible snow-capped mountain views, guided treks to Mount Toubkal, yoga and cultural workshops. The kasbah supports local education and healthcare through the Association Bassins d'Imlil, donating 5% of profits. Highly recommended. Kasbah du Toubkal, Imlil 42152. kasbahdutoubkal.com bookings@discover.ltd.uk +212 661-918598

31.1324, -7.91885 £££

19 AZZADEN LODGE, AÏT AÏSSA

The luxury Azzaden Trekking Lodge is a spectacular and traditional lodge perched on the mountainside in the village of Aït Aïssa (1,820m) and is reached by trekking from the village of Imlil in the neighbouring Ait Mizane Valley or from Ouirgane lower down the valley. Imlil BP31 Asni 42152. highatlastrekkinglodge.com +212 661-918598

31.1341, -7.9748 £££

18

20 BERBER FAMILY LODGE, IMLIL

A lodge built around a traditional family home, carved into the side of the mountain. It offers seven rooms, tastefully decorated with natural materials in a muted yet stylish manner. Hiking, mule and horse-riding excursions in Asni were available. Delicious food. Free Wi-Fi. Douar Aguersioual, Imlil BP21. berberfamilylodge.com +212 609-785427

31.1603, -7.9255 ££

21 AUBERGE AMSOUZARTE AÏT STIDAR

Simple but super-friendly hostel close to the start of the trail to Lake Ifni. Good food and hot showers. A spring with clean fresh water emerges outside the hostel with pleasant views over the valley from the roof terrace. Amsouzart, Toubkal 83175. belgddimyoussef00@gmail.com +212 641-170601

31.0144, -7.8335 £

16

14

19

20

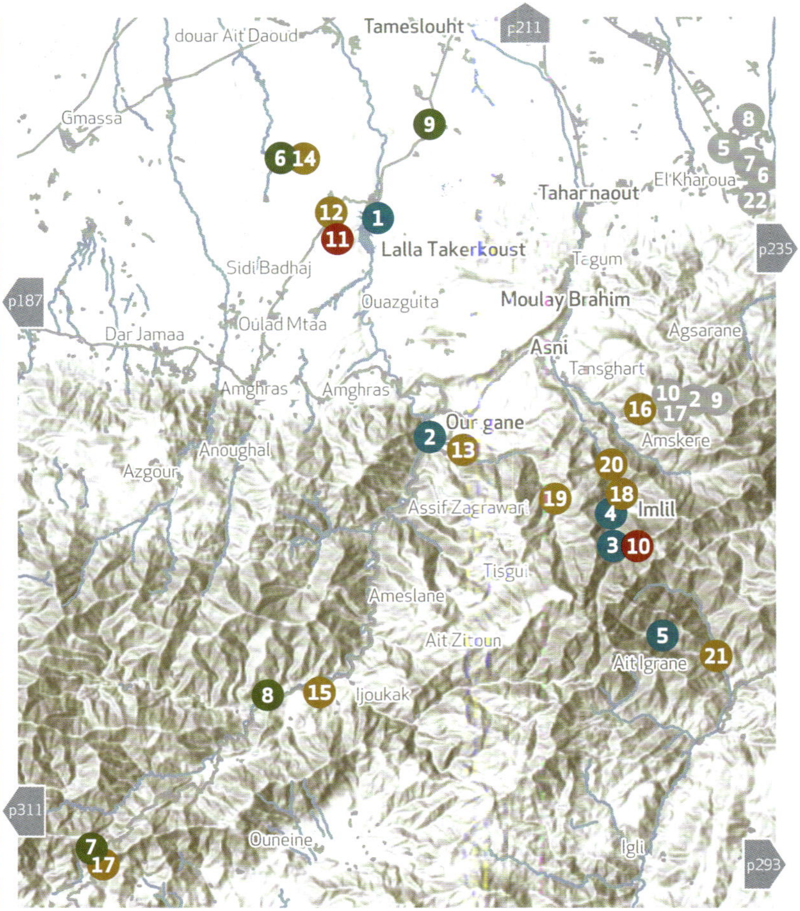

17

OURIKA VALLEY & CENTRAL HIGH ATLAS

Our perfect adventure

- **Climb** the seven waterfalls of Setti Fatma and experience the ecstasy of cold mountain water cascading over you
- **Seek** spiritual solace at Setti Fatma Mausoleum, where an enigmatic female saint rests
- **Rest** your head at Auberge des Jeunesse Les Cascades with panoramic views over the Atlas Mountains
- **Adventure** through a wonderland of art and plants at Anima (André Heller Garden)
- **Discover** the baths, palaces and mosaics of the Aghmat Archaeological Site
- **Drive** round hair-raising hairpin bends of the Tizi n'Tichka Pass, flanked by cedar and pine forests
- **Visit** the ancient mountain village of Megdaz and experience an authentic Amazigh homestay
- **Marvel** at the glorious sunset over the High Atlas mountain peaks at the Oukaïmeden Lookout Point

'What induces you… to depart from your home in town, to leave parents and friends and go to the countryside over mountains and valleys, if it is not for the beauty of the world of nature?'

Leonardo da Vinci

The Ourika Valley, located 30 km south of Marrakech in the High Atlas Mountains, is known for its natural beauty and diverse wildlife. The Ourika River is the lifeblood of the agricultural terraces cultivated by Amazigh farmers. Hiking trails crisscross the valley, winding through olive and almond groves, past waterfalls, and up to scenic viewpoints. Oukaïmeden, Africa's highest ski resort at 3,273 m, was a highlight of our journey. We parked our campervan at the summit, captivated by the views across the mountain peaks, and spent the night under the stars.

Setti Fatma's seven waterfalls attract many visitors. We embarked on a challenging guided trek, ascending the steep trail past all seven waterfalls. Reaching the highest and final cascade and taking a dip in the pool brought immense satisfaction and pleasure. Seventh heaven. The valley has a vibrant arts scene. Local artist Abdelhaq Elyoussi's sculptures, which capture Moroccan life and family bonds, deeply resonated with us and we bought one of his pieces. The valley's botanical gardens, including André Heller's Anima Garden, seamlessly blend art and nature, creating an evocative and dreamy experience.

In spring, wildflowers blanket the valley, while higher elevations are covered with juniper and pine forests. Birdwatchers twitch for species such as the Barbary partridge and Moussier's redstart. Traditional Amazigh markets, such as the Saturday market in Asni, offered a genuine insight into regional life, bustling with locals trading produce, crafts and animals. In September 2023, an earthquake hit Marrakech and parts of the High Atlas, including the Ourika Valley, causing damage to infrastructure and homes. At the time of writing, many families were still living in tents, but efforts to rebuild the resilient communities are well underway.

Journeying to the southern slopes of Mount Toubkal, we explored the Oued Zat Valley, where vibrant greenery meets the stark, arid terrain. Traditional Amazigh villages cling to the mountainsides, sustained by the Zat River. We shared tea with a local family and explored a weekly souk, a meeting place for villagers. High in the Atlas Mountains, at the ancient village of Megdaz, we were treated to great hospitality, sublime views and a trek to a 30m waterfall, passing fields of wildflowers and glades carpeted with wild mint en route.

LAKES & RIVERS

1 SEVEN CASCADES OF OURIKA

Waterfall one is ten metres high and thunderous, the white water cascading into a pool where adults and children paddled and took selfies. The first waterfall was a 30-minute hike from Setti Fatma. Although the climb was quite steep and rocky in parts, it was easy to find without a guide. Many hotels in Marrakech offer day trips to the waterfalls and it can get busy, particularly in summer. Arrive early to avoid crowds. We took a round trip to Setti Fatma by following the path to the right of the café, alongside the cliff and back down to the village. Waterfalls two to four are viewable from the café opposite the first waterfall. In Setti Fatma, cross the river at the bridge for Cafè Restaurant Azarg (31.2271, -7.6729); climb uphill through the stalls and shops until you come out by small river; follow stream to falls; if in doubt, ask for 'cascades'.
30 mins, 31.2212, -7.6710

Waterfalls four to seven cascade down through a near-vertical cliffside to waterfalls two and three. Climb down to the pool of waterfall four for a paddle. Abseiling down to the first waterfall can be organised with canyoning groups.

From the first waterfall, walk up to the steps to the café; walk through the restaurant to the R and upwards; turn L up the steps (from here look up to L to see waterfalls 2, 3 and 4); walk up and L along the path; keep L at the fork in the path and you will arrive at the fourth waterfall.
30 mins, 31.2205, -7.6697

Waterfalls five and six were simultaneously a challenge and a fantastic experience;
we recommend hiring a guide to make the climb as the trail was very difficult and the waterfalls harder to find.
20 mins, 31.2196, -7.6687

For waterfall seven, we hired a guide as this was a much longer and more dangerous trek. There had been a clear path, but the 2023 earthquake covered its tracks. The seventh cascade features a huge, displaced rock that forms a tunnel over the pool. Together with Mohammed, our guide from Auberge des Jeunesses Les Cascades, we climbed over the rocks and thrust our heads in the cold, intense waterfall, then bathed in the pool. Lola perched on the fallen rock in the sunshine – in pure ecstasy.
40 mins, 31.2178, -7.6618

2 LAC D'OUKAÏMEDEN

Snow in Africa. Located near a ski resort, Lac d'Oukaïmeden sits at an elevation of about 2,600m – one of the highest lakes in north Africa. During the winter months, the area is a wonderland, attracting skiers and snowboarders. In the summer, the landscape is perfect for hiking and picnicking. The lake itself was relatively small, yet its crystal-clear waters reflected the surrounding mountains like a mirror. Fed by mountain streams, the shores were dotted with wildflowers. The road up to Oukaïmeden was long and twisting, but the views over mountains, villages and terraced valleys more than made up for the challenging

ascent. As we waited for an excavator to clear fallen rocks from the road, a young man on a motorbike drove past with a live sheep on his lap. From Talghoumt, head SE on P2017 toward P2010 for 18km; slight R at signs for Oukaïmeden on to P2030 for 29km.

2 mins, 31.2088, -7.8527

3 MEGDAZ NATURAL POOLS

As we ventured to the waterfall, the trail unwound through hillsides covered with wildflowers. The trek itself was a challenging endeavour, which required us to cross rivers, scramble up steep hillsides and acrobatically cross narrow ledges. We took a wild dunk in a popular swimming hole where the river had sculpted pools into the rocks then continued to Cascade d'Megdaz. We recommend using Muhammad at Dar Megdaz as a guide, as he was familiar with the complex route.

35 mins, 31.3834, -6.7928

4 MEGDAZ WATERFALL

An hour after leaving Magdaz Natural Pools, we arrived at the 'small' cascade, which was actually 30m high. The waterfall tumbled down enormous, red boulders and the air was filled with the sweet aroma of wild mint and the melodic songs of birds. Perfect for a picnic and a moment of contemplation. We crossed fields and passed a tiny douar (hamlet), where villagers collected water from a stream. They offered us mint tea. If you are looking for a longer trek, the large waterfall is worth a visit, Muhammad from Dar Magdaz will show you the way.

95 mins, 31.3787, -6.7950

GARDENS

5 ANIMA (ANDRÉ HELLER GARDEN)

A whimsical oasis where art and nature come together to create a vibrant wonderland. Passing through a palm tree-lined corridor garlanded with oleander and bougainvillaea, we arrived at a wooden door adorned with intricate geometric patterns and silver Hands of Fatima. The garden's unique blend of art and nature include a striking display of African-style copper masks mounted on simple stone carvings, surrounded by a tastefully designed landscape featuring tall bamboo, palm, olive and banana trees. The soothing sounds of birdsong added to the ambience as a vast pair of blue eyes stared at us from a pink, bougainvillaea-covered archway. Aloe vera plants create artistic patterns and giant cacti towers above the landscape. Even the dustbins are terracotta in pastel hues. Café Paul Bowles serves fresh juices, including a refreshing homemade lemonade flavoured with ginger and

4

6

7

mint, and you can sit on the rooftop terrace overlooking the mountains. Douar Sbiti Ourika. anima-garden.com

2 mins, 31.4005, -7.8260

6 JARDIN BIO-AROMATIQUE DE L'OURIKA

A herbal haven with a peaceful atmosphere full of sweet fragrances and melodious birdsong. A charming wooden structure on a raised stone platform, draped with Virginia creepers, provided a welcome retreat from the sun. Flower beds are edged with roses all labelled for identification. Twenty deep-blue mosaic sinks offer foot baths with nectarine bath salts infused with bitter-orange essential oil. Wooden furniture crafted from tree trunks and chairs made from curved metal added rustic charm to the scene. Traditional meals available if ordered in advance. Garden is closed in August. Tnine Ourika Douar Elhaddad Haouz, Marrakech. jardin-bioaromatique-ourika.com +212 650 963661

2 mins, 31.3799, -7.7842

7 PARADIS DU SAFRAN

Saffron only blooms in late October to November, but Christine Ferrari, the visionary owner of Paradis du Safran, has cleverly extended the normal experience. More than 200 herbs and plants, labelled in multiple languages, grow in tastefully landscaped gardens. Peacocks and hens roam freely among life-sized camel sculptures. Long, fragrant rosemary hedges line the walkways between the saffron fields and gardens. On our visit, the natural birdsong mixed with the sweet sounds of children chanting at school nearby. The farm grew apples, mangoes, pomegranates and avocados. Alongside the fishpond, we found a set of pétanque balls and an invitation to 'kick back and relax'. The barefoot textures walk – wood, pinecones, leaves and stones – culminated in pots infused with soothing herbs and argan oil to dip the feet. To cap it all, we savoured a warm cup of saffron tea alongside tasty herb bread. Over-12s only. BP 58, MA-42452 Ourika/Maroc - km 31, Douar Takateret/ Ourika. paradis-du-safran.com +212 628 796979

2 mins, 31.3886, -7.7961

ANCIENT

8 AGHMAT ARCHAEOLOGICAL SITE

Aghmat was a major city during Idrisid rule (eighth to tenth centuries). It was captured by the Almoravids, who came from the desert with fundamentalist beliefs and a disciplined army. An excavation, led by French archaeologists, uncovered a vast complex of buildings, including a mosque, baths and palaces, plus impressive mosaics and ceramics. The site is considered one of the most important archaeological sites in Morocco. Contact the guardian (+212 624-870724) to gain access for a small fee; otherwise, look through the fence at the ruins. From the roundabout in Aghmat, head N for 190m; turn L and the ruins will be on the R after 250m. Visible from the road. Park at (31.4233, -7.8047).

5 mins, 31.4229, -7.8041 ££

8

9 OUKAÏMEDEN ROCK CARVINGS #1

Oukaïmeden is renowned for its ancient rock art. Petroglyphs scattered throughout the valley are believed to date back to the mid-third millennium BC when cattle were brought to the valley in summer as the Sahara dried. Carvings included cattle, snakes, elephants, daggers and maps. As the demand for pasture increased, disputes over grazing rights became common, leading to the widespread use of circular symbols representing shields. We recommend you enlist the services of a guide to help find the petroglyphs, as they are difficult to spot unless you know what you are looking for. Directions as for Lac Oukaïmeden, the sign is beside the road, opposite the lake.

5 mins, 31.2091, -7.8526

10 OUKAÏMEDEN ROCK CARVINGS #2

More rock carvings can be found on boulders around the valley. A guide showed us where they were, for a small fee. Or you could try looking for them yourself. From the Oukaïmeden Lookout Point, follow the small, winding track downhill for about 500m until it takes a sharp turn to the L; turn R and walk around the boulders to find carvings.

15 mins, 31.2036, -7.8718

11 TELOUET KASBAH

A nineteenth-century fortress, once the stronghold of the Glaoui dynasty. Its walls are adorned with intricate tilework and ornate ceilings. The surrounding gardens feature ancient olive trees and cacti. Now a museum, the kasbah contains exhibits on the history of the Glaoui family and their reign. Nearby is a women's co-operative shop selling traditionally made carpets. At the time of writing, due to the 2023 earthquake, the kasbah was closed for renovations. Telouet Kasbah, P1506, Telouet, Morocco.

5 mins, 31.2865, -7.2367

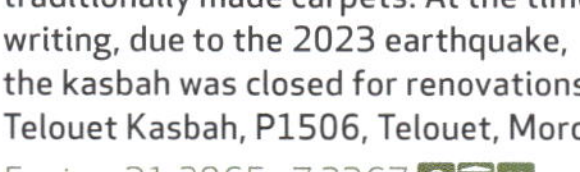

11

10

11

12 MEGDAZ

The ancient village of Megdaz is at the end of the road. The village is renowned for its traditional adobe architecture and scenic mountain views. Picturesque houses grow from the red rock on the mountainside. The contrast between orange trees, golden wheat and colourful schools on hillside slopes created a picturesque scene. Down on the village football pitch, children played with energy and passion, some barefoot, others in flip-flops, united in their joy. Two ancient kasbahs, one built 800 years ago and the other 200 years later, serve as a testament to the community's history and ingenuity. Originally constructed to protect families from rival villages that would pilfer their grain, these fortified structures still store food for the villagers. Everyone we met was warm and welcoming, and greeted us in either French or English. The village had a few small shops, a fruit and vegetable stand and a co-operative selling nuts – but surprisingly, no one sold bread. When we asked a shopkeeper about buying bread, he told us to come back later. We returned to find him waiting for us with a warm loaf from his own kitchen.

5 mins, 31.3912, -6.7926

13

14

CULTURAL HOTSPOTS

13 LE SAVO'ART FER

On our way to Setti Fatma, we stopped by this free art gallery and discovered Abdelhaq Elyoussi's creative genius. Created from recycled metal, his works have been displayed in Marrakech, London and Dubai. His sculptures, known for their dynamic and expressive forms, reflect Moroccan culture and daily life, as well as social issues such as climate damage.

KM 43 Asguine Road of Ourika; Al Haouz province. le-savoart-fer.com

2 mins, 31.3241, -7.7592

14 SETTI FATMA MAUSOLEUM

In the heart of the Ourika Valley, the village of Setti Fatma bears the name of a revered and enigmatic saint whose legacy has left an indelible mark on the region. The mausoleum is in a small, unassuming building on the mountainside overlooking the village. Despite the scarcity of historical records, traditions told a rich story of Setti Fatma, a pious woman remembered for her unwavering faith, wisdom and selflessness. The term 'Setti', used for female saints (analogous to 'Sidi' for males), signifies respect. Setti Fatma is celebrated for her miracle-working, including creating a spring that birthed the Seven Waterfalls of Ourika, plus solving marital and fertility problems.

Her tomb, alongside those of two of her daughters, remains a pilgrimage site where people seek blessings and spiritual solace. Annually, on 11 August, villagers gather to celebrate a moussem (festival) in her honour, reflecting her enduring influence and veneration. From the village of Setti Fatma, head E on the P2017, opposite the first house on the R cross the bridge (31.2244, -7.6819), follow the path through the woods for 200m; bearing L and walk 200m to the small red house on the hill.

10 mins, 31.2235, -7.6792

15 HOUSE OF SETTI FATMA

Not often highlighted in guidebooks, this site holds significant cultural and spiritual importance. Anyone can come and seek solace here; they will be fed and looked after, contributing only what they can afford. We were given soup, bread and tea; we donated some money. Three meals a day are cooked on ancient stone fires and someone is always here to talk to visitors. There were mattresses where people could stay overnight and pray. Walk 500m past end of village of Setti Fatma until you see a few houses and a red sign in Arabic on the R with an arrow; go through the open space and turn R towards the house.

1 min, 31.2233, -7.6875

ADVENTURES

16 BUREAU DES GUIDES VALLÉE D'OURIKA

Based in Setti Fatma, the team of 30 experienced official tour guides are available for any kind of hiking, walking and climbing in the Ourika Valley. Open from 9am to 7pm, seven days a week. WP 11 Bus Stop, P2017, Setti Fatma.
ourikatravels.com +212 663-292756

2 mins, 31.2257, -7.6748

VIEWPOINTS

17 OUKAÏMEDEN LOOKOUT POINT

Dominated by Jbel Toubkal, north Africa's highest peak at 4,167m, this is one of the best places to watch the sunset over the High Atlas. Toubkal's snow-capped summit contrasted with the twin peaks of Jbel Ouanoukrim and Jbel Aguelzim: the rugged giants created a striking silhouette against the early evening sky. We camped out in our campervan and woke up to a glorious sunrise. Unforgettable. From Oukaïmeden, turn first R up a narrow concrete road, which becomes a track for about 600m; you will see a roped-off with two information signs where you can take in the view.

3 mins, 31.2001, -7.8700

ROAD TRIPS

18 OUED ZAT VALLEY

To experience rural Morocco, we took a road trip through the towering peaks of Oued Zat Valley, green and lush, and full of olive groves, almond trees and fig orchards. The P2016 road follows the course of the river upwards, past isolated Amazigh villages. School children, women working in fields and laden donkeys were common sights. Variable road quality, with regular potholes. Motorhome accessible.

- To/from: P9 > OuedZatValley
- Distance:30km
- Roads: P2016
- Scenic stop-offs: Tighedouine Wednesday Souk (31.42775, -7.52526); Azgour Park – Imi N'Ouzerg – weir, food stalls during summer (31.34878, -7.49907); Picnic stop by river (31.3865, -7.5179); park and garden – small orchard and a part of the river dammed to create a small pool (31.3287, -7.4990); Café Azgour – riverside snacks (31.3492, -7.4988)

19

19 TIZI N'TICHKA PASS

Tizi n'Tichka crosses over the Atlas Mountains, connecting Marrakech with the Sahara. During the medieval period, the pass was an important trade route for merchants and travellers, including the renowned explorer and scholar Ibn Battuta, who traversed the area in the fourteenth century. The well-maintained road curved irresistibly towards the summit through a series of seemingly endless hairpin bends and switchbacks. At its peak, we were treated to vertiginous and breathtaking views of the surrounding mountains and valleys; we stopped to breathe in the vistas and take photos.

The pass is flanked by towering Atlas cedars and green pine forests, which thrive at this high altitude. Roadside cafés and stalls served tea, coffee and orange juice. The road is generally open year-round. However, from November to March access may be restricted by snow.

- To/from: Marrakech > Ouarzazate
- Distance:193km
- Elevation: 2,205m
- Roads: N9
- Scenic stop-offs: Tizi n'Tichka Pass summit (31.2858, -7.3808)

20 OUARZAZATE TO MEGDAZ

The drive north was like being in a film. Our route began appropriately at Atlas Film Studios and soon led us to a Tatooine-like landscape of orange sandy hills, which gradually transitioned to yellow with dark, Imperial-grey rocky peaks as we climbed far, far away up into the mountains. The sinuous road alternated between smooth tarmac and rough terrain. The Oued Tassaout River, enclosed with silver birch and orange groves, provided the cinematic backdrop. Villagers transported crops on donkeys across cultivated patchwork fields that completed the bucolic landscape.

- To/from: Ouarzazate > Megdaz
- Distance:100km
- Elevation: 1,160m to 1,900m
- Roads: N10, R307, unnamed road
- 31.2253, -6.8176

20

19

20

21

CAFÉS & EATERIES

21 CAFÉ HUSSAIN

First stop on N9 after leaving Marrakech on your way up to Tizi n'Tichka Pass. This café has great views down the valley from the roof terrace.

31.4855, -7.4316 £

PLACES TO STAY

22 LA CLÉ DES OLIVIERS

Shimmering in the morning sunlight beneath the canopy of olive trees, the very long, slender swimming pool at La Clé des Huiles beckoned. Day tickets available. En suite chalets and larger family bungalows are available for overnight stays. Kilometres 35 Route, Ourika 42452. lacledesoliviers.com +212 667-516455

31.3663, -7.7884 ££

23 AUBERGE DES JEUNESSES LES CASCADES

The hostel boasts panoramic views and is en route to the first of the Seven Cascades of Ourika. Saïd, our host, welcomes couples, singles and groups. Clean and spacious, quiet and peaceful, with excellent showers and facilities, including good Wi-Fi, so an excellent hangout for digital nomads. Saïd and his colleague Mohammed, a the house of Setti Fatma and mausoleum plus treks to all seven waterfalls. 8C3J68FG+WW, Setti-Fatma gitelescascades@gmail.com +212 707-4360…

31.2247, -7.6726 £

24 SETTI FATMA GUARDIAN PARKING

Campervans or motorhomes can park overnight in the car park at the end of the village for a small fee. No facilities.

31.2258, -7.6749 £

25 ESCALE FORÊT

Wild camp in a charming wood set within red, earthen hills with glorious views over the valley. From Marrakech head E on N9 for 45km; turn left down unnamed road (31.5434, -7.5351) for 800m; park on your R.

31.5477, -7.5289

26 MAISON D'HÔTES AGDAL

A much-needed stop-off on the way to Telouet Kasbah. The hotel has seven clean and spacious family rooms, along with four smaller rooms. In the gardens adorned with vines, we ate a delicious cumin-infused omelette, complemented with fried onions and tomatoes. The views of the surrounding mountains enhanced the flavour even further. 7M5C+9M8, Aït Ali Ouroho, Telouet 42252. From Telouet,

23

26

27

head SW on P1506 for 12km; hotel on the L. atlas.auberge@gmail.com +212 667-595952
31.2583, -7.3280 ££

27 DAR MEGDAZ

Reaching the hostel involved a moderate climb up the side of a small waterfall, but the breathtaking view from the terrace made it all worthwhile. From the rooftop, we enjoyed great views of the village. Breakfast was a delightful spread: freshly baked bread, eggs, olives, honey, jam and olive oil. Shared bathroom and free Wi-Fi. 96R5+2Q Megdaz. +212 697-277953
31.3901, -6.7905 £

26

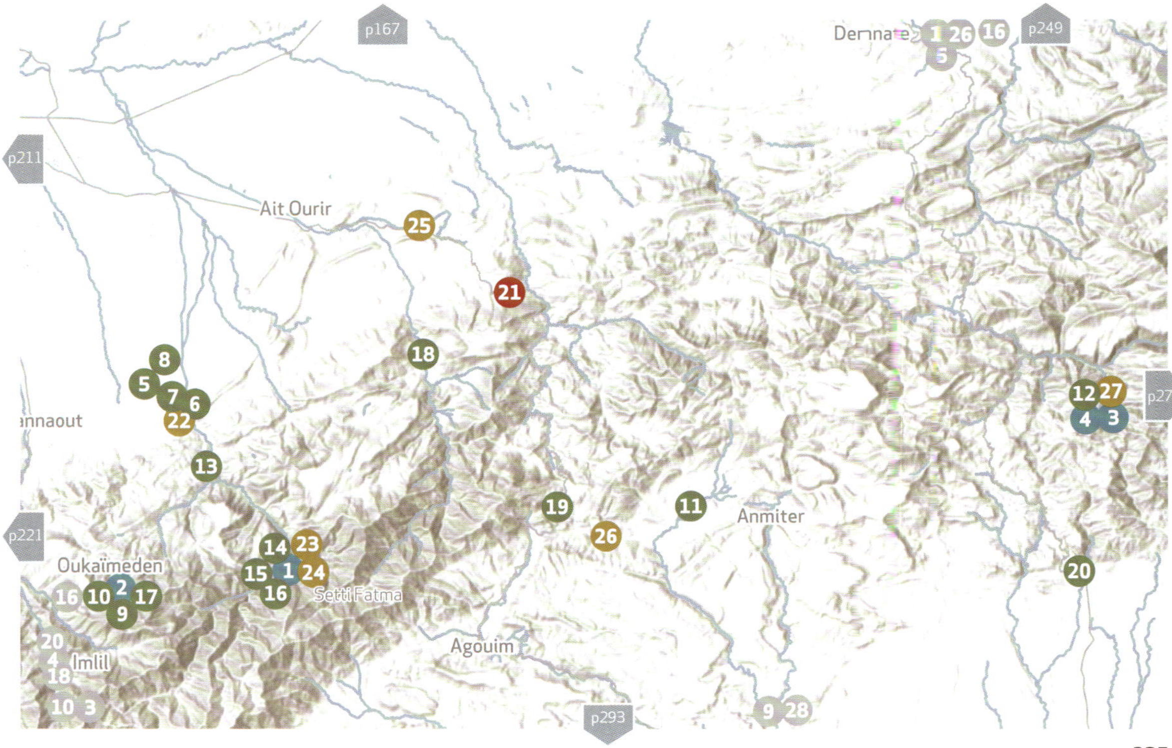

Demnate
Ait Ourir
Oukaïmeden
Setti Fatma
Imlil
Agouim
Anmiter

p167 p249 p211 p277 p221 p293

11

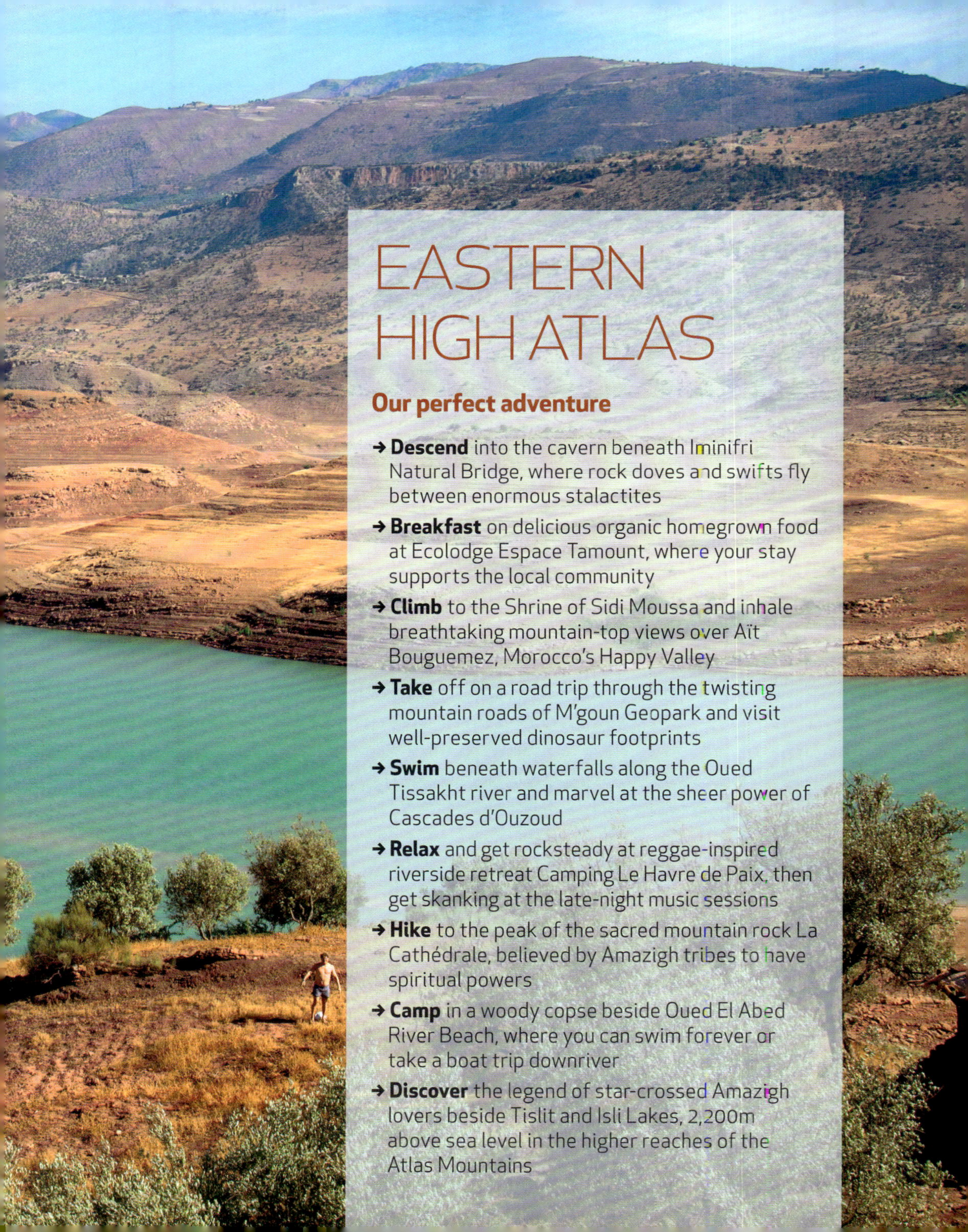

EASTERN HIGH ATLAS

Our perfect adventure

- **Descend** into the cavern beneath Iminifri Natural Bridge, where rock doves and swifts fly between enormous stalactites
- **Breakfast** on delicious organic homegrown food at Ecolodge Espace Tamount, where your stay supports the local community
- **Climb** to the Shrine of Sidi Moussa and inhale breathtaking mountain-top views over Aït Bouguemez, Morocco's Happy Valley
- **Take** off on a road trip through the twisting mountain roads of M'goun Geopark and visit well-preserved dinosaur footprints
- **Swim** beneath waterfalls along the Oued Tissakht river and marvel at the sheer power of Cascades d'Ouzoud
- **Relax** and get rocksteady at reggae-inspired riverside retreat Camping Le Havre de Paix, then get skanking at the late-night music sessions
- **Hike** to the peak of the sacred mountain rock La Cathédrale, believed by Amazigh tribes to have spiritual powers
- **Camp** in a woody copse beside Oued El Abed River Beach, where you can swim forever or take a boat trip downriver
- **Discover** the legend of star-crossed Amazigh lovers beside Tislit and Isli Lakes, 2,200m above sea level in the higher reaches of the Atlas Mountains

'Atlas, whose strength is beyond measure, who supports the heavens and the stars.'

Pindar, Odes

The Iminifri Natural Bridge, near Demnate, is a rock arch, sculpted over millennia by the underground currents of the Tisslet River. This colossal structure forms a massive tunnel, home to swifts, rock doves and artistic stalactites. After climbing over narrow plateaus, we emerged into sunlight at the lower end of the bridge to find natural rock pools, where we joined local youngsters for a refreshing dip in the cool waters.

Perhaps the most famous natural attraction in the Eastern High Atlas is the Cascades d'Ouzoud, a spectacular series of enormous waterfalls that plunge from more than 100m into rocky pools below. Situated near Tanaghmeilt, these falls offer hiking trails that follow the river upstream. Our explorations took us further downstream, revealing smaller, less-frequented cascades and secluded natural swimming pools. We stopped for tea with 'Rasta Mohamed' at a reggae-themed café before trekking further to discover hidden pools and a 'mystic' cave where two rivers meet in a brackish confluence.

The brilliant turquoise waters of the vast Bin El Ouidane reservoir stood in stark contrast to the surrounding red hills and the pink glow of evening skies. A popular destination for water sports, fishing and boating, we watched as teenage boys dived from a floating pontoon; they invited us to share a homemade, lakeside tagine. Along the banks of Oued El Abid, which feeds the lake, we found a shaded river beach beneath tall pines, where boatmen offer river trips.

Ain Asserdoun, with its ornate gardens, natural springs, fountains and the historical Castle of Béni Mellal, sits high above the city, offering panoramic views over the plains and mountains. Water cascades down aqueducts to supply the town below. Meanwhile, in the Imsfrane Gorge, we marvelled at 'La Cathédrale', an imposing rock formation whose towering cliffs resemble cathedral spires. Campers flock to this gorge, both in organised sites and wild camping spots, surrounded by tall oleander bushes and the flowing river. A solo, Moroccan, female hiker joined us on a lively trek climbing waterfalls and paddling through the shallow waters of the lower gorge.

Finally, we ascended to the Haut Atlas Oriental National Park, 2,200m above sea level, to discover the 'Lakes of Love'. According to legend, these twin lakes, Isli and Tislit, were formed from the tears of two star-crossed Amazigh lovers, their eternal bond immortalised.

MOUNTAINS & HIKES

1 IMINIFRI NATURAL BRIDGE

Descending into the small gorge of the Iminifri Natural Bridge revealed a landscape where massive boulders were seemingly piled haphazardly by giants. A river trickled down between the rocks, while swifts and doves darted above us. Trailing ferns draped the cliffside, interspersed with intricate stalactites and a tapestry of green stone. Beneath the natural bridge over the river waters, a vast red rock tunnel was filled with cool air and the echo of bird calls. Careful navigation over slippery rocks led to a ledge at the far side of the cave where the cavern's enormity became evident. Steps descended into the depths where streams fed small pools and waterfalls and clusters of moss coloured the rocks. The climb back to the road consisted of 213 steps and conveniently placed benches provided resting spots for weary feet. Guides are available at the top of the bridge though not strictly necessary. Negotiate prices beforehand. From the parking spot in Iminifri (31.7241, -6.9715), walk 10m to the W until you see a gate and a path leading down to the cave; guides are available if needed.

5 mins, 31.7242, -6.9714

2 LA CATHÉDRALE IMSFRANE

Known for its unique rock formations made up of limestone and dolomite and sumptuous scenery, Imsfrane is a popular destination for trekkers and nature lovers. The mountain resembles a vast cathedral, hence the nickname, La Cathédrale. The hike to the peak typically takes about two to three hours, depending on the route taken, and offers breathtaking views over the village of Tilouguite and the Targa Valley below. Imsfrane is home to a variety of flora and fauna, including olive trees, juniper trees and several species of birds. The area was considered sacred by Amazigh tribes, who believed the mountain had spiritual powers. The ascent can be dangerous and it's easy to lose your way. We recommend you contact the local guide Farid (+212 678-039407), as you can easily get stuck on the mountain and be unable to find your way up or down. If you don't fancy a trek up the mountain, drive up the mountain track near Maison d'Hôte Dar Tawda for a wonderful viewpoint. We found a couple of benches and a table to have a picnic while we took in the beauty of our surroundings. We walked over the hill behind the hotel for a sublime sunset. Follow the R302 towards Imsfrane (be aware that this road is in bad condition in places and deteriorates to a stony track towards the end): turn R up a dirt track (31.9942, -6.1561); drive round the narrow twisting track for 2.7km until you see the picnic spot on your R.

2 mins, 31.9900, -6.1516 (viewpoint)

3 GORGES DE L'OUED AHANSAL

A natural wonder characterised by dramatic rock formations and the meandering Ahansal River. Rich in biodiversity; resilient juniper trees, wildflowers and hardy shrubs thrive in the challenging conditions. From October to April, the gorge attracts rafting enthusiasts for adrenaline-fuelled rides (berberraftingadventures.com). During the summer, when water levels recede, explore the gorge on foot. Bring water shoes. Park at Chez

Said Aziz (31.9880, -6.1254); turn off R302 (31.9880, -6.1242) and walk towards the river keeping the line of trees on your R; after 60m you will see a path with a steep bank on the L; follow the well-marked path by the side of the river for 1.5km until river turns sharp R and you will see gorges; walk alongside the river the gorge.

60 mins, 31.9755, -6.1147

4 PASSAGE BERBÈRE

We didn't undertake this trek. It looked far too scary. Our courageous Moroccan friend Zineb did and this is her report (not for the vertiginous): 'A narrow, challenging path carved into the towering cliffs. This remote area is defined by its sheer landscapes – limestone cliffs and deep gorges – and provides a breathtaking yet intimidating environment for hikers and climbers. Historically, paths such as this were used by the indigenous Amazigh people to navigate the rugged terrain, linking isolated communities. Setting off early, with no safety equipment in sight, we began our journey from the village of Taghia. The hike to the Passage Berbère took two hours and the path, barely wide enough for a single person, was nerve-wracking. The drop below was more than 300m and, at one point, fear gripped me so tightly I couldn't move. Thankfully, Soulaimane, our guide and a local climbing enthusiast, helped me through, turning a terrifying experience into a personal triumph. Though Taghia is largely unknown to foreign adventurers, its peaks, including Timghazine, offered incredible challenges. Next time, I hope to tackle the passage alone, but I'm aware of the risks. Proper hiking shoes and sticks are essential for anyone attempting this demanding, yet rewarding, journey.' (Zineb Khaidach). From Taghia follow track SE towards Gîte Taoujdate Taghia and turn right before gîte; follow dry river path for 80m to end of a piece of rocky ground; turn L following a rabbit path through the trees; then head up the side of the mountain; trekking guide strongly recommended (Soulaimane +212 657-875223)

120 mins, 31.7769, -6.0702

5 AÏT BOUGUEMEZ

Also known as 'Happy Valley', this is a wonder of nature and the starting point for treks and cultural discoveries. The area is known for its apples, barley, wheat, apricots and figs, and medicinal plants. We spoke to Victor Demurs, who spent some time with fellow Canadian students volunteering in the valley: 'We spent a day with local rammed earth artisans, learning about the building technique. After working, we shared a meal and tea on a wooden plank. We also spent a day in the mountains with a young shepherd who guided us through grazing areas. The quality of the sheep's diet

directly influenced the quality of their wool. Our experience continued at a women's co-operative, where we observed the intricate wool processing, from shearing to weaving carpets. Each stage revealed the artisans' skills and the traditional tools still in use. Finally, we trekked to M'Goun Peak. Supported by a dedicated team, we embraced the challenge of the ascent and revelled in the breathtaking views at the summit.' If you're interested in any of the activities in the Aït Bouguemez region, contact Anne at Alliance Berbère (allianceberbere.com).
31.6447, -6.4672

RIVERS & LAKES

6 IMINIFRI NATURAL POOLS

At the end of the Iminifri Natural Bridge, we found some rock pools where boys took advantage of the cool sweet water to swim beneath oleander bushes and between huge boulders. Further downstream, there were more pools, where the water was salty. A small shack at the end of the cave sold tea and snacks. The pools are at the end of the Iminifri Natural Bridge walk or you can walk down the 213 steps by the parking spot.
10 mins, 31.7228, -6.9715

7 CASCADES D'OUZOUD

Huge and impressive waterfalls well worth chasing. However, the main falls were very touristy, with a vast array of cafés and restaurants to provide refreshment while visitors marvel at their magnificence. We prefer things a bit wilder and more adventurous, so we walked down the steep path past the trinket shops to find the smaller falls. Among the oleander bushes and flora are small riverside campsites and cafés. We swam at the first falls in a big natural pool (easy entry through Camping Africa). The intense power of the falls made for a joyous and energising swim, as well as a proper workout, as we tried to swim beneath the torrent of water. The further we walked along the river, the wilder the place got. Keep an eye out for monkeys. Paid parking near the main falls for a small fee; we drove to at the end of the cul-de-sac and parked on the road where there were green and white markings (32.0143, -6.7188 free parking); from the bridge over Oued Tissakht, face downstream and turn R then first L; at the end of the cul-de-sac, follow the concrete path down to stalls, then go R towards the main falls or downwards towards the river for the small falls and beyond.
15 mins, 32.0170, -6.7241

11

9

8

8 HAWAII NATURAL POOL

A deep natural pool and waterfall further downstream of Ouzoud. There was a six-metre rock to jump from; we watched a local jump first. Cross to the opposite side of the river from Camping Le Havre de Paix; climb up to the higher path and follow for 750m; turn down steps on L to Hawaii pool.

10 mins, 32.0244, -6.7282

9 LES GROTTES DE CASCADES D'OUZOUD

Stalactites and a large rock in the shape of a shark's mouth filled the centre of this ten-metre-high cave. The silence was palpable and we were impressed by the artistic formations of nature. Some stalactites have reached the floor to form powerful columns. From the opening, we could see a brackish line in the river where the river Oued Tissakht and a tributary meet – one green, one brown. From Hawaii Natural Pool, follow the river and the yellow arrows to the end where you come to a round flat area like a T-junction where you overlook the meeting of the two rivers; you are now standing above the cave; climb down the rocks to the right facing the rivers and come back to the left, and you will see the opening.

30 mins, 32.0285, -6.7272

10 OUED EL ABED RIVER BEACH

A picturesque destination, perfect for a swim and a relaxing day out. Upon arrival, we found a shaded wooded area to plot up and escape the sun's rays. As we slipped into the water, we were surrounded by lush greenery and towering cliffs. We took a moment to lie on our backs to gaze up at the sky, painting the landscape with warm hues. We camped overnight and bought our own food and water, as there were limited options on site. The access road was a tight squeeze in the van but the swim was well worth it. Guided boat tours of the river available. The current can be strong due to the nearby dam. From the Barrage Bin El Ouidane Dam, head W on N25 toward R306 for 2.4km; take the turning on the L (32.1081, -6.4853) and follow the road downhill for 280m until you find a place to park.

2 mins, 32.1070, -6.4850

11 BARRAGE BIN EL OUIDANE

At 1,700m high up in the High Atlas Mountains, this mesmerising turquoise reservoir stretches its tentacles invitingly around the orange hillsides: a great spot for paddleboarding. No shade, no facilities and no lifeguards, so we took plenty of water, snacks and sun hats. We found a pontoon and some pebbly ground to get in the water as the bank was muddy in some places. We arrived at the same time as a group of teenage boys, who promptly started jumping and diving in. They had two tagine pots on the go and invited us to eat with them. From Bin El Ouidane, head SE on R306 for 5km; turn R at 40 speed sign just before bridge (32.1126, -6.4171); drive 850m down rocky track to lakeside and park (32.10594, -6.41749); walk W for 1km and turn L towards pontoons for 150m.

15 mins, 32.1017, -6.4239

11

12 CASCADES D'AKAHOUDEN

The clearly defined trail to this little-known but picturesque waterfall took us alongside the river Oued Ahansal, lined with pink oleander trees. The path turned upwards into woods past pine, carob and wild olives. Tiny waterfalls tumbled over rugged limestone as we climbed. The final clamber led us to our prize. As for Gorges de l'Oued Ahansal, continue following the path as it turns upwards; keep the tributary on your RH side; finally, after 600m cross the water and climb over rocks to reach the waterfall.

100 mins, 31.9794, -6.1107

13 TISLIT LAKE

There she lay, radiant and resplendent; a sapphire cradled in the rugged folds of the grey Atlas Mountains. According to Amazigh legend, Tislit, a young woman from the Aït Yaâza tribe, fell deeply in love with Isli, a shepherd from the neighbouring Aït Brahim tribe. Their love was forbidden by their feuding families (sound familiar?). Yet, they couldn't resist their passion and would secretly meet at a spring between their homes. Unable to bear the constant

10

12

separation, the Amazigh Romeo and Juliet fled into the mountains where their tears of sorrow formed the two lakes, now known as Tislit and Isli, symbols of their undying love. Overwhelmed with despair, they drowned themselves in the lakes rather than live apart. Moved by the tragedy, the tribes eventually reconciled. In honour of the lovers, an annual moussem (festival) is held in the region, where young people from the once acrimonious tribes are encouraged to meet and form connections, to atone for the long-ago feud that kept the lovers apart. If you camp by the lakes, some say that on moonlit nights, you can see the spirits of Tislit and Isli rise from the waters, reunited in death as they could never be in life. Follow N12 S from El Ksiba for 107km; the road is good but gets increasingly steep, with hairpin bends up to the lake; bear R round the lake past the Auberge Camping Amskou Imilchil on the R; a small gravel path on your L leads to the lake.

3 mins, 32.1929, -5.6338

14 LAKE ISLI

Turquoise-blue and rumoured to be 100m deep, Lake Isli sat among brown mountain peaks. Herds of white sheep and black goats followed their shepherds towards the water's edge. Lola took a dip in this wild and lonely lake. See Lake Tislit for the legend. Directions as for Tislit Lake (118), but follow the track to the other side of lake where it meets at a T-junction with a stoney track; turn R and follow the track for 9km until you see Lake Isli; park where you can and walk down to the lake.

3 mins, 32.2216, -5.5498

15 AIN ASSERDOUN, BÉNI-MELLAL

A freshwater spring and water source for the city of Béni-Mellal, channelled through a cascade on garden terraces. The spring has been a vital water source for centuries, contributing to the region's agricultural prosperity. The site includes landscaped gardens, waterfalls, walking paths and the historical Castle of Béni Mellal, which overlooks the spring. We saw groups of young boys escaping the summer sun by damming up small pools and jumping in. Free entry. Le Circuit Touristique, Béni Mellal. Paid parking (32.3230, -6.3402) for 5dh.

5 mins, 32.3250, -6.3356

ANCIENT

16 DINOSAUR FOOTPRINTS

M'goun Geopark covers more than 5,000km2 of the High Atlas Mountains. The area features diverse geological formations such as limestone plateaus, deep gorges and ancient Mesozoic sedimentary rock formations that revealed its

17

prehistoric marine environment. A significant site is a set of well-preserved dinosaur footprints that can be clearly seen in the red clay. The 30x25cm prints were made by a megalosaurus, a bipedal theropod (three-toed) dinosaur, a very, very long time ago. From Iminifri, head E on R302 for 7km; park on L by gates (31.7264, -6.9086); walk 100m to the house and ask for the key; you will be let in to view the prints for 10dh.

2 mins, 31.7265, -6.9087

17 SHRINE OF SIDI MOUSSA

Sitting 200m atop a natural circular pyramid, this agadir (granary) was constructed about 200 years ago to protect the riches of three surrounding villages. The granary boasted 34 rooms, each equipped with strong wooden doors locked with intricate wooden keys, which would have stored grain, dried foodstuffs and important documents. The granary also contained the tomb of Sidi Moussa, a Jewish saint (marabout) believed to have worked in the area and possessed special healing skills. The Amazigh tribes venerated Sidi Moussa, and women still visit the site to pray for fertility and tie ribbons or wool to the door as an offering. A wooden ladder led to the roof from where the guardians had a 360-degree bird's eye view to spot potential threats from other villages or tribes. A small fee for entry, mint tea and a guided tour. From Alliance Berbère, drive past the house on the L; turn L at the small track towards the house with red garage doors; turn L up the rabbit path towards the red-and-white communication antenna/pylon; walk up the path to the summit.

30 mins, 31.6585, -6.4333

18 CASTLE OF BÉNI MELLAL

A seventeenth-century fortress built by the Alawite Sultan Moulay Ismail in a strategic location from where he could look out for invaders and monitor activity in the city of Béni-Mellal below. Directions as for Ain Asserdoun; look for the path leading up to the kasbah opposite the park.

10 mins, 32.3243, -6.3376

ROAD TRIPS

19 IMINIFRI BRIDGE TO AÏT BOUGUEMEZ

Setting off from Iminifri Bridge, the road twisted and turned alongside rugged mountains and rocky terrain that had once formed an ancient seabed. Approaching M'goun Geopark, we crested the brow of a hill and suddenly a vast valley sprawled out before us, the road winding elegantly with steep ascents and heart-pounding drops. Sparse villages dotted the landscape. The rocky terrain transformed

17

18

20

20

21

22

into dark-red soil adorned with silver-leaved olive trees, almond trees and fields of cereal crops. Aleppo pines clung to the mountainside. In need of a beverage and a rest, we stopped in Aït Blal Village; where we bought olives, nuts and raisins and were warmly welcomed. In a linguistic mishap, Lola requested tea 'with mint' (b'nana) and the owner, eager to assist, disappeared and soon returned with a kilo of bananas (banaanaat). As we ascended in altitude, the landscape shifted dramatically. The fertile land gave way to oak and juniper trees, along with alpine meadows. The quality of the road deteriorated and demanded our full attention. Finally, we arrived at Aït Bouguemez, affectionately known as 'Happy Valley'. The scenery was filled with fields and orchards and the M'goun River snaked through the landscape.

- To/from: Iminifri Natural Bridge > AïtBouguemez
- Distance: 64km
- Roads: R302
- Stop-offs: Aït Blal for drinks and snacks (31.6912, -6.7170)

20 AÏT BOUGUEMEZ VALLEY TO OUZOUD

From Aït Bouguemez, the mountain road passed through ancient villages and agricultural terraces. We took the well-maintained R302 via Tamda. As we climbed higher into the mountains, we were met with a procession of trucks, all overloaded with onions. After a seemingly endless descent, we finally reached the bottom of the valley, where a tiny stream trickled alongside us. The road seemed disinterested in fulfilling its function and disintegrated, leaving only a narrow strip of Tarmac at its centre. We ascended the opposite side of the valley, entering a new landscape populated by plane trees and a thickly spread layer of yellow gorse. We stopped for coffee and watched the world go by in the little town of Aït M'Hamed on market day (Thursday). The road reverted to its narrow but well-surfaced state, albeit with a massive drop on one side, as we continued towards the Ouzoud Falls.

- To/from: Aït Bouguemez Valley > Ouzoud Waterfalls
- Distance: 100km
- Roads: R302, P3105
- Stop-offs:Aït M'Hamed for refreshments (31.8782, -6.4738); panoramic view (32.0072, -6.6650)

21 BÉNI MELLAL TO LAKE TISLIT

As we set off on the N8 from Béni-Mellal, silver olive groves flanked the road. After an hour, we reached Taghbalout, a forest with springs, a lake and a children's playground. Driving higher, we stopped occasionally at viewpoints to admire the mountains behind us. The road was well-maintained with two lanes and soon we descended into a green valley where people were harvesting their crops. The earth here was yellow and the mud houses blended seamlessly into the landscape. As we ascended ever higher, the trees began to thin and the mountains' colour transitioned from yellow to grey. Gradually, great folds emerged in the terrain and the road narrowed and became steeper. The twists and turns grew sharper and all vegetation vanished. Just when we thought we'd reached the sky, we turned a bend where Tislit Lake shimmered beneath us.

- Length 160km
- Road:N12
- Elevation:620to 2,119m
- Stop off: Taghbalout (32.5545, -6.0144)

22 OUED EL ABED VIEWPOINT

Great viewpoint along the gorges of the Oued el Abed river. Directions as for Dar l'Eau Vive, stop at top of road before hotel.

1 min, 32.1081, -6.48102

CAFÉS & EATERIES

23 AÏT BLAL CAFÉ

One of the few options for a cup of tea or coffee on the R302 en route to Aït Bouguemez. The shop next door sold olives, nuts and sugary snacks.

31.6912, -6.7170

24 CAMPING LE HAVRE DE PAIX

Sitting beside one of Ouzoud's waterfalls, this reggae-inspired retreat has been a haven for relaxation and revelry for 20 years, thanks to Rasta Mohamed's dedication. The colourful restaurant and campsite were a feast for the senses, with its bright-red, gold and green hues. Unwind for a day or two, or simply stop for a mint tea and a dip in the natural pools. Inside, a room filled with musical instruments awaited their next night of use. Amenities were basic but comfortable; separate facilities for toilets and showers. Campers will feel at home, with options to bring your own tent for a fee, including breakfast. Cabins also available. Whatever your choice, you'll be surrounded by good vibes. Walk 230m downstream from small waterfall by Cascades d'Ouzoud.
+212 067-0402257

32.0188, -6.7245

25 DAR L'EAU VIVE

We had an excellent lunch overlooking the river. Staff were attentive and welcoming. Small cabins of wood and bamboo clung to the mountainside, with verandas lined with flowers and olive trees. Kayaks available to rent. N° 84, Maison d'Hôte Dar l'Eau Vive, Dr Zitone, Bin El Ouidane 22200.
darleauvive.com +212 666-642183

32.1070, -6.4791

24

24

PLACES TO STAY

26 ECOLODGE ESPACE TAMOUNT

A unique project combining sustainable tourism with community development. Comfortable en-suite rooms. Camping and campervan parking is available. Large, shady garden with tables for dining. The ecolodge was mainly self-sufficient, generating power through solar panels and producing its own olives and vegetables. Built entirely with local materials and artisans, the ecolodge supports the community through employment and the sale of handmade carpets. A small museum traces humanity's development from the Stone Age and a large meeting space hosts community projects such as music lessons.
International charities base their operations here to work with rural mountain communities.
Km 6,5, Iminifri, Demnat 22300
+212 668-498677

31.7244, -6.9674

27 CHEZ HAMED RAHICH

Basic gîte and campsite on the R302. Very picturesque surroundings of red mountains. Douar Iglouane, Ait Bouli.
+212 659-384868

31.6160, -6.5810

26

29

30

31

28 CAMPING TAGHBALOUTE

Simple auberge and campsite by the river with space for a small campervan. Douar Iglouane, Ait Bouli. +212 668-394887

31.6163, -6.5809

29 ALLIANCE BERBÈRE

A stylish house from which the family farm a flock of an endangered variety of sheep, bred specifically for the quality of their wool. The landscaped courtyard features vines, herbs and plants used for making tea. Organic food was varied, creative and delicious. Rooms are tastefully designed in natural colours. Call in advance to arrange activities and food preferences. Anne, the owner, has contacts with local guides who organise short and multi-day treks. Alliance Berbère, Imelghas, Vallée des Aït Bouguemez, Tabant 22450 allianceberbere.com +212 618-322429

31.6638, -6.4279

30 LE DOMAINE M

Comfortable hotel above the Ouzoud Falls. Chef Fatima made a mean vegetarian pasta and a first-class breakfast. Lovely swimming pool, especially when it was illuminated at night. Cascades d'Ouzoud 22000. +212 661-931677

32.0105, -6.7273

31 DAR DIAFA

Two apartments with wonderful views over the reservoir. Hicham and his wife provided meals, a washing service and did everything they could to ensure that we had a pleasant stay. We scrambled down the hill for a cheeky swim in the lake (32.1025, -6.4411). The entry was muddy, but the water was smooth and luxurious. R306, Marruecos. From Bin El Ouidane, head SE on R306 for 2km; turn off R (32.1068, -6.4419) down a steep and narrow track to the house +212 616-734171 (Abdul).

32.1072, -6.4403

32 MAISON D'HÔTE DAR TAWDA

If you're looking for a peaceful hotel with incredible mountain views, this is the place to come. The house is decorated with varnished pine and the eco-domes in the garden are stylish. Saïd was a wonderful host and his wife, Malika, an excellent cook; her orange cornbread with homegrown apricot jam was delicious. In the garden, they grew onions, tomatoes, peppers, courgettes, corn and pomegranates. We parked our campervan and used the hotel facilities. The access road was too narrow for a motorhome. Cathédrale Imsfrane, Tilouguite 22602. Follow the R302 towards Imsfrane (be aware that this road is in bad condition in places and deteriorates to a stony track towards the end: turn R up a dirt track (31.9942, -6.1561); drive round the narrow twisting track for 2.7km until you see Dar Tawda on your R. dartawda.ma contact@dartawda.ma +212 661-897813

31.9905, -6.1525

33 CAMPING CATHÉDRALE IMSFRANE

Campsite by the Oued Ahansal offered a rustic experience. Wild camping spots could be found on the other side of the river. The valley was full of towering pine trees, bright-pink oleander bushes, some the size of small houses. Adjacent to the campsite, there was an area suitable for parking a campervan. On the opposite side of the campsite lay an abandoned wood factory, notable for its derelict red truck, which has become a curious tourist attraction. XVR8+C3, Temga. +212 667-772551

31.9927, -6.1367

34 CHEZ SAID AZIZ

Simple budget auberge and campsite without electricity or mod cons, but fantastic views of La Cathédrale Imsfrane in the heart of the countryside. Run by a kind and friendly owner. From Tifouina, head NE on R302 for 30km; turn L off R302 on to track (31.9880, -6.1264); continue for 100m. +212 667-226935

31.9880, -6.1254

35 GÎTE TAGHIA ZOUHAIRI

Run by Saïd Zouhairi and his family, this gîte offers budget-friendly accommodation in the picturesque village of Taghia. Featuring traditional home-cooked meals made from locally sourced ingredients and unlimited mint tea. Rooms had en suite bathrooms and free Wi-Fi. Saïd, an experienced guide, can organise treks and climbs tailored to your needs and

32

33

34

provide local information. The gîte supports sustainable tourism through its use of local resources and promotion of low-impact activities. Call ahead to arrange your itinerary and dietary requirements. From Zaouiat Ahansal either walk or drive the 7km winding piste to Taghia. Public transport: CTM bus from Beni Millal to Azilal, from there by transport rural Mercedes 207 to Taghia
gite-taghia.com +212 656-647507
31.7869, -6.0728 £

36 MAISON D'HOTES AÏT BOU IZRYANE

A homage to art and recycling. The decoration at this family-run hotel, just outside Béni Mellal, was quirky, eclectic and amazing, lovingly created by the host, Ali. Well worth a visit just as an exhibition of modern art. The rooms are large and colourful, with walk-in showers and sofas. All food was grown and prepared on-site, including bread, jam and olives, and was of the highest quality. Call ahead to specify dietary requirements. Coffee was traditionally-made with added spices and herbs to keep the body healthy. Free Wi-Fi, private parking and facilities for disabled guests. Bicycle rental, cookery classes, walking tours and many other activities can be organised with advance notice.
Highly recommended. Timoulilte 22700.
+212 662-681618
32.2167, -6.4658 ££

37 AUBERGE CAMPING AMSKOU IMILCHIL

Set on a hillside above Tislit Lake. Rooms are en suite and spotlessly clean, as is the dining room. Campervans and tents can stay on the veranda, and an Amazigh-style tent was on the lower level. Saïd, a former trekking guide, was kind and helpful and dished up good food.
Bikes were available for hire and guides for treks of more than two days can be organised to the three surrounding summits and Lake Isli. R317, Imilchil 52403. +212 668-518479.
32.1901, -5.6387 £

36

36

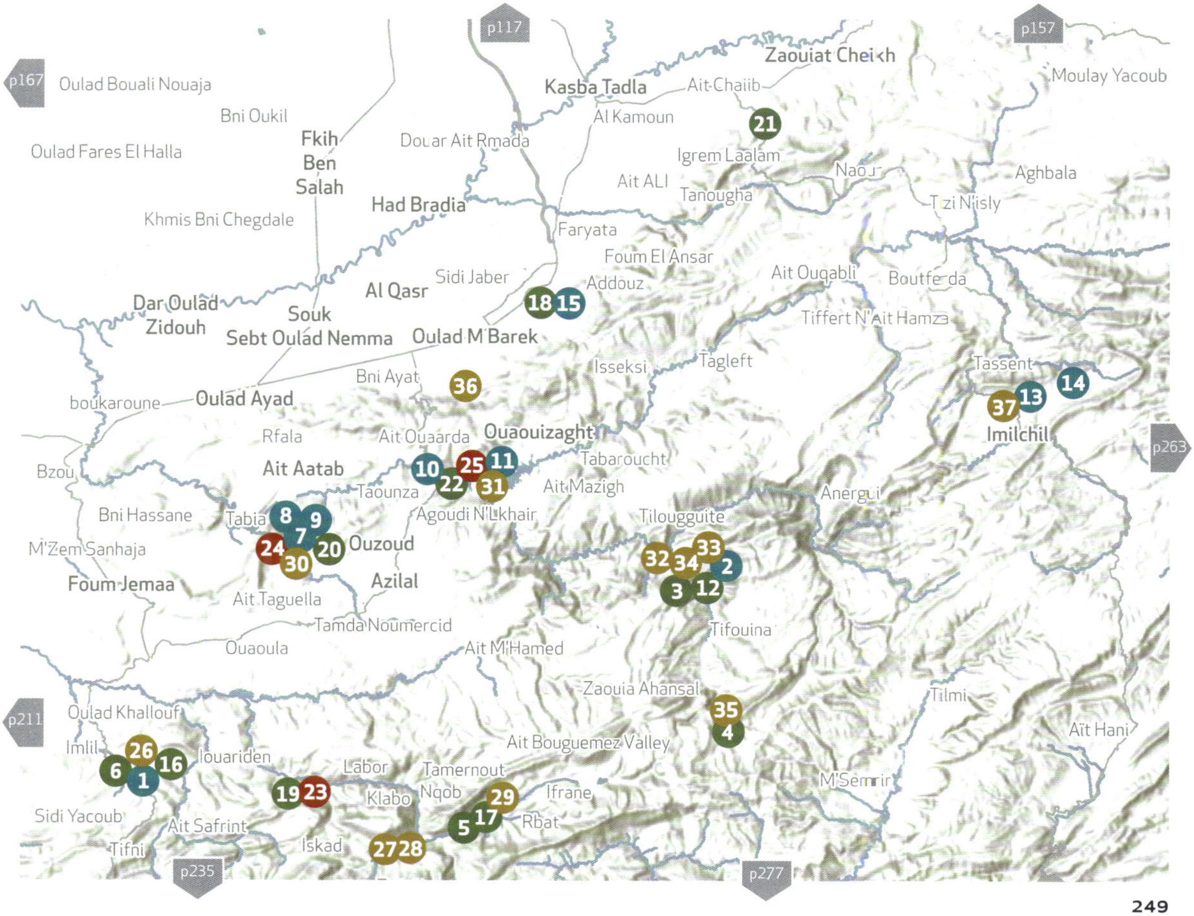

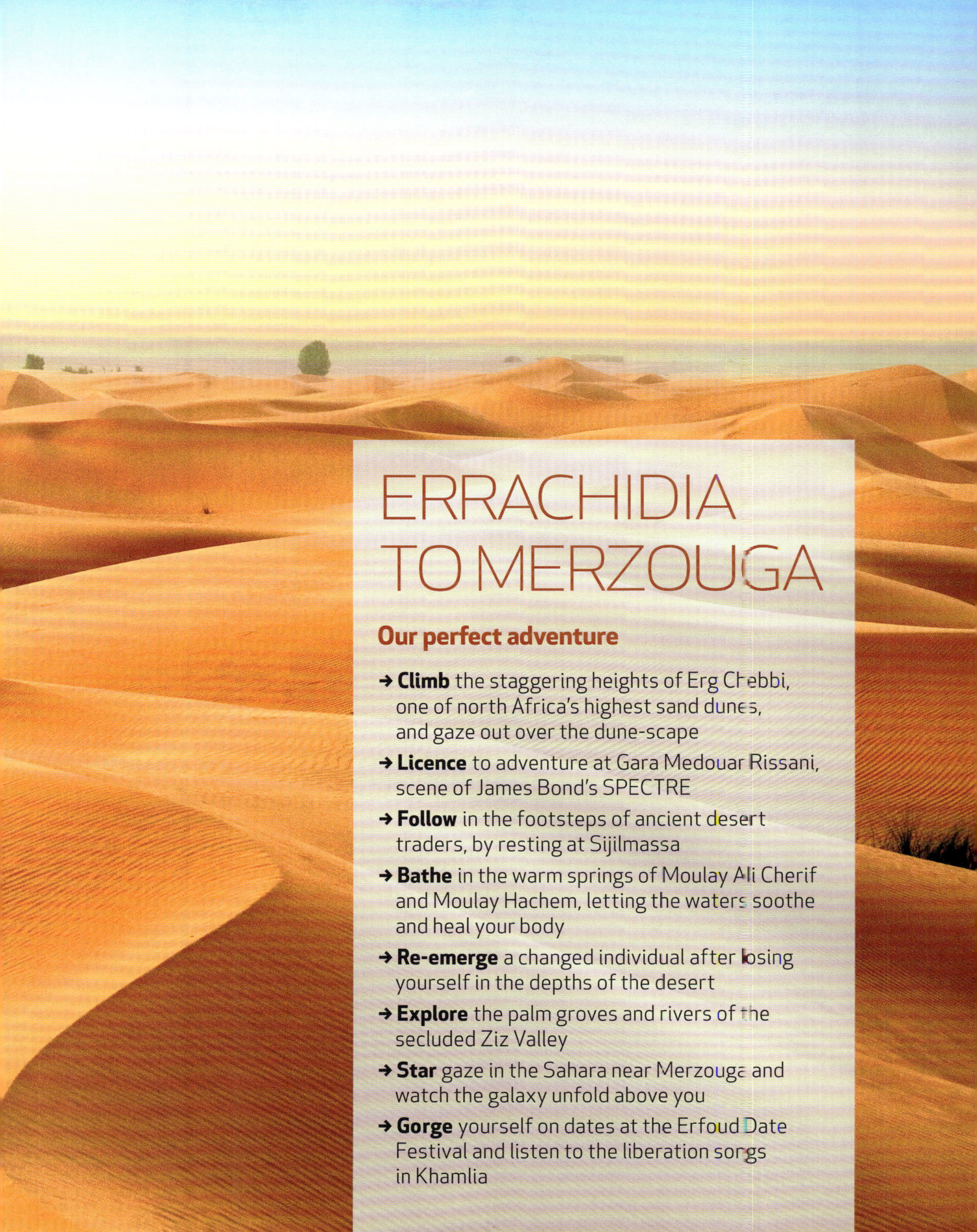

ERRACHIDIA TO MERZOUGA

Our perfect adventure

- **Climb** the staggering heights of Erg Chebbi, one of north Africa's highest sand dunes, and gaze out over the dune-scape
- **Licence** to adventure at Gara Medouar Rissani, scene of James Bond's SPECTRE
- **Follow** in the footsteps of ancient desert traders, by resting at Sijilmassa
- **Bathe** in the warm springs of Moulay Ali Cherif and Moulay Hachem, letting the waters soothe and heal your body
- **Re-emerge** a changed individual after losing yourself in the depths of the desert
- **Explore** the palm groves and rivers of the secluded Ziz Valley
- **Star** gaze in the Sahara near Merzouga and watch the galaxy unfold above you
- **Gorge** yourself on dates at the Erfoud Date Festival and listen to the liberation songs in Khamlia

'My road leads into the desert. I can see it. If you'll have us, we will come.'

Paul Atreides, Dune Part One

Merzouga and its northern neighbour, Sijilmassa, were the ancient gateways to the Sahara, with the latter representing the terminus of the trans-Saharan trade routes, linking north Africa with sub-Saharan Africa. Sijilmassa flourished for centuries, serving as a melting pot of cultures and a testament to the economic prowess of medieval Morocco. We followed the path of silks and precious gems from the medina of Marrakech to the sands of the Sahara over high mountains and through the clutches and dramatic backdrops of river valleys.

The Oued Ziz has carved its way across this landscape over millions of years, creating vast canyons and gorges that leave deep, beautiful scars on the face of this region. Vast, verdant palm groves follow the lines of the river, adding another layer to the colour palette of the Ziz Valley, starkly contrasting with the deep red of the surrounding rock walls. Rivers such as these give life in tough landscapes and here is no different. Ancient kasbahs and villages such as Kasbah Amjjouj and Ifri line the course of the Oued Ziz, their ruined magnificence a reminder of fallen fastnesses, while the intricately decorated porticos of Bab Jdid stand testament to an ancient skill and beauty. Alternatively, take a break from historical introspection and bathe yourself in the natural thermal springs at Moulay Ali Cherif, whose waters are claimed to be remedies for a wide array of ailments.

Soaring high up the skyline, the sandy dunes of Erg Chebbi stand defiantly, mirroring the rocky peaks of the nearby mountains that make up the border with Algeria. These dunes don't seem to fit in with reality, appearing to be painted, almost cartoon-like on the landscape, an artist's afterthought rather than part of the original design. Standing over 150m tall, Erg Chebbi is a sight not to be missed, literally or figuratively. Danny took a quad bike tour into the heart of the dunes, where even camels cannot venture due to the steep slopes. Over the roar of the engine, nothing was audible, yet when he paused on a peak, silence descended squarely upon his head. Yesterday's gusts carved enticing curves through the sands, only to be erased by the winds of tomorrow. The vast seasonal waters of Dayet Srij were also visible from its peak, a resting place for avian migrants and an ancient watering hole for camel herders. In the valleys of the dunes, where great walls of sand obscured the horizon, the only signs of life were tiny bushes, stoically clinging on in this harsh environment or the occasional, tiny, hopping footprints of an unknown bird, tracking its way across the dunes.

RIVERS, LAKES & OASES

1 MOULAY ALI CHERIF NATURAL SPRINGS

Situated in a riverside village, naturally occurring hot springs burst forth and draw visitors year-round. Known for their therapeutic properties, according to researchers these waters are reported to alleviate conditions such as constipation, digestive sluggishness, obesity, rheumatic pain and arterial issues.
A portion of the spring water is directed into a spa building (hammam), accessible with a paid entry. However, most visitors prefer a more natural experience, wading into the river where hot and cold streams converge for an outdoor spa treatment. We joined a group of men seated in the warm waters, exchanging salaams and being warmly welcomed into what, for some, was a cherished daily ritual. The springs operate on a gender-segregated schedule, with designated times for men and women.
Each gender alternates on the hour, waiting patiently on the hillside as one group exits and the other enters, upholding a respectful and harmonious flow. From Errachidia, head N for 39km, springs are on your L. Walk down to the river to discover the riverside springs. The drive to Moulay Ali Cherif is spectacular.

5 mins, 32.1809, -4.3671

2 OUED ZIZ SWIM SPOT

Beneath the bridge over the Oued Ziz, a path winds down from the road to the riverbank, inviting weary travellers to cool off in its refreshing flow. A couple of local boys splashed about in the turquoise shallows, laughing and leaping through the currents. From Errachidia take the N13 N for 29km. Park on N side of the bridge on L and follow the path behind rocks on R down to river.

3 mins. 32.0806, -4.3837

3 BARRAGE AL-HASSAN ADDAKHIL #1

Clear-blue waters are nestled in the mountains above Errachidia, their middle studded with a single rocky island. Although swimming is forbidden in these inviting waters, this shoreline spot down is great for a mid-road trip picnic. From Errachidia take N13 N for 15km. Eoad through the village is for residents only. However, there's a dirt track on the R down to water at (32.0193, -4.4789).

2 mins. 32.0142, -4.4714

4 BARRAGE AL-HASSAN ADDAKHIL #2

Perched on a cliff overlooking the reservoir below, this roadside viewpoint offers a panoramic vista of sparkling waters and deep-red mountains topped with ancient watchtowers. If you fancy a closer look, there is a walkable path down to shore. From Errachidia take N13 N for 14km.

10 mins. 32.0010, -4.4897

5 RISSANI PALMERAIE

Winding roads lined with well-watered palm trees pass ancient houses and a mosque in the heart of this desert palmeraie. The solar power station deep within the groves provides sustainable power to the kasbah. Water channels cut through the palmeraie, the tinkling water providing a soothing backdrop to the day. Take N13 W out of Rissani for 4km, then turn R at roundabout. Continue for 1km before turning L on to N12. Follow for 2.5km before turning R on to paved road, which becomes a dirt track. Follow for 3km into palmeraie.

2 mins, 31.3076, -4.3141

6 WADI GHAREES

Lying on the western edge of the Rissani Palmeraie, Wadi Gharees flows lazily through the arid landscape. Once much fuller, its muddy banks showing signs of the past touch of water, it remains an artery of life on the outskirts of the desert. From the parking at the bridge (31.3076, -4.3141) walk back along the road to (31.3071, -4.3160) where there is a bridge across a deep irrigation channel. Walk N for 600m until you see the river.

20 mins, 31.3108, -4.3170

7 HASSILABIED OASIS

A small sliver of an oasis beside the soaring sand dunes, borders fringed with defiant cacti. Heavily laden with bundles of harvested crops, women in bright abayas crisscross the slow trickle of a river that waters their fields. As we awaited our turn to cross the stepping stones, an elderly gentleman on crutches made the crossing towards us. Filled with respect, we hopped, skipped and jumped our way into the oasis, where men and women toiled under the shade of palm trees. The scorching sand of Erg Chebbi poked its head above the parapet of foliage, a silent sentinel to the hard day's work. From Merzouga take the R702 north for 14.4km. At the main square take the second R and park in the open space 100m on your L.

2 mins, 31.1416, -4.0214

8 LAC DAYET SRIJ

A seasonal lake that forms only in the winter months, the shores are lined with families and their picnics, alongside feathery visitors; migrating ducks on their way back south for the winter. These ephemeral waters are a stop-off for camel herders, with a group of 20 of the humped creatures arriving at the shoreline with us, their throaty roars mixing with the herder's insistent calls. From Merzouga, take the N13 north for 3.6km before turning R at the Bakery Remal Merzouga. Follow the road for 250m before bearing R at the fork. This road continues for 1.6km until turning into a dirt track. Follow the track for 1km to reach the shoreline.

1 min, 31.0984, -4.0471

9 LAC YASMINA

Forming at the base of the Erg Chebbi desert, this lake appears once a decade after intense rainfall, as in October 2024. Normally the starting point for camel rides into the dunes, this once-dry bowl was transformed into a watering hole, complete with migrating storks and herons, overlooked by the soaring heights of Erg Chebbi. A good case study for global warming. Hurry up, it might still be there. Only accessible with 4x4.

2 mins, 31.2135, -3.9827

MOUNTAINS & GORGES

10 TUNNEL ZAABAL VIEWPOINT

Mountain roads straight out of The Italian Job cling to the rockface and wind their way up the Ziz valley. Just before entering the Tunnel Zaabal from the south, look out for a gorgeous vista of red mountains, contrasting with the deep blues and greens of the Oued Ziz far below. On days like these, the mountains stare at their own reflections in the water, while a pair of hawks wheeled and dove through the air, hunting an elusive pigeon. From Errachidia, take the N13 N for 50km.

1 min, 32.1704, -4.3684

11 ZIZ CANYON OVERLOOK

Cresting the final cliff, the Ziz Canyon lies at your feet, its floor filled with palm trees, stretching off into the distance. Take a moment during your journey to appreciate the view. Parking available onsite. From Errachidia, take the N13 S for 27km.

1 min, 31.7897, -4.2382

12 OULED CHAKER LOOKOUT

A conveniently placed viewpoint on the road between Errachidia and Erfoud, offering a spectacular vista of the Ziz Valley, and the palm groves flowing along its base like a green river. From Errachidia, take the N13 S for 29km.

1 min, 31.7837, -4.2274 

DESERT

13 ERG CHEBBI

Though commonly called Merzouga, this changing landscape is actually Erg Chebbi, a desert made entirely of sand dunes. 'Chebbi' is the name, and 'Erg' refers to this specific type of desert. The more typical desert, hard and stony with little sand, is known as a hamada. Erg Chebbi is one of Morocco's most famous deserts, spanning about 30km by 8km, with dunes reaching up to 150m high. We suggest staying at one of the numerous desert camps surrounding the enormous sand dunes.

Don't enter the dunes without a guide unless you have a lot of experience as it's very easy to get lost. From Merzouga take the R702 N for 22km. The heights of the dunes are visible from the road, but are only accessible on foot, by motorbike and by quad bike. Even camels struggle with the steep slopes and shifting sands in these dunes.

30 mins, 31.1457, -3.9677

13

ANCIENT

14 IFRI KASBAH

Lingering by the highway, the remains of an ancient kasbah stand sentinel over the impending encroach of modernity. A brightly hijabed woman emerged from the shadowy doorway, pulling a reluctant donkey in her wake. She gave us an inquisitive salaam before heading on her way. Neighbour to the kasbah is the village's cemetery. Do its ghosts wander the halls of their old kasbah home, lamenting what they have lost? From Errachididia, take the N13 north through the Ziz Valley for 32km.

1 mins, 32.1233, -4.3650

15 KASBAH AMJJOUJ

Perched on a cliff above a bend in the Oued Ziz, the ruins of the once-imposing Kasbah Amjjouj stand as a testament to the past. Walking through its crumbling passageways is like stepping back in time, retracing the lives of its former inhabitants. With a mosque, homes, and communal kitchen areas, this kasbah once accommodated between 20 and 50 people. Its broken walls now open on to sweeping views of the nearby mountains and the river valley below. From Errachididia, take the N13 N for 27km. After crossing the bridge across the Oued Ziz, take first R up a dirt track for 100m before turning R on to a paved road. Follow it for 5km to the kasbah.

2 mins. 32.0507, -4.3808

16 BAB JDID

Stand and marvel before this exquisitely decorated and multicoloured front gate into a 300-year-old, still-occupied kasbah. Adorned with ceramics and Quranic verses, the building highlights the beauty and skill of Moroccan architecture. The kasbah itself was built using traditional 'rammed-earth' methods. This technique ensures that the buildings stay warm in the winter and cool in the hot summer. From Erfoud, take the N13 N for 27km before turning L on to a paved road, follow this road for 6.3km before turning L onto a dirt road. Parking available at the end of this road. From the parking head N on the street for 100m, take the second L and follow this path for 150m to reach the entrance to the kasbah.

5 mins, 31.6384, -4.2139

17 L'ESCALIER CÉLESTE

Hannsjörg Voth is celebrated for his three Land Art installations in the Moroccan desert. Drawn to the desert's vastness, his first major project, Himmelstreppe (Stairway to Heaven), was built between 1980 and 1987. Constructed using traditional Moroccan rammed-earth techniques, this structure reaches nineteen metres in height with 50 steps. A vertical slit faces the stars, reflecting Voth's fascination with astronomy. The narrowing side walls create unique shadow patterns and the interior is accessible, containing several rooms. Voth's work weaves together his formal art education, ancient architectural inspiration, and his father's architectural legacy. The three installations are only accessible by 4x4, to arrange a visit, contact Hassan at Desert Trip Tour: contact@deserttrip.com.

5 mins, 31.5815, -4.4775

18 SPIRALE D'OR

Hannsjörg Voth's Golden Spiral is a nautilus-shaped stone structure in the Moroccan desert, inspired by the Fibonacci Sequence. This mathematical pattern, where each number is the sum of the two before it, is reflected in the spiral's expanding radii across nine-quarter circles. The design also incorporates the Golden Ratio, a proportion seen in nature, from tree branches to seashells, where the smaller-to-larger section equals the larger-to-whole ratio. Voth's work beautifully merges art and mathematics, celebrating the desert's majesty and the harmony between natural patterns and artistic expression. For directions, see L'Escalier Céleste.

3 mins, 31.5919, -4.5350 

17

16

18

19 LA CITÉ D'ORION

The third creation in Hannsjörg Voth's 'magic triangle' of monumental works, La Cité d'Orion is an earthly tribute to the constellation, inspired by the architecture of Moroccan kasbahs. Voth envisioned this installation as a three-dimensional map of Orion, with seven towering structures crafted from rammed earth, symbolising the Orion's brightest stars, while smaller towers represent the fainter ones. The precise positioning and scale of each tower align with the stars' locations and luminosity, creating a terrestrial reflection of the night sky. For directions, see L'Escalier Céleste.

4 mins, 31.6131, -4.5253

15

20 SIJILMASSA ARCHEOLOGICAL SITE

A medieval trade hub hugging the Sahara's northern edge. Established by Sufrite Kharijites after Amazigh revolts, Sijilmassa grew into a critical terminus for the trans-Saharan trade route, facilitating commerce between north Africa and sub-Saharan regions. Sijilmassa's prosperity drew famous visitors such as the chroniclers Ibn Hawqal and Ibn Battuta (regarded as the world's first travel writer), who praised its wealth and beauty.

After Almoravid and Almohad rule, Sijilmassa fell to decay, only briefly revived in the 18th century under Sultan Moulay Ismail, before falling to Ait Atta tribes in 1818. Parking onsite. From N side of Souk Rissani, head W for 100m before turning R. Follow road for 200m until reaching roundabout on N13.

Cross N13 and follow road for 300m until reaching entrance to site on L.

2 mins, 31.2855, -4.2742

21 RISSANI CITY GATE

A beautifully decorated arched gateway into the town of Rissani, the crossroads between the northern and southern Morocco. The town was once the meeting point for trans-Saharan caravans and camel trains, bringing spices, silks and precious metals from across north Africa to Morocco.

10 mins, 31.2824, -4.2705

19

21

22 GARA MEDOUAR

A horseshoe-shaped limestone formation near Sijilmassa, fortified in the 11th century, to protect the city and nearby trade routes. The fortress included a 12m-high wall at its only entrance, additional defensive structures and dams to collect rainwater. The wall into the fortified interior is pierced by a single track, leading up to the summit of the formation, from where spectacular views of the surrounding mountains stretch out into the distance. Since the 1999 film The Mummy, Gara Medouar has become a popular filming site and tourist attraction, featuring in the James Bond film SPECTRE and drawing visitors for its cinematic and off-roading appeal. Take the N13 west out of Rissani for 4km before reaching a roundabout. Turn R and follow the N13 for a km before turning L on to the N12. Continue for 14km before turning off at the ruined hut at (31.2704, -4.4033) and follow the dirt trail for 3km.

8 mins, 31.3006, -4.4000

VIEWPOINTS

23 THERMAL SPRINGS OVERLOOK

Before descending into the healing waters of the Moulay Ali Cherif hot springs, take a minute to sit above the town and take in the lazy curves of the river below you, framed by the vast red cliffs that soar above you. From Errachidia take the N13 N for 43km through the Ziz Valley.

1 min, 32.1795, -4.3631

24 THE DAM'S LANDSCAPE

Take a break from your road trip through the Ziz Valley and from high on the cliffs stare out across the sparkling, blue waters of Barrage Al-Hassan Addakhil.
From Errachidia take the N13 N for 16km.

1 min, 32.0463, -4.4103

25 ERFOUD PANORAMIC VIEWPOINT

From a rocky promontory by the river, get a bird's-eye view of the town of Erfoud and its surrounding mountains. Palm trees perforate its patchwork skyline, providing a balance between natural and manmade. In the heart of Erfoud, a mosque sticks its pale-blue minaret defiantly into the sky, while a three wheeled tuk-tuk transports palm logs down the road surrounding the town and out into the plains below the mountains. Take the R702 E out of town for 1.3km, before turning L on to the Route de Borj. Follow this dirt track up the hill for 650m to reach the viewpoint.
Not suitable for longer vehicles.

10 mins, 31.4353, -4.2189

22

CULTURAL HOTSPOTS

26 ERFOUD DATE FESTIVAL

Every October, Erfoud hosts the vibrant Date Festival, celebrating the harvest of nearly a million date palms in the region. Over five days, visitors enjoy traditional music, dance, food and a variety of date-centric activities, including a fashion parade, the crowning of the Date Queen, and thrilling dromedary races. Exhibits from local producers and co-operatives showcase more than 100 Moroccan date varieties, including the prized Medjool, Deglet Noor, and Halawi dates. The Medjool, known as the 'King of Dates', offers a rich, caramel-like flavour. Visitors can stay in Erfoud hotels but bookings are essential due to high demand. Historically vital to Moroccan cuisine and culture, dates are significant to the economy, with 90,000 tons exported annually. The festival has become a bustling carnival atmosphere, with food stalls, music and activities attracting tourists and locals alike. Park where you can.

5 mins, 31.4371, -4.2337

27 TAHIRI MUSEUM OF FOSSILS

For a comprehensive introduction to Morocco's fossils, visit Brahim Tahiri's private museum. Here, scientifically significant specimens are showcased alongside more common fossils, some of which are available for purchase. Brahim Tahiri's dedication to highlighting Morocco's rich geological heritage has earned him international recognition, including the naming of a trilobite species, Asteropyge Tahiri, in his honour. The museum is easily identifiable by the life-size dinosaur skeleton replicas at the entrance. Watch out for the T-rex.

Less rare fossils and jewellry carved from locally found rocks available in the gift shop. Parking available onsite. Take the N13 from Erfoud S for 11km towards Rissani, the museum will be on the L.

+212 602-325856

1 min, 31.3497, -4.2907

28 SOUK RISSANI

A bustling market filled with goods of every description, from bright-red chilli peppers and sparkling, silver jewellery to hanging animal carcasses and leather workshops. This market is a feast for the senses, with sights, sounds and smells fighting for your attention, echoing the ancient markets of Sijilmassa, when caravans from across north Africa brought their precious wares to these same streets. From Hassilabied, take the N13 north for 37km to reach Rissani. Park where you can.

3 mins, 31.2813, -4.2660

29 DAR GNAWA

About four miles from Merzouga lies Khamlia, a village known as the 'southern gateway to the Sahara'. This small community is home to Gnawa musicians who have their residence at Dar Gnawa, at the southern end of the village. Originally nomads from Erg Chebbi and the Sahara, the Gnawa people migrated to Khamlia in the 20th century from Sudan, Mali, and Niger. Their music, characterised by chanting, jumping and clanking, symbolises freedom from slavery. Grab a glass of mint tea and a tagine, and enjoy the traditional music and dancing: the soundtrack to Morocco. From Merzouga, take N13 south for 5.5km to Khamlia. Parking available onsite.

1 min, 31.0329, -4.0070

30 GALERIE CHEZ LES ARTISTES

Khamlia is home to the art gallery of local and international artists. Lahcen Mahmoudi and his wife, Johanna, opened Chez Les Artistes 15 years ago, creating art from recycled materials left on the roadside. Stars of the collection include a replica 1950s film camera made from a jerry can and an abstract piece on water conversation made from discarded pipes and taps. Together, they work with local poetry groups and design the covers for their anthologies, and translate them from Arabic into French. Mint teas, juices and coffees are available from the café while you take a deep drink of the local culture. From Merzouga, take N13 south for 5.5km to Khamlia, turn L at the sign of the paintbrush. Parking available onsite.

1 min, 31.0339, -4.0055

ROADTRIPS

31 ERRACHIDIA TO MERZOUGA

As the sun rose over Errachidia, we embarked on an adventure to the shifting sands of Merzouga, the gateway to the dunes. The lush Ziz Valley greeted us with a breathtaking panorama of palm trees and ancient kasbahs. Weaving through the landscape, the Oued Ziz creates a vibrant contrast to the ochre hills. We had a date to keep in Erfoud, where we stopped for coffee and a scenic detour of the panoramic views of the town. Time to hit the road to Merzouga. As we arrived at the spectacular Erg Chebbi, the landscape transformed: the towering dunes appeared like ripples of gold in the sunlight. Nowhere on Earth will you find a more breathtaking sight than the sunset over the Erg Chebbi dunes.

- From/to: Errachidia > Merzouga (31.0999, -4.0175)
- Distance: 130km
- Roads: N13
- Scenic stop-offs: Ziz Valley, Erfoud, Erg Chebbi

33

34

CAFÉS & EATERIES

32 CAFÉ VUE PANORAMIQUE

A handily placed snack shop overlooking the Ziz Valley. For directions see Ziz Canyon.

31.7898, -4.2393 £

33 CAFÉ DESERT

Despite what the name suggests, this mobile café has its home on the shores of Lac Dayet Srij. Cool, refreshing drinks and light snacks to those who fancy an afternoon by the water. Only open in winter when lake is full of water. For directions see Lac Dayet Srij.

31.0987, -4.0472 £

PLACES TO STAY

34 GÎTE LUNA DEL FUEGO

A warm and welcoming family-run auberge decorated in bright colours and traditional Moroccan style. In the heart of the Ziz Valley, the dark-red stone walls of the valley rise on either side of you, a dramatic backdrop to your evening tagine. The Oued Ziz flows through the palm groves, calming background music to your stay. Parking onsite. From Errachidia take N13 N for 31km, turning L at signs for the gîte, follow road for 550m. +212 666-537706

32.1134, -4.3679 ££

35 GITE-CAMPING-CARAVANING HAKKOU

A family-run campsitef ocusing on genuine interactions and sustainability. The campsite has its own vegetable gardens, chickens and a herd of goats. Water comes from the river and electricity from solar panels. Space for campervans, tents and cabins, they can also organise cultural evenings and local tours. From Erfoud, take N13 N for 27km before turning L on to paved road; follow for 3km. +212 655-237554

31.6732, -4.2013 £

36 RIAD LGHIAM

A gorgeously decorated hotel on the outskirts of Rissani, made with traditional rammed-earth building methods to keep the interior warm in the winter and cold during the summer. Complete with a pool and multicoloured reflections of stained-glass windows. Halima, the owner, revealed the healing powers of the desert sands, said to be a cure for arthritis and rheumatism. Rissani Num 5 près de Ksar Lamrani et de Moulay Ali Cherif, Rissani 52450. +33 666-695916

31.2773, -4.2540 £££

34

35

37

37 BELDI CAMP

An oasis on the outskirts of the Erg Chebbi dunes, this camp offers a taste of desert living with a few creature comforts. Tents are equipped with showers and toilets, and a hearty Moroccan breakfast and delicious dinner are made with locally sourced ingredients. Nightly fireside performances of traditional Gnawa music under the stars add to the enchanting atmosphere. The camp can organise quad bike and camel tours into Erg Chebbi, making it a great place to watch the sunrise. Powered exclusively by solar energy, Beldi Camp also offers the opportunity to stargaze among the dunes. Meeting point to leave your car (31.2099, -4.0237), where you will be picked up by Ashraf in a 4x4 to take you to the camp. From Hassilabied take the R702 north for 9.7km before turning R onto the dirt track at the sign for Hotel Café du Sud. Continue for 700m and park outside the hotel.
beldicamp.com +212 622-168172

31.2010, -3.9378 £££

38 ARTISTES CAMPERVAN STOP

A campervan park and an art gallery all for the price of one. Take in a bit of local culture on your way to or from the Sahara and chat with the lovely Johanna and Lahcen Mahmoudi about their incredible project. See Chez les Artistes Art Gallery for more info and directions.

31.0342, -4.0051 £

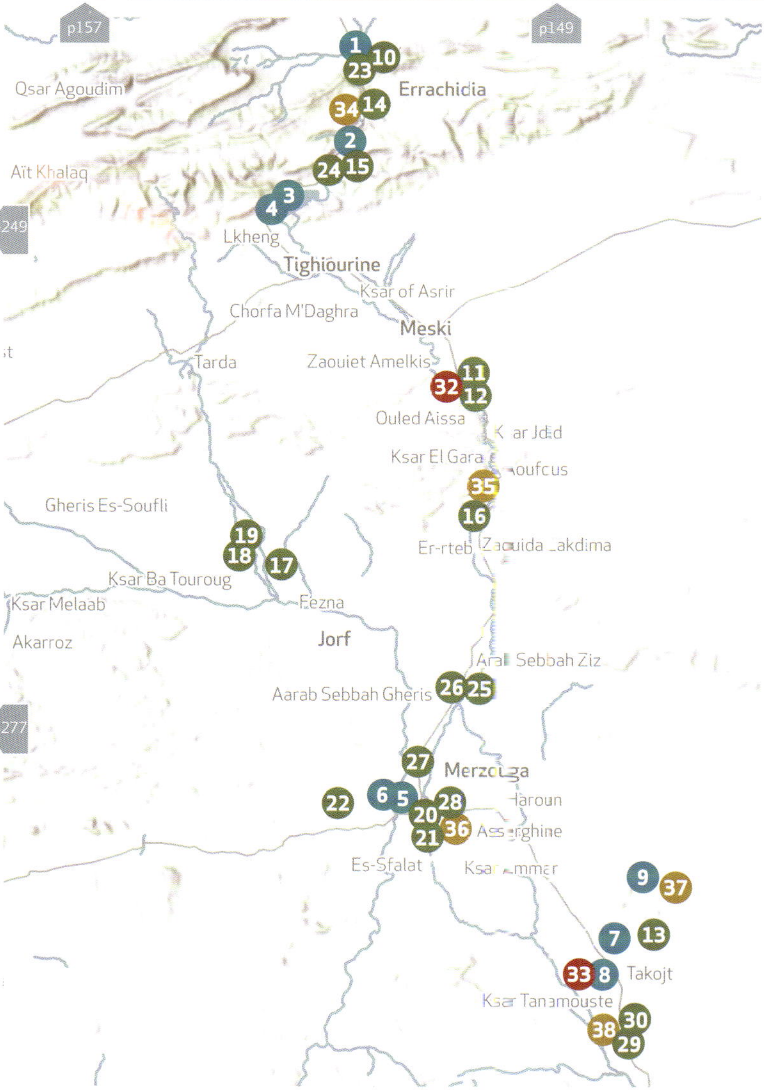

TODRA GORGE TO ZAGORA

Our perfect adventure

- → **Climb** sheer rock faces and put your body to the test in the Todra Gorge
- → **Meet** the Nomads who live all year round in the heights of the Atlas Mountains
- → **Stroll** through gardens and vast palmeraies in Tinghir and Skoura
- → **Wave** back at the Monkey Fingers in the mountains around the Dadès Gorge
- → **Hold** your nerve on the tricky twists and turns of the Tisderine Bends
- → **Take** the load off and enjoy the comfort and tranquillity of the Riad Gabsi du Dadès
- → **Greet** the new day from the top of Erg Chigaga, north Africa's tallest sand dune
- → **Learn** about the traditional Moroccan way of life at Musée d'Art et de Traditions near Zagora
- → **Glide** down towering dunes on a sandboard, feeling the rush of Saharan adventure beneath you

1

5

5

'The camel never sees his own hump, but that of his brothers is always in his eyes.'

Moroccan proverb

Where Morocco's mountains begin to give way to the desert, there are a myriad of adventures to be found. Valleys and gorges cut their way through the landscape, creating dramatic and majestic vistas. The Todra Gorge, just north of Tinghir, is a haven for hikers and climbers, with countless routes through, over and up cliff faces and mountains lying waiting to be explored. Neighbour to Todra is Dadès Gorge and a fierce rivalry exists between the communities who live in the gorges, each claiming theirs is the most magnificent. We would never dare come down on either side of the divide, but a hike around the strange geological formations, the 'Monkey Fingers', that resemble primate paws in the Dadès Gorge, certainly grabbed our attention.

It's not all rocks, however. These gorges have been carved over millennia by rivers and have fed vast palmeraies that spread out as far as the eye can see. Walking from Todra Gorge down to Tinghir was a magical experience: small gardens bisected by streams reminiscent of Hobbiton gave way to vast palm groves dotted with the ruins of ancient kasbahs and fortresses. The palmeraie in Skoura dwarfs its Tinghir counterpart, stretching out across the plains, studded with kasbahs still lived in by families and communities. Between these two oases of palm leaves lies the pink beauty of the fertile Valley of the Roses, where each year a sea of roses carpet the land.

Zagora serves as the gateway to the vast Sahara. Its iconic sign, *52 days to Tombouctou*, recalls its historic role as a major starting point for trans-Saharan caravans. We visited mud-brick structures and intricate designs of Amezrou Ksar, reflecting Amazigh, Arab and Jewish influences. Amezrou was once a vibrant hub for Jewish communities, evident in the remnants of synagogues, traditional homes and silver manufacture.

At a desert camp in the Iriqui National Park, we ate traditional food, some of the best in Morocco, by the campfire and watched the stars come out at night. Waking up early the next morning, we plotted up on the top of the 150m-high Erg Chigaga dune, the largest in north Africa. Watching the sunrise over the Sahara was a profound experience that will stay with us forever. The first light of day spreading orange and gold hues over the undulating sea of sand was mesmerising and felt like a personal gift.

MOUNTAINS & GORGES

1 TODRA GORGE

Deep in the Atlas Mountains, along the route to the Sahara, lies the Todra Gorge. This natural wonder boasted canyon walls that soared to more than 400m – taller than the Empire State Building. A premier destination for photography enthusiasts, climbers, bikers and hikers.
An ideal stop for an overnight stay or a longer retreat between Marrakech and the desert. From Tinghir head N on R703 for 15km through the mountains; passing through Tizgui Village, the gorge is 1km further on; park by gorge.

2 mins, 31.5878, -5.5931

2 TODRA GORGE CLIMBING

A rock climbers' paradise, with something for every mountaineer. The conditions and quality were close to perfect, with sunshine all year round. The best time to climb in the area is between March - May and September - November. When climbing, always wear helmets, as there was loose rock on the top of the gorge, occasionally displaced by the nomads and their goats on the clifftops. Bring your own equipment, or hire from climbing shops on the main road. Directions as for Todra Gorge.

5 mins, 31.5878, -5.5931

3 ROCK N YOGI

If you're an inexperienced climber or don't have a climbing partner, we recommend booking a guide through Rock n Yogi Adventures, based in Todra Gorge. They had a wealth of experience in climbing and the local area and were UK-qualified rock-climbing instructors, mountain leaders and first-aid trained. Climbing and hiking with them for four days; I felt in such good hands and had an unforgettable time, on and off the climbing wall. +212 634-474184 rocknyogiadventures.com

6 mins, 31.5788, -5.5877

4 DADÈS GORGE

Stretching for 45km between the towns of Boumalne Dadès and Msemrir, the gorge is renowned for its dramatic red rock formations, steep cliffs and traditional Amazigh villages. The road through the gorge offers incredible views and is popular with photographers due to its unique geological formations, the 'Monkey Fingers', and the rock faces' vibrant colours. The area is a haven for hikers and adventure enthusiasts, with trails leading to hidden oases and ancient kasbahs. From Tamellalt, head NE towards Gorges du Dadès/R704 for 17km and park by Camping Berbère de la Montagne (31.5574, -5.9094); walk S towards gorge for 100m.

1 min, 31.5548, -5.9082

5 THE MONKEY FINGERS

This towering cliff face, with long vertical sections of rock that look like 'digits', was a unique part of the gorge. As the name suggests, it resembles a monkey's paw rising up from the river, waving 'hello' to those that pass. Viewing platform on the road or you can hike around the Fingers. From Boumalne Dadès, head N for 16.6km on R704; viewpoint is on R after Tamellalt Village.

2 mins, 31.4492, -5.9702

6 VALLEY OF THE ROSES

Carved by the Assif n Im'Goun River, the valley wound its way to Kalaat M'Gouna along a scenic 30km paved road offering views of red rock and green valley landscapes. Each April and May, local women gather 3,000 to 4,000 tonnes of roses, quickly picked and sent to nearby factories to be made into products like shampoos and creams. Even when the roses are not in bloom, a walk through the fertile green oasis on the valley floor, especially in early spring, is a fragrant and lively glimpse into a local industry. Villages such as Tabarkhachte or Hdida give easy access to the valley floor, or you can arrange for a guided tour via local hotels. From Kalâat M'Gouna, head N on Vall. des roses for 7km.

15 mins, 31.2879, -6.1492

HIKES

7 THE NOMAD LOOP

If you don't fancy climbing, the Nomad Loop provides a welcome alternative. This non-signposted hike took roughly four hours and traversed mountain plateaus, complete with Amazigh symbols traced out in stones. We recommend going with a local guide, such as Rock n Yogi Adventures (rocknyogiadventures.com) or ask at Auberge Tizgui, as there are sections where you can get lost. At the mountain's summit, you can meet Aicha and Ahmed, an elderly nomadic couple who live here year-round, in caves chiselled from the rock, living off the herding and tending of goats. Although advanced in age, Aicha, especially, moved with the agility and speed of a woman half her age, gained from a lifetime of hard work in the mountains. Ahmed, whose wrinkled face was quick to crinkle into a broad smile, has striking blue eyes, in stark contrast to the dark brown of his weather-beaten visage. I took a moment to have some tea with them and listen to their stories; their way of life is coming to an end as this generation will most likely be the last that lives in the mountains full-time. Their children and grandchildren are coming down from the mountains to study and work in the local towns, then trying to find work in Morocco's growing cities. While this may be a bitter pill to swallow for those enamoured with this off-the-grid lifestyle, tea is there as a sweet soother to your sadness. It's made from thyme that grows wild in these mountain passes and complete with serious amounts of sugar. It was the perfect fuel for the second half of the journey back down into the town. The hike finished in the abandoned Todra Kasbah. Directions as for Todra Gorge, but continue through the gorge for 40m, the parking will be on your R (31.5891, -5.5963).

10 mins, 31.5891, -5.5966

8 THE MONKEY FINGERS LOOP

Descending into the green valley of the river, pink blossoms lay on the banks and small footbridges crisscrossed its blue-green path. The villages were a mix of ancient and new, with old kasbahs and outposts sharing walls with modern houses and sheep pens. Emerging from the past, I arrived at the secret pool and took a moment to appreciate the calm serenity of its tranquil waters. Leaving the openness of the river behind, I entered the clutches of the mountain, winding my way through canyons and gullies carved by years of passing water. Some passages were completely blocked by earthquakes and rock falls, forcing me to climb. Finally emerging from the claustrophobic clutches of the mountain, and after a scramble up a steep escarpment, I was granted a panoramic view of the Fingers and the gorge. Take lots of water and sturdy shoes. Can be done without a guide but not for the faint of heart. From Boumalne Dadès, head N on R704 for 18.5km, through the gorge and past the Monkey Fingers rock formations; the trail start is on the right of the road just before the town of Aït Sedrat. Trail start: (31.4604, -5.9724): starting on the bridge from the main road into the village of Aït Arbi, take the first right as you enter the town and follow that path for 1.8km past the ruined tower of Aït Ouglif (31.4541, -5.96607) until you reach the Secret Lake (31.4505, -5.9662). From there, take the path on your left leading out of the clearing and follow it for 300m until you reach the entrance to the gorge; from here the trail is very difficult and some may require a guide, particularly after the recent earthquake. Follow the gorge for 2km before emerging into a wider stretch of canyon. In front of you will be a steep slope upwards. Climb it to reach the Monkey Fingers' viewpoint (31.4547, -5.9466). Then follow the path back on the clifftop to your right, following the route of the canyon, for 2.5 miles; this path then rejoins the trail by Aït Ouglif and you can retrace your steps back to the bridge.

180 mins, 31.4604, -5.9724

FORESTS, PARKS & GARDENS

9 TODRA GORGE GARDENS

Hidden gardens crisscrossed with footpaths and partitioned by the Todra River. Groups of men and women sat in the gardens and drank tea and ate Amazigh pizza – flatbread topped with tomato, onion and ground beef, which they were more than happy to share with me. This was a lovely spot for a picnic on the way to and from the gorge. From Tinghir take the R703 N for 15km through the mountains; passing through the village of Tizgui, park next to the mosque (31.5787, -5.5873) in the centre of the village; follow the signs for the Secret Garden through the houses and into the gardens.

3 mins, 31.5781, -5.5861

10 TINGHIR PALMERAIE PANORAMA

A bird's eye view of the vast expanse of the Tinghir Palmeraie, cut through by streams and dotted with the dark-brown fastnesses of ancient kasbahs. Surrounded by mountains and with the town of Tinghir below, this was an awesome sight in the truest sense of the word.

Take the R703 N out of Tinghir for 5km, the viewpoint is just after the village of Aït Ojana on the R.

1 min, 31.5417, -5.5664

11 PALMERAIE DE SKOURA

A unique intersection between the Sahara, the High Atlas Mountains and the Jbel Saghro mountain. The palmeraie's ecosystem, with 25km² of palm groves and olive trees, protects and nourishes other vegetation. This landscape supports a traditional way of life where families cultivate crops and participate in local markets. At least 157 constantly occupied kasbahs still stud the green expanse. Difficult to explore by car due to the narrow tracks and sharp turns. We recommend exploring it on foot or by bike, which can be arranged by contacting Camping Skoura Amridil. Directions as for Kasbah Amridil, but turn right at the fork and explore the Palmeraie.

5 mins, 31.0518, -6.5848

ANCIENT

12 TODRA KASBAH

A sprawling fortified village set on a cliff above the Oued Todra, with panoramic views of the surrounding mountains and the Todra Gorge Gardens. Although the kasbah was completely abandoned, with inhabitants constructing modern concrete homes on the eastern bank of the river, some are returning. Directions as for Todra Gorge, but park outside Tizgui mosque (31.5785, -5.5870). From parking, walk E for 450m along R307; turn R at opening between the houses and follow gravel path for 250m until you reach stream; cross it using footbridge and entrance to Kasbah will be on your R.

15 mins, 31.5759, -5.5854

13 PALMERAIE DE TINGHIR

The palmeraie spilt down through the mountains, from the Todra Gorge to the old French garrison city of Tinghir. The vast green expanse was cut through by small streams, and dotted with the ruins of ancient kasbahs and working farms. Hiking from Todra Gorge Gardens down to Tinghir was an incredible journey; the palmeraie expanding from a small strip of land by the Oued Todra, to a sprawling mass around Tinghir.

7 mins, 31.5478, -5.5655

13

14

15

14 THE ABANDONED KASBAH OF TINGHIR

Within a stone's throw of the main road, the Tinghir valley held a secret; hidden among palm leaves, bushes and crops, an ancient stronghold sat in stoic silence. An Amazigh castle built to protect the town of Tinghir and the vital water source from neighbouring tribes. Ramparts that once supported fierce Amazigh warriors, now sunned themselves idly, no enemies threatening their now-crumbling exteriors. One watchtower still stood proudly above the palm leaves, a testament to the castle's former strength. Yet bushes and weeds were clawing their way up its walls, threatening to drag it down into obscurity. Not on Google Maps, so it took a bit of effort to find. Park near the Jardin Publique (31.5204, -5.5325) in the centre of Tinghir, walk on to the N10 and turn R; follow road for 630m until the palmeraie appears in front of you and a bridge crossing the river valley; at the roundabout head straight on for 100m and there will be a path to your R leading down into the palmeraie; follow paths through the fields from here towards the ksar, which is 500m NNE of you.

15 mins, 31.5295, -5.5306

15 IKALALNE AFANOUR MOSQUE

This 600-year-old mosque was nestled in the centre of an ancient ksar across the river from the modern town of Tinghir. The beating heart whose arteries have now run dry, as the buildings around it lay in ruins. New buildings have sprung up around its edges. From the roof of the ancient mosque I was granted views of the ksar, Tinghir and the green belt of the palmeraie. Jutting up arrogantly above the skyline was the minaret of the new mosque. This new and younger model, only 400m from its predecessor, was tactlessly named the New Ikalalne Mosque, a slap in the face to the original that had survived so many years.
In the shaded halls of the ancient mosque, the prayer hall, granary and toilet stalls have been carefully preserved by its caretaker, Abdisalem, who, for what he lacks in teeth, makes up for with his passionate love of this sacred place. Park in the open space on the R of the N10 as you enter the village (31.5318, -5.5285) follow the white arrows painted on the walls, they will lead you to the kasbah.

20 mins, 31.5282, -5.5244

16 KASBAH AMRIDIL

One of the most impressive kasbahs in the country – it once featured on the Moroccan 50dh note. Founded in the 17th century by a Saudi Arabian family, it initially served as a fortified village (ksar) at a strategic river location. In the late 19th century, it was expanded into its current state to provide Quranic educational facilities for the families' sons. The Kasbah, still owned and partly occupied by the Nasiri Family, is the most prominent structure in the area, featuring traditional Amazigh architecture, with rammed earth construction and square corner towers adorned with geometric designs. A museum showcases traditional artefacts and local architecture. Also appeared in the 1962 film Lawrence of Arabia. Café on site. Take the N10 SW out of Skoura for 2km; turn R at signs for Kasbah Amridil for 600m before bearing slightly L at outskirts of the palmeraie; here the track becomes rocky, but it's only 300m from here to the Kasbah.

8 mins, 31.0463, -5.5812

17 AMEZROU KSAR

The ochre-coloured structure is a labyrinth of narrow, largely covered and dark alleys, once providing shelter and security to its inhabitants. Established in the 18th century, the ksar covered an area of 41,800m^2.
The mosque was built in the 15th century and featured a well used by the village. The ksar's architecture includes traditional palm wood and bamboo-supported ceilings, as well as tamarisk wood doors. Despite the scarce rainfall, wooden drainpipes and covered passageways were notable features. The community, once home to around 500 Muslim and Jewish families, thrived on its silversmithing craft, especially

16

within the Jewish quarter, the mellah, with its own synagogue. Although the last Jewish family left in 1962, the synagogue can still be visited by requesting the key from the family across the street. Park where you can in Amezrou and explore the medina.

3 mins, 30.3074, -5.8215

DESERTS

18 ZAGORA 52 DAYS TO TOMBOUCTOU

The 52 Days to Tombouctou sign in the town of Zagora, was erected in the 1960s and is an emblematic monument. Commemorating the town's historical role in trans-Saharan trade, it marks the arduous journey caravans undertook to reach Timbuktu, traditionally taking 52 days by camel. Well worth a photo. Located on Avenue Mohammed V near Hôtel la Palmeraie.

1 min, 30.3236, -5.8409

19 DUNES DE TINFOU

A sample-sized taster of the Sahara. Way smaller than its big brother, Erg Chebbi, Tinfou was a perfect introduction to the desert's magic. Arriving early in the morning at the sand dunes near Tamegroute allowed us to experience the tranquillity of the dunes before the crowds arrived. The only sound was the wind blowing around us. Nearby Tamegroute is renowned for its green-glazed pottery, with shops and workshops where visitors can see the distinctive pieces being crafted. From Zagora take N9 E; After 16km straight over roundabout to stay on N9: after 7.6km turn L on to track at sign for Dunes de Tinfou; bear R and follow track to dunes.

5 mins, 30.2396, -5.6015

20 ERG CHIGAGA

This is Al-Kabeer (The Big One) and the trek across the Sahara to reach the dune was a meditative and arduous expedition. Climbing north Africa's largest sand dune was no easy feat. Find your balance and dig in, keep your body low, zigzag to preserve energy and use short, fast steps near the ridge. Standing atop the 150m-tall dune at sunrise blew our minds. Come the dawn, each peak was kissed by the sun, glowing amber as golden waves of sand rippled beneath us. We felt closer to the heavens than to civilisation. Time stood still and the silence overwhelmed us. Lying on our backs and staring up at the sky, we felt unable to move for what seemed like an eternity. Possibly the most memorable and humbling moment of our trip to Morocco. Nearest road is about 60km away – we recommend staying at Camp Al Koutban. Dunes 60 mins from the camp, ask them for directions or find a camel and a guide.

60 mins, 29.8419, -6.2370

17

19

20
20
20
20

ROADTRIPS

21 TISDERINE BENDS

This series of hairpin bends and switchbacks next to the Oued Dadès could prove a test for even the most skilled drivers, forcing even the nippiest of Moroccan speed junkies to slow their pace. Make sure you give a loud honk before you start your climb, especially if you're in a campervan or motorhome, to let drivers coming the other way know you're coming and to give you space. If the climb proves too much for your nerves, there's a conveniently located café and auberge at the top of the bends. While you sip on a beverage you can watch others attempt to make the same climb. The most entertaining, or stressful (depending on your temperament), is when a typically overladen Moroccan lorry makes the ascent/ descent, taking impossibly wide turning circles to make its bulk pass smoothly through the tight curves. Additionally, when two drivers meet right on a switchback, an interesting dance is performed as they squeeze past each other. The driver ascending the bends is 'usually' given priority. From Boumalne Dadès, head N on R704 for 25km until you see the road bend in front of you.

- From/to: The Dadès Gorge > Boumalne Dadès(31.3745,-5.9895)
- Distance: 33km
- Roads: R704
- Scenic stop-offs: Dadès Gorge, Tisderine Bends Viewpoint (31.5296, -5.9253), The Monkey Fingers

30 Mins, 31.5273, -5.9253

CULTURAL HOTSPOTS

22 WORKSHOPS AND SILVER CRAFTING

A community-driven workshop with a portion of the profits supporting local families. For an exceptional door made from tamarisk wood inlaid with camel bone and other decorations, visit Barzouk Douini, the 'King of Doors'. The co-operative also offers wooden mantelpieces, bowls, decorative necklaces and camel-milking tools. One room features women embroidering kaftans, which can be quickly adjusted as required. Nearby, a silver gallery showcases rings, bangles, necklaces, mirrors, plates and daggers. Additionally, there are carpets, plates and bowls on display. Prices are negotiable. Ksar Amezrou +212 668-943982 (silver shop).

5 mins, 30.3068, -5.8226

23 MUSÉE D'ART ET DE TRADITIONS

A captivating museum that showcases tools, keys, agricultural implements and water-carrying devices. Featuring green pottery from Tamegroute and a variety of wooden doors, smoked to protect against insects. Signs explain the distinction between a ksar and a

23

26

29

kasbah, illustrating the fortified villages of southern Morocco. Exhibits include a guest reception room with teapots, traditional palm-leaf carpets and teas. Prehistoric tools, traditional clothing and musical instruments are also on display. The Haratine tribe's history and the influences of Romans, Jews and Andalusians on local culture are highlighted. The museum also features old guns and metal castanets. The museum guide, Boujmaa, is descended from Sahrawi Nomads. From Amezrou, head N on N10 for 10km; turn R at sign for the museum and park in dedicated parking spot on L.

2 mins, 30.3967, -5.8596 £

PLACES TO STAY

24 AUBERGE RESTAURANT TIZGUI

An authentic home-from-home guesthouse run by the village chief's two sons, Mohammed and Faisal, who have excellent language skills, and knowledge of the area and went over and above to ensure that I had the best experience possible. Delicious food, amazing hospitality and big smiles. I cannot recommend this place highly enough. Tizgui Toudgha El Oulia, Tinerhir 45800. +212 699-177938

31.5764, -5.5830 ££

25 HÔTEL RESTAURANT CAMPING BERBÈRE DE LA MONTAGNE

Rooms are available, along with space for motorhomes. The camping area features pleasant, shaded spots by the river, located just beyond the narrowest section of the gorge. Clean bathrooms and hot showers. Free Wi-Fi. Gorges du Dadès, Dadès Gorge, Boumalne Dadès 45150. Directions as for Dadès Gorge. +212 615-270374

31.5573, -5.9094 £

26 RIAD GABSI DU DADÈS

A gorgeous riad at the heart of the Dadès gorge with a variety of rooms and delicious food on offer. A central courtyard with a swimming pool, lined with arches offers panoramic views of the gorge. Conveniently located across the road from the start point of the Monkey Fingers hike. Location, location, location.
From Boumalne Dadès, head N on R704 for 8.5km, through the gorge and past the Monkey Fingers rock formations; the riad is on the L of the road just before the town of Aït Sedrate. riadgabsidades.com +212 672-581780

31.4621, -5.9736 ££

27 CAMPING SKOURA AMRIDIL

With comfortable rooms decorated in traditional style, delicious Moroccan cuisine and a warm, welcoming atmosphere, this place was a pleasure to stay in. My host took me on a guided e-bike tour of the palmeraie and kasbahs. Swimming pool, space for motorhomes and free Wi-Fi. Amridil, Skoura 45500. Directions as for Kasbah Amridil but after turning off the N10, follow the road for 500m before turning R at sign for the campsite; entrance is 150m in front of you. +212 608-676182

31.0499, -6.57592 £

30

28 AUBERGE CAMPING BASSOU

Simple but tastefully decorated en suite rooms around a lovely, green courtyard with lots of birds. Ibrahim – who speaks English and is extremely knowledgeable about the area – and his sister are friendly and helpful. Wi-Fi is good in places. Live music can be organised, as can treks to Jbel Saghro mountain to meet with Aït Atta nomad tribe or to the Neolithic Aït Ouazik carvings. Campervans and motorhomes welcome. Handy stopover if you're on your way to or from the Sahara or visiting the nearby town village of Nkob, boasting no less than 45 kasbahs and a vibrant Sunday souk. Talat nw Akiwne, Nkob 47072.
aubergebassou.com +212 658-385291
30.9070, -5.8889 ££

29 RIAD SOLEIL DU MONDE

A family-run guesthouse in Zagora, nestled amid lush gardens filled with date palms and bougainvillaea. Emphasising sustainability, they grow their own organic produce, including vegetables, fruits, fresh goats' cheese and eggs, ensuring farm-to-table freshness. Two swimming pools. Accommodation options include air-conditioned rooms and charming cabins for longer stays, decorated with designs inspired by Amazigh writing. Parking is available. Contact in advance if arriving in a large campervan as the road is very narrow. The Riad Soleil du Monde prides itself on employing local staff, supporting the community and can organise trips to the local kasbah, as well as to the desert. Riad Soleil du Monde, 45900 Zagora.
riadzagora.net +212 661-687131
30.3124, -5.8312 ££

30

30 CAMP AL KOUTBAN

Situated beneath the towering dunes of Erg Chigaga, Camp Al Koutban offers an unparalleled escape into the heart of the Sahara. Hocin and his team provide warm hospitality and delicious home-cooked meals. Hummus in the desert was an unexpected treat. With a maximum of 24 guests in 12 tents, the camp maintains an intimate atmosphere. Activities in the dunes include guided hiking, camel trekking, sandboarding, sunset/sunrise vantage points and stargazing. The nearest road is a two-hour journey away; the closest light pollution 60km away. Open from 1 September to 15 June. Unless you have your own 4x4, arrange transport with the camp who can arrange transfers from Marrakech and other nearby airports. Highly recommended.
campalkoutban.com +212 679-006221
29.8556, -5.2268 ££

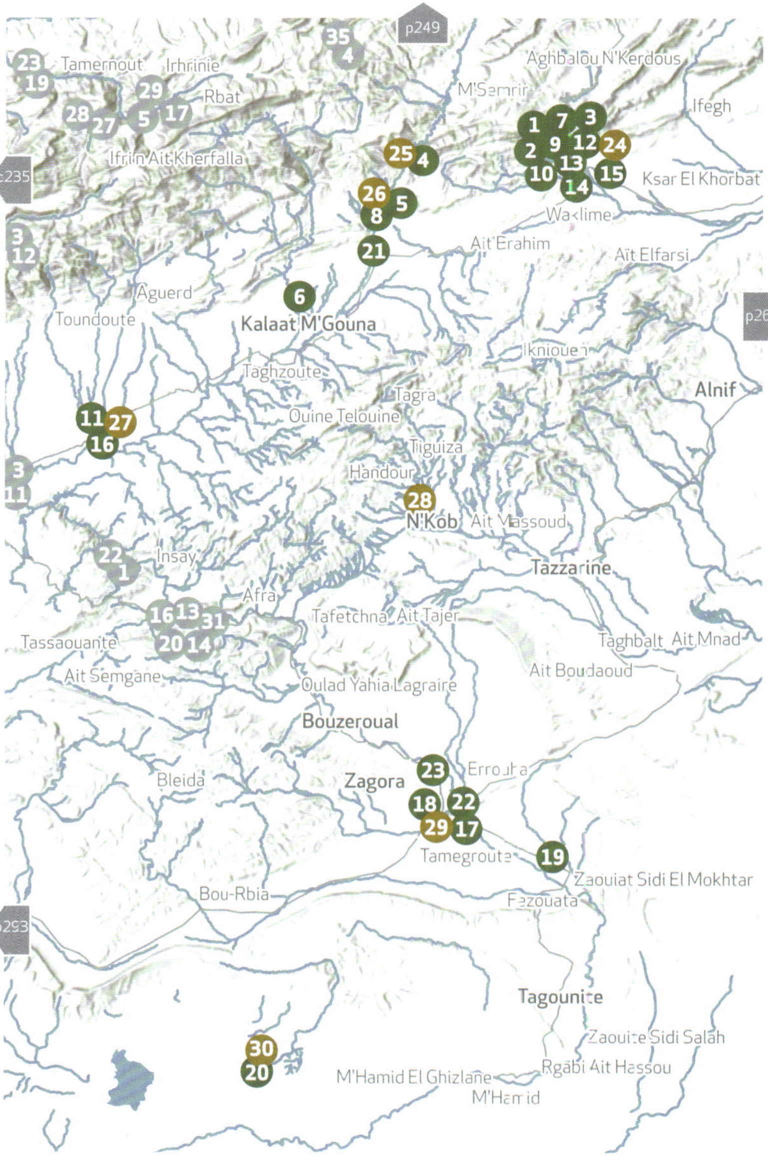

AÏT BENHADDOU TO OUED DRAA

Our perfect adventure

- → **Dive** into crystal-clear pools beneath the Cascades Attiq at the edge of the desert
- → **Marvel** at the Martian-esque landscape of the Tissint Gorge
- → **Disconnect** from the world in the Amoudou Lodge Camp and swim a river in the desert
- → **Admire** the vast palm groves of the Draa Valley at Agdz Oasis viewpoint
- → **Discover** impressive graffiti next to a historical building at Street Art Kasbah Tamnougalt
- → **Purchase** spice's red gold, saffron, from women's Coopérative Souktana du Safran and support local farmers
- → **Release** your inner gladiator in the ancient, fortified village of Aït Benhaddou, the backdrop for many warrior movies
- → **Explore** Agadir Ifri Imadiden storage granary, built into the cliffside about a thousand years ago and decorated with stalactites
- → **Enjoy** tasty traditional cuisine at La Terrasse de Délices while gazing out over date palms, fig trees and olive groves of Fint Oasis

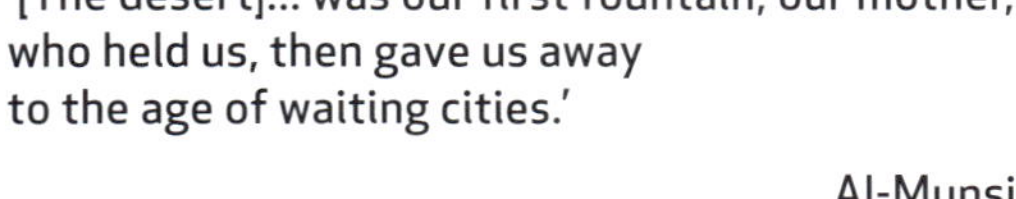
**'[The desert]... was our first fountain, our mother,
who held us, then gave us away
to the age of waiting cities.'**

Al-Munsif al-Wahaybi, The Desert

From Lawrence of Arabia to Gladiator and Game of Thrones, the ancient ksar and UNESCO World Heritage site of Aït Benhaddou, has provided the ochre backdrop for many a great film. Standing for centuries as a key stop along the caravan routes linking the Sahara to Marrakech, the ksar features typical earthen buildings and steep, intricate kasbahs. Meanwhile, Ouarzazate is the strategic crossroads where ancient sub-Saharan trade routes met those from the Mediterranean. We're in a gladiatorial and dramatic mood, so can't resist a visit to Atlas Studios, the Hollywood of Morocco, where we explore famous film sets and star in our own short film.

At Fint Oasis, we experienced traditional farming practices, partook in bread-making and enjoyed an overnight stay in a family-run hostel. In the morning, we took a dip in the natural oasis. Along the famous Oued Draa, the longest river in Morocco, rugged terrain, sedimentary rocks and dry riverbeds have sculpted lunar-looking landscapes, with date palms marking the waterways. From our vantage point in Agdz, we gazed over the palm groves of the Draa Valley, imagining camel caravans laden with goods destined for northern markets. The town's name, meaning 'resting place' in Tamazight, aptly reflects its historic role as a waypoint for traders.

Ancient meets modern at Kasbah Tamnougalt, a fortress atop a hill that was once the residence of the local governor and a centre of power in the region. On a building next door, large street-art creations from Igloo Hong's urban art project contrast colourfully with the ageing yellowstone. Below Ksar Tamnougalt lies a 16th-century fortified city that once housed 300 families. The well-preserved kasbah of the last Caïd now serves as a museum, showcasing Amazigh decor and history.

Passing through Taliouine, the saffron capital of Morocco, we vow to return for the 'festival of red gold' at the end of October. Baking in the lunar landscape of the remote village of Tissint, on the edge of the Sahara, we spend a lazy afternoon swimming in a river that runs through the parched, red gorge. Later, we dine on tagine and dates by candlelight in the silent, star-filled desert night. We're a long, long way from home.

WATERFALLS

1 LES CASCADES DE TIZGUI

A charming waterfall surrounded by pink oleanders. Behind the restaurant, stairs lead to another waterfall, requiring some wading and climbing. Wild camping is possible in the car park at the top of the stairs. From the car park in Tizgui (30.7782, -6.5289), turn L at the sign and walk along the path to the wall; descend more than 100 steps to reach the waterfall and the café.

5 mins, 30.7759, -6.5289

2 CASCADES ATTIQ

A must-see, must-swim destination. The deep pools were crystal clear and ideal for swimming. We were mesmerised by the local boys diving and performing acrobatics into the water. Surrounded by tall cliffs and the vast, open sky, the river was a hidden place where, for centuries, the Amazigh people had escaped the harsh desert environment to cool down. We joined them in this ancient tradition. From Tissint head N on P30/N12 for 600m; at the roundabout, take the first exit; after 75m park where you can; walk L to the metal handrail to the cascades and the river.

2 mins, 29.9057, -7.3154

LAKES & RIVERS

3 BARRAGE EL MANSOUR EDDAHBI

Calls of migratory birds filled the air as we stood by the shimmering waters of the reservoir, with the dramatic backdrop of the Anti-Atlas Mountains. Created by damming the Drâa River in 1972, this is more than just a scenic spot; it is a testament to human ingenuity in transforming barren landscapes into fertile farmland. Named after the Saadian Sultan Ahmed el-Mansour, the barrage plays a vital role in irrigation and water management for the surrounding arid regions. Marked by sedimentary rock formations and sprawling desert vistas, its geological landscape provides a haven for flora such as tamarisk trees and bird species, including flamingos and herons. We parked by a curious, abandoned swimming pool, ready to explore around the water's edge and find a good picnic spot. From Ouarzazate, head N on N10 for 13km; turn R off P10 on to a dirt track opposite Mosquée Kchaite (30.9760, -6.7582); follow the track for 2.5km, bearing L until you reach a flat parking area by a building with a disused swimming pool.

5 mins, 30.9611, -6.7557

4

7

4 TISSINT RIVER SWIMMING

River swimming in the desert. Tall cliffs overlooked soft, yellow sand and water as clear as an epiphany. A magical scene. Could have been a mirage. We floated on our backs, mesmerised as black and white ducks flew overhead, their quacks punctuating the still air. The gentle rustling of palm trees and the distant murmur of the river completed the symphony. Here was the perfect picnic spot on a sandy beach, complete with nature's own swimming pool. If you've had lunch, or are staying at Amoudou Lodge Camp, Ali will provide you with tea and cosy blankets. This was one Moroccan swim we won't ever forget. Walk across from Amoudou Lodge Camp or walk W for 1km along the river from Point de Vue Tissint.

5 mins, 29.9101, -7.3388

5 FINT OASIS

This tranquil river oasis features palm groves, traditional Amazigh villages and serene landscapes, providing a perfect escape from the desert's harshness. A deep, natural pool at the entrance to the oasis is bordered by a beach to sit and contemplate the mountains and palm trees. We joined local kids swimming and jumping from rocks. Pink oleander decorated the pool. At weekends, local families come to swim and picnic. Walk along the river to see crops cared for using traditional methods. The car park guardian informed us that we were welcome to park overnight, for a small fee. From Ouarzazate continue to Av. Moulay Abdellah for 1.3 km; take N9, P1516 and P1507 to P1509 for 17km; parking is on R at the bottom of the hill; walk across sand to the oasis.

3 mins, 30.8308, -6.9515

ANCIENT & CAVES

6 MESSALIT CAVES

Created over millennia through the natural process of erosion, these limestone caves are characterised by orange stalactites and stalagmites, expansive chambers and narrow passageways. Historically, these caves served as shelters for local Amazigh communities, providing refuge from the harsh desert climate and the threat of occasional raids. Artefacts unearthed in the caves suggest a long history of habitation, with evidence tracing back to prehistoric periods. A haunting and beautiful silence permeates the caves. Take P1805 N from Tata for 6km until you see a sign on the right for Les Grottes de Messalit.

10 mins, 29.8124, -7.9885

7 AGADIR D'AÏT KINE

Built in the 18th century from clay, with ceilings of palm trunks, this is a fantastic example of an oasis-style agadir. Carefully restored by local artisans in 2008 with government funds, the granary, still in use today, is defended by two watchtowers and a thick wall. Barley, dates and other foodstuffs are stored in the small rooms on three levels in the same way they have been for generations, as are important documents such as deeds and marriage certificates.

In the case of a raid, villagers could seek shelter here, where they would find food to survive.

A platform in the centre of the courtyard is used in marriage celebrations. To enter, call the number of the guardian, which you can find by the door. 2RF9+P6, Aït Kine. Park where you can in Aït Kine.

5 mins, 30.0242, -8.1819

8 AGADIR IFRI IMADIDEN

Many hundreds of years old, according to the guardian, the agadir (granary) is a remarkable structure built directly into the cliff face of the Anti-Atlas Mountains. Featuring approximately 200 rooms, this agadir is still used by local Amazigh villagers to store grain, food and important documents. The 100m-wide granary protrudes dramatically from the cliff. Small doors are ingeniously wedged into the clay and wooden beams, along with ladders, connect

10

the different levels. Long clay stalactites hung down from above, creating a magical and otherworldly appearance. When we drove into the village, locals approached us, offering to guide us to the granary (which is hard to find) and fetch the key, expecting a small payment for their service. Drive into the village of Ifri (30.4504, -7.8446) and find a parking spot; someone will offer to guide you to the agadir.
5 mins, 30.4445, -7.8378

9 KASBAH DU GLAOUI DE TAMDAKHTE

A notable, albeit lesser-known, fortified palace situated near Aït Benhaddou. Built in the 19th century, it served as the residence of the influential Glaoui family during the French protectorate. The kasbah featured traditional Amazigh architecture and a glimpse into the opulent lifestyle of its former inhabitants. Guided tours were typically led by a guardian who appeared magically upon our arrival. The kasbah has been used as a filming location for movies such as The Mummy and Gladiator. Directions as for Kasbah La Cigogne; walk 200m S.
2 mins, 31.0854, -7.1455

10 AÏT BENHADDOU

Located along the ancient caravan route between the Sahara and Marrakech, Aït Benhaddou is a fortified village dating back to the 11th century. Aït Benhaddou has been used as the backdrop for numerous films, including: The Man Who Would Be King (1975); Lawrence of Arabia (1962); Game of Thrones (2011-2019) and Gladiator (2000). We explored the narrow streets and alleys and the views from the top across the Oued El Maleh were superb; the sunsets can be magnificent. Aït Benhaddou is a UNESCO World Heritage Site and rightly so. From the centre of town, follow signs and cross bridge over river Oued El Maleh. NB not wheelchair accessible but great view from the opposite side of the river.
5 mins, 31.0476, -7.1301

11 KASBAH TIGREMT N'AÏT IDAR

Kasbah Tigremt N'Aït Idar stands alone on an island in the Barrage El Mansour Eddahbi reservoir, a romantic and haunting presence. Constructed in the late 19th century, it was once home to five Amazigh families: the Aït Idar, Aït Kassi, Aït Jabbour, Aït Oujamaa and Aït M'hamed. These families lived here until they were displaced by the reservoir's construction in 1972. On New Year's Eve 1999, a music festival near the kasbah apparently drew revellers in their thousands. Directions as for Barrage El Mansour Eddahbi. Viewpoint: (30.95856, -6.75577).
2 mins, 30.9525, -6.7599

12 KASBAH OF TAOURIRT

An excellent example of Amazigh architecture, constructed primarily in the 19th century by the influential Glaoui family. This sprawling fortress features intricate carvings, winding corridors and more than 300 rooms. Once a vibrant centre of commerce and trade, it stands as a symbol of the region's rich history. The kasbah's walls echo the tales of the past, from the powerful Thami El Glaoui's rule to the bustling market days. For a small fee, we were taken around by a knowledgeable and friendly guide, who explained important parts of the building. He also tells us the Amazigh meaning of 'ouar' – without – and 'zazate' – noise – suggesting that this was a 'calm place'. W492+RJF, Av. Mohammed V, Ouarzazate 45000.
2 mins, 30.9203, -6.8992

13 TAMNOUGALT KSAR

A fortified city dating back to the 16th century, which was once the vibrant capital of the Draa region. A bustling trade hub, it served as a meeting point for nomadic caravans exchanging goods. Unlike a kasbah, typically associated with a single family, a ksar is a village comprising multiple families. The old village is a three-tiered labyrinth with impressively thick walls for insulation. The synagogue mirrors the mosque's architecture

with arches and an outdoor oven once used by the Jewish community. The old ksar had four entrances: one for Jews, one for the garden, one for the market and one for caravans. Today, the well-preserved kasbah of the last Caïd, Ali, houses a hotel, restaurant and museum. Its central square, shaded by a bamboo trellis roof, was historically a men's domain, while women gathered in the gallery. The second floor offers guest rooms and the restored roof terrace displays Amazigh decor. Tamnougalt showcases a variety of architectural styles through its different kasbahs. You'll probably meet a guide outside offering their services or you could phone the well-informed Jamal (+212 709-422021). From Agdz, head SE on N9 for 4.5 km, turn L onto Palmeraie de Tamnougalt for 1.5km and park where you can (30.6756, -6.3915).
5 mins, 30.6745, -6.3886 ££

14 KASBAH TAMNOUGALT

The climb up the hill to Kasbah Tamnougalt rewarded us with a breathtaking panorama of the kasbah, the surrounding mountains and the palm groves below. Constructed in the 16th century, this kasbah is a captivating blend of Amazigh, Islamic and Andalusian architectural styles. While in a state of disrepair, with missing ceilings and rubble-strewn floors, the kasbah's towers and outer walls, punctuated by defensive openings,

remained impressively intact. Early morning offered the best opportunity to appreciate the kasbah's grandeur. The solitude, accompanied by the chorus of birds and the amazing view, was enchanting. As we wandered through the central courtyard and labyrinthine passageways, it was easy to envision the kasbah's former glory. Directions as for Tamnougalt Ksar and park near the football pitch opposite Kasbah Itrane; follow the obvious path up to the kasbah on the hill

15 mins, 30.6771, -6.3970

VIEWPOINTS

15 VIEWPOINT OF AÏT BENHADDOU

An excellent spot for sunrise and sunset photographers to capture the magnificence of the UNESCO World Heritage Site. Can get a little windy at times. At the SE end of Aït Benhaddou, park on your L where you will see the viewpoint

2 mins, 31.0410, -7.1260

16 PALM GROVES OF DRAA VALLEY

The palm grove at Agdz is a remarkable example of traditional Moroccan agriculture and life. Stretching along the banks of the Draa River, the oasis is a patchwork of date palms, gardens and terraced fields, nurtured by ancient irrigation systems known as khettaras. These underground channels are essential for sustaining life in this arid region, drawing water from the distant mountains. Take a stroll through the palm groves or head to the viewpoint for captivating views.
The road trip along N9 from Zagora to Agdz Oasis was equally impressive, winding through the expanse of ochre desert and the green Draa Valley. For the viewpoint, from the roundabout in centre of Agdz, take E exit for 630m keeping R towards Office De La Municipalité.

2 mins, 30.6924, -6.4429

17 TISSINT GORGE

Stood on a huge rock, looking out over the Martian-esque terrain, we felt like Major Tom, separated from the world below us. The Tissint Gorge is a striking geological formation, its arid landscape characterised by undulating plains and protruding peaks. The gorge's distinctive orange hue is due to the iron-rich sandstone that is prevalent in the regionand created a spectacular panorama. A unique feature was the presence of two rivers, one fresh water and one salty evidence of the area's ancient maritime past. Turn off P30/N12 on to a sandy track (29.9053, -7.3452); walk between rocks and find one to climb.

1 min, 29.9035, -7.3481

14

14

17

19

19

18 POINT DE VUE TISSINT

A pretty bridge spans the point in the oasis where two rivers flow; one fresh and the other salt water. They come from sources upstream and meet below the Amazigh village of Douar Akka Nait Sidi perched on a clifftop overlooking the canyon. From Tissint town head N on P30/N12 for 850m; at the roundabout, take the 2nd exit and stay on P30/N12 for 850m; turn R towards the bridge.

2 mins 29.9094, -7.3302

CULTURAL HOTSPOTS

19 ATLAS FILM STUDIOS

If you like films, Atlas Film Studios is a must-visit. Founded in 1983 and renowned as one of Africa's largest film studios, it is a fascinating place. Countless movies and series have been shot here, including Gladiator, Prince of Persia, Game of Thrones, The Living Daylights, Aladdin and The Mummy. Our guide was both humorous and well-informed, explaining why Atlas Studios is a filmmaker's dream. Ouarzazate's consistently good weather ensures uninterrupted shooting, while low labour costs make it budget friendly. The diverse landscapes – desert, mountains and forests – offer endless possibilities. Moreover, the Moroccan government's support, including streamlined contracts, boosts the local economy through job creation. Our guide expertly led us through various film sets, detailing their transformation for different movies. The tour's highlight was a surprise: the guide directed us in a short scene, an unforgettable souvenir. BP 28 Route de Marrakech (Mohammed V), Ouarzazate 45000. ouarzazatestudios.com

2 mins, 30.9402, -6.9668 £

20 STREET ART KASBAH TAMNOUGALT

Street art is a rare sight in Morocco, so discovering some on a building adjacent to Kasbah Tamnougalt was a delightful surprise. The graffiti, characterised by large, circular designs and a vibrant colour palette, was both

19

unique and thought-provoking. This open-air gallery is the result of the 2016 Igloo Hong Urban Art Project, by acclaimed American artist David Choe. Choe, along with a group of international artists, transformed the area's walls into a captivating showcase of contemporary art. This project introduced a fresh perspective to the historical site, harmoniously blending traditional Moroccan architecture with modern artistic expression. Directions as for Kasbah Tamenougalt; walk 100m N.

15 mins, 30.6778, -6.3966

CAFÉS & EATERIES

21 COOPÉRATIVE SOUKTANA DU SAFRAN

Saffron is harvested by hand in autumn. Each bloom yields three red stigmas, which are quickly dried to preserve their quality. With 150,000 flowers needed for 1kg of saffron, it's among the world's most expensive spices. This women's co-operative supports traditional methods, ensuring fair prices for local farmers. A museum details the process and a shop sells organic saffron and saffron-based products. The harvest and annual festival occur in late October to early November. Centre, N10, Taliouine 83500. +212 528-534452

30.5310, -7.9156

22 CAFÉ RESTAURANT CHEZ OMAR

Run by Omar and Issa and located at the base of the Tizgui waterfall. We enjoyed mint tea, tagine and brochettes. Basic rooms available for overnight stays for 400dh, which includes dinner, bed and breakfast. Directions as for Cascade de Tizgui.

30.7759, -6.5289,

23 VUE PANORAMIQUE MUNÉS

Sit and drink tea with cinematic views over Aït Benhaddou. 2VWC+Q6G, Aït Benhaddou.

31.0469, -7.1294

23

31

25

30

PLACES TO STAY

24 DAR INFIANE

A restored kasbah, sitting in a palm grove in the ancient town of Tata, which combines traditional architecture with eco-conscious practices. Using locally sourced materials and solar energy, the owners aim to minimise environmental impact, while its design promotes natural cooling. The modest pool, set within local stonework and native plants, offers a refreshing retreat. Water-saving practices and eco-friendly treatments maintain the pool. Guests can enjoy panoramic views, traditional Moroccan meals and a terraced garden featuring desert plants that support local biodiversity. Free Wi-Fi. Dar Infiane Guest House; Douar Indfiane, BP221 Tata 84000. darinfiane.com +212 610-932524

29.7339, -7.9756 ££

25 LA TERRASSE DE DÉLICES

A charming guesthouse nestled in the scenic Fint Oasis with a restaurant offering fantastic views of the mountains and the green oasis below. The landscape was dotted with date palms, fig and pomegranate trees, cornfields and olive groves. Equipped with a pretty garden, 15 rooms with modern amenities and a swimming pool. Activities, including treks and trips to nearby desert camps, can be organised. Oasis de Fint, Tarmigte 45000, Ouarzazate terrassedesdelices.com

26 30.8237, -6.9441 ££

27 CAMPING TOUBKAL

A serene escape in the heart of Morocco's saffron capital. Set amid picturesque landscapes, the campsite promoted eco-friendly practices such as solar power and waste recycling. Accommodation options include motorhome/campervan pitches, tents and bungalows with modern amenities. Traditional Amazigh hospitality, a restaurant and a medium-sized swimming pool as well as organised trips to explore nearby attractions such as the Toubkal National Park. G4F4+49 Taliouine. +212 528-534343

30.5226, -7.8936 £

28 KASBAH LA CIGOGNE

Conveniently located 5km from Aït Benhaddou. All rooms are equipped with a private bathroom. Douar Tamedakhte Aït Benhaddou, Ouarzazate 45100. kasbah-cigogne.com +212 524-890371

31.0857, -7.14591 ££

29 ECOLODGE L'ÎLE DE OUARZAZATE

Situated a few miles outside Ouarzazate, the ecolodge is built around gardens and a swimming pool on the edge of the Barrage El Mansour Eddahbi. Rooms are large with en suite and air conditioning. Wi-Fi is available throughout. The owners invest a percentage of revenue back into community projects. Tours and activities included bike hire. Talat Tarmigt Ouarzazate 45000. +212 666-177610

30.9064, -6.8573 £

30 AUBERGE LA ROCHE NOIR

Experience life in an Amazigh home in this charming hostel located near Fint Oasis. The hostel welcomes guests into a warm, familial atmosphere and invites them to participate in daily activities, such as helping prepare traditional meals. We helped bake the morning's bread. If you're interested in exploring the oasis, Rachid and Idriss offer guided tours, showcasing how locals cultivate their crops. November visitors can witness the date harvest. Desert excursions to bivouac camps or guided treks can be arranged. Accessing is via a narrow, winding track. We managed with our six-metre campervan, but the road is unsuitable for larger motorhomes. Oasis de Fint, Tarmigte, 45000 Ouarzazate.
larochenoire-oasis-fint.com +212 671-519962

30.8212, -6.95037 £

31 BAB EL OUED

The beautifully designed gardens of this luxurious eco-lodge are a refreshing oasis in the arid Draa Valley, complete with tranquil pools inhabited by terrapins. Situated within the UNESCO-designated Biosphere Reserve of Southern Morocco's Oasis, this pioneering lodge seamlessly blends tradition with sustainability. The solar-heated outdoor pool offered a cooling retreat. Built by local craftsmen, Bab el Oued's architecture blend Amazigh and nomadic influences, utilising earth bricks produced on-site. The interiors featured an eclectic mix of African and Oriental aesthetics, adorned with local antiques and African artefacts. Home to more than 250 plant varieties, including edibles, aromatics and medicinal herbs, the lodge cultivates ingredients for its organic, additive-free cuisine. Guests can explore the surrounding area on organised walks and treks. Palmeraie de Tamnougalt, Mezguita – Agdz, Ouarzazate. ecolodgemaroc.com afrikamath@hotmail.fr +212 684-678051

30.6743, -6.3965 ££

32 KASBAH TISSINT

A luxurious retreat that seamlessly integrates eco-friendly practices, with solar panels providing renewable energy. The kasbah is built using traditional adobe and local materials, ensuring natural temperature regulation without excess energy use. Organic gardens supply fresh produce for traditional Moroccan dishes and a water-recycling system conserves valuable resources. In the ferocious heat, the large swimming pool provided a welcome

escape, as did the air conditioning in the comfortable en suite bedroom. Free Wi-Fi. Commune Rurale Tissint, 84053.
+212 667-991338
29.9065, -7.3169 ££

33 CAMPEMENT AKKA NAIT SIDI

A luxurious nomadic bivouac nestled in a gorge just outside Tissint, offering a genuine desert experience with minimal environmental impact. The camp uses solar energy for its lighting and hot water needs and serves dinner by candlelight to reduce electricity use. With no Wi-Fi, the focus is on nature, where the lunar landscape and star-filled skies create a serene

34

escape. Comfortable tents are equipped with water-saving toilets and showers. Camp Akka Nait Sidi Sarl, Sis Douar Akka Nait Sidi – CR de Tissint – Cercle Foum Z'guid.
cans-akkanaitsidi.net +212 610-932524
29.9246, -7.3428

34 CHEZ LAHCEN

An authentic Amazigh stay with a focus on eco-friendly practices. Constructed with traditional adobe and local materials, the building naturally regulates temperature. Each room features handcrafted Amazigh decor. The terrace offers panoramic views of the surrounding mountains and lush palm groves. Douar Akka Nait Sidi, Foum Z'guid, Tissint 84053.
chez-lahcen-maroc.com +212 610-932524
29.9101, -7.3321

35 HOTEL BAB RIMAL

If you find yourself driving near Foum Zguid and in need of delicious food, a break from the arid heat or a dip in a crystal-clear swimming pool, then look no further. The warm desert wind gently swayed the palm trees as we indulged in a delightful spread of vegetarian dishes. Savour spiced lentils, grilled green peppers, fluffy rice, and much more. Experience luxury in the desert. Friendly staff and welcoming atmosphere. Tastefully designed bedrooms. Campervan, pitches available, with added charges for electricity and a nominal fee for short stays.
30.1283, -6.8679

36 ERG KINGDOM

Wild and remote camping spot between the towering cliffs and impressive rock formations near Foum Z'guid. Bring your own everything as there aren't any shops or services for miles around. Unless you have your own 4x4, arrange camp and transport with Camp Al Koutban (campalkoutban.com).
29.9188, -6.8361

37 AMOUDOU LODGE CAMP

This authentic desert escape embraces eco-friendly living without electricity or Wi-Fi, allowing you to disconnect from the world. Savour home-cooked meals or learn to cook like a Moroccan. Genuine hospitality and delicious tagines. Ali can also organise excursions to visit Neolithic carvings and walks in the desert. Check out the swim from nearby river beach. From Tissint head N on P30/N12 for 900m; at roundabout, take 2nd exit and stay on P30/N12; after 3km destination will be on R; look out for signs for Amadou Lodge Camp, turn on to sandy track to parking; follow steps down to camp.
+212 658-256710
29.9093, -7.3387

29

36

37

35

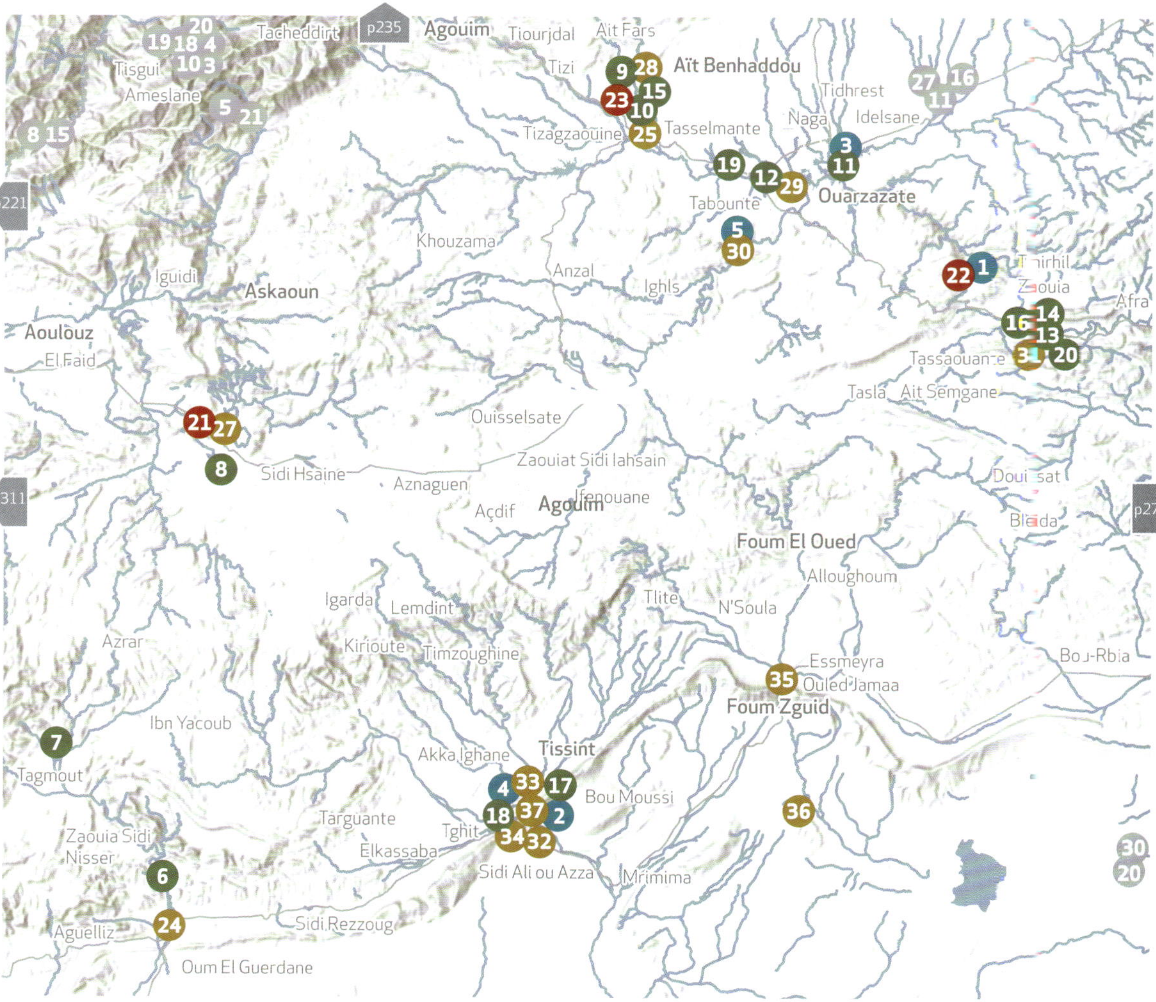

p235
Agouim
Tiourjdal
Ait Fars
Tacheddirt
Tisgui
Ameslane
Tizi
Aït Benhaddou
Tidhrest
Naga
Idelsane
Tizagzaouine
Tasselmante
Ouarzazate
Tabounte
p221
Khouzama
Anzal
Ighls
Iguidi
Askaoun
Aoulouz
El Faid
Afra
Tassaouante
Tasla
Ait Semgane
Ouisselsate
Zaouiat Sidi Iahsain
Sidi Hsaine
Aznaguen
p311
Açdif
Agouim
Ifenouane
Foum El Oued
p277
Alloughoum
Igarda
Lemdint
Tlite
N'Soula
Azrar
Kirioute
Timzoughine
Essmeyra
Bou-Rbia
Ouled Jamaa
Foum Zguid
Ibn Yacoub
Akka Ighane
Tissint
Tagmout
Bou Moussi
Targuante
Zaouia Sidi
Nisser
Tghit
Elkassaba
Sidi Ali ou Azza
Mrimima
Aguelliz
Sidi Rezzoug
Oum El Guerdane
19 18 20 4 10 3 5 21 8 15 9 28 23 15 10 25 27 16 11 3 11 19 12 29 5 30 22 1 16 14 13 31 20 21 27 8 35 7 4 33 17 18 37 2 34 32 36 6 24 30 20

ANTI-ATLAS MOUNTAINS

Our perfect adventure

- → **Rappel** down rocks and climb through canyons in Tanelt Canyon
- → **Drive** through the dramatic landscapes of Les Gorges d'Aït Mansour
- → **Lie** back in the water and relax in the gentle grip of the mountains in the pool of Aït Mansour
- → **Explore** the pure paradise of Boutboukalt, Oued Tessaout where we swam with inquisitive terrapins
- → **Enjoy** shimmering water framed by the silhouettes of olive trees, pink oleanders and green palm fronds at Takoucht Chtouka
- → **Hike** to La Rivière Amtoudi accompanied by birdsong and the babble of rivers and waterfalls
- → **Discover** ancient agadirs (fortified communal granaries) perched high on a rocky outcrops
- → **Camp** beneath a star-filled sky near the blue rocks of Tafraoute

1

1

3

'Certain nights, words are not enough.
You must step out of your room and walk toward the sky.'

Tahar Ben Jelloun

Extending from the Atlantic coast to the edge of the Sahara, the Anti-Atlas Mountains present a stark contrast between lush oases and valleys, rocky gorges and arid plains. The mountain range features ancient sedimentary rock formations, including limestone and sandstone. The flora includes hardy plants such as thyme, rosemary and argan trees, which are adapted to the harsh climate, as well as date palms in the oases, highly valued for their sweet, nutrient-rich fruit.

We visit Agadir Inoummar, a traditional fortified granary. You'll find agadirs all over Morocco, particularly in the Amazigh regions. These structures were used to store grain and valuable goods, symbolising collective wealth within communities. Built from stone and clay, agadirs are often perched on hilltops or cliffs, providing protection from invaders and natural elements. Each family had its own compartment within the agadir, which also served as meeting places for village elders. A guardian will explain the history and serve mint tea for a small fee.

Thrillseekers should head to Tafraoute for trekking, climbing, cycling and canyoning in the surrounding mountains. The Tafraoute Almond Festival, usually held in the second week of February, features presentations of the centuries-old ahwach dance, showcasing rhythmic movements and soulful melodies. Meanwhile, the Tifawin ('light' in Amazigh) Festival of Village Arts, held in August includes a mix of musical performances, traditional dances and cultural displays including tbourida (equestrian performances celebrating ancestral rites). Buy delicious amlou, a mixture of ground almonds, honey and argan oil, at the Tuesday or Wednesday souks, alongside spices, food, clothes, jewellery and much more. While waiting for our van's brakes to be fixed, Lola asked a young man for help charging her SIM card. A couple of hours later, he returned with couscous made by his mum – another of the many open-hearted gestures we received in Morocco.

MOUNTAINS & HIKES

1 TANELT CANYONING

If you're in the Anti-Atlas Mountains or anywhere near Tafraoute and feeling fit and adventurous, canyoning is an absolute must. Tanelt is high on the list of abundant canyoning spots. Over millennia, the mountain waters have cut deep into the rock, leaving a string of pools for the adventurous traveller to rappel down using ropes and harnesses and remind themselves that they are in fact, truly, alive. Unless you're an experienced canyoner with your own ropes, helmet and wetsuits, don't attempt this on your own. A local guide can provide you with all the equipment and instruction. The descent into some of these canyons is nearly 50m and cannot be attempted without harnesses. We recommend Anti-Atlas Adventures (anti-atlas-aventures.com). Its guide, Ahmad, is a consummate professional, a self-proclaimed 'man of the mountains'. The local guides also make up the Mountain Rescue Team in this area (+212 673-701247) and are well-equipped to keep you safe on your adventures.

240 mins, 29.7871, -9.0945

2 LA TÊTE DU LION

An original and striking rock formation created by millions of years of erosion. This natural wonder has a distinctive shape, resembling a lion's head with its 'mane' of rocks and its 'nose' of a pointed peak. Best viewed from Camping Tête de Lion or the roof of Auberge Kasbah Chez Amaliya.

5 mins, 29.7710, -8.9543

3 JBEL TAGTOUT

They say that no good thing is easy and the climb up Jbel Tagtout, stands true to this maxim. The view from the 1.3km-high summit took away the little breath I had left, as the valley unfolded before me, clenched tightly in the fingers of the surrounding mountain peaks. Unless you're an experienced climber, don't attempt this on your own, or tell someone that you're going. Ahmad at the Tagtout Auberge is a lovely man and will be more than happy to keep an eye out for you and give you advice on the ascent. Don't believe him if he tells you this climb is 'quite easy'; he's only doing it to motivate you. Bring water, food, suncream and a torch. Start hike behind Tagtout Auberge; start point is 200m L of auberge between two large boulders (29.7243, -8.9897). No well-worn path to guide you up this mountain, you must rely on your own good sense and judgement, or hire a guide; climb up and R to the base of the first ridge and then traverse along its base until you can begin heading up and R towards summit.

180 mins, 29.7227, -8.9885

4 CAPPELLO DI NAPOLEONE

A striking natural rock formation that resembles a Neopolonic hat (cappello is Italian for 'hat'.). This unique geological formation has been carved out by the forces of nature over millions of years, creating a dramatic and surreal landscape. Surrounding the rock tower are devastating views of the surrounding mountains and valleys, making this a popular spot for photographers. From Tafraoute, head S on R107 for 2.5km; Cappello di Napoleone is on your R. Park where you can.

5 mins, 29.69685, -8.9668

5 PAINTED ROCKS OF TAFRAOUTE

This may not be the Taj Mahal, but it's the symbol of a man's love for his dead wife. The rocks were painted in 1984 by Belgian artist Jean Verame, a tribute to his late wife. With the help of the Tafraoute Fire Department, a remarkable 18 tons of blue, pink, red and black paint were used to bring this romantic monument to life. You can also wild camp around the rocks. From Tafraoute, head S on R107 for 7km; turn R at sign for PAINTED ROCKS; continue for 1.5km; park in the shade behind the red and the blue rocks (29.6655, -8.9721); walk N or W for 500m to see the rocks.

5 mins, 29.6710, -8.9740

5

6

6 AOUKERDA GORGE

We embarked on a three-hour hike along Aoukerda Gorge, a natural marvel carved over many millennia. On our trek along the dusty riverbed, we found a small pool (29.35697, -9.02553), lined with palm trees and oleander, where we stopped to rest and cool our feet. We navigated and forged our way through dense vegetation and enjoyed further watery interludes (29.3492, -9.0179 and 29.3448, -9.0163), where we dunked our sun hats and soaked our feet in the idyllic oases. The towering orange rock formations are a testament to Earth's ancient history while small shrubs and palm trees cling precariously to the gorge's walls. Bring plenty of water and snacks and wear sturdy footwear. Start from the Aoukerda Village and follow contours of the valley for 6.5km; alternatively, you could start at Igmir and walk to Aoukerda, make sure you have someone to pick you up from Aoukerda. Park where you can in Aoukerda; we left our van in Igmir and organised a lift to Aoukerda from Hassan (+212 611-828204)

220 mins, 29.3644, -9.0283

LAKES, RIVERS & POOLS

7 PISCINE TIOUT

Tiout's huge, unheated, stream-fed swimming pool sits beside a palm grove. Divided into two sections: one measuring 30m x 40m and the other 25m x 30m, one area is shallow and the other deep enough to dive from a 5m wall. The water was naturally clear and fresh; we saw with an army of frogs blithely floating by the steps leading into the pool; their protruding eyes surveying the fun around them. Children's laughter filled the air as they jumped, dived and played, while others sat around chatting. Busy on a Sunday afternoon, so visit on a weekday morning to have the place to yourself. No lifeguards. Ignore Google maps; from Tiout Village, head S for 1.5km until you reach car park (30.3819, -8.6977); pool is on your R.

1 min, 30.3819, -8.6984

10

8 BARRAGE AHL SOUSS

Peaceful lake among the hills where families come to have picnics and spend time. The air was full of birdsong and the sound of children having playground fun. A paved waterside walkway made for a leisurely stroll around the lake. From Aït Baha, head SE on R105 for 2.8km; park on R; follow path to playground and lake.

3 mins, 30.0635, -9.1248

9 GARDE FORESTIER AMAGOUR

Nature took on an artist's guise, sculpting volcanic rocks and caves into twisted forms and gnarled crevices that evoked the work of a surrealist sculptor. Amid this dramatic landscape lay a small, shimmering, natural pool, a relic of volcanic activity. We stumbled upon a group of boys revelling in unbridled joy, launching themselves into the pool with spirited abandon, their laughter ringing around the cave. How they managed to avoid colliding mid-air was a mystery. Later, as we ventured into the nearby village, helpful locals mended our flat tyre. Park in Amagour Village; path is difficult to navigate, best bet is to ask one of the local kids to show you the way.

20 mins, 30.2404, -8.8505

10 BOUTBOUKALT, OUED TESSAOUT

Pure paradise. The Oued Tessaout meandered gently towards the Youssef Ibn Tachfin reservoir, with inquisitive terrapins poking their heads above the water. The riverbanks were lined with vibrant, pink oleander bushes and graceful palm trees. Cool water invited us in, while a gentle breeze caressed our skin. Birds sang softly, filling the air with a melodious swirl. A perfect end to a long, hot, dusty drive. Some friendly workmen offered us food and tea. From Agadir, follow N1, P1714 and P1009 for 77km; turn L on to Rte Vers Sebt Aït Milk for 14.4km; park where you can by side of road (29.8106, -9.3932); walk E along the riverside path until you find a good spot to get in the water.

15 mins, 29.8081, -9.3861

11 TAKOUCHT CHTOUKA AÏT BAHA

The shimmering water was framed by the silhouettes of olive trees, pink oleanders and green palm fronds. We took a walk downstream and found a weir built by locals, which formed a swimming pool. Exploring upstream revealed more hidden pools. Couldn't have been more idyllic if it tried. From Tafraoute, head N on R104 for 3.5km; turn R on to Amzkhsane-Tanalt road for 43km; park just after bridge (29.7918, -9.1753); walk back over and follow track by river for 200m

5 mins, 29.7924, -9.1731

11

12

13

12 RIVER OF AÏT MANSOUR

Behind the palm trees lining the road and down a short dusty path, lies the River Mansour, gently stretching itself out along the valley, like a cat in the hot sun. Dappled sunlight dances along the series of small pools lying beside the road, setting the water alight, and revealing the small fish beneath. Austere and imposing, the mountains that gave this river its source stand above it, like a parent watching over a wayward child. This spot is ideal to dip your toes in before heading on to the main attraction, the Pool of Aït Mansour. From Souk N Tasrirt, head S for 11km to parking (29.5478, -8.8771); cross road and follow small path through break in trees to your R, or ask guardian for directions.

1 mins, 29.5476, -8.8773

13 POOL OF AÏT MANSOUR

Fringed by palm trees and peaks, the silence of this man-made pool in the River Mansour is only broken by the gurgle of the water as it trickles downstream. This pool is a patch of watery paradise in the otherwise unbroken rocky beauty of the Anti-Atlas, a perfect place to decamp for an afternoon swim on your way through the mountain passes. Directions as for River of Aït Mansour, but from parking, walk 100m S down road and pool will be on your R.

2 mins, 29.5475, -8.8759

14 LA RIVIÈRE AMTOUDI

Walking along the riverbed, among the shady palm trees, the layered orange walls of the vast gorge towered above us and we felt insignificant compared to these eternal monuments. We were serenaded by birdsong as we headed for the water source, a vital lifeline that keep the palm and argan trees lush and green. Soon we started to climb and began to see some small pools emerge between pink flowering oleanders, and the babble of a waterfall drifted to our ears. The water was deep, transparent and full of fish and small children, accompanied by a watchful mother. Following the children's example, we jumped off a rock and swam through the narrow channel. Further on, we discovered another pool where we dived again into the depths of the cool, clear water. Park where you can in Amtoudi; walk along the path E from Amtoudi on the LH side of the palmeraie; cross over to other side at the rock with Arabic writing, bearing the legend 'Marhaba' (Welcome). Follow the route of the aqueduct and the channel of the riverbed until you reach the pools; there are a number of rocks to clamber over and beware of slippery mud; 11km there and back; 890m elevation gain.

90 mins, 29.2309, -9.1684

6

FORESTS, GARDENS & PARKS

15 OASIS TIOUT

Walking through Oasis Tiout in spring was a unique experience and filled our senses: the sweet sound of birdsong; the freshness of the moisture-filled air; the early morning sun rising over the distant mountains. The palmeraie is home to 20,000 palm trees and a multitude of bamboo-framed gardens and well-tended flowers. Aqueducts flow unceasingly, bringing the water that nourished such unusually riotous plants. A variety of cafés, complete with carpets and cushions, offer tea and we bought cheap but delicious freshly fried doughnuts or sfenj from a small stall. Directions as for Piscine Tiout; enter the palmeraie to the R of the pool.

2 mins, 30.3827, -8.6990

16 TARGUA N'TOUCHKA

As we walked through the palm groves, we noticed abundant cultivation – bananas, papayas, dates and lemons grew. Birdsong filled the air, mingling with the gentle sounds of water. If you want to explore further, the Sentier Targua N'Touchka offers a 9km circular walk: a map is displayed at start of walk.
A souk is held in the centre of Targua N'Touchka village every Sunday. From the parking spot in the village of Targua N'Touchka (29.8843, -9.2060), walk N for 250m; take first R for 120m to beginning of palm grove and start the circular walk.

5 mins, 29.8864, -9.2035

VIEWPOINTS

17 IMCHIGUEGUELN VIEWPOINT

Great roadside spot to watch the sun set. From Aït Baha, head SE on R105; after 550m turn L on to Vers Taallat – Hilala; after 2.5km park where you can by the road.

2 mins, 30.0972, -9.1322

18 VIEWPOINT TIZOURGANE

Panoramic view over Kasbah Tizourgane and the surrounding area. Best viewed at sunrise. From Izougne, head SE on R105 for 1.6km and park by the side of the road.

1 min, 29.8909, -9.0023

19 BARRAGE YOUSSEF IBN TACHFINE

From the viewpoint, the reservoir was laid out before us like a vast green tablecloth. The sky was hazy, but nonetheless the view was immense on this dusty, hot day. A small café with a sunshade on a wooden platform overlooks the lake. Abdullah serves sugary mint tea, which he calls 'Berber Whisky'.
No Swimming signs everywhere. From Agadir, Follow N1 S for 40km; after the petrol service

station turn R and follow the road for 20km; drive over the dam and continue for 2km to the viewpoint on your R.

2 mins, 29.8427, -9.4980

20 GRAND CANYON PARK

As canyons go, this one is grand and spectacular. Enjoy the view.

Directions as for The Window of Life.

2 mins, 29.3790, -9.0328

21 THE WINDOW OF LIFE

Massive square that nature and time have chiselled out of the vast, red, rock walls of the Aoukerda Canyon. We got dropped off at the top of the canyon (see Aoukerda Gorge) and walked down to Aoukerda, the start point of the canyon hike back to Igmir; The Window of Life is about halfway down. Be sure to take a look through it. From Tahouaout, head S on R107 towards Agoujgal Nord for 4.0km; turn L for 350m; slight L for 450m; slight L for 700m; turn R and The Window of Life is on your L after 7.4km although you may see it before from the other side of the rocks; park where you can by the road.

1 min, 29.3707, -9.0311

22 POINT DE VUE GORGES

Incredible canyon views along Aoukerda Gorge on a very steep road in and out of Igmir.

From Igmir, head NW on R107 for 1km; park where you can.

2 mins, 29.3380, -9.0110

ANCIENT

23 AGADIR INOUMMAR

This 300-year-old stone building is said to be the largest collective granary in the western Anti-Atlas. The impressive hilltop structure was built to store the valuables of 13 surrounding villages. Until 1900, the agadir also functioned as a governing space for village representatives and provided refuge during tribal conflicts. Today, it focuses on storing cereals, food and important documents.

Each family contributes grain for the guardian, mosque and less-fortunate villagers.

The knowledgeable guardian, Abderahman, offers informative tours, complete with mint tea and biscuits, for a small fee. From Agadir, follow N1, P1714, P1009 and R105 for 62km; turn L at fork (30.1619, -9.1298) for 3km; turn R at sign for AGADIR INOUMMAR; park by kasbah and walk S for 200m to the granary.

5 mins, 30.1668, -9.1075

24

28

28

29

24 AGADIR IKOUNKA

Just a ten-minute drive from Aït Baha, we discovered the remarkable Agadir Ikounta. This was the first agadir (grain store) we encountered that wasn't situated on top of a mountain, making it easily accessible. Upon our arrival, we found the door locked. As if by magic, a young man appeared, something we'd come to expect in Morocco. He opened the gate and gave us a tour. A watchtower was used to keep a lookout for anyone attempting to steal foodstuffs or important documents. We walked through a 7m-long stone tunnel, where approximately 130 rooms rise three stories high on each side of the corridor. Stones jut out from the walls, acting as steps for villagers to easily access their stores. The metre-high wooden doors were intact and in good condition. Take R105 N towards Biougra; after 8km turn off R at sign for the historical granary by the shop and fire station (30.10248, -9.20076); continue for 1.4km; agadir on R.

2 mins, 30.1139, -9.2009

25 AGADIR IMAIZEN

Perched on a hill, this traditional fortified granary served as a vital storage facility for grains and agricultural products. Interconnected passageways on multiple floors pierce through the expansive structure, which we explored with the knowledgeable guardian, Hassan. A climb to the top of the guard tower offered amazing views over the surrounding countryside. In the village of Imaizen, head NW to the top of the hill.

10 mins, 30.1043, -9.1124

26 AGADIR IMHILEN

A traditional fortified granary. This communal structure was designed to store grain, oil and other valuable resources, safeguarding them from thieves and harsh weather. Perched on a rocky outcrop, Agadir Imhilen is an impressive example of Amazigh architecture, with thick, stone walls and narrow passageways and small family storage spaces on three levels. Flat stones jut out as stairways. Ask for Abdou in the village: he holds the keys and is very knowledgeable. Directions: as for Café Abdelmounaim; follow the zigzag path from the side of the café up to the agadir.

10 mins, 29.9149, -9.0018

27 KASBAH TIZOURGANE

A thirteenth-century fortress perched atop a hill in the western Anti-Atlas Mountains. This ancient stronghold exhibits a unique blend of Arab and Amazigh influences. We explored the ramparts and towers, where its strategic location offered us panoramic views of the surrounding hills and valleys. In the courtyard, we appreciated the intricate stone carvings and the tranquil silence of the surroundings. The kasbah proved to be a resilient place; following a period of severe drought in the 1970s and 1980s, it experienced a significant decline in population as its inhabitants abandoned the area. Despite this, the site's historical significance and cultural value prompted restoration efforts. Public and private funding enabled the restoration of much of the structure in the early 2000s. However, not all of its structures have been fully restored, and some remain in a state of disrepair. It looked amazing from a distance at sunrise. From Izougne, head SE on R105 for 2.5km; turn R on to Rte Kasbah Tizourgane for 270m to parking spot; walk up steps.

2 mins, 29.8870, -9.0019

28 AGADIR ID AISSA

Built high on the hillside overlooking Amtoudi, the granary features hundreds of small, stone rooms where families stored essentials such as grain, dates and almonds, as well as important documents. Beehives and honey were also stored. Flat stones jutting from the walls hinted at where defenders once stood, protecting against marauding tribes. Muhammad, the guardian, showed a stone once used for crushing gunpowder. Low doors suggested the original inhabitants were much shorter. Despite recent renovations, most original features remain, including wooden doors and rock-carved steps – a testament to the hard work done with just hand tools and donkeys. From Hôtel Camping Amtoudi in Amtoudi, follow the path up the hillside to the agadir. If Muhammad the guardian isn't there, give him a call: +212 635-496084

40 mins, 29.2463, -9.1854

29 AGADIR AGUELLOUY

One of the most impressive examples of the granary-citadels of Morocco. Agadir Aguelloy was uniquely fortified, perched high on a rocky outcrop, accessible only via steep paths which offered natural protection. The design reflected the community's need for both security and communal storage, featuring original oak beams and small rooms arranged in a circular pattern. The Amtoudi granaries (Aguelloy and Id Aissa) were restored in 2007 with funds from the South Agency and the Wilaya of Guelmim and again in 2015-16 with support from Prince Claus and the Global Heritage Fund. Architect Salima Naji led these efforts, working with local craftspeople and the community to preserve the site. Although some modern materials, such as concrete, were used in the restoration, much of the original structure remains. Enjoy the panoramic views of the palmeraie and the red-walled gorge from the roof. In Amtoudi,

30

go to the mosque at the E end of the village; turn R and follow the white trail up the hillside; if you want to go inside you will need to contact Fernando so that he can open up for you: +212 061-146004

30 mins, 29.2398, -9.1727

CULTURAL HOTSPOTS

30 ALMOND BLOSSOM FESTIVAL

The festival, held annually in Tafraoute in February when the trees are at their blossoming peak, celebrates the bloom of almond trees in Tafraoute. Featuring folk music, traditional dance and local crafts. Savour delicious local cuisine, including almond-themed dishes. Bloomin' marvellous. Check local websites for the date of the next festival.

5 mins, 29.7202, -8.9719

31 PALAIS CLAUDIO BRAVO

The former residence and art studio of the Chilean hyperréalisme painter Claudio Bravo (1936-2011), renowned for his meticulous attention to detail and innovative techniques, Palais Claudio Bravo is now a hotel and museum. Quite expensive to visit, so we opted to pay the smaller fee to explore the pristine gardens. In the mausoleum, pots and vases from varying eras are on display, along with two traditional-style paintings by the artist. A few abstract sculptures are exhibited in the garden, including one that clearly represents the 1656 painting Las Meninas by the leading artist of the Spanish Baroque period, Diego Velázquez. Secreted away in the grounds, we found a glorious swimming pool with an art deco-style diving board. Prepared with bathing costumes, we took a hyperrealist dip. From Taroudant, head N on P1727 for 9km; turn L on to Rte Palais Claudio Bravo (signposted) and continue for 2.7km. Route de Tamaloukt, Agadir 83000. palaisclaudiobravo.com +212 808-502827

2 mins, 30.5478, -8.8775

31

32

31

ROADTRIPS

32 THE AMELN VALLEY

Setting off from Tafraoute, we were surrounded by pink granite rock formations interspersed with almond and olive groves. The terrain changed quickly through rugged valleys and steep, winding mountain passes. Precipitous cliffs and sheer rock faces offered dramatic vistas at every turn. We marvelled at the changing colours of the landscape – from the earthy tones of the rocks to the lush greens of the fertile valleys. The undoubted highlight of the journey was the wild swim and mint tea stop at Takoucht Chtouka. As we approached Aït Baha, the landscape softened into rolling hills and more verdant ground, with occasional palm groves lining the river. All things must pass and we rolled into the riverside town.

- To/from: Tafraoute > AïtBaha
- Distance:100km
- Roads: R105
- Scenic stop-offs: Takoucht Chtouka Aït Baha

33 LES GORGES D'AÏT MANSOUR

These dramatic gorges stretch 25 km across the Anti-Atlas region. The scenic route winds through steep cliffs, a meandering river, and lush palm trees. The contrast between rocky terrain and greenery creates an incredible visual effect. Some consider it one of Morocco's most scenic drives, but we'll let you be the judge. From Taloust Village, take the first R as you enter and follow road for 11km until you enter the gorge.

- To/from: Taloust > Aflalghir
- Distance:23km
- Roads: Unnamed
- Scenic stop-offs: Viewpoint (29.5544, -8.8780); River of Ait Mansour; Pool of Ait Mansour; Tamsaout Palm Grove (29.5402 -8.8629); children's playground & rainwater pool (29.5276, -8.8511); Gdourt Palm Grove (29.5214, -8.8409)

32

CAFÉS & EATERIES

34 ASDIM RESTAURANT BIOLOGIQUE

Family-run restaurant focusing on organic, locally-sourced ingredients, growing most of the vegetables and herbs in their own gardens. The menu features traditional Amazigh dishes, such as tagines, couscous and fresh bread, prepared with care and respect for local methods, although burgers are also available. Abdel Majid and his family have created a peaceful setting in the shady garden surrounded by the natural beauty of the mountains. Hay Asdim, Aït Baha 87100.
+212 660-451118
30.0720, -9.1686 £

34

38

38

38

38

35 CAFE RESTAURANT TIZI

Cheap and cheerful place to get food in town (opposite Hôtel Al Adarissa). Fantastic lentil dishes. Veggie friendly.
Av. Mohamed V, Aït Baha 87100.
30.0717, -9.1542

36 CAFÉ TAKOUCHT CHTOUKA

Seasonal, riverbank tea shop beneath a canopy of foliage. Serving coffee (when available); sweet mint tea (always); soft drinks (sometimes cold). Food appeared to be limited to a stack of long-life cakes and a tower of tinned sardines. Fine riverside dining. Directions as for Takoucht Chtouka Aït Baha.
29.7920, -9.1750

37 CAFÉ ABDELMOUNAIM

Welcoming roadside café where you can unwind and enjoy coffee, tea and other refreshments before or after visiting Agadir Imhilen. From Tasila N Tbnanat, head N on R105 for 1.4km; café will be on your R
29.9153, -9.0043

PLACES TO STAY

38 AFENSSOU VALLEY HOMESTAY

Hamid's house offered an authentic experience of traditional Amazigh life. Under the shade of an orange tree we drank saffron tea along with home baked flatbread, amlou (almond, argan and honey spread), sesame powder and large nibs of pollen and carob. Everything served was locally picked, so the sweetest and most freshly squeezed orange juice inevitably followed. Hamid can organise local treks to an olive press, a 100m waterfall or further afield to Jbel Aoulime. We explored the area, walking past small fields where men, women and donkeys worked beneath fruit trees. You can participate during your homestay. From Taroudant, head N on P1727 for 45km; expect narrow winding mountain roads; the last few kilometres not suitable for motorhomes nor the faint-hearted driver. +212 628-587615
30.7817, -8.7652

39 LES TERRASSES DE L'ATLAS

A stay deep in the mountains for lovers of nature, authenticity, trekking, gastronomy and relaxation. Solar panels provide much of the hotel's energy, while water conservation systems minimise waste. Locally sourced, organic ingredients feature in their restaurant, supporting nearby farmers. Rooms are thoughtfully designed using traditional Moroccan materials. Guests can enjoy nature hikes, guides are available if required. P676+R6 Afenssou.
terrasses-atlas.com +212 661-090604
30.7144, -8.7894

40 HÔTEL AL ADARISSA

If you're travelling to or from Tafraoute on the R105, this hotel in Aït Baha makes a great stopover. En suite rooms and modern amenities, including free Wi-Fi and secure parking. Friendly and helpful staff. Av. Mohamed V, Aït Baha 87100 +212 662 094789
30.0722, -9.1541

41 MAISON D'HÔTES OASIS DE TIOUT

A beautifully designed hotel and gardens. Rooms and communal areas were spotlessly clean and the view from the roof was magnificent. On each floor, there were wooden sun loungers and carpeted areas to drink tea. Guests can take an hour-and-a-half walk or a longer trek up to the mountains to a small spring-fed Berber village. Certified guides available if required. Visitors can also go to a local hammam or visit the women's co-operative in the village. Cookery classes available. Douar Azour, Tiout 83000. +212 528-551890
oasistioute.wixsite.com/oasis-de-tiout
30.3911, -8.6914

42 CAMPING TÊTE DE LION

Friendly campsite with great views of La Tête du Lion rock formation. Cute swimming pool and possibly the best Amazigh omelette we ate in Morocco. The campsite is open all year round. From Tafraoute head N on R105 for 4km; at the roundabout take the second exit; after 150m campsite is on R. camping-tafraoute.com +212 670-388723
29.7529, -8.9666

43 AUBERGE KASBAH CHEZ AMALIYA

Comfortable rooms and a Moroccan tent overlooking the pool. The perfect base to discover nature, hiking, cycling and mountain climbing. Great views of La Tête du Lion rock formation from the rooftop. B.P. 41, Tafraoute, 85450 chezamaliya.com +212 052-8800065
29.7529, -8.9681

44 TAGTOUT AUBERGE

Rooms, camping and space for motorhomes, with a terrace where you can sit and eat tagines or drink tea with views over the entire Ameln Valley. Rooms were cosy and clean and Ahmad was extremely helpful. I only planned to stay here for three days and ended up staying for six. A great place to base yourself and explore the surrounding area. Take the R104 E out of Tafraout for 1km before turning R on to a dusty track (29.7178, -8.9842) by the Camping Granite Rose; follow the track for 100m until reaching the fork by the palmeraie; take a L and follow the track for another 250m until you reach the auberge.
tagtout.com +212 661-388336
29.7212, -8.9872

34

34

36

38

39

42

41

41

43

41

45 WILD CAMPING BLUE ROCKS

Vans, buses and tents congregate near the famous blue rocks. From Tafraoute head SE on R107 for 7km; turn R at sign for PAINTED ROCKS; head SW 600m along track; slight L for 260m; turn L; continue to blue rocks for 3.5km.
29.6718, -8.9724

46 CAMPING VALLÉE TARSAOUTE

Situated in a charming Amazigh village at the edge of the desert, surrounded by pink granite mountains at an altitude of 1,200m. The campsite hotel features a variety of amenities, including Wi-Fi, games room, tea room restaurant and swimming pool. Guided tours of the region can be organised. On the R107 in the village of Tarsouat. +212 766-954756
29.5781, -9.0226 ££

47 CAMPING TINNOUGBA

Well-maintained campsite with impeccable toilets and showers. 57PC+CXQ, Bouizakarne.
29.1861, -9.7273 £

48 AMTOUDI AVENTURE

Homestay in an Amazigh house. Good home-cooked food. Hassan can organise treks around the area. Great starting point for visits to the Amtoudi agadirs and the gorge. Aidaissa, Amtoudi. +212 611 828 204
29.2436, -9.1827 £

49 HÔTEL CAMPING AMTOUDI

Campsite with restaurant and hotel rooms amid amazing surroundings. Great starting point for hikes to the oasis and agadirs. Id Aissa, Amtoudi. hotelamtoudi.com +212 672-050963
29.2429, -9.1924 £

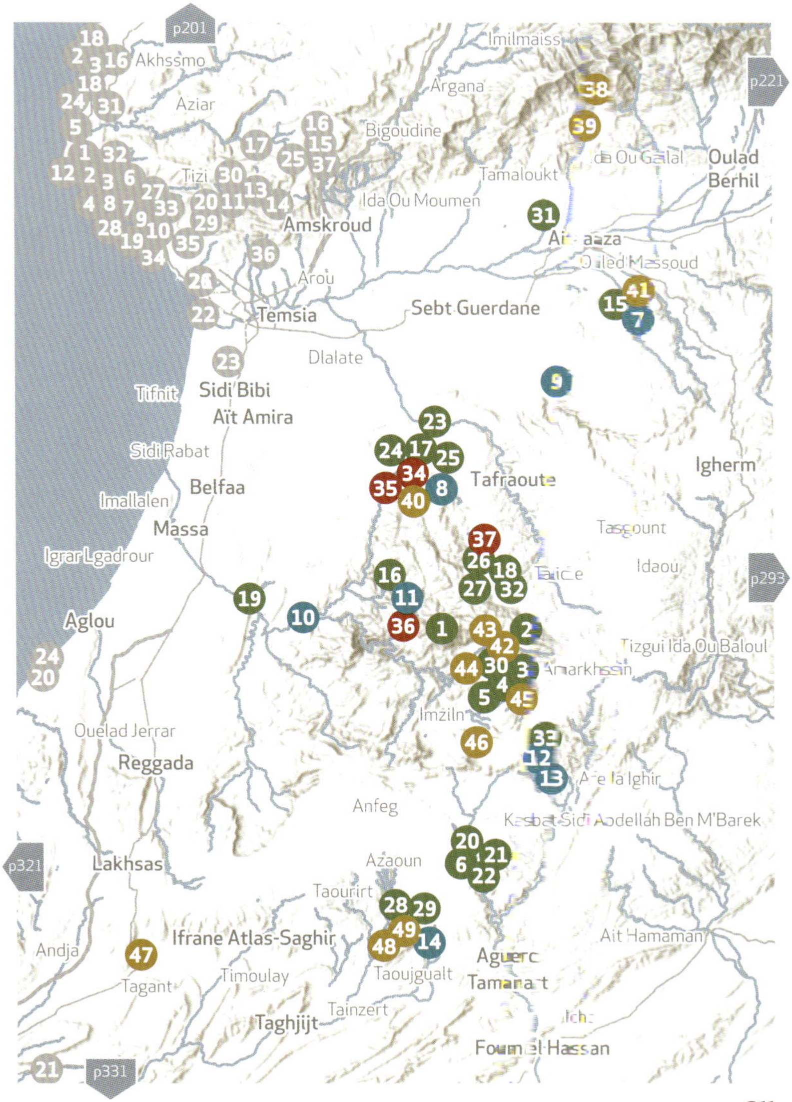

49

41

TIZNIT TO PLAGE BLANCHE

Our perfect adventure

- **Fly** like a bird in the sky from the paragliding hotel at Nid d'Aigle
- **Escape** the cares of the world on the remote, golden sands of Sidi Boulfdail
- **Step** down to Plage Tamhrouchte, locally named 'La Plage Sauvage' (The Wild Beach)
- **Wonder** at nature's creative artwork – the vast red Arche of Legzira
- **Devour** grilled fish while watching the sunset over the waves at Simo Farina, Legzira Beach
- **Picnic** in a wildlife paradise Barrage Khenfouf Assif Iboudrarn
- **Rent** rustic rooms and eat fresh fish on the beach at the eclectic Le Rayón Vert in Foum Assaka
- **Dance** on top of the dunes with nomads at Plage Blanche Camp, miles from civilisation

1

2

3

'The fingers that I customarily hide in the sand
are drowning in kindness
that overtakes me.'

Aziz Azrhai, The Last Confessions of a Rhinoceros

There is an abundance of wild beaches on this stretch of coastline; so if you want to be alone with the waves, head south. Near Tiznit, we stumbled across the aptly named Nid d'Aigle (Eagle's Nest), perched atop a cliff with infinite views over the Atlantic Ocean. Danny ventured on an accompanied paragliding flight and was blown away by the experience. Further south, we discovered Mirleft, an under-the-radar surfer hangout; we plotted up in the tiny courtyard of Camping Gîte Le Nomade, where they helped us find a local electrician/rapper who mended the fridge in our campervan – vital for cold water in this part of the world.

We marvelled at the huge, natural, red-stone arch at Legzira Beach. The walk was long, we refused offers of lifts on quad bikes and were rewarded with the sight of the sunset through the vast, curved tunnel. On the way back, we stopped at a group of beach restaurants and were served delicious freshly caught grilled fish, seasoned with chermoula for a very reasonable price. After eating, we chatted to the staff and were treated to a performance of songs mixing traditional music with modern rhythms, accompanied by skilled guitar playing. At their invitation, we drummed out beats on empty plastic tubs.

The wildest beach on this stretch of coast, perhaps anywhere, was surely Plage Blanche; 40 kilometres of virgin shoreline, where the Sahara meets the sea. We were driven along the seashore in a boneshaker of a Land Rover to our camp at the base of a colossal sand dune. After the obligatory climb to the top and the exhilarating descent, we were treated to campfire food traditional music and delightful company from our exceptional hosts. Staring up at the clear and eternal night sky, we felt a long way from home in our 'million-star hotel'.

Inland at Barrage Khenfouf Assif Iboudrarn, a watery paradise full to the brim with coots and frogs, we had another taste of Moroccan hospitality. Four young men from Tiznit had been playing football by the lake and invited us over to eat with them. Conversation flowed in different languages as we learned about each other. A tasty tagine was eaten from a shared pot with pinched bread for utensils, followed by mint tea and copious amounts of fruit: watermelon, oranges, bananas. All leftovers were given to a passing shepherd..

BEACHES

1 SIDI BOULFDAIL

A wide expanse of golden sands, devoid of life except for a fisherman trying to catch his dinner from the headland. There are two sections to this beach, bisected by a rocky headland. The first is accessible by a path down the rocks on the northern end of the beach. The second is reached via a set of stairs next to a fisherman's hut. From the town of Mirleft take the R104 N for 7km, before turning L on to the P1905 near the town of Gourizim; follow the road for 7.6km until reaching the village of Boulfdail; parking spot on L (29.6788, -9.9586); walk along the path into the village, then take the first L and then the first right; follow this road for 60m before taking the LH fork at the intersection; follow this path for 2km until you reach the sea; first access point is down through the rocks (29.6889, -9.9666); second via the stairs (29.6817, -9.9747).

30 mins, 29.6828, -9.9736

2 SIDI BOULFDAIL COVE

A secluded spot for a solitary swim, sheltered from the winds that race up and down this coastline. From Mirleft, take the R104 N for 7km, before turning left on to the P1905 near the town of Gourizim; follow the road for 7.6km until reaching the village of Boulfdail, parking area will be on your L; take the path into the village, then take the first L and then the first R; follow this road for 60m before taking LH fork at the intersection; follow path for 2km until you reach sea; turn L and head S along the cliffs for 2km until you reach cove.

35 mins, 29.6798, -9.9766

3 PLAGE AFTASS

Nestled away on the side of a headland covered with Alpine plants and sea lavender is a small beach with a café and a small children's playground. Graduated entry into the sea and protected from the open sea by a headland. From Mirleft, head E on Bd Legzira and Rue Las Palmas for 1.5km to parking overlooking beach (29.5773, -10.0468).

5 mins, 29.5781, -10.0479

4 PLAGE TAMHROUCHTE

Beautiful sandy beach surrounded by hills just south of Mirleft known locally as 'La Plage Sauvage'. Ninety-five steps down to the beach. Gentle entry into the water. From Mirleft, head S on R104 for 3.2km; take a slight R (29.5613, -10.0534) and continue for 500m to parking spot (29.55783, -10.0555); walk down steps to beach.

5 mins, 29.5562, -10.0558

5 SIDI EL WAFI

A wild escape down a rough track with a rivulet running down its length. An abandoned house loomed to our left; a forgotten relic. The beach revealed a vast expanse of untouched beauty where waves crashed, fierce and untamed. Not a soul in sight. You could linger here for a month under the infinite sky. From Sidi Ifni head NE on R104 for 24km; parking spot will be on your L (29.5375, -10.0570); walk along the track to the beach for 1.25km.

15 mins, 29.5401, -10.0640

5

6 PLAGE FTAYSA RKOUNT

Time stood still on this sandy beach, encircled by hillsides adorned with resilient yellow-flowered launaea bushes. From Sidi Ifni, head NE on R104 for 21km; turn L (29.5142, -10.0574) for 1.2km to parking (29.5164, -10.0693); walk down 47 steps or a steep concrete ramp.

3 mins, 29.5152, -10.0706

7 YASSCOBAR BEACH

Just to the right of the well-known Plage Legzira, we discovered a small, secret beach where we escaped from the crowds. Beware of the tides as you could easily get cut off here. Make sure you know your way out and what time the tide comes in. From Legzira Beach turn R and climb over red rocks by sign for ZONE NON GARDE.

5 mins, 29.4488, -10.1146

8 ARCH OF LEGZIRA

We walked the whole length of Plage Lagzira to the arch. The beach itself was incredible – huge and sandy, featuring one of the most impressive natural monuments in the world. There were plenty of quad bike taxis for those who didn't want to walk. We were in awe of the beauty of nature as the sun set over this magnificent red stone monument while waves crashed incessantly ashore. Apparently, there had been a second arch, but it had fallen into the sea. Eat great grilled fish in the cafés. At Plage Lagzira, turn L for 1km.

20 mins, 29.4398, -10.1210

9 PLAGE LEKRAYMA

Wild, pebble beach. Good for a few days in a campervan and sea fishing. You may be lucky enough to find a fisherman willing to cook you a fish supper. From Sidi Ifni, head SW on P1901 for 15km; turn right on to dirt track where road bends sharply to left; follow track down to beach.

10 mins, 29.2812, -10.2558

10 PLAGE SIDI OUERZEG

Below the fishing village of Sidi Ouerzeg, with its traditional square houses, is a huge dune leading to a wild, sandy beach. Beloved of surfers, Sidi Ouerzeg has been the venue for local championships. From Auberge Maison Diyani walk down stone steps to the dunes; follow your footsteps in the sand to trace your route back up; turn L at end of steps.

5 mins, 29.2656, -10.2839

11 ARKSIS BEACH

A sand dune rose above the waves, while a scattering of rocks in the sea created a beautiful contrast with the dark-red headland to the left. When we arrived at midday, we found the beach deserted. From Sidi Ifni, head SW on P1901 for 26km to parking spot (29.2274, -10.3259); follow track down to beach.

10 mins, 29.2314, -10.3294 

12 PLAGE SIDI CHAAB

A quiet beach nestled near a tiny fishing village. From Sidi Ifni, head SW on P1901 for 33km; turn R on to Coral Road (29.1748, -10.3521) and park just before beach.

5 mins, 29.1803, -10.3807

13 FOUM ASSAKA

Getting closer to the Sahara, we felt pretty conspicuous driving a big white van across the open, flat, deserted landscape. The first part of the road to access this beach was rocky and steep, but it soon improved. We didn't drive our van up the rough terrain but you easily could in a car. We walked along the road beside the river, which opens into a wide lagoon, home to a diverse array of birds who'd left their tiny talon prints all over the beach. Pebbly, sandy and surrounded by barren hillsides, the area was full

of fossilised dunes. From Sidi Ifni, head SW on P1901 for 40km; turn R at sign for Foum Oued Assaka; drive or walk for 1.2km.

5 mins, 29.1408, -10.4062

14 OUED REMLA

Small beach with pristine sandy shores and calm, clear waters in front of a fishing village. Surrounded by rugged, natural landscapes. Directions as for Plage Sauvage Takomba, but 1km further down P1901 to parking (29.0537, -10.4788).

5 mins, 29.0585, -10.4799

15 PLAGE SAUVAGE TAKOMBA

Wild, crescent-shaped beach wrapped in solitude. A refuge from modern life, where the rhythmic crash of waves against rocks drowns out the background noise in your head. For the patient angler, the beach promised rewards. From Sid Ifni, head SW on P1901 for 52km; the road deteriorates soon after Foum Assaka, and is not marked on Google maps, but we drove down the imaginary road. Turn R on to beach and park (29.0486, -10.4866).

2 mins, 29.0493, -10.4872,

16 PLAGE BLANCHE

The start of this 42km pristine 'white beach' was a paved road leading to a small, square car park where we were invited to drink mint tea by a French/Moroccan couple. The last place you can access this famous beach with an ordinary car, but still remote, wild and rugged with desert shrubs, succulents and tamarisk trees. Migratory birds, including flamingos, flock to this untouched coastline, as well as desert foxes and reptiles. We saw camels on the beach. Directions as for Plage Sauvage Takomba then drive 14.4km further until crossroads at (28.9603, -10.5624); turn R and follow road for 4km to parking spot (28.9612, -10.6063).

5 mins, 28.9628, -10.6146

17 PLAGE BLANCHE WILD CAMP

Atop a towering sand dune, we stood and overlooked the spot where the Atlantic Ocean meets the Sahara. The contours in the sand resembled the stretch marks that grace a woman's belly after childbirth. Rolling waves behind us enhanced the mesmerising beauty of the pristine sand. We were miles from the distractions of civilisation; forget about a phone signal. After a while – could've been longer – we ventured down from our dune and went for a swim, mindful to stay at waist height, as the area is notorious for riptides. As night fell, a fire blazed in the sand. Nomads beat large water containers, singing in the style of the Tuareg, also known as the desert blues.

One fellow traveller aptly remarked, gazing at the expanse above us, 'this is our million-star hotel'. In the morning, we scaled the dune once more, greeted by a transformed landscape. While it is possible to reach Plage Blanche alone in a 4x4, the solitude of this place is stark. Should anything go wrong, help would be far away, with no phone signal to call for assistance. The campsite had been licensed due to its proximity to an army outpost, ensuring a level of safety. Guides were required to have at least two vehicles for emergencies. To visit Plage Blanche with professional guides we recommend going on an overnight camp with Auberge Maison Diyani (+212 659-586700). If you have a 4x4 and know what you're doing, turn off N1 on to track at 29.0389, -10.4974 and drive south 39km along the beach at low tide until you see a huge dune on L and a small river ahead; turn L between the dune and the river and the camping spot is about 100m behind the dune.

60 mins, 28.8436, -10.8416

LAKES & RIVERS

18 BARRAGE KHENFOUF IBOUDRARN

A long, green stretch of water surrounded by palm trees with hundreds of coots on the river. Wild tobacco grew in abundance along the banks. We considered a bit of wild swimming, but the water appeared too weedy. Frogs and coots scattered at our approach, the air filling with the sounds of their croaks and calls. Four young men who'd been playing football sat down on a rug in the shade and beckoned us over to join them for lunch. They offered us their food and we dipped into the same tagine pot of vegetables, raisins, prunes and freshly shelled peas. Friendly conversation flowed, followed by copious quantities of watermelon, oranges and nectarines. Inevitably, they served mint tea. While we were eating the fruit, a shepherd passed by with his flock of goats. The young men gave him leftover loaves of bread and fruit; the lamb to his dogs. From Sidi Ifni, head NE on P1901 for 1.8km; at roundabout, take second exit on to R104 for 1.8km; turn R on to P1918 for 12km; park on R (29.4018, -10.0631) and look for path down to river.

2 mins, 29.4028, -10.0630

VIEWPOINTS

19 MIRLEFT

A fantastic spot to watch the sunset over the Atlantic. From the town of Mirleft, walk W for 1.5km towards the sea or park near Plage Aftass (29.5771, -10.0466).

5-20 mins, 29.5812, -10.0476

17

18

24

23

27

21

20 NID D'AIGLE

Let the world fall away as you stand on the edge of a cliff and stare out at the vastness of the Atlantic Ocean far below. Paragliders from the nearby activity centres will lend some action to your view and the sunsets from here are magnificent. Take the R104 west out of Tiznit for 14.3km. Take a R off the main road at (29.6721, -9.8550); follow road for 9.5km; pass through the village of Tamellalt, park by the viewpoint (29.7007, -9.9310) at end of village on the cliff edge. Alternatively, get the number 18 bus from Tiznit Bus Station (29.6908, -9.7197), ask for Club Evásion; from the bus stop (29.7051, -9.9369), take the road to your left up the cliff; it's a 2.3km walk with many switchbacks so put that hitchhiking thumb to good use; when you've reached the top of the cliff, the viewpoint is on your R.

3 mins, 29.7014, -9.9302

25

26

30

CAFÉS & EATERIES

21 SPOT-M

Laid-back café and surf school overlooking the expansive Plage Tamhrouchte and wild Moroccan coast. This enthusiastic outfit also provides surf holidays and packages. Spot on. Directions as for Plage Tamhrouchte, on your L at bottom of steps spot-m.com +212 672-882661

29.5568, -10.0551

22 SIMO FARINA, LEGZIRA BEACH

Delicious, freshly caught grilled dorado (sea bream) and salad from friendly waiters who speak English and French. Imbibe an incredible sunset over the Atlantic Ocean with your mint tea or strong espresso coffee. If you are lucky, waiters, cooks and friends will sing for you. +212 653-111546

29.4460, -10.1161

PLACES TO STAY

23 AUBERGE MAISON DIYANI

Cosy accommodation, warm hospitality, delicious, locally caught fish, and vegetarian options. Imbibe panoramic sea views from the communal area and rooftop balcony. Can organise camping trips to Plage Blanche. In Sidi Ouarzeg - you can't miss it. +212 659-586700

29.2646, -10.28252

24 NID D'AIGLE PARAPENTE

If you're seeking thrills, this is the place for you. Perched atop the cliffs and looking out over the Atlantic, this hotel and activity centre offers you the chance to fly. Taking off from a runway in the middle of the hotel, visitors can take tandem paragliding flights with the instructors, or solo flights if qualified. Soaring above the world, weightless and free, contrasting with the wind pressure, my pilot took us in fast downward spirals, which was beyond exhilarating. Run by a lovely Belgian/Moroccan couple. Chalets are cosy and comfortable and the restaurant provides an array of delicious food. Parking available for campervans & motorhomes. Free Wi-Fi. Eagle's Nest, Tamellalt, Tiznit. Directions as for Nid d'Aigle, the hotel is at the end of the village on the cliff edge. nidaigle.com +212 658-458223

29.7006, -9.9315

25 VEGAS GUEST HOUSE

Beachfront café and guesthouse. Enjoy fish, veggie tagines and sublime sunsets. Directions as for Plage Aftass. +212 649-177108

29.5790, -10.0478

26 CAMPING GÎTE LE NOMADE

Small-scale campsite consisting of a yard area with a shared kitchen and a couple of showers. Kind and helpful staff. A pleasant seating area with shaded cover to eat or simply relax under with a cup of tea. One French gentleman spends six months of the year there in a tent on top of his car. 13 Quartier d'Aftas, Mirleft 85352 +212 528-719137

29.5799, -10.0436

27 CAMPING SIDI OUARZEG

Laid-back campsite with swimming pool and playground for children about 800m from Plage Sidi Ouerzeg. From Sidi Ifni, head SW on P1901 for 20km; campsite is on L. +212 670-177745

29.2542, -10.2803

28 LEGZIRA CAMPER PARK

No-frills campervan stop overlooking Plage Legzira. Toilets and showers in nearby abandoned-looking holiday resort. At end of Rte Lagzira.

29.4462, -10.1147

29 CAMPING GRAN CANARIA

Large, secure, sandy campsite with good showers. Out of clean clothes, we made an emergency wash stop. Before the cycle had even started, we were invited to tea by some Moroccan ladies, including the owner, sitting at a nearby table. Rue des Plages, Sidi Ifni. +212 528-876321

29.3838, -10.1726

30 LE RAYÓN VERT, FOUM ASSAKA

The Green Ray is a remote and eclectic beachfront restaurant, the walls adorned with guitars and 45rpm records. We drank mint tea and browsed through the paperbacks at the international book exchange. Views of the beach were fabulous, possibly one of the finest places to catch the sunset in Morocco. Locally caught grilled fish was a speciality. Rustic rooms are available to rent, all with a sea view. Directions as for Foum Oued Assaka, turn R at village for 500m. +212 662-166051

29.1454, -10.4033

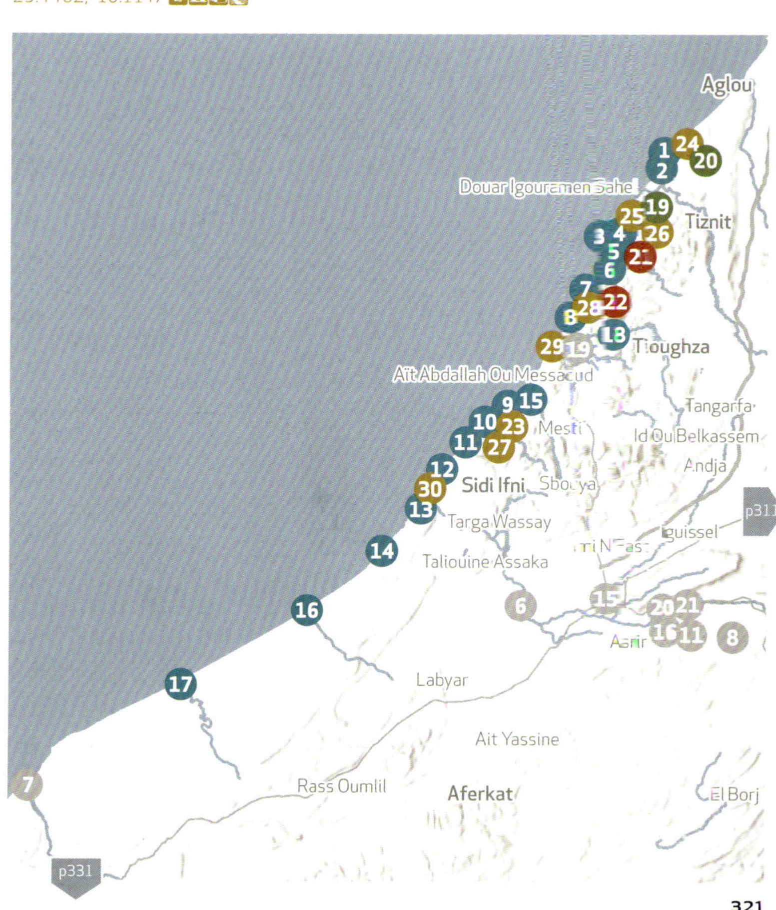

7

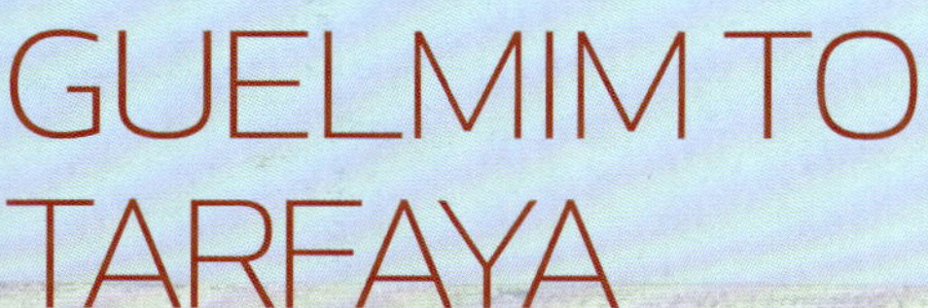

GUELMIM TO TARFAYA

Our perfect adventure

- **Wallow** in therapeutic mud at Mineral Eye Hot Springs, there's nothing quite like it for cooling the blood
- **Delight** in audaciousness tales of aviation and derring-do at the Antoine de Saint-Exupery Museum
- **View** desert, mountain and oasis from the roof of Tarmguist Homestay, then peruse stars with incredible clarity
- **Stroll** along the mouth of the Draa Estuary, where Morocco's longest river meets the sea, a crucial habitat for migrating birds
- **Contemplate** the mystery of Grotte d'Akhfennir Ajeb Lah, a natural wonder also known as the 'Devil's Hole'
- **Watch** wildlife or take a boat out on the tranquil waters of Naila Lagoon, a wetland haven for nature lovers
- **Wild** camp overlooking the untamed beauty of Naila Lagoon in Khenfiss National Park
- **Discover** the history of Sahrawi nomads at Kasbah Caravansérail in the Tighmert Oasis
- **Savour** barbecued fish at Restaurant Casa España in the one-street town of Akhfennir, somewhere between Paris and Dakar

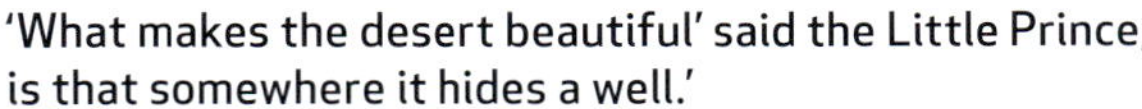

'What makes the desert beautiful' said the Little Prince, is that somewhere it hides a well.'

Antoine de Saint-Exupéry

In Morocco, it is said that the further south you go, the stronger and sweeter the mint tea becomes; there was only one way to find out. Famed as the 'Gateway to the Sahara', Guelmim is located between the Anti-Atlas Mountains and the edge of the Sahara. This vibrant town is predominantly Amazigh, boasting rich cultural ties to the nomadic Sahrawi tribes who have roamed the surrounding landscapes for centuries. Guelmim is also renowned for its lively weekly camel market, where traders and locals still come together to barter for camels and stallholders sell textiles, pottery, local produce and handicrafts.

Nearby Tighmert Oasis was filled with palm trees and traditionally built homestays, where you could easily imagine yourself as a nomad. We visited Kasbah Caravansérail, a beautifully preserved 300-year-old family home belonging to Habib. His museum offered a glimpse into the region's heritage, featuring a fascinating mix of traditional tools, utensils, clothing and both past and recent history related to the travelling traders who once traversed these arid lands. Jardin Botanique Anna and Alessandro came as a verdant surprise, a cool, and fragrant botanical garden slap-bang in the middle of the arid oasis.

After miles and miles of little but sand, sea and camels, Naila appeared like a mirage – one of the largest saltwater lagoons in Morocco, home to hundreds of thousands of migratory birds. By the jetty, we met a cheerful French-Belgian lady, wearing a vibrant and intricate Senegalese dress and sporting an infectious smile. She was headed north. She pulled a wooden xylophone from the back of her van and played to her heart's content. Fishermen arrived in their boats, wearing their distinctive yellow rubber trousers, and deposited their catch before heading back out to sea.

Listening to an audiobook of Wind, Sand and Stars by Antoine de Saint-Exupéry (The Little Prince), we motored along the new N1 road south.

In this autobiography, the author recounts heroic tales of pioneering postal service flights in rickety planes over the Sahara. The quiet, windswept town of Tarfaya, where the famous French aviator and writer was stationed, commemorated this magnificent man with an intriguing museum. Meanwhile, at the beach, the setting sun burst through the ruins of the Casa del Mar, built by the British in 1802 and subsequently taken over by the Spanish colonisers. A trader conversed in Spanish while serving hrira and dates in the souk. This is as far south as we went.

BEACHES

1 OUED CHBIKA BEACH

A small spring trickles into the lagoon by the path as gulls swoop, dive and circle overhead. We had the beach all to ourselves. From Tantan 82000, head NW on N1 for 29km; turn R on to track (28.4406, -11.3764) and park on cliff top overlooking beach; and down track to beach.

5 mins, 28.4456, -11.3767

2 OUED MA FATMA

An important place for diversity in biology and ecology; the mouth of the river is a favourable location for Audouin's gulls, sandpipers, sanderlings and other sea birds. A great spot for camping. From Tantan, head E on N1 for 83km; turn R down unmarked road (28.2036, -11.7820) and follow a track round to beach for 700m.

5 mins, 28.2081, -11.7842

3 SIDI WAAR

Golden sands and gentle waves, surrounded by rugged cliffs. No facilities, few people. Great for swimming and walks. From Tantan head E on N1 for 90km; turn R (28.1694, -11.8894) and follow road for 2.2km and park on L (28.1726, -11.8708); walk down to beach.

5 mins, 28.1758, -11.8710

4 SANTA CRUZ DE LA MAR PEQUEÑA

When you've had enough of drooling over Naila Lagoon, jump into the landscape and head over to the beach for a swim. 360° of beauty and pleasure. Keep an eye on the tides because the water will come in very, very quickly. Directions as for Naila Lagoon; walk down stairs and head R for 2km to water's edge.

30 mins, 28.0380, -12.2239

5 CAPE JUBY

A vast, untouched stretch of beach just outside Tarfaya. Its windswept sands offer solitude and a sense of wild beauty, while hundreds of wooden stakes are a distinctive feature of the landscape, adding to its rugged, historical ambiance. These stakes, often weathered and worn by the elements, likely once served practical purposes related to the fishing industry or as boundary markers for specific areas of the coastline. The beach is famous for strong winds, making it popular among windsurfers and kite surfers, though its rough waters are generally unsuitable for swimming. From Tarfaya head N on Ave Ahmed Hadar; turn L at (27.9452, -12.9058) on to track for 600m and parking is on R.

5 mins, 27.9541, -12.9024

LAKES & RIVERS

6 MAKITA AL-SAFI, NOUN RIVER

An area of outstanding natural beauty. Layers of slate in shades of grey, interspersed with orange hills, have been eroded by a dark-green river, to form steps of varying heights. The river meanders through, shaped by the sharp, slate edges into melodic waterfalls, while the calls of frogs and birdsong blended with the burbling water. From Guelmim head NW on Bd Hassan II/ N12; go through two roundabouts; after 1.8 km at roundabout, take 2nd exit; after 10km turn R; after 8.1km, park on R before bridge.

5 mins, 28.9705, -10.2281

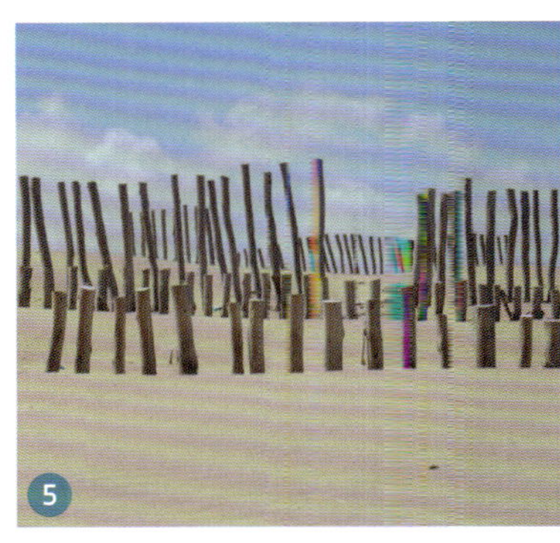

5

9

7 DRAA VALLEY ESTUARY

An immense drive through orange sandy scrubland punctuated by the occasional grazing camel. We stopped at the clifftop, we could go no further and looked down at the Oued Draa's inevitable exit to the sea, which opened wide between the dunes – a blue ribbon edged by patches of green. Shallow curving steps descend towards the sea to a platform where we ate lunch and watched the waves meet the river. We were told it wasn't possible to camp in the car park because a nearby army post would send people to check our passports and ask us to move in the evening. However, we learned that we could drive a couple of kilometres back up the road, turn off onto a side track and wild camp for the night without any issues. No shops or water available, so we were glad we had come prepared. A magnificent place to spend some time marvelling at the beauty of nature. From El Ouatia head E on N1 for 16km; turn L at Restaurant Ben Khlil and continue for 23km to the parking spot overlooking mouth of Draa Valley.

5 mins, 28.6750, -11.1236

8 MINERAL EYE HOT SPRINGS

Mud, mud, glorious mud. Renowned for its therapeutic properties, the spring was warm and rich in minerals. According to local lore, the hot spring was discovered centuries ago by shepherds and nomadic tribes who roamed the region. These early inhabitants stumbled upon the warm, bubbling waters while tending to their flocks and searching for water sources. The track to the spring is unpaved and quite difficult to find. Bamal is an interesting and informativeguide, speaks great English and will help you find the springs (+212 618-514152). Camping spots available nearby. From Tighmert (28.9525, -9.9254) follow the sandy track SE for 9.7km.

3 mins, 28.9205, -9.8444

9 NAILA LAGOON

You must, must, must pass through here if you are heading north or south. Naila Lagoon is home to some 20,000 birds in winter. Water, mud flats with flamingos, sand dunes and the sea beyond. Walk down to the lagoon where you can swim, fish, take a boat ride from Naila Lagoon Boat Dock, or walk around the shoreline towards the dunes. No facilities. Best at low tide. From Akhfennir, head W on N1 for 21km; turn R (28.0044, -12.2416) for 2.7km to end of the road.

2 mins, 28.0288, -12.2394

CAVES

10 GROTTE D'AKHFENNIR AJEB LAH

The highlight of this stretch of coast is Grotte d'Akhfennir Ajeb Lah, also called the Devil's Hole. It's a beautiful and mysterious cave created by the waves of the Atlantic Ocean. From Akhfennir head NE on N1 for 750m; you will see a track on your L (easy to miss); follow for 600m till you see the Trou du Diable on your L.

2 mins, 28.1070, -12.0378

ANCIENT

11 KASBAH CARAVANSÉRAIL

Fascinating museum of nomadic history. Sahrawi Habib took us around and explained all the objects on display. There was a plethora of saddles and other camel-related items, including a woven breast-covering for female camels to prevent their babies from drinking all their milk, allowing the nomads to share it. Utensils, tools, woven baskets, metal-tipped arrows and manacles filled the space. The house, over 300 years old, included a 5m by 7m underground cell for miscreant slaves. There were 12 rooms stuffed with objects from both past and present nomadic tribes, including Sahrawis, featuring an outfit worn by Habib's father when he was 12 and made entirely of camel hair. A variety of square brushes and combs used for separating camel hair into strands for weaving were among the items Habib enthusiastically described. One interesting item was the water timer. It amused us to think that while we used sand timers, the nomads used a small bowl with a tiny hole in a bucket of water to measure the hour each family was allowed to take water from a well or spring. Finally, we enjoyed the inevitable mint tea, poured and repoured by our flamboyant host. We noticed that the tea was getting stronger the further south we travelled. Directly opposite Maison Etoile du Desert.

2 mins, 28.9413, -9.9588 £

12 CASA DEL MAR, TARFAYA

The peaceful white beach of Tarfaya is far from the busy tourist resorts, has a mild climate all year round and is ideal for sunbathing, swimming and walks. Of particular interest was the historical Casa del Mar, a former Spanish fortress built on a rocky outcrop offshore in 1882. Although in ruins, it offers a glimpse into the town's colonial past. Spectacular as the sun sets behind it. In the evening take a stroll around the souk, which was teeming with life and where you could buy fruit, vegetables and tagine pots. Stand in front of Plage Tarfaya – you can't miss the House of the Sea.

5 mins, 27.9437, -12.9299

CULTURAL HOTSPOTS

13 ANTOINE DE SAINT-EXUPÉRY MUSEUM

A charming museum adorned with a vivid depiction of the Little Prince on the front door. If your only connection to Saint-Exupéry is through The Little Prince, we recommend reading Wind, Sand and Stars before your visit. This autobiography captures Saint-Exupéry's thrilling years as a pioneering pilot, navigating skies from Toulouse and Barcelona to Casablanca, later extending to South America. In these golden days of aviation, brave pilots flew fragile planes, often encountering peril, especially over the Pyrenees. The museum documents their stories through photos, French descriptions and original airmail letters. Life-size cutouts of Saint-Exupéry and Jean Mermoz stand beside models of the planes they flew and informative posters chronicle Exupéry's life. Closed on Fridays. From the seafront boulevard in Tarfaya, head SE on Ave Mohamed V toward Ave Moulay Abd El Azize for 120m; the museum is on the L.

2 mins, 27.9438, -12.9249

15

14 SAINT-EXUPÉRY MONUMENT

The Antoine de Saint-Exupéry monument in Tarfaya pays homage to the aviator and author. The statue features a model of a Bréguet XIV biplane, the aircraft Saint-Exupéry flew during his time as a pioneering airmail pilot, flying mail routes between Toulouse, Casablanca and Dakar. The monument is on the seafront and easy to find; a fitting tribute to a literary and aviation hero. Par avion. Par excellence.

2 mins, 27.9450, -12.9258

15 SOUK AMHIRICH, GUELMIM

One of the largest weekly markets in the region, famous for its camel trade, now offering a blend of traditional and modern wares. Historically, Guelmim was a key point along the trans-Saharan trade routes, where merchants from various African regions would converge to exchange goods such as dates, salt and textiles. Each week, traders still gather to sell livestock, crafts and local produce. Visitors can also find artisanal jewellery, leather goods and spices. The market usually starts about 8am and continues until the afternoon, typically closing by 2pm or 3pm. Arrive early to witness the camel trading. Saturdays only. From Guelmim take the N1 towards the W; market is on R just before the first roundabout

1 min, 28.9821, -10.0741

FORESTS, GARDENS & PARKS

16 JARDIN BOTANIQUE, TIGHMERT

An oasis within an oasis built by Italian Anna and Alessandro. We entered the botanical gardens to discover an area of great beauty with well-labelled beds full of diverse plants including agave variegata and other native cacti. A series of circular sculptures represented the moon and the landscaping was exquisite. A fountain and a small pond with a model wooden sailboat added to the charm and made the garden feel cool; a welcome escape from the dusty heat outside. A tiny swimming pool was adorned with a metal statue of an eagle poised to dive into the water. The gardens are open from 9am – 12.30pm, and from 3.30pm to 6.30pm. If the door is locked, knock, wait and someone will surely come

16

16

W2WQ+344, Tighmert – we parked at gates, then turned L, immediately followed by a R down a very narrow street; we followed wall around to find entrance. +212 528-772856

2 mins, 28.9445, -9.9622 £

CAFÉS & EATERIES

17 RESTAURANT CASA ESPAÑA

Late-night, no-frills fish restaurant, popular with families and truckers heading north and south. Also dishes up chicken, lamb or vegetable tagines. A nearby sign for Hotêl Paris Dakar is a reminder that you're on the route of the famous motorsport event and somewhere between Paris and Dakar. 3WVW+P45, Akhfennir +212 609-240701

28.0943, -12.0546 £

18 HRIRA STALL, TARFAYA

Hrira is a tomato, lentil and chickpea soup, often accompanied by dates, flatbread or hard-boiled eggs. The food Moroccans traditionally break their fast with during Ramadan. The owner, Houssein, spoke to us in Spanish - Cape Juby, including Tarfaya, was ruled by Spain from 1884 to 1975. A couple of young girls offered us some of their msemen, a delicious pancake-like, square savoury pastry, which was so good that we bought more from a nearby shop, and treated them to their soup. Next to Arrahma Mosque.

27.9396, -12.9246 £

PLACES TO STAY

19 GRAN CANARIA CAMPSITE

Large, secure, sandy site with good showers. Out of clean clothes, we made an emergency wash stop. Before the cycle had even started, we were invited to tea by some Moroccan ladies, including the owner, sitting at a nearby table. Rue des Plages, Sidi Ifni. +212 528-876821

29.3838, -10.1726 £

20 MAISON ETOILE DU DESERT

Traditionally built, family-run guest house offering an authentic oasis experience. Set within a shady garden, a tea tent and sun terrace offer relaxation. Rooms are en suite and the locally sourced food was well-prepared. Built using traditional construction methods the guest house blended in with the environment. Despite its remote location, it has strong Wi-Fi, making it possible to work remotely. Friendly and affordable. Douar Tighmert, Commune Asrir, Tighmert, 81000. etoile-du-desert.wdro.net +212 630-518984

28.9412, -9.9592 £

21 TARMGUIST HOMESTAY

The desert, mountain and oasis view from the rooftop is spectacular, especially at night with stars in their millions. Authentic family atmosphere, rooms with en suite. Friendly and helpful staff. Enjoy mint tea in an authentic nomad-style tent. English is spoken. Space for campervans. Guelmim 81000. +212 667-916530

28.9725, -9.9265 ££

22 HOTEL CAMPING ATLANTIQUE TANTAN

Large, well-maintained campsite beside the ocean with clean showers, toilets and electricity. Rooms are also available. Great meeting point for travellers heading either north or south. FMV7+JF, El Ouatia 82000 +212 717-36[illegible]298

28.4934, -1[illegible].3365 £

23 AKHFENNIR BEACH

Great place to park your vehicle overlooking Akhfennir Beach. Report to the nearby police station, show your passport and get free camping.

28.0971, -12.[illegible]495

24 KHNIFISS NATIONAL PARK

Parking overnight is possible too for a small fee. A photo of your passport will be taken for security reasons. Directions as for Naila Lagoon.

28.0278, -12.2416 £

25 ROTEL RESIDENCE CANALINA

Clean rooms and apartments available with en suite. One of the few places to stay if you're in Tarfaya. Friendly, helpful staff and good Wi-Fi. Handy if you're visiting the Antoine de Saint-Exupéry Museum. Ave Mohamed V, Tarfaya 70050. +212 541-785521

27.9412, -12.[illegible]228 ££

Sidi Kaouki Beach (p181)

Index

Wild Guide Morocco
Adventures Through Mountain, Coast & Desert

Words:
Lola Culsán
John Weller
Danny Weller

Photos:
John Weller, Danny Weller & and those credited

Editing:
Andrew Brassleay

Design:
Gary Nickolls, John Weller, Tania Pascoe & Daniel Start

Distribution:
Central Books Ltd
50, Freshwater Road
Dagenham, RM8 1RX
020 8525 8800
orders@centralbooks.com

Published by:
Wild Things Publishing Ltd.
Freshford, Bath
BA2 7WG

Author acknowledgements
John: Mum & Tony; Dad; sisters April, Caroline & Angela; Bobby, Rowan and Jody; Richard, Tom & Tat; Andy Small; brother Khalid Aribi; Michael Breitung at Wild Morocco; Markus & Oliver - sons of the desert; **Lola:** Mum, Dad & Denise & familia Culsán for making me a citizen of the world; my sisters Suzie, Anna, Elise & Marie; Vincent, Claire & my grandson Finn Tobin; Niblings: Emilia, Ronnie, Jessie, Louna, Bump, Celeste & Galatée; Fran, Brett, Paul & Anthony for encouragement and being a loving family. Darren Guttridge and everyone at Edward Wilson for being supportive and accommodating. **Danny:** to my family and friends for supporting me and encouraging me to complete this book; Shemaiah Rose for posing for photos in the desert; Giulia Frinzi for helping me with my adventures; Mohammed, Stefan and Aicha at Authentic Moroccan Homestay for opening their home and hearts to me; Natalie & Dan at Rock N Yogi for keeping me safe while mountain climbing; a massive thank you to all those who hosted me on my travels and who deepened and immeasurably improved my Moroccan experience. **Writing contributors:** Layla Benesallem, Zineb Khaidach & Victor Demurs. **Friends old and new we met along the way:** Achraf who took Lola on his motorbike to get a replacement tyre; Ali and Amagour village who replaced our wheel; Anna Bala and her balafone playing at Naila Lagoon; Nina and Hugo for late night mountain-top laughter and fridge fixing; Mounia and Raja'a who shared msmen with us in Tarfaya; Saad, who brought us food from his house in Tafraoute; Mohammed who gave us a lift in Azrou, then invited us to a family picnic; the amazing women Lola went hiking with in Skoura M'Daz; and Yousef & Anas who guided us. **Ali Kamel** for teaching Lola Darija; providing and checking information and translations; putting Danny up and being Our Man in Morocco. **To the people of Morocco**, thank you for making our journey special; for the directions, roadside help, endless offers of tagine and mint tea, and most importantly, for your incredible hospitality and open, kind hearts.
Gary Nickollsfor design and layout. **Andrew Brassleay** for editorial.
Finally, thanks to **Daniel and Tania at Wild Things Publishing** for your continued belief in us and making this book possible.

Health, Safety and Responsibility:
The activities and places in this book have risks and can be dangerous. The locations may be on private land and permission may need to be sought. The authors and publishers have gone to great lengths to ensure the accuracy of the information but conditions and circumstances change all the time so the responsibility to assess each place for safety and legality falls to the reader.

Published in the United Kingdom in 2025 by Wild Things Publishing Ltd, Bath, BA2 7WG, United Kingdom. ISBN: 1910636517.